KV-731-665

The French Left and the Fifth Republic

The Discourses of Communism and Socialism in Contemporary France

John Gaffney

Lecturer in Modern Languages
Aston University

MACMILLAN
PRESS

© John Gaffney 1989

All rights reserved. No reproduction, copy or transmission
of this publication may be made without written permission.

No paragraph of this publication may be reproduced, copied
or transmitted save with written permission or in accordance
with the provisions of the Copyright Act 1956 (as amended),
or under the terms of any licence permitting limited copying
issued by the Copyright Licensing Agency, 33–4 Alfred Place,
London WC1E 7DP.

Any person who does any unauthorised act in relation to
this publication may be liable to criminal prosecution and
civil claims for damages.

First published 1989

Published by
THE MACMILLAN PRESS LTD
Houndmills, Basingstoke, Hampshire RG21 2XS
and London
Companies and representatives
throughout the world

Printed in Hong Kong

British Library Cataloguing in Publication Data
Gaffney, John
The French Left and the Fifth Republic:
the discourses of communism and socialism
in contemporary France.
1. Socialism—France—History—20th
century
I. Title
333′.00944   HX264
ISBN 0–333–43231–2

QUEEN MARY
COLLEGE
LIBRARY

THE FRENCH LEFT AND THE FIFTH REPUBLIC

Also by John Gaffney

INTERPRETATIONS OF VIOLENCE: The Handsworth Riots of 1985
FRANCE AND MODERNISATION (*editor*)
ESSAYS ON POLITICAL CULTURE IN FRANCE AND WEST
  GERMANY (*editor with E. Kolinsky*)
THE LANGUAGE OF POLITICAL LEADERSHIP IN THE UK

For Melissa

Contents

Acknowledgements

First, I must thank the ESRC who funded the initial research for this book. I should also like to thank the staff of Sussex University library and the staff of the libraries, documentation departments and archives of the Assemblée Nationale, La Conféderation Française Démocratique du Travail, La Documentation Française, La Fondation Nationale des Sciences Politiques, L'Institut de Presse, Le Parti Communiste Français, Le Parti Socialiste and L'Université de Paris I, and, in particular, Marianne Delmaire of the French Socialist Party and Guy Pélachaud of the French Communist Party. I should also like to thank Editions Stock for permission to quote from *Pour le socialisme* (Editions Stock, 1974), and Editions sociales for permission to quote from G. Marchais, *Pour une avancée démocratique* (PCF, 1979) and G. Marchais, *L'Espoir au présent* (Editions sociales, 1980). I also wish to express my gratitude to the many academics, journalists, political advisers and practising politicians who gave me information and advice while I was doing my research. I want to thank, for their critical interest in my work and for their comments on specific chapters: David Bell, George Craig, Pamela Gaffney and Peter Newman. I should like to extend my thanks to the Department of Modern Languages at Aston University and my colleagues there for their help and co-operation while I was writing this book. I particularly want to thank Claire Allan who typed and corrected the manuscript, and whose continuous help ensured that the publishers received the text on time. Finally, and most of all, I want to thank Professor Bruce Graham of Sussex University, my research supervisor, whose encouragement in the early stages of my postgraduate studies and whose intellectual guidance were invaluable, and whose friendship and continued interest in my work I have appreciated greatly.

JOHN GAFFNEY

List of Abbreviations

CERES	*Centre d'études, de recherche et d'éducation socialistes*
CFDT	*Confédération française démocratique du travail*
CGT	*Confédération générale du travail*
CNPF	*Conseil national du patronat français*
CPSU	Communist Party of the Soviet Union
FEN	*Fédération d'éducation nationale*
GAM	*Groupes d'action municipale*
MRG	*Mouvement des radicaux de gauche*
MRP	*Mouvement républicain populaire*
PCF	*Parti communiste français*
PS	*Parti socialiste*
PS (SFIO)	*Parti socialiste (Section française de l'internationale ouvrière)*
PSU	*Parti socialiste unifié*
RPF	*Rassemblement du peuple français*
RPR	*Rassemblement pour la république*
SMC	State Monopoly Capitalism (theory of)
UDF	*Union pour la démocratie française*
UNR	*Union pour la nouvelle république*

Account for the Statistik
THIS IS A BOOK TO SEND YOU TO SLEEP
(RECOMMENDED READING BY THE INSOMNIACS ASSOCIATION)

1 Presidentialism and the Fifth Republic

The near-universal acceptance of the presidency of the Fifth Republic as the central authority in the French State set in motion political changes of fundamental importance. In this book I shall analyse the effects of a strong presidency upon the political parties of the French Left, and especially upon their modes of discourse. My principal argument is that in coming to terms with presidential politics the Left adapted its doctrines, practices and public discourse to new and unaccustomed forms, and that, in consequence, the character of the French polity has begun to alter in unexpected ways.

The purpose of this chapter is to survey the dominant themes and approaches of the literature which has analysed the nature and characteristics of the Fifth Republican regime.[1] We shall see from our survey that the themes of this literature change markedly over time. The early preoccupations with the problem of whether the new regime was or was not republican were replaced by quite different ones which were themselves centred upon the problems of explaining how and why the new regime was extending its organisational and administrative range. The preoccupation of the early period was with republicanism; that of the later period, with how a centralised, technocratic State could be constructed with little effective resistance from parties and social groups, and possibly with their acquiescence. Schematically, we can say that the later preoccupation simply replaces the earlier one, but literature, since it is continuous and interactive, reflects this shift in perspective by degrees as specific themes and subjects rise and fall on the scale of attention. This produces characteristic styles, which belong to distinguishable phases in the literature. Attention to these phases, styles and themes will tell us a great deal about the manner in which the regime has been understood.

The first phase, between 1958 and 1962, was characterised by interpretative writing which analysed de Gaulle's actions from within the theory that France was inherently republican.[2] Because of this interpretation, writing – whether critical or supportive of de Gaulle – was governed by what we might call the principle of reversion, that is to say, the principle that the regime, despite its contingent

1

temp measure

presidential characteristics, would be restored to or would converge upon the republican norm once the Algerian emergency had been ended.[3]

The critical literature argued that republicanism would reassert itself and force de Gaulle away from power after an Algerian settlement. The supportive literature was based upon the same principle, but differed in its interpretation, which was that, because de Gaulle was himself a republican protecting the republic from the extreme Right, he would facilitate a return to an effective republicanism once the crisis had been surmounted.[4]

In spite of the quality of its discussion, however, the interpretative writing of the period took the nature of republicanism itself as relatively unproblematic. For the writers, the task was one of understanding de Gaulle rather than of questioning the frame of reference – France's republican tradition – within which or in contrast to which his actions were interpreted. Many questions, however, were rarely addressed. How was it, for example, that de Gaulle could be both acclaimed and condemned by groups claiming allegiance to the same tradition? How was it that de Gaulle rallied support from republicans and from non-republicans? How was it that de Gaulle was acclaimed by half of the Left, condemned by the other half? If the principle of reversion was valid, how would the presence of de Gaulle, or the legacy of his intervention, impinge upon republican practice? These kinds of questions were rarely asked because, irrespective of whether de Gaulle was or was not seen as acting within the republican tradition, that tradition itself was generally accepted as relatively unambiguous, and was understood as one which was deeply inscribed in France's political culture and was approved of and understood by the near totality of the French population.

In the post-1962 period, however, it became increasingly difficult to sustain the reversion principle. In the first place, the anti-government and anti-regime 'republican' parties were unable to persuade the electorate to reject de Gaulle's proposal for amending the Constitution to provide for the election of the President by direct universal suffrage. This was approved by a referendum on 28 October 1962 by 61.7 per cent of the votes cast. Immediately following this, the republican parties were defeated in the general elections of November 1962 by the *Union pour la nouvelle république* (UNR), the Gaullist party. Three years later, in December 1965, de Gaulle won the first presidential election to take place under the new constitutional provisions against a republican contender, François Mitterrand. In 1967, the opposition parties again failed to win a majority in the general elections to the National Assembly. When the regime was eventually faced with a major demonstration of social unrest, in May–June 1968, this was expressed through the trade unions and through student groups, and not through political parties identified with republican values.

It was these unexpected developments within the regime, coupled with the continuing weakness – and in some cases eclipse – of the older republican parties, which were the conditions of a major thematic, formal and stylistic change in the writing about the regime.

Political writing during this period and retrospective analysis of that period became increasingly attracted to narrative forms of exposition, culminating in what were virtually chronicles of the regime[5] or speculative works about what French politics would be like without, or after, de Gaulle.[6] It was as though both Caesarist and republican (and Left–republican) interpretations had become theoretically inadequate or irrelevant in the context of the consolidation of an apparent Caesarism within an apparent republicanism. Interpreting the Fifth Republic gave way to simply chronicling it.

Interpretative writing still appeared, partly as the result of the development of the political clubs in the early 1960s. Although these works do not share the necessarily repetitive aspect of the chronological works, all of the writings of or about the 1960s period share the tendency to abstract de Gaulle from the rest of politics. In the case of the chronologies, this separation takes the form of an inordinate focussing upon de Gaulle and the presidency. In the case of the more interpretative analyses, it takes the form of discussions or debates which, although they do not ignore his contemporary significance, ignore his future one.[7]

We can see, therefore, that the thematic and formal change in the literature of and about the period from 1962 onwards is underpinned by an implicit belief that the principle of reversion was arguably still valid, but that it would not take effect until after the departure of de Gaulle from political life. Neither the chronologies nor the more interpretative writing of the 1960s – the first by ignoring republicanism, the second by ignoring de Gaulle – came to terms with the problematic nature of the relationship between presidentialism or personal leadership on the one hand, and an apparently impersonal republicanism on the other.

After de Gaulle resigned from office in 1969, chronological

'instant histories' remained a strong feature of political analysis, but with the Pompidou period (1969–1974) a different approach becomes more marked. P. Williams and M. Harrison's *Politics and Society in de Gaulle's Republic*[8] is something of a watershed in this respect. The book has the traditional chronological structure, but also a synchronic emphasis upon the political and social institutions of the period, which – treating the French polity as less unpredictable and mutable – anticipates the literature of the 1970s.

General de Gaulle left office in April 1969. His successor was Georges Pompidou, who had been de Gaulle's Prime Minister between 1962 and 1968. His support in the National Assembly was based upon the landslide majority that the Gaullists had gained in June 1968 in the wake of the events of May. Pompidou's presidency lasted until his death in office in 1974. His successor, Valéry Giscard d'Estaing, an Independent Republican, was President between 1974 and 1981. His parliamentary base remained secure, thanks to the success of the Right-wing parties in the elections to the National Assembly in 1973 and 1978.

The literature of and about this period remains essentially descriptive, now not so much of passing events but of political institutions.[9] The 1969–1981 period coincided with a consolidation of the regime and was a period of relative political and economic stability, after the rapid political evolution and economic expansion of the 1960s. One would expect, therefore, the development of a more synchronic approach and a move away from the emphasis upon the dramatic style of political leadership characteristic of de Gaulle. However, there was not, as one would also expect, a revival of interest in republicanism, nor a shift of focus away from the presidency itself, nor any significant discussion of the French polity's failure to revert to a more unequivocally republican form. The reluctance to return to the discussion of republicanism is associated with a readiness to pursue two closely related themes concerning the nature of the regime.

At the level of politicians' public statements, the major concern is with claiming a legitimacy from an enclosed and limited conception of republicanism, that of the Fifth Republic, which implicitly incorporates de Gaulle's conception of presidential rule. At the level of political analysis, attention has been directed almost exclusively towards the exercise of power from the presidential centre, rather than the expression and maintenance of the principles of republican authority in the making and implementation of policies. This shift in focus has been sustained by an implicit scepticism about the value or importance of the issues raised by the interpretative discussions of the earlier period. There are strong similarities between this approach to French politics in the 1970s and that of Marxian explanations of the way in which dominant classes maintain their domination of society and the polity.[10]

The political changes that occurred, therefore, have been explained as the result of the extension of the influence of the presidential office. Political change is reduced to institutional change, and institutions are portrayed as sites of power which are relatively unhampered by the republicanism which gave rise to them.

The two major literary forms of descriptive political analysis, the chronological and the institutional, have further encouraged the proliferation of two other related forms, both of which express the conviction that the formal practices of institutional politics are, at best, a series of ritual exercises, devoid of serious content, or, at worst, elaborate deceptions which hide the real nature of the political processes of the regime. The chronicle form has encouraged the significant growth of memoirs, accounts and other detailed descriptions offering insights into the 'behind the scenes' play of power relationships.[11] The focus upon institutional description has fostered a more systematic, less personalised literature, but this is based, explicitly or implicitly, upon the same principle: that political appearance and political reality are distinct entities, and that the maintenance of the one by the other is effected through control, manipulation, the reproduction and interrelation of elite groups and the internal structural characteristics of organisations like the bureaucracy. This mode of explanation, once the domain of Marxism in Europe and political sociology in the United States, now extends to all areas of French political analysis.[12]

The two dominant literary forms, chronicle and institutional description, have reinforced one another and have fostered a characteristic empiricism based upon the idea that the constant accumulation of data is necessary both to present and future understanding. Much of this literature, therefore, dates very quickly, and is either superseded or updated or implicitly criticised by new, corrective descriptions of the way politics in France is working under a different President or in the light of a new, detailed description of a major institution of power relationship. Traditional models for the depiction of the political system have indeed been recognised as inappropriate or difficult to apply: during the Fourth Republic, an academic writer could safely devote the major part of a book to the political parties and institutions of the regime, and a minor (and renewable) part to the more informal and less permanent processes, such as conventions governing the making and unmaking of governmental coalitions, the activities of pressure groups, or the social context of electoral politics.[13] Under the Fifth Republic, the assumed importance of informal politics, the fluidity of the party system and the stresses within the institutional framework have rendered such an exercise much more difficult.

The main problem facing political writers is not so much the rapidity of the change as its direction. The polity, by liberal, republican or socialist standards, has evolved along a quite unexpected path, judged by what occurred in earlier instances of regime change or development, and this raises questions concerning the interpretation of recent French history. One of the major questions concerns the assumption – or the denial – that the basic elements of organised politics (the political parties, leadership, the making and application of laws, the exercise of authority and the expression of degrees of allegiance to such authority) are contained within a popular republican tradition that is a coherent and unambiguous tradition exclusive of others.[14]

In spite of the corpus of theoretical literature on the problematic nature of democratic processes in political parties[15] and an even more critical Marxian analysis of their function,[16] the theoretical approach which explicitly or implicitly informs the great body of analysis of Fifth Republican politics in all periods is a simple one which we can call the tension theory, that is to say, an approach which sees the dynamic of politics and political change as a tension or conflict between two conceptions of the organisation of power, the one involving a drive towards democracy (and reliance upon the parties and parliament) and the other a drive away from it (towards the presidential or other executive office and the practice of presidential rule). The second of these conceptions involves greater emphasis upon the authority of the State and the independence of its action. It is this aspect of the theory which links it to a more general theory of French history variously described as a conflict between republicanism and the Empire, republicanism and the State administration and, in the twentieth century particularly, republicanism and the political representatives of modern capitalism.[17] The experience of the Fifth Republic raises questions which concern both conceptions of the organisation of power in a republic and the nature of the latter's place in French history as a whole. The politics of the Fifth Republic in fact bring to the fore the ambiguities contained within the notion of republicanism.

Advocates of the republican form of government, considering it a more or less perfect expression of representation, have invariably presented it as the adversary of unrepresentative authoritarianism.[18] In this way republicanism has been presented not only as a form but as a synonym of democracy. However, both within republicanism and outside it, other claims are made to legitimate forms of representation, often in contradistinction to an assumed lack of representativeness in republicanism itself. To the Left of it – normally represented in the twentieth century by the French Communist Party – a claim to a more representative republicanism exists in the idea of the *régime d'assemblée*. To the Right of it, and based upon a claim to more effective representation, lies another tradition, that of the *régime présidentiel*. Both of these claims, though broadly republican, draw heavily upon a plebiscitary notion of representation. Moreover, the *régime parlementaire* itself – which is what is traditionally signified in the modern period by republicanism – has its historical roots, much of its doctrine and a great deal of its modern rhetoric within this plebiscitary tradition. As we shall see in greater detail in the next chapter, the main representatives of this tradition, and in particular the French Socialist Party, are not only concerned with constitutional prescription, but are sustained by claims to a tradition which is part delegatory, part plebiscitary.

It was this shared heritage which allowed de Gaulle to make a claim to a more thoroughgoing form of representation by accentuating various elements within it. In this way, de Gaulle and the Fifth Republic distorted still further the political parties' relationship to their traditions, but now from within republicanism itself. (Ironically, de Gaulle depicted them as the modern versions of the pre-republican *féodalités*.) One of the ways that the political parties of the Left have responded to this double constraint (their dual heritage and de Gaulle's treatment of it) is not, as we shall see, through the abandonment of republicanism and the development of a bleached, historically insensitive political discourse, but through the accentuation of some of their earlier traditions.

During the early years of the Fifth Republic, de Gaulle's defence of the new constitution included not only an assertion of its republican credentials but also a denial of the claim, derived from the Third and Fourth Republics, that parliamentarianism was the equivalent of republicanism. Given the eclecticism of the republican, as distinct from the parliamentary, tradition it was difficult to counter both the assertion and the denial.

The essential point here is that it is far more difficult to specify the boundaries of republicanism than those of parliamentarianism.[19] Where did de Gaulle's legitimacy come from if he was merely the beneficiary of a plebiscitary phase in the evolution of republicanism? How could he claim authority in areas specific to the republican tradition? Equally important, and outside the reference of the mainstream republican view although crucial to an understanding of the nature of authority, was the question of the relationship between the rights and the personal style of rule of the presidential office-holder and the relationship of these to modes of representation.[20]

The failure to confront theories of republicanism with the problematic nature of authority and representation was present, not only in the writings and speeches of political actors, but also in press comment and in academic work. And what emerges when we look at the political analysis of the first thirty years of the Fifth Republic is a gradual shift away from a concern with republican practice towards a concern with the exercise of authority, rather than the elaboration of the nature of the relationship beween the two.

In the most reflective writing, the republican-authority/non-republican-authoritarianism opposition was, and has continued to be, expressed essentially as an institutional drama, in which the scope of the presidency was extended at the expense of parliament (and indirectly of parties) by administrative and technical means. Within this drama, however, the republican legitimacy of the strengthened presidency is seen as having been accepted,[21] though mainly on the grounds that it contributes to the strength of the State's executive functions. The acceptance of its capacity to establish popular support within the domain of representative politics, and to maintain such support after de Gaulle's departure from office, has been tardy and incomplete. The conflict between the presidency, as a representative as distinct from executive office, on the one hand, and the parties and parliament on the other, has often been treated as an elaborate game with a fixed volume of resources, in which the presidency's gain is the parties' loss. The inadequacy of this interpretation is evident, however, when we see that, on the one hand, the traditional parties (and realigned centrists) as well as the Fifth Republican Gaullist party have maintained their strength at all levels of national election, particularly at the municipal level and that, on the other, the parties have themselves become the base from which most presidential candidates emerge.

The hypothesis which presents itself, therefore, is that the parties are not in decline but are instead adapting themselves to a regime in which presidential and parliamentary politics are intertwined. If this is the case, then a related hypothesis proceeds from it: that not only de Gaulle, but subsequent presidential figures; Pompidou, Giscard d'Estaing and Mitterrand, have acquired a representative standing and a significance in French politics which goes far beyond the phrase 'personality politics' which has hitherto been used to deal with the half-perceived phenomenon that lies behind it. If this inadequacy is recognised, then it is the case that both of the above hypotheses are in need of searching examination. Our central conviction, therefore, is that a clearer understanding of the nature of the relationship between different party doctrines and their relationship to republican traditions and to what we shall define in the next chapter as political personalism does facilitate an understanding of the nature of regime change in the Fifth Republic.

The explanations concerning the central importance of the presidency which we find in the literature on the Fifth Republic are not misplaced but they are incomplete, and this incompleteness is the result of an understressing of the parties' traditions in relation to presidentialism and to French political culture, which has in turn led to a misperception of the nature of allegiance to the office of the presidency and the person of the President.

Generally speaking, the political parties in the Fifth Republic have been studied from two related perspectives. In the first instance, they are seen as units in a system of coalition building (with the presidency as the formative and constraining condition).[22] Secondly, *all* the parties from the 1960s onwards are seen as having orientated themselves towards a 'catch-all' strategy,[23] reminiscent of the UNR. Both of these approaches neglect or diminish the role of doctrine and tradition in party behaviour and dispositions, and treat parties as having been drained doctrinally in order to operate effectively in a presidential regime. That the realignments in the party system are due to the presidency is not in doubt. What is lacking in an analysis of the political party and the regime, however, is an understanding of how such alignments occur, indeed, how they are *possible*, for, as we shall see in chapters 4, 5, 6 and 7, parties not only represent interests directed towards the attainment of power, they also and still represent wide-ranging philosophies of French history and politics.

Parties claim to represent people, and do represent them in two quite different senses: on the one hand, they represent shifting and internally mobile assemblages of social and economic interests at any one point in time and, on the other, they represent and express enduring, though mutable, ideas about the general nature of French society and the polity. The latter form of representation was, except in the case of the Gaullists, predominantly anti-plebiscitary and anti-authoritarian, while containing an awareness and guarded acknowledgement of the functional nature of claims to plebiscitary legitimacy. What has happened under the Fifth Republic is that these party traditions have been, as it were, twisted on their axes to accept the values of presidentialism and political personalism as legitimate means of representing collective desires and ideals.

To sum up, we can say that the analyses and commentaries concerning the Fifth Republic initially assumed that the authority of the office of the presidency would revert to 'republican' institutional practice once the Algerian crisis had been resolved or, failing that, after de Gaulle had left office. When it became clear that the presidency was maintaining, and even increasing, its dominance, the focus of analysis became that of understanding how the presidency had asserted itself and how the parties and other institutions and practices had been forced to respond. Underlying this shift in focus is the abandonment of preoccupation with the republican tradition and with the manner in which the presidency accommodated, and still accommodates, to it, and the subsequent emergence of the functionalist view that one political institution (the presidency) refused power to a second (parliament), with the result that the institutions which were the sources of the second's strength veered away from this constraint. According to this view, they did so by developing majority coalitions, emptying themselves of doctrinal content and historical sensitivity and amplifying their rhetoric with the slogans and images appropriate to the projection of modern 'dynamic' and essentially apolitical party leaders on French television screens.

There are elements of truth in this view, but it fails to incorporate an understanding of the conditions and process of change. In particular, it fails to take into account the effect and process of regime change upon organised politics, particularly upon the political parties, which undergo considerable doctrinal and organisational stress as a result of their cultural, philosophical and organisational traditions, traditions which must be involved if the parties are to be drawn into the normative parameters of the new regime.

The approach adopted in this book raises the question of modalities of such change and adaptation, and it is here that attention to political ritual and discourse becomes significant. In doing so, it raises further questions concerning the manner in which both republicanism in general and the Fifth Republican regime in particular have been portrayed and understood.

All political organisations are sustained by their ritual mode. In modern representative democracy, moreover, they all practise public discourse, the medium through which a significant portion of political exchange is operated, whether through the media, at congresses, rallies, in speeches in parliament, in communiqués or in other discursive forms.

The following chapters will examine how public discourse and public political ritual have been crucial in the subtle and complex adaptation of the political parties of the Left to the regime, how discursive and ritual forms have themselves led to other changes in the parties and in the regime as a whole, and how such central roles appropriated by discourse provide insight into the nature of representation in general and leadership in particular within the context of the parties' doctrinal and organisational traditions.

2 Political Leadership and Political Theory

As the previous chapter has shown, much of the writing on French politics ties interpretation of political reality and explanation of political change to the principle that France is inherently republican, that the nature of republicanism, however disputed, is not within itself contradictory, and that deviations from this norm either revert to republican forms in a short space of time or else remain deviations, unable to establish proper legitimacy. It is argued that deviations from the republican norm are sustained by a concentration of power and/or systematic ideological manipulation that is antithetical to republicanism. At the heart of this interpretation – and this is why the discussion of republicanism disappears from the analyses of Fifth Republican presidentialism – is the conviction that modes of rule and forms of government involve mutually exclusive categories (such as monarchical, Bonapartist, republican, socialist or communist forms),[1] and that each category expresses distinctive and coherent principles of rule.

Closer examination reveals that the principle of reversion to republicanism rests upon three empirically-supported theoretical considerations: first, that personalised power is always ephemeral and exceptional; second, that it is incompatible with republicanism; and, third, that republican forms of institutional order have become normative in both French political and civil society.[2]

However, having been elected President on 21 December 1958 by the restricted electoral college, de Gaulle consistently acted to sustain the institutions of the Fifth Republic against anti-republican movements. He defended them against the extreme Right and against elements of the army, most dramatically in January 1960 and in April 1961. He also allowed the emergency powers conferred upon his office by article 16 of the 1958 Constitution to revert to parliament after the period of emergency in 1961.

In late 1962 fears of a shift towards institutionalised authoritarianism were raised once again when de Gaulle successfully amended the Constitution by means of a referendum to allow for the election of the President of the Republic by direct universal adult suffrage. Some observers argued that the use of universal suffrage for the election of the President would set up a rival process of representative legitimation to that provided by elections to the National Assembly, would emphasise their local and sectional character, and would deny them their claim to represent the national interest exclusively.[3]

Given the principle of reversion underlying the republican view, however, it was still argued that the Fifth Republic could – within the framework of the 1958 Constitution – revert to type, with the parties of both the majority and the opposition steadily asserting themselves as parliament explored its implicit powers, and the President's dramatic interventions in the political process became less frequent and less appropriate. Reversion, even after 1962, was still seen as likely but was now presented as occurring in the post-de Gaulle period rather than simply in the post-Algerian phase. Once this tendency to reversion had reached a certain stage, it was argued, the non- or anti-republican elements of the Constitution, such as article 16, could be deleted or allowed to fall into disuse, as had been the case with certain of the provisions of the Third Republic's Constitution, and rival claims to democratic legitimation could be co-ordinated so that the presidential elections become a function of parliamentarianism and the proper application of the Constitution.

However, the absolute majority gained by the Gaullist party, the UNR, and its allies in the National Assembly elections of November 1962 enabled the Assembly to work smoothly within the framework of the amended 1958 Constitution. Even though de Gaulle, from 1962 to 1969, still asserted his authority according to his interpretation of the 1962 constitutional amendment,[4] the parliamentary majority was able to act as if it constituted a party of government, and as if the Council of Ministers and the Prime Minister were accountable to it to an important degree. Many of the problems raised by uncertainties in constitutional practice appeared to have been solved or else postponed until the regime was stable, providing that de Gaulle's parliamentary majority could be sustained beyond his departure and/or the Left came to power within the framework of the regime. If this proved to be the case, the government, nominated by the President but responsible to parliament, might preside over the return to a regime which was in the direct tradition of the Third and Fourth Republics, only strengthened now by the existence of a coherent governing majority and party programmes. Therefore, although throughout the 1960s de Gaulle continued to assert his executive authority and central position in the polity, the full range of political parties remained active. However, this progressive adaptation of the Fifth Republican parties to the regime has involved, not only a gradual acceptance of and allegiance to the Constitution, but also the development of a series of political practices which themselves have been prompted or encouraged by the continuing development of presidential power.

It is this latter adaptation which has often been misinterpreted and imperfectly understood. From the 1965 presidential campaign onwards, the parties of the Left increasingly experimented with the methods of launching political personalities into the competition for presidential power, at first as a matter of prudence or pragmatic necessity, and later as a matter of organisationally justified and considered principle. In effect, parties began to compete for the presidency and to organise themselves in relation to such competition. One result was a profound alteration in the balance of party behaviour, produced mainly by the tendency of actual and aspiring leaders to borrow and later to use systematically the doctrines and organisational structures of political parties as vehicles for presidential campaigns and by the parallel tendency of party organisations themselves at first to allow and later to encourage such usage. Parties which had hitherto accepted the republican norm that political parties should not be drawn into personalist 'adventures', and that, if they were, they ceased to be parties in the true sense of the word (and would soon cease practically to be so), had now to deny one part of their inherited nature and behave, in part, as non-parties. It is at this point of party adaptation that personalism – which we shall discuss in detail below, but which can be represented here as overtly stressed personal leadership – begins to impinge upon party processes.

The acceptance of personalism by parties entailed an extension of hitherto suppressed and contradictory ideas within their own traditions. For example, most parties combine liberal notions of democratic processes involving the representation of pluralistic aggregates of interests and clientele with Rousseauistic notions of their embodying or epitomising a unified social whole. However, the latter tradition, with its stress upon the idea of organic community, has affinities with the idea that personal leaders can, in some mysterious way, also epitomise and represent the community as a whole. This shifting of the dual focus of the perceived political site of community towards a leader has, in fact, often occurred within republican regimes even though it has never been given theoretical consideration. Each of the major French party lineages in the twentieth century has examples of leaders who have presented themselves or have been presented as personally and simultaneously representing their political tradition and the wider community: Léon Blum for the Socialists in 1936, Maurice Thorez for the Communists in 1944–6, Antoine Pinay for the Conservatives in 1952 and Pierre Mendès-France for the Radicals in 1954–6.

However, it was one thing to allow a leader unusual scope for action in exceptional circumstances and accept the occasional presentation of the party leader to the wider public as the symbol of an ideal community, but quite another to accept personalism as a permanent principle of party activity. Logically, the adaptation to personalism can be represented as simple, involving little more than a rearrangement of existing principles, and an adjustment of the margins of acceptable conduct (stress upon the affinities between the party and the wider or ideal community, assertion that the leader 'speaks for the party', implicit acceptance of the 'logic' of modern media coverage of politics). Normatively, each party needed to reach back into its traditions to heighten and emphasise particular themes and principles. Organisationally, however, the consequence of these shifts meant profound changes in party activity, organisational life and party orientation and a further and more dramatic revision of principles and norms.

This is the essence of the way French party politics 'adapted' to the Fifth Republic, but the manner in which change occurs is complex. It can be characterised as involving the interplay of organisational practice, political strategies, doctrinal heritage and leadership, mainly through the agency of discursive exchange, and in the context of the revision of leadership status.

The approach adopted in this study is that of detailed analysis of particular political texts, placed in their doctrinal, ritual, organisational, strategic and more immediate political settings. Such an approach presupposes a series of theoretical standpoints and perspectives which we shall discuss under three broad headings: leadership, political organisation, and public discourse.

LEADERSHIP

Let us examine three theoretical approaches which, more than any others, have influenced and shaped the Left's response to the phenomenon of personal leadership and the leadership/democracy dichotomy: those of Marx, Trotsky and Weber.

Before criticising Marx's arguments in *The Eighteenth Brumaire of Louis Bonaparte*[5] let us abstract the main lines of that argument. Firstly, he sets out to demonstrate that 'great man' theories of history are misplaced, but concedes that historical processes may work through forms of personal power. Secondly, he acknowledges that personal power and authority exist relationally between leader and led, but argues that the personal qualities of the leader do not explain the relation. Thirdly, he concedes that the concentration of power achieved by Louis Napoléon, following his *coup d'état*, effectively breaks or interrupts various sequences of historical development, and principally the development of class conflict. Fourthly, he points out that Louis Napoléon's establishment of the Second Empire has the ultimate effect and purpose of reasserting class power in a new institutional form.

Marx's study is an analysis of the events leading to Louis Napoléon's *coup* of 2 December 1851. He spares no effort to diminish the historical role and personal qualities of the new Emperor. In his preface to the second edition, Marx specifically condemns Victor Hugo's equally hostile preoccupation with the personality of Louis Napoléon which 'makes this individual great instead of little'. Conversely, Marx attacks Proudhon's determinism which, depriving human actors of autonomy, serves as an indirect apologia for the Emperor. Interpreting history as class struggle, Marx wishes to emphasise the social and historical conditions which have allowed 'a grotesque mediocrity to play a hero's part'.[6]

For Marx, Caesarism is to be distinguished from Bonapartism by the differing conditions of Rome in the first century BC and Paris in the middle of the nineteenth century. However, for us, this affirmation of underlying difference and surface resemblance is not in itself explanatory, for if the social conditions of Caesarism and Bonapartism are not comparable, what then is it that causes the assumed though misplaced affinity?

This leads us to a more fundamental objection to Marx's treatment of his subject. He describes Bonapartism as a 'cardsharper's trick'.[7] Characteristic of Marx's approach is an explicit contempt for a person 'who hides his commonplace repulsive features under the iron deathmask of Napoleon'.[8] It is, in fact, implicit throughout the *Eighteenth Brumaire* that there are, for Marx, collective and individual heroes whose greatness is truly recognisable. Louis Napoléon is commonplace because he built his reputation upon what amounted to a parody of his uncle and not upon his own integrity or genius. This attitude to real heroism or its absence is not restricted to those individuals history has produced to create or consolidate class power. Marx treats Blanqui and other revolutionary leaders as the potential focus of true and effective leadership, but who were removed from the political stage too early to influence events.[9] Not only, therefore, is the false consciousness which generates adherence to either of the Napoleons not addressed, but there is an easily discernible belief, expressed in Marx's account, in a personal leadership capable of rallying the people and which does not distort the consciousness of the revolutionary class. With regard to the presidential elections of December 1848, which Louis Napoléon won overwhelmingly, voting behaviour is explained in terms of the voters' response to their objective interests rather than to their subjective desires. Marx argues that ideas expressed by the Napoleonic doctrine (concerning property rights, strong government, the role of the Church, the police, and the army) coincided with the interests of the peasantry: 'the most numerous class of the French people'.[10] There is a dualism in Marx's approach to the nature of political allegiance. And it is this dualism – the assumption that political allegiance is uncontentious when in the interests of the progressive classes on the one hand, and the instrumentalist treatment of it when it is interpreted as an adjunct to class domination on the other – which reduces the explanatory power of the analysis.

Marx's seminal work therefore emphasises the relational aspect of personalised leadership but is only tangentially concerned with the reasons for and form of its widespread acceptance, in 1848 as in 1851, and with the nature of leadership authority.

Another of the classic and most influential Leftist studies of the phenomenon of Bonapartism is Leon Trotsky, *The Revolution Betrayed*, an analysis of the basis of Stalin's power in the USSR.[11] In a manner similar to Marx's reaction to Hugo's preoccupation with Louis Napoléon's personality, Trotsky is reacting to the idolatry of Stalin by Western socialists such as Sidney and Beatrice Webb.[12] Like Marx, Trotsky is debunking a myth by identifying its functional role, rather than explicating it. For Trotsky, Stalin is the personification of the bureaucracy.[13] He does not mean, however, that Stalin symbolises a social force, but simply that he is the political instrument used to defeat the Bolsheviks. Stalin brings to the protection of the bureaucracy the prestige of an old Bolshevik leader,[14] but, surrounding himself like Louis Napoléon with mediocrities, he is accepted as safe by the administration. The 'secret of

Stalin's success'[15] is, for Trotsky, that he promotes the interests of the bureaucracy without interfering with it. Trotsky does not examine either the nature and dynamic of the symbolic protection offered, or why, once accepted, Stalin is deified by substantial sections of the Soviet population. What, for example, is the nature of the prestige of an old Bolshevik, and where does such prestige link up with forms of allegiance in political and civil society? What is the dynamic of Stalin's rise above and domination of a politically atomised society?[16] Within the tradition of Marxian interpretation, Trotsky sees the cult of Stalin as the bourgeois form of Caesarism adapted to a revolution. which Russia was ill-equipped to carry through to socialism.

For Marx, Napoléon III triumphed in France over underdeveloped social forces. For Trotsky, Soviet Bonapartism triumphed in the Soviet Union, as did Fascism in Italy and Germany, because of the 'dilatoriness of the world proletariat in solving the problems set for it by history'.[17] Both Marx and Trotsky define Bonapartism in terms of the social and political traditions which apparently give rise to it. As if to deny Stalin's leadership a reality because he considers it evil, Trotsky defines neither the rationale of Stalin's position, nor the relationship of the leader to his popular support, nor the reasons why committed or contractual supporters believe he will be so supported. To argue that individuals come to prominence in situations in which social forces are undeveloped is to characterise those forces but not their relationship to leadership. Marx's ridicule of the farcical nature of modern history's self-conscious re-enactment of the past through mimicry, parody and reference to analogous events only further begs the question of the nature and role of the re-enactment.[18]

Both Marx and Trotsky deliberately understate (and thereby indicate by default) the 'qualities' of leadership, representing them as functionally instrumental in a process of mystification which, once exposed, can be shown to have concealed deeper social processes. Neither writer, however, questions the assumption that social classes or groups of people will follow leaders, and it is the dynamic of this aspect of politics which requires examination.

Weber's notion of charismatic authority in (modern) society arises from his examination of how and why societies produce various forms of authority in moments of social change. For Weber, the modern industrial period is characterised by the development of rationality in governmental and other social practices and is manifest in the development of bureaucracy and in a concomitant mode of authority which is itself rational.[19] Charismatic authority, incarnated essentially in charismatic individuals, occurs at moments of social regression or transformation wherein a movement of allegiance to a leader is set up in opposition to other authority modes:

> *The term 'charisma' will be applied to a certain quality of an individual personality by virtue of which he is set apart from ordinary men and treated as endowed with supernatural, superhuman, or at least specifically exceptional powers or qualities. These are such as are not accessible to the ordinary person, but are regarded as of divine origin or as exemplary, and on the basis of them the individual concerned is treated as a leader.[20]*

There is a problem raised by Weber's own treatment of charisma which is discernible in the definition itself. The emphasis is clearly and deliberately upon the notion of the ascription of qualities, and therefore upon the idea of charisma as a perceived phenomenon rather than one which, of itself, possesses identifiable qualities. There is, however, an area of uncertainty in Weber's definition. It is true that, for Weber, charismatic authority is not exclusive to individuals. Other forms of authority also possess a transcendental, extraordinary quality.[21] But what we can say, and what Weber clearly sensed, was that when an individual is perceived as the focus of charisma, it is attractive to conflate charisma with, and difficult to distinguish it from, the assumed possessor of it. To stress the relational aspect of Weber's treatment of charisma goes some way towards reconciling the ascription/possession duality in the phenomenon. This, however, does not address the question of why the ascribed or possessed quality of 'charismatic individuals' is so compelling, nor does it identify the rationale behind the ability of charismatic individuals to rival and sometimes replace other forms of authority. Both of these characteristics are related to the notion of individuals as the personification of ideas and, as we shall see, it is in discourse and through its rhetoric that such a notion can be elaborated so effectively.

Much of the discussion of the questions posed by Weber has concentrated upon the theoretical adequacy of the term 'charisma'.[22] The use of the term, however, masks a series of imagined events which we can represent here as a triptych: (i) the conferring of grace (by God); (ii) acknowledgement by the community (or Church or State or organisation) that a gift of grace-receiver exists; and (iii) acceptance that the possession of grace endows the receiver with a peculiar authority to act. In secular, political processes this triptych raises three related questions. What is to be taken to represent political insight in a given community? How is the insightful person to deport him/herself, personally and discursively, in order to gain acknowledgement? What are the possibilities open to (and the constraints upon) the insightful individual when he or she embarks upon political action? By concentrating upon charisma as a form of authority, Weber's definition distracts attention from the question of how any political order, whether legal, rational or traditional in form, has to deal with constant *discursive appeals* to an alternative and metaphysical idealism. And within a representative democratic polity all maintenance of or changes in exchange, custom and control are operated initially through discourse.

In the political history of modern France, there are numerous examples of political leaders who have appealed for support by referring to a vision of an ideal society, and who have suggested that existing institutions could be transformed under inspired leadership. It is also the case that such idealism is often expressed in transformational rather than in revolutionary or insurrectionary language, that is to say, that the political task is presented as that of making institutions work for an ideal purpose rather than that of replacing them with new institutions.

The latter observation highlights a further difficulty with the Weberian notion of charisma, namely, its implication that charismatic authority is inimical to other forms of authority.[23] As a result, when Weber concentrates on the notion of charismatic individuals, he sees their success and failure as a function of the establishment and eclipse of a charismatic authority.[24]

Our approach to the study of leadership in politics begins, not from a notion of authority, but from a notion of a claim to personal insight or vision and the transmission of this claim through discourse. If politics is considered as a rational process, consisting of the statement of interests, the expression of those interests through associations, and the working out of policies by the careful recognition and co-ordination of claims upon resources, then leadership here becomes a matter of expert knowledge of, for example, how the complex system works, how interests are articulated, and which resources should be deployed for what results. In short, a strong managerial element is the basis of its authority. This view of politics is underpinned by the assumption that the general interest is served by the expression of specific interests, and that political institutions are the reflection in organised form of cultural and social entities. It is this view that is challenged by individual leaders who lay claim to a vision of what the community could be ideally, and who claim to encompass a concern, not only for the articulation of the rational expression of interests, but also for deeper inarticulate expressions of anxiety and desire. Such leaders do not necessarily claim that existing institutions are inherently bad, only that they do not function properly but would do so under inspired leadership. These leaders and potential leaders offer a symbolic commitment to an alternative validation of politics and to a particular form of legitimacy, but not necessarily to an alternative form of polity.

In representative democracy, the focus of this mode of discourse normally involves an imagined view of the State and the form of leadership appropriate to it. Political leadership within the State is characterised as working in a series of close relationships with political organisations which are themselves competing for influence within the polity. Here, the exercise of leadership may be defined as a set of activities carried out within a prescribed office. From our analysis, however, it is clear that Bonapartism, Caesarism and charismatic authority are all inadequate in the characterisation of it because they proceed from the premise that personal leadership is exclusive of this initial political leadership relation. We shall therefore define personalism as the intrusion of a leader's persona into prescribed organisational activities, by means of his/her claim to a particular insight, an intrusion which sees a concomitant response on the part of the political organisation to this claim, either because of the actual influence of the intrusion or because of the assumed response of the wider community. Both esoterically and exoterically, therefore, political personalism is the organisational, doctrinal and discursive opposite to the impersonalist claims of and within the political process of representative democracy. Nevertheless, it has always constituted part of that process. The role of the leader of a political organisation is deducible from the function of the office, but is always in some form of relationship, or potential relationship, to leadership in a transcendental sense.

Political personalism is therefore two things: it is the intrusion of persona into party practice, and it is an implicit or explicit claim to insightful leadership, actual or potential.[25]

LEADERSHIP AND ORGANISATION

From the above discussion, we can see that the question of personal leadership and its relationship to organisation in political theory is problematic and unresolved. Within republicanism, moreover, the problematic nature of personal leadership is compounded by the fact that the principles of representative democracy are always expressed in impersonal terms. Indeed, theories of representative democracy, whether or not they incorporate the mediation of interests via political parties, are themselves based upon a form of impersonalism. However, because individuals are distributed throughout the polity and because representation presupposes representatives in the form of spokespersons and leaders, of factions, parties and governments, the emergence of political personalities in some form is automatic.

Constitutionally, representative democracy entails the formation and maintenance of associations and institutions in which formal procedures obviate the anti-democratic expression of personal interest and private ambition as well as the domination of the polity by sectional interests. Paradoxically, the broadening of the suffrage and the evolution of democratic politics and channels of political communication have increased the practical and symbolic roles played by individuals to the point where they speak for a wide range of accessible opinion, and therefore represent organised interests, while they also symbolically embody or are potentially capable of embodying the less easily identifiable range of changing hopes, anxieties and desires which we mentioned earlier.

The rationale of modern political parties in representative politics is twofold. Traditionally, they have restricted and regulated the personalism of unreconstructed representative politics that is characterised by either parliamentary factionalism, patronage or lack of accountability, all of which were perceived as misrepresentations of electors by the elected. Secondly, parties purport to represent structurally the interests of various sections of society and, by extension and in differing degrees, the interests of present or future society as a whole. This double process of regulation and organisation has involved the parties in the reconciliation of expanding constituencies with the representative process, in the inclusion or exclusion of rival elements that run counter to constitutional prescription, and in the induction of a massive electorate into the procedures and strategies of political accountability, consensus and compromise.

The evolution of representative democracy in the modern period, therefore, has placed the parties under characteristic and continuous strain. They mediate between large sections of society and representative institutions. They also incorporate into their own affairs a version of the representative process which reflects the ethical imperatives which inform them as well as their idea of political relations in an ideal society. This tension between the party as the organised representation of sectional interest and as the symbolic representation of the whole or ideal society is particularly acute during national election campaigns. In order to maintain itself as a (public) organisation, the modern political party has developed a series of ritually expressed, organisational cycles, routine practices and procedures of internal differentiation. Its efforts, therefore, to convert itself into a self-contained and self-sustaining political group within the State run counter to its declared purpose, which is to represent only, as if in unreconstructed form, a substantial part of, or else the whole of, the electorate. One part of its organisation is directed to mobilise mass support and another designed to prevent such support from dominating it. We can say, therefore, that in order to appeal to communitarianism the party must also organise against it. These contradictory drives are normally represented as a constellation of political actors of which the party is the core. In French politics, the connotative elaboration of terms like *militant, membre du parti*, or *inscrit, clientèle* and *électorat*, which are portrayed as interdependent and varying parts of an organic whole, is an attempt to lend coherence to the highly problematic questions raised by the simple notions of party affiliation and allegiance.

Such a traditional model might be justified if the first in this series of related terms, *militant* (activist), were in a direct relation to all the other terms, and could be portrayed as successfully expressing the interests and values of other party members and the wider constituency. The activity of the *militant*, however, is not directed outwards but inwards towards specialisation, the development of party programmes and other necessarily esoteric acts in the self-maintenance of the political party, a process which therefore strengthens the party while separating it organisationally from its supporting interests and potential electorate. This being the case, the burden of accommodation between the various expressions of the political party and the party's perceived constituency falls upon the main party leaders and their discursive performances.

In relating the internal concerns of their party to the external politics of the regime, party leaders work within a complex framework of discourse, observing the language both of impersonal associational politics and the transcendental communitarianism associated with rally politics.[26] In a party such as the RPR (*Rassemblement pour la république*), this leadership/organisation dichotomy is minimised by the tradition of overt personal allegiance within Gaullism. Parties of the Left are far more constrained doctrinally in this respect. Apparent leadership submission to or involvement in projects, programmes and party plans or, conversely, the appropriation by leadership of party discourse are practices which minimise the contradiction of personalism within a party whose doctrinal base is anti-personalist and/or egalitarian. Parties of the Left, therefore, will either allow the balance within the party to shift towards, or else will attempt to domesticate, personalism within an associational range. The tension, however, is always present.

The nature of the regime will directly affect the play of this tension. Where the electoral process is channelled mainly towards a legislature which in turn provides the basis of executive power, interest groups and social groups will accept and exploit the party's central mediating role between government and civil society. Electoral choice, moreover, is far more likely to be expressed in the impersonal forms of party programmes and mandates. Where the electoral process is also directed towards the election of a President whose office is the basis of executive power, the tension will increase dramatically and the political parties will reorientate themselves in order to remain politically relevant. Moreover, interest groups may enter into direct corporate relations with the executive power and administrative institutions. In order to redress or maintain the balance of the party's relationship to its constituency and to prevent non-partisan leaders from impinging upon the political relations within the polity, the political parties will be forced to release their leaders from associational constraint and present them as candidates for presidential power whose potential legitimacy is drawn from the people at large. They will simultaneously present the leader as the representative of themselves and (therefore) themselves as the representatives of the wider community.

Regime changes in post-war France have demonstrated the contingent nature of party leadership. Under the Fourth Republic, the parties of the Third Force (1947–51) – the Socialists, Radicals and the *Mouvement républicain populaire* (MRP) – defined themselves and their alliances within parliament as proceeding from a dedication to the parliamentary regime, the essence, in their view, of the republican tradition. Their main task, therefore, was to resist attempts by groups representing other traditions, namely the Gaullist RPF and the Communists, to force the Fourth Republic towards, respectively, a *régime présidentiel* and a *régime d'assemblée*. For the same reasons, these parties sanctioned personalist politics within their own ranks, and emphasised the virtues of impersonal institutional rule.

The 1958 Constitution was not a repudiation of this tradition, but the 1962 constitutional amendment, which provided for the election of the President by direct universal adult suffrage, created the effective basis for a further regime change. The parties which under previous republics had constrained leaders, keeping them from crossing the boundaries of associational politics were now obliged to allow them much more scope to 'represent' not only the interests, values and myths to which the parties deferred, but also those which were foreign to their own conception of their republican identity. The Fifth Republic witnesses the significant intrusion into party discourse, via the personalist leader, of another discourse which purports to represent the collective beliefs, interests, desires, anxieties and expectations of a much wider constituency.

Party leadership has therefore become personalist but its role has become more diffuse as these changes occur. For the *Parti socialiste* (PS) in the 1970s, for example, François Mitterrand, the First Secretary of the party, was not simply the elected leader, nor just the main spokesperson for the Union of the Left, nor the potential President of the Republic (or the potentially defiant Socialist Prime Minister in a Giscardian regime), nor the modern interpreter of a Socialist and republican tradition. He was *all* of these things combined. Within the party, moreover, he also came to represent the threat that, should he lose the leadership, the rally of opinion around the Socialists would ebb away and the Socialists lose the chance of gaining power for the foreseeable future. His authority, therefore, was polyvalent and ill-defined, going far beyond his official function. In broad terms he represented not only the party's esoteric traditions but also those attributed to a wider electorate. In this way he became the focus of two broad sources of legitimacy. In the Fifth Republic, however, the second potential source, the exoteric, has become greatly strengthened and has edged the party towards a rally purpose, heightening and extending the significance of esoteric aspects of the party and adapting them to personalism.

The party leader has thus become a rally leader not intermittently and imperfectly, as under the Third and Fourth Republics, but continuously and explicitly. Political personalism thus becomes a permanent feature of Fifth Republican politics, and the parties, having surrendered their leadership and much of their ritual and organisational rationale to such politics, are also constrained to define themselves as rallies in some respects, oriented towards relative success in presidential elections and towards the discursive and symbolic enactment of community which that orientation entails.

In the Fifth Republic, therefore, two major changes occur in the nature of political parties, changes which inform theories of political leadership and of party organisations: first, within the republican notion of representation, impersonalism gives way to personalism; and, second, the associational tradition gives way to the rally tradition. The progress of their relation will be marked in discourse and ritual. These too undergo substantial change and their public expression becomes significantly more central in the life of the political party and in the support they lend to the personalist and rally undertaking.

THE DISCOURSE OF POLITICAL PERSONALISM

We shall take political discourse to mean the verbal equivalent of political action: the set of all political verbalisations, and expressible forms adopted by political organisations and political individuals. It generates response which may range from indifference, through hostility, to enthusiasm and which may or may not lead to political action. It is as complex in its interrelations as political action is. The significance of any instance of political discourse will be affected by its overall relation to political action. And together discourse and action constitute political practice.

The constant endeavour of public political discourse is to give meaning to activity. It does so, however, in contexts which themselves supply meaning in and to discourse. A central contextual element is the relationship of the speaker or writer to his/her audience. This in particular will define the modalities of the discourse, and the explanation of the relationship will normally be one of the constituent themes of it. The wider context, and one which distinguishes political discourse from many other forms, is the profusion and elaborateness of previous discursive expressions.

The immediate and wider contexts of political discourse are both controlled and enhanced by a further context of discourse in modern representative politics, namely, ritual. It too defines and characterises, as, for example, in the case of the speaker/audience relationship and the status of the speaker in the press conference. Ritual constrains, moreover, in that through it public political discourse is normally one-way. This one-way aspect of ritual is compensated for by the fact that ritual, in the context of public discourse, obviates self-indulgence on the part of the speaker while extending the possibilities for collective participation and celebration. When the audience of a given moment of leadership discourse is the political party itself, one of the functions of ritual and aims of discourse is the alignment of external and internal party relations to which leadership, and especially personalist leadership, is the key. Ritual is, therefore, the necessary condition of party politics itself, a formative condition of public political discourse, and the central context of leadership discourse.

The case of the French Communist Party (PCF) congress is a good example of this. The PCF congress is the traditional and exemplary occasion of a highly controlled ritual. At the 23rd Congress (see Chapter 4), however, discourse has the effect of overtly demonstrating the compatibility of traditionalism and the new personalism. Here, ritual not only facilitates personalism but, through the discursive alignment of a traditional and a novel ritual significance, actually celebrates it. This is not to say that elaborately ritualised practices are the only places where such discursive intrusions can take place, rather that the change in the nature of ritual occasions is itself an indication of a more generalised transformation.

Like discourse, ritual is itself problematic. The presence of ritual in political occasions is often disguised by an apparent spontaneity or other function, but its role is crucial. The French Communist Party congress is, in fact, the most important practical moment of party activity, where the leadership is elected and a *projet de résolution* amended and voted upon in order that the party define its political orientation for the next three years.

The conflation of the ritual and the practical has been attested in anthropological studies and, it is often argued, adds to ritual effect by its own hidden nature. We shall argue, however, that ritual is not only practical (and functional) in a Durkheimian manner but, through its discourse, facilitates change.

This brings us to a central point: that the fundamental feature of this contextualised mode of personalist political discourse is its symbolic enactment of revelation. Such revelation involves an assumed change of consciousness whereby the community recognises itself as the embodiment of a past or future community of free individuals. One of the fundamental characteristics, therefore, of personalist discourse is its reference to myth.

From the case studies examined in Chapters 4, 5, 6 and 7 we shall see that myth is in fact a strong element in this form of political discourse. A very wide range of myths are perpetually signified by political discourse. They inhabit the presupposed and the understood as well as the said of discourse and can therefore be implied, alluded to and transformed without explicit reference. They are often discursively expressed in the form of fables or parables but equally often implied, referred to or signified in less explicit form. Political myths are held by groups and organisations to have a history and therefore a traditional legitimacy. They are, moreover, treated as public property and are held to be widely believed or implicitly subscribed to. They are held as being true without being scientifically demonstrable. They are not, however, opposed to rational thought but, like it, are held to be opposed to formlessness of thought and aimlessness of political action. Like rational thought, they possess logic, self-evidence and reasonableness, which are themselves often strengthened by implicit political axioms. They therefore orientate political action. They do not of themselves resolve problems but can point towards their resolution. They invite reference in ritual and, like ritual, can remind and reassure, thus inducing or strengthening belief in them. Moreover, because of the nature of discourse, they may intrude upon particular political discourses which logically and traditionally have been considered as alien to them.

Another feature which they share with ritual is their use of symbols; in ritual these are visual, in the deployment of myth, discursive. Symbols are crucial in political discourse because they can encompass a situation or refer to myth without the necessity of exposition.[27]

Myths appear in an infinite variety of ways in political discourse and the amplifications of reference, juxtaposition and degrees of allusion may give them political strength or effect in different contexts. They are therefore a rich resource in discourse, not least because of their ability to be invoked through suggestion. By the same token, they are difficult, though not impossible, to subvert. Inappropriate deployment, trivialisation, over-use and counteraction by other forms of argument are all discursive possibilities which can contribute to the disenchantment of myth. Because they are discourse-dependent and not self-dependent, they do not form a system themselves, although they have affinities with one another and can therefore imply one another.

We can see, therefore, that the use of myths lends political discourse a dense and complex texture, indeed many of the qualities of poetry and poetic drama; their scope, their range of reference, their use of metaphor and symbolism, allusiveness, ambiguity and other conventions.

Some of the complexities of personalist discourse can be resolved into a number of component themes or motifs: a statement of community, the interpretation of experience, a claim to a sense of purpose, and an appeal for authority for future action. These four elements do not often appear as explicit claims. Much of their strength is in fact derived from the elusive and allusive nature of the claims made.

Personalist discourse has the capacity to absorb political myths and to accentuate those aspects of them which stress the ability of individual leaders to influence events decisively. In Marxian discourse, for example, the myth of the 1917 Revolution can be converted from one signifying the dialectical forward movement of class antagonisms, causing and surmounting a revolutionary crisis, into one in which the leadership of Lenin and Trotsky, and the vanguard role of the Bolsheviks, are treated as the crucial causal elements. In Bonapartism, the myth of degenerate republicanism can be deployed and a leader presented who is able to restore the State's integrity. The strength of these and other myths is drawn in part from the juxtaposition of a supposed mythic order – universal characteristics expressed through recurring dramas – with its logical opposite, a voluntarism which enables inspired individuals to present themselves as able to achieve changes in that order by a sustained exercise of will. In personalist discourse, voluntarism in leadership action is the ultimate promise that an apparent determinism (usually referred to as *une fatalité*) can be arrested and transformed. The notion of the inspired leader as the manifestation of voluntarism is linked to the idea that such a leader acts to change *une fatalité* without communicating what the future itself will bring in precise terms. He or she therefore stands in an ambiguous relation both to the order of things and to future society.

It is in the nature of parties to produce detailed and discrete myths of political occurrences. It is in the nature of the personalist leader's function to produce, from these myths and from elsewhere, generalised myths which are widely subscribed to. It is not that political personalism is transcendental and political organisation not, but that the elements of transcendentalism and reference to myth (often only latent or severely constrained by organisational practice) which pre-exist in party discourse and doctrine can be displaced onto or appropriated by personalist discourse in certain circumstances.

3 Methodological Issues in the Analysis of Texts

The introduction into our argument of the notions of discourse and ritual brings us close to paradox: in order to answer the questions raised by our survey of the historiography of the regime (Chapter 1) and those raised by studies of leadership and of organisation (Chapter 2), we need to alter the focus of our discussion. The present chapter will explain this change of focus and outline the methodological approaches adopted in Chapters 4, 5, 6 and 7. In order to do these things, three discussions are appropriate: an explanation of the choice of texts to be studied, a discussion of the problems of analysis, and the exposition of the analytical approach adopted in the present study.

CHOICE OF TEXTS

In order to identify texts which will elucidate the problems raised by our analyses in Chapters 1 and 2, certain initial constraints impose themselves, some of which refer to the exclusive nature of the analysis, some to its inclusiveness. In the first place, in order to demonstrate how presidentialism, within the context of a strong party tradition, has encouraged the *generalised* emergence of personalism on the Left, and what its effects have been, I have chosen to analyse texts which do not emanate from the presidency itself.

Furthermore, analysing texts from a period of relative regime stability will show: firstly, that personalism is not restricted to periods of political crisis; secondly, that it is as much a discursive claim as it is a political process; and, thirdly, that such a claim does not necessarily involve a call for radical regime change.

In one of our case studies (Chapter 6), the analysis of two texts, neither of them texts emanating exclusively from the leadership, will enable us to illustrate how an accepted discourse, which is elaborated in order to facilitate allegiance to one leader, may be deployed by a contender for the leadership, thus indicating how personalism can become both a strategy of and a resource within the political party.

A final consideration is the desirability of including in our analysis texts which are not themselves speeches. This will demonstrate that although personalism is often deployed and exhibited orally and oratorically, the political speech is not its only site and mode.

Four considerations, therefore, govern the choice of texts. Firstly, in order to study personalism in the context of discursive traditions, it is necessary to choose texts that are rich and complex and where the assertion of personalism is made within an elaborate discussion of tradition. Secondly, such texts are more likely to be produced in relative calm than in a major crisis. Thirdly, the status of a text as a leadership text is not a primary consideration. More important is the association of a personalist claim with reflection upon tradition and future-oriented activity. Finally, the study of both speeches and other discursive forms will indicate the extent to which the 'rhetoric' of personalism extends beyond the boundaries of the oratorical. The texts are:

1. The Report of the Central Committee, given by the party's General Secretary, Georges Marchais, to the French Communist Party's 23rd Congress at Saint-Ouen, Paris, on 9 May 1979 (Chapter 4).
2. The text of Georges Marchais' book, *L'Espoir au Présent*, published in 1980 before the presidential elections of May 1981 (Chapter 5).
3. The integral texts of the Assises du socialisme (*Pour de socialisme*), held in Paris on 12 and 13 October 1974, and Motion C (Rocardian) of the French Socialist Party's Congress held at Metz between 6–8 April 1979 (Chapter 6).
4. The text '*Modernisation et progrès social*' adopted by the National Convention of the Socialist Party in December 1984 (Chapter 7).

With this choice of texts to be studied, given the requirements outlined above, a series of problems arises. First of all, even though we are concentrating upon detailed analysis of specific texts in each case study, we still need to be aware of the traditions involved in each of the literary forms analysed. These shape the texts to a considerable degree, both in terms of past practice and in terms of audience expectation. In the case of the first Communist Party text we need to be aware of the Report in relation to its immediate predecessors – in particular the congress in 1976 – but also in terms of its being traditionally the close oral counterpart of the congress resolution, which itself is part of a tradition which goes back beyond the creation of the Communist Party in 1920 to the early socialist movements of the nineteenth century. In the case of the Socialists and the *Assises*, these latter have been infrequent in the Socialist Party, normally held at times when the party's organisation and/or doctrine is under scrutiny, as in early 1959. *Assises* in the Socialist Party, therefore, taking place outside the normal organisational and ritual cycles of the party, can be seen as having both an anti-organisational and a doctrinal significance. And we shall see in Chapter 6 how the anti-organisational sentiment of the 1974 *Assises* is incorporated into the normal ritual occasion of the 1979 congress. To appreciate the special nature of the *Assises* and of the Rocard motion compared with standard motions, we therefore have to be aware of the normal expectations of party life, the tradition of statutory and non-statutory meetings within both the *Parti socialiste* and the SFIO (*Section française de l'internationale ouvrière*), and the ritual which surrounds the proposing and considering of congress motions, and their function in leadership contests.

TEXTUAL ANALYSIS

From the above we can say that, although our analysis consists essentially of the detailed study of the texts themselves, we should not treat them as drawing their significance exclusively from within themselves: they have a provenance which is their formative condition. Moreover, they have a function, that is to say, they communicate a message or messages.

The two levels of message we are concerned with here are that of the texts' ostensible form and content and that of their signifying of personalism or other related phenomena. In terms of those messages evoked by the form and signalled in the content of the texts, these always involve both less and more than their intention. Less, in that the deliberate intention prompting any text or speech never guarantees the complete control of a text's effects by those involved in its production; political actors and speech writers have to contend with the variables of audience (of which we shall say more in a moment), unintended meanings, media distortion – unintended or deliberate – and with the characteristics of discourse itself. More, in that the total significance of a text and the nature of discourse itself will impinge upon ostensible meaning and add to it. It is a commonplace with which we do not disagree that the sender/receiver metaphor is of importance in the analysis of texts, and therefore that all of our texts have a relational, and therefore variable, meaning or meanings. Over and above this, however, we shall be concerned to reveal the rhetoric of the texts to be examined. This will be studied in terms of the texts themselves rather than in terms of audience response. The rhetorical effects of our texts, therefore, will be inferred from their rhetorical qualities.

Even though we shall not be concerned with measuring audience response, a point of major importance is that the nature of audience-in-discourse is itself highly problematic. For each of the texts studied, and in varying degrees, there is an actual audience and a set of other audiences: journalists, political adversaries, the politically uncommitted. The actual audience, moreover, will itself consist of a multiplicity of political actors with a greater or lesser degree of allegiance to the text or speaker. Nevertheless, because of the one-way nature of the discourses studied and their ritualised settings, the audience signified within them shifts in nature and status. We shall see that attempts to influence or manipulate this shifting nature and status is one of the primary rhetorical devices of political discourse.

Given our dual concern with communication and persuasion, and our insistence upon the need to establish a text's provenance and immediate political context, there is one other condition which it is important to establish and to which we referred in the previous chapter: the ritual context of public political discourse.

The main point concerning ritual is that the roles of the actors involved are prescribed, not only by exclusive definitions, but also by the careful specification of action and response within a named series of ritual acts. Ritual excludes certain styles of verbal and acted behaviour and therefore confers privilege upon others. The point here is that a Report, for example, needs to be in all respects precisely what it purports to be, as does a congress motion, and so on. The paradox here is that this constraint makes certain other things possible. In the case of our texts, for example, the highly elaborated ritual and ritualised modes which surround them are often the essential agencies of personalism.

Let us now examine our own specific approach to the analysis of our selected texts.

EXPOSITION OF ANALYSIS

As we have indicated, the conditions of a discourse impinge upon and orientate it. The relative influence of these formative conditions, however, will differ considerably from party to party: differing party traditions will contain differing discursive implications; differing emphases upon ritual will constrain and facilitate discursive shifts to differing degrees.

These differing emphases will be reflected in the different preliminary discussions in each chapter. Similarly, these differing emphases will also affect the form of textual exposition in each chapter. However, the essential factor governing the exposition of the texts is the need to respect as far as is analytically possible their narrative form: firstly, in order not to depart from the spatio-temporal relationship in the texts' actual delivery or reading; secondly, in order to demonstrate the effects of discourse: at the most banal level, for example, the cumulative effect of simple repetition; finally, and most importantly, in order not to reduce the texts to the status of effects of other processes, whether ideal or material. This problem of interpretation is a constant one in literary analysis, partly because any effective thematic elucidation will distort the narrative quality of the text. Awareness of it, however, will reduce the inevitable distortions which analysis entails.

In conclusion, therefore, the approaches adopted in this study are not tied to any *a priori* analytical method, because our first concern is to respect the detailed form and structure of the texts, not to deform them. Neither theoretically nor methodologically, moreover, can we make assumptions beforehand about the strict relationship between elements of form, structure and content; on the contrary, it is more likely that this relationship will vary markedly from text to text and from party to party. Even though we pay great attention to the provenance of our examples, the values and significance of them can only emerge from the interrelationships of the texts' internal structure within the context of their narrative quality or discursive rendition.

Two distortions of major hermeneutical importance are inevitably brought about by our analysis: the first, the conversion of a discursive event into a text for analysis; the second, the distortion of meaning through a certain analytical mode. Strictly, it is only on purely analytical texts that the analytical mode can operate without distortion. The several formal and conceptual difficulties stemming from this are recognised in, say, poetry criticism. It may well be that the problems posed by interpretation are not ultimately resolvable. They can, however, be mitigated: in the first instance, by establishing the provenance of a text, while recognising that such provenance comprises the contingent and formative conditions of a discourse but does not constitute its cause; in the second, by respecting the text's form in order that the ideas contained within it and signified by it – its connotations, allusions, the issues it raises and does not raise, the metaphors and other figures it uses and does not use – may be properly expounded and given due weight.

4 Discourse and Tradition: The Communists

The *Parti communiste français* (PCF) exists within a polity where personalism is encouraged by the formal political institutions and the personalisation of politics is encouraged by the media. These political conditions within the regime are not easily accommodated to in the discourse of Marxism and Marxism–Leninism, and run counter to the conscious wishes of most French Communists. The PCF, therefore, in spite of an organisational structure and vocabulary which it shares with other Communist parties, operates in circumstances which distinguish it from other Communist parties, from other parties within its own polity, and even from its own identity in previous French republics.

This chapter will analyse the French Communist Party's Central Committee Report which was presented by the General Secretary, Georges Marchais, on the first day of the party's 23rd Congress which took place at the Sports Centre at Saint-Ouen in the Ile-St-Denis near Paris between 9 and 13 May 1979.

The 23rd Congress of 1979 had to deal with a crisis in the party's strategy. At the time of the preceding congress, in 1976, the party appeared to have established a course of action that would substantially increase its power within the regime; it was in electoral and potentially governmental alliance with the *Parti socialiste* (PS) and the *Mouvement des radicaux de gauche* (MRG) with whom it had agreed and signed a Common Programme of Government in 1972. The PCF vigorously supported François Mitterrand, the PS leader, in the 1974 presidential elections, and the parties to the alliance had developed comprehensive arrangements for mutual support in election campaigns. In the space of two years, however, this pattern was broken. An attempt to bring the Common Programme up to date failed in September 1977 and the combined Left did not succeed in its attempt to gain an overall majority in the legislative elections of March 1978. At this point the PS (and MRG) and the PCF broke decisively away from each other.

The 23rd Congress dealt with the strategic consequences of these events by means of the discursive reconciliation of the traditional and expected reflex of *repli* with a radical departure, an implicit commitment of the party to personalism as a means of creating an explicit rally around itself and its leader. In the present chapter I shall argue that the true significance of the 23rd Congress cannot be understood unless it is seen in its contradictory relationship with the 22nd; that this contradictory relationship is reconciled by virtue of the nature and particular use of discourse within the framework of a highly symbolic moment of party activity; and that the discursive conflation of *ouverture* and *repli* facilitated and was facilitated by the development of personalism.

In order to situate the text within its wider context, I shall examine the unusual place of the 22nd Congress in the progressive formulation of party doctrine, and the immediate setting of the 23rd.

1 THE 22ND CONGRESS

The 22nd Congress of the PCF, held between 4 and 8 February 1976, marked the high point in the PCF's internal harmony and self-confidence in the 1970s. The congress took place at a time when the party was still associated with the Common Programme along with the PS and the MRG. The congress resolution emphasised that the party was preparing with its allies to appeal to a potential majority of the electorate, which would include social groups often considered beyond the party's reach. The General Secretary himself was portrayed in the media as an urbane, even liberal figure. The congress was seen as marking historic change within a party now wide open to ideas and influences. The resolution itself strengthened this impression by seldom referring to past congresses and past events except in the most general terms. The party appeared to have been transformed and to have acquired a new but approved style of leadership. The main evidence of a willingness to change was the proposal at this congress that the next congress should ratify the removal from the party statutes of the term 'dictatorship of the proletariat'. The congress received extensive media coverage and its atmosphere was, and was seen to be, open and relaxed.

The significance of the congress, however, was ambiguous and little analysed – indeed, the most common observation was that it was 'significant', as if simply the notion of PCF *ouverture* entailed sufficient significance for it to be communicated or understood without being explained. Apart from that of the extreme Right and extreme Left, nearly all newspaper comment intimated or stated the apparently irreversible nature of this stage of party development. Although there was no examination of what *ouverture* meant doctrinally, organisationally or strategically, the media emphasised the element of spectacle and the efficiency of an organisation capable of staging such an event.

For all these reasons, one can clearly see how the PCF could, to a certain extent, be seen as 'born again' in 1976, just as the PS had been in 1971. It is interesting to note in this context that the references to documents, tracts and other discursive inspiration are restricted to (a) recent, (b) non-statutory, and (c) French works. A further factor in the developing adaptation of the PCF was its independent, if not insolent, attitude to the USSR and the CPSU.

Nearly all of the interventions at the congress, whether made by the young or by veterans such as François Billoux,[1] referred to and supported the abandonment of the dictatorship of the proletariat,[2] usually by referring explicitly to the text of the draft resolution or to the Report or to Marchais in particular. This rejection was, however, implicitly qualified by three factors: (i) Georges Marchais' defence of the theory of Marxism–Leninism; (ii) André Vieuguet's contribution concerning the need to continue and develop democratic centralism; and (iii) Paul Laurent's declaration of PCF allegiance to proletarian internationalism, all code expressions for the party's traditional allegiances.

The overall result was to signify a rejection of Leninism as a theory of post-revolutionary government while confirming it as a theory of political organisation. The unstated Leninist approach to organisation was underpinned by a decisive call to increase the number of workplace cells, as well as CGT representation, workplace cells being not only more authentically socialist than others, but also more subject to central control. Doctrinally, the position of the proletariat was further strengthened within the notion of the *Union du peuple de France* by the ascription to it of its *rôle dirigeant*. The party's organisational form was, therefore, seen as an unquestioned tradition within the party even though the party was presenting itself as being clearly in favour of change. This is not to say (although it has been said by critics at the time and since) that Leninism is abandoned in theory though not in practice, but rather that, through the naming of a specific rejection (here, the dictatorship of the proletariat), a flux in ideas, their implications and interconnections is created in which the specific focus upon an interim period of political strategy is removed. Furthermore there is a suggestion that the fundamentals of a doctrine may change where they never before seemed to do so. The consequence for leadership is twofold: in the case of the creation of a flux in ideas, leadership is seen as being eventually able to offer solutions and reassurance where there was debate and uncertainty. Secondly, there is enhancement of the prestige of a leader who has presided over doctrinal changes and issues perceived as being as important as those which were made in 1920.

The press commentaries, without exception, described the 22nd Congress as Marchais' congress. Let us look a little more closely at this media description. Marchais announced on 7 January 1976 on *Antenne 2*,[3] one month before the congress, that the notion of the dictatorship of the proletariat no longer corresponded to the nature of French society and the role of the PCF within it, and that the forthcoming congress would recommend the deletion of the term from the party statutes. At the same time he emphasised his belief in a *socialisme aux couleurs de la France*. During the congress itself, Marchais gave an extensive press interview, clarifying and elaborating upon points raised at the congress. A further speech was made at the *fête populaire* which followed the congress. On each occasion, Marchais remained the only significant party spokesperson. The personalist development here is not in opposition to the party, the apparatus, collective leadership or congress but is, as it were, a parallel expression of the party in personified form. On each occasion the General Secretary discussed only the ideas found in the draft resolution and only answered other questions which concerned his relaxed state of mind and the state of his health (he had suffered a minor heart attack in January of the previous year). Marchais was, in 1976, the articulation of specific, widely held beliefs within the party and outside it, and at no time was he presented as going beyond the limits of organisational tolerance regarding doctrinal, organisational and policy *content*. The parallel course taken by the General Secretary outside official party meetings is therefore a *formal* one. The leader was not portrayed as imposing his will upon the party, but as presenting the party's own ideas, to itself (at the congress) and to the outside world, before, during and after the congress. This does not mean that the impression was not created that the present General Secretary might be capable of changing party orientations, but that on this occasion his ideas were the articulation of consciously held majority opinion.

The political atmosphere surrounding the 22nd Congress was imbued with ideas about Eurocommunism and saw the party denouncing the Soviet labour camps and psychiatric hospitals and speaking out in defence of the Soviet dissident, Leonid Plioutch. It was in this context that the General Secretary called for *discussion animée* in the preparation for the congress. The congress itself, however, saw virtually no disturbance or questioning of the party's (changing) orientations. All the interventions took the usual form: PCF life at local level and endorsement of leadership decisions. The congress was an impressive and apparently effortless demonstration of party unity. In his Report, Marchais put the party on guard against a cult of personality, yet the 22nd Congress facilitates the appropriation by the leadership of the definition of the party's identity. This later facilitates a more radical personalist appropriation within a Communist framework. At the 22nd Congress the office of General Secretary was not simply being used to effect a particular line; rather the nature of the office itself was being modified.

2 THE 23RD CONGRESS

The Setting

The combined total of the seats won by the PCF, PS and MRG in the National Assembly after the legislative elections of March 1978 fell just short of an absolute majority. Although the parties of the Left had, once again, increased their representation, their failure to achieve the long-awaited victory was perceived as a major, even historic, defeat. It was generally accepted that the cause of defeat was the breakdown of the alliance after September 1977 when discussions to translate the Common Programme into specific campaign policies produced dissension and finally convinced disagreement. The PCF placed the entire responsibility for this failure on the PS. However, some Communists dissented from this interpretation and also complained that the leadership was taking decisions without reference to the party members. The media, too, held the PCF leadership responsible for the defeat. Unrest within the party took the form of absenteeism at cell meetings, the expression of disillusionment among activists, sometimes in the bourgeois press, and further active dissent, particularly among the party's editorial staff, some *permanents* and intellectuals.

It was against this background that the preparations for the 23rd Congress were set in train. The leadership now faced the problem that both dissenters and ordinary party members attached two kinds of value to the 22nd Congress of 1976: in the first place, it was valued as an affirmation that party congresses had become occasions for making policy decisions to an extent never envisaged in the history of the party; and in the second place, congresses had now acquired (with their grand use of space, publicity and transcendental themes) major symbolic importance. In a sense the preceding congress had become the discursive and doctrinal base of the party. It would, therefore, have been extremely difficult for the leadership to reject the themes or the significance of the previous congress and operate its traditional *repli* strategy in the wake of the breakdown of the Common Programme alliance and the Left's failure to secure victory in the legislative election of 1978.

In traditional PCF strategy, *ouverture* is justified if there are signs of a rally and a relative ascendancy of the PCF over the Socialists. *Repli* is justified if the Right are ascendant or if the Socialists are gaining in relative strength on the Left. During the 1970s there was evidence to support both interpretations of events. By the mid-1970s, moreover, the party had weakened values which made a decisive *repli* possible. Personalism, however, can be adapted to progress or retreat. Moreover, *ouverture* and *repli* have certain common characteristics which facilitate their discursive coexistence: organisational unity, trade union solidarity and strong leadership (in the first case to lead, in the second to protect). Personalism, therefore, can break the alternating pattern of *ouverture/repli*. In terms of one of the specific registers that personalism exploits at the 23rd Congress, I shall discuss nationalism in the main analytical section of this chapter. Here we may note that the European elections of June 1979 allowed nationalist themes to be exploited in a dramatic manner, while allowing the General Secretary to avoid the overtly personalised mode of the next national election to fall before the following (24th) congress, the presidential elections of 1981, and to concentrate upon a cause, that of French patriotism and the defence of French sovereignty.

The symbolic significance of the 23rd Congress was heightened by the congress's treatment of the Report as an event of the utmost importance. It was referred to ceaselessly. At the start of the congress, on Wednesday 9 May, Etienne Fajon, a veteran of the party, made a short speech greeting the 2000 delegates of the ninety-eight federations and the representatives of eighty-eight other Communist parties and National Liberation movements. He then introduced Georges Marchais. After Marchais' speech and for the next four days all subsequent interventions were short, measurable in minutes. Contributions from the floor all fell within predictable formats – the forms and outcomes of local struggles, the role of the party in such struggles, the expressions of unanimity at federal and other conferences, and basic work and activity in local cells and sections. Those who spoke were ordinary workers, academics, feminists, economists, seamen, Catholics, immigrants, peasants, regionalists or *permanents* reporting on party finances and newspapers. Many of the interventions concerning local struggle took the form of a story or incident illustrating the virtue of the party and justifying its overall role in the polity and society. These interventions were interwoven with those expressing the language of scientific socialism, theoretical erudition or straightforward conference business. Including the *interventions non-prononcées*, there were sixty-two altogether. Whatever the type of intervention, the references to Georges Marchais, his Report and the draft resolution were incessant. Marchais' own speech was about 30 000 words long and took 5 hours to deliver.

The General Secretary's Report takes place at the beginning of the congress and the voting upon the various texts takes place at the end, four days later. In both its form and its content the Report is attuned to the draft resolution. Having been, as it were, the property of the party members and delegates, the draft resolution is transferred to another plane. The General Secretary becomes its custodian and presents it to the congress through the Report. The General Secretary literally interprets the draft resolution orally, reflecting and accentuating its themes and structure. Through this act, the draft resolution and the General Secretary are linked so that the final act of its voting is an implicit ratification and endorsement of the General Secretary himself. Given its proximity to the election of offices, which also takes place at the end of the congress, it indicates that the leadership is the keeper of the party spirit for the next few years until, in response to external influences and the concomitant need for redefinition of purpose and the mutation of the party within its structurally defined limits, the Central Committee initiates the elaboration of a new resolution, addresses it to its members and prepares the ground for another act of consecration. In the role of *rapporteur*, therefore, the General Secretary, at this moment of party activity, fulfils several symbolic functions. As *rapporteur* he is linked to the Central Committee, but transcends this function as General Secretary of the whole party. As interpreter of the draft resolution he also becomes symbolic of the unity of party opinion and the personification of effort and of hope.

In this context, the congress, apart from being the most important official meeting of the party, symbolically demonstrates that individual isolation is punctuated by assembly and that periods of isolation have drained neither will nor faith. The arrival of the draft resolution is the first tangible sign that a new gathering has begun. This in part explains why, as many observers have noted, the draft resolution invariably takes the same thematic form, even though it will refer to contemporary events and issues. Within this classical form, one section will describe the savagery of capitalism and its creation of the conditions of its own destruction. Another will highlight the role and history of the PCF in this context. The other sections will look at the party's aims, its strategy, its organisation. There will be slight variations on this recurring form and it is within the constraints of this form that those who draft the resolution and the Report must attempt to confirm or revise doctrine, legitimate and initiate changes and continuously adapt the party to the regime.

The delivery of the Report therefore does two things, or rather one in the context of another: it transmits (i) old and new information; and (ii) the presence of leadership. In terms of the audience, therefore, the Report has two characteristics: (i) it is recognisable, and therefore acceptable and reassuring, either of convictions or of prejudices; (ii) it possesses new elements and so involves risks and departures on the part of the listener. In this way 'understanding' the Report which involves some form of acceptance of it can alter the significance of known Communist discourse.

The position of a *rapporteur* in a Communist party is complicated by two things. First, Communist parties have an organisational structure such that only in exceptional circumstances can a leader be – or even be imagined as being – free of organisation. Second, Stalinism and destalinisation have inoculated Western Communist parties against overt forms of the cult of personality. Therefore, Marchais' position in the Fifth Republic differs from the personality cult developed around Thorez not only because of the leader's role outside the party (presidential elections, publicised tours, television appearances) but also because of the influence of the past. A present-day Communist leader's position is conditioned by the fact that: (a) the personality cult is now consciously disdained within the party; (b) more generally, such explicit demonstrations of allegiance are perceived as politically naive; and (c) the actual personification of politics outside the party justifies a certain use within and by the party of the modern methods of capitalist domination, on condition that personal power should be explicitly denounced by the party.

For these reasons the personalism of the PCF in the present period is different from the cult of personality because it is unstated. Marchais does not need to be – indeed should not be – presented as physically robust and a culture-seeking son of the people. The fact that he lacked these qualities ascribed to Thorez facilitates the surreptitious introduction of personalism into the party by means of the discourse of the party itself. Marchais, perhaps even more than Thorez, is seen as the creation of the party apparatus. This conflation of organisational background with a shift towards the play of personality within a discourse creates the conditions for the initial acceptance of a personalist venture.

Acceptance is further facilitated because the Report is, after all, only the report of the party to itself. The resolution, of which the Report is only an echo, is, in its most democratic interpretation, the child of every active member of the party. It is because of this that the speaker is able to impinge upon a general perception of the resolution which he refers to by name in the Report twenty-four times. As *rapporteur*, therefore, the General Secretary is not only perceived as the party's leader, but is also its most humble servant, its executive officer. Hence the justification for his being *seen* to work harder (speak for longer) than anyone else. For the same reasons the protagonist in the Report is ostensibly the party, or else the nation. The first person singular pronoun, however, is used in the 23rd Congress *rapport* seventy times, and this in a speech where the ambiguous first person plural, itself used innumerable times, often signifies the speaker himself.[4]

The Text

At the beginning of his speech, by immediately naming the 22nd Congress: '*Il y a trois ans, ici même, se tenait notre XXIIe Congrès*', the speaker makes it the point of reference for the 23rd. The 22nd Congress is thereby endowed immediately with certain qualities: it is recent, it is historic and it is exemplary. The three intervening years are thus presented as not having diminished the immediacy of the previous congress. Only in the second paragraph does Marchais refer to the painful experience of the 1978 elections which separates the two events:

> Cette épreuve a suscité une réflexion approfondie, un grand débat, des interrogations et, parfois, ici et là, du désarroi. (p. 1)[5]

He thus names and characterises what has been a major source of anxiety within the party. However, failure to reduce the 1978 elections to a familiar scale could break the symbolic link being established between the 22nd and the 23rd Congresses, reduce the possibilities for effective reference and thus make the former less than exemplary or the latter a deviation from it. Hence Marchais' immediate affirmation that what happened in 1978 confirmed rather than questioned the ideas and orientations contained within and supplied by the 22nd Congress.

> Dès avril 1978, l'analyse que nous avions entreprise nous conduisait à cette conclusion que, bien loin de remettre en cause la ligne du XXIIe Congrès, la situation nous commandait de la confirmer, de la prolonger, de l'enrichir, de donner une ampleur nouvelle à sa mise en oeuvre. (p. 1)

The opening lines of the Report therefore relate the 23rd Congress conceptually and discursively to the notion of the 22nd Congress *en marche et vivant*. Its decisions and pronouncements are accepted and offered as rigorously correct and beyond reproach and, as such, provide the 23rd Congress and the 1976–9 period with their major normative framework of reference and, from it, justification. Upon this implicit basis, Marchais outlines the new Report. Using the first person singular, he says:

> Je veux, dans ce rapport, revenir sur le choix soumis à notre congrès à partir des cinq grands ensembles de questions que la discussion préparatoire a mis en avant. (p. 1)

The ensuing Report is in this way legitimated by reference to the preparatory discussion from which it springs. The '*ensembles*' around which the speech is organised are: '*I.   Le socialisme démocratique: issue de la crise*'; '*II.   Notre stratégie internationale*'; '*III.   Les pays socialistes et nous*'; '*IV.   L'Union pour le changement démocratique*'; '*V.   Quelques aspects du développement du Parti et de son activité.*' From these subdivisions of the Report it is clear that the form of the Report remains traditional and, as such, complements the draft resolution. It is, therefore, through an accepted discursive format that new orientations will be projected.

Part I

In order to demonstrate that the party determines its strategy, not by unsystematic reactions to economic and political events, but by sensitive analysis of the underlying problems, the speaker reminds his audience that the 22nd Congress itself had directed attention to democratic socialism as the means of transcending the crisis, adding that: *'nous n'avons pas fait un choix artificiel, arbitraire'*. (p. 6) Defined, therefore, in terms of the grand objective, the two congresses and their decisions become direct emanations of the more generalised and universal struggle against capitalism. On the other hand, events such as the 1978 elections and the break with the Socialists assume their proper perspective as surface political phenomena. This positing of levels of activity, and therefore of significance, is a traditional one in Communist thought and frames the notion of choice and decision within the base/superstructure metaphor.

Marchais then goes on to define the crisis in terms of its effects, rather than its deeper level of significance;

> *La crise, c'est aujourd'hui un chômage massif et durable....*
> *La crise, ce sont les machines neuves que l'on casse et les usines que l'on ferme. Ce sont des villes, des régions entières que l'on asphyxie....*
> *La crise, c'est la baisse du pouvoir d'achat ....* (p. 6)

He further notes that *'Une bataille politique et idéologique intense'* (p. 7) is being waged which concerns the causes and solution of the crisis, and affirms that, in opposition to the ruling power's attempts to shift cause and solution to other contexts:

> *A cette question, nouse répondons: la crise est avant tout, nationale.* (p. 7)

The *'nous'* here refers to the party as a collectivity but is a clear indication of a *'nous/moi'* (here we reply in the form of my voice) which will reappear in various and functional forms throughout the speech. And in the next paragraph, Marchais makes a surprising personal observation:

> *Cette réponse a fait l'objet d'une discussion importante, mais – permettez-moi de le dire – encore insuffisante à mes yeux. Car il est*

évident qu'une évaluation correcte de la crise, une compréhension exacte de ses causes, de son caractère, de son mouvement sont indispensables pour définir et mettre en oeuvre une juste politique, basée sur la realité et non sur des spéculations hasardeuses ou des schémas préétablis. (p. 7)

In the above passage, the General Secretary is pointing out that a proper evaluation of the crisis (that which had, until this point in the text, been taken as known) is needed in order that *'une juste politique'* be developed. The mention of *'discussion'*, which he himself considers inadequate, and of policy based not on the analysis of the real, but upon *'des spéculations hasardeuses ou des schémas préétablis'* is a warning that grave and unexpected error is linked to uninformed doctrinal or doctrinaire responses to present events. Simply by naming a deficiency, the speaker is indicating that what is required is exceptional sensitivity to events and apparently unorthodox judgement in the delineation of policies. Marchais thus gives a first indication of the offer of himself as intercessor between past and future forms of party as one who has a developed sense not only of what form the future will take but also of what may inhibit such development. The advice given and its implications, therefore, are prudential while manifesting a guarded projection of the self. In the above passage, the personal judgement of the speaker is, in effect, a response to a perceived counter-analysis which is deemed to be both illusory and perfidious and, what is more, is deemed to originate within the party.

Here then, we have the rejection of the previously assumed sense of communion with the audience which involved its acceptance of a mutually assumed yet imposed interpretation (of *'la crise'*). The desired momentary aimlessness of the audience born of the security of the assumed communion, is now replaced by its (the audience's) own anticipation of an explanation (*'encore insuffisante'*). Now, however, it will not be an apparent mutual explanation but the speaker's own, given that, in contradistinction to the idea of communion hitherto projected, a claim of inadequacy and of strain now exists and is reflected in inadequate *'discussion'*. Moreover, the word *'discussion'* in the quotation carries an important double significance. It signifies an insufficient discussion among the activists which may be instrumentally rectified by the speaker's discussion of the subject. It further connotes discussion as being, till this moment, qualitatively inadequate. In both cases, the first explicit, the second implied, the presence and ideas of the General Secretary are necessarily highlighted.

From this *mise en garde* against falling into error, Marchais, beginning with a '*Je pense que*' (p. 7), elaborates, in orthodox party manner, the rejection of the French government's claim that the national crisis is the result of external factors, such as the 1973/4 rise in oil prices. The first proof offered of the fallacy is that '*les dirigeants du pays*' (p. 7) argue their case with such desperate eagerness (and herein lies a warning to those within the party who might be sympathetic to such theses). Facts and figures are then given in refutation before a deeper discursive distancing from the audience is established:

Cela dit, il faut, bien sûr, aller plus au fond des choses. (p. 8)

This warning of the need for further and more scientific reflection precedes an account of one of the most difficult paradoxes in Marxism–Leninism as regards decisions about appropriate political strategy: that although capitalism is an international system, the class struggle is invariably engaged within the framework of the nation–state. This duality is maintained while greater emphasis is given to the national dimension: '*Les nations, les Etats existent.*' (p. 8) Given this attribution of near-ontological status, the ground is prepared for the justification of party activity at national level and an implied *allegiance* to the nation–state.

The devices used in this sequence of passages place the audience in a rapid succession of positions and roles *vis-à-vis* the speaker, each of them conferring a different value on the *rapporteur*. The explanation as revelation which follows the explanation-as-refutation of government policies and the '*Cela dit*' statement is unambiguous and uncontentious. That the crisis predates 1973/4 and that there are international dimensions to national conditions (pp. 7–9) are truisms of Communist Party thought. In effect, Marchais constructs, in the presence of the audience, an imagined interlocutor who first agrees, then fails to understand, anticipates explanation, is warned, then is finally reassured. The speaker thus becomes central to his own text, effortlessly articulating, moving beyond and returning to the thoughts and opinions of the audience.

Two passages from this part of the Report will serve to illustrate the developing centrality of the speaker. The first shows how the resolution, in theory a more sacred text than the Report itself, is used to legitimate the Report and then is rendered secondary to the speaker. They both follow the acknowledgement of the international dimensions of the crisis.

Par ailleurs, comme l'expose fort bien le projet de résolution, la crise comporte des dimensions spécifiquement internationales qui influent sur le développement des crises des différents pays. J'y reviendrai, car tout cela est naturellement très important.

Here the resolution is invoked as justification of the speaker.

Here the speaker appropriates the resolution and offers himself as able to modify it.

Pour autant, ce serait une très lourde erreur, ce serait tomber dans le piège qui nous est tendu que de tirer de toutes ces données réelles la conclusion que la crise vient du dehors, qu'il n'y a d'approche du problème sérieuse qu'à l'échelle internationale. (p. 8)

Here the resolution is made secondary to a more urgent issue: that of a *mise en garde* by the speaker against error on the part of the audience.

The second passage concerns the assertion of the national dimension of the struggle:

Les nations, les Etats existent. Ils ont une histoire, une réalité profonde et durable. Ils connaissent entre eux, des contradictions. Ils sont eux-mêmes l'enjeu de la lutte de classes. Ne pas prendre tout cela en compte serait mortel pour le mouvement révolutionnaire.

Nous l'avons dit, mais il faut le répéter sans cesse: c'est dans chaque pays que naissent et se développent les crises qu'ils subissent. (pp. 8–9)

The national/international paradox is converted into a formula by the maintenance of the ambiguity between nations as States on the one hand (in the contractual, Gaullist sense) and on the other by the depiction of the State as the conflictual '*enjeu de la lutte*', Marxian sense, wherein the State is itself one of the principal sites of struggle. Again the audience is placed at a distance by an implicit threat ('*ne pas prendre tout cela en compte serait mortel*') which carries both a tactical and a normative charge. The confusions and conflations which do arise from the State/nation dichotomy and, by extension, the national/international paradox, are dissolved by the *process* of explaining which itself is given a personal dimension: '*Nous l'avons dit, mais il faut le répéter sans cesse*' means, in this context, 'I must repeat it to you' as well as the explicit 'We must repeat it' (to outsiders).

The national/nationalist argument is reinforced and developed by the assertion that, although there is an international crisis, its form in France is of a particular kind which affects all aspects of social life (p. 9) and is therefore *'une crise nationale au plein sens du terme, une crise de la société française.'* (p. 10) France is thus presented as both vulnerable (to American, German and Japanese pressure (p. 9)) and yet possessing a treasure and a strength (*'originalités'*, *'personnalités nationales'* (p. 9)) which must not be squandered. The nation–state is therefore confirmed not only as a reality but as natural and desirable, but not the use to which it has been put.

At this point, the argument enters a new phase and develops the idea that *in order* for capitalist internationalism to masquerade as national it must indeed be a strategy which involves the successful adoption of a political method whereby capitalist relations may be successfully reproduced and the multinational groups may *'se tailler une part dans la nouvelle répartition des zones d'influence'* (p. 10). That is to say that a process of legitimation is applied via the national bourgeoisie. The major weapon in this strategy is the politics of personal power. This has been alluded to earlier when reference is made to Giscard d'Estaing, Barre and Ceyrac (at this time, respectively, President, Prime Minister and leader of the employers' organisation, the CNPF) and by the use of the adjective *'giscardien'*.

It is here that Marchais begins to introduce the notion of *'la voie'* and to supply supporting words and phrases (*'stratégie'*, *'presser'*, *'plier'*, *'issue'*, *'avancer'*, *'aller de l'avant'*, *'prendre le chemin'*). Over four pages of the speech (pp. 12–15) one conscious course of action or *voie* (bad) is confronted with a second (good) in which developments will be determined by the will of the party itself to struggle against the forces ranged against the nation. The important point is that a *voie* is not the consequence of impersonal or structural economic or social forces in which political groups enact predetermined roles, but is the result of calculated and specifically directed action by politically motivated groups and individuals. A theory of voluntarism involving all political actors is thereby implied at the same moment as the personal dimension of capitalist politics is evoked:

Sous couvert d'adaptation au monde, les dirigeants de l'économie et de l'Etat veulent ainsi presser, plier, on dirait aujourd'hui plus savamment 'destructurer', la France pour la soumettre à leurs besoins. Délibérément, ils organisent son déclin. (p. 11)

Significantly, responsibility is then placed, not on the political bourgeoisie alone, but on the more tenuous '*classes possédantes*' (p. 11):

Une fois encore, elles sont prêtes à vendre la France pour garder leurs privilèges, leurs châteaux et leurs gros sous. (p. 11)

Casual reference is made to: '*cette tradition d'abandon et de capitulation*' (p. 11), thus summoning up, though not stating, the eternal treachery and anti-national sentiments of the powerful: the *émigrés*, the Thermidorean reaction, the bourgeoisie of 1848, the Versaillais, Vichy and the collaborators. By the same token, the alternative tradition is implicitly appropriated for those represented by the text: the revolutionaries of the Great Revolution and those betrayed and massacred in the June Days, the Communards and the Resisters.

Marchais next notes the paradox that such a reactionary and voluntarist strategy cannot be maintained without its being assured of '*un consentement populaire suffisamment large et stable*' (p. 11) This is obtained by a '*pression idéologique*' (p. 12) which involves all the means of persuasion, communication and (mis)information at the disposal of the ruling classes. Here the PS is named as an accessory to this collaboration. At the core of the argument is the claim that the essential feature of *le pouvoir* is its personal character and that the strategy of decline cannot be relied upon in a democracy without shifting all the articulated interests of a class and the strategies of the ideological war into the care of the personal/ authoritarian leader. By extension, personal power is seen, for all practical purposes, as synonymous with (though in Marxian theory only in that it is traceable to) all of the social processes which call it into existence.

By implication, the audience is being referred to the problem first stated in Marxist writing in *The Eighteenth Brumaire*, namely, that the development of class conflict can be arrested by Bonapartism. In the Fifth Republic, '*le pouvoir et le patronat*' (p. 12) are trying to destroy the workers' capacity for resistance and struggle, a process which entails:

le renforcement progressif et systématique du caractère autoritaire et personnel du pouvoir, de la mise en cause progressive et systématique des droits et libertés démocratiques. (p. 12)

However, just as there is a synonymity of oppression, so too do the forces of progress cohere and produce '*la liaison intime – je dirai presque la fusion – qui s'opère aujourd'hui entre les intérêts de la nation et les intérêts de la classe ouvrière*' (p. 13). By extension this liaison extends to the party and the discourse of its leader.

Thus far in the Report, Marchais has diminished the importance of superstructural phenomena (1978) and emphasised the fundamental infrastructural processes and their direct consequences (*la crise*). He next re-establishes the importance of the political (superstructural) in negative form by emphasising its direct links with capital. This re-establishing is essential to his subsequent claims concerning his own and the party's political activity. At this point, he claims that a whole range of social groups, classes and institutions desire more justice, more equality, more liberty, more personal choice, more participation: '*En un mot, ce qui est nécessaire aujourd'hui, c'est plus, toujours plus de démocratie.*' (p. 13) It is explicit here that it is capitalism that impedes this development. Implicitly, however, Marchais is referring to a widely-held theory of society in which it is normative that the extension of democracy is a perpetual and inexhaustible desire or social force.

Here and until the end of the section, the Report becomes more future-oriented. It is here that *autogestion* is introduced into the argument as a vision of a future ideal society in which the truly democratic aspirations will find expression. Thus socialism and democracy are presented as coincident. In the past, the term and the notions signified by *autogestion* had been treated with circumspection by the PCF. The term, once named, is repeated four times in rapid succession and is supported by several references to the draft resolution and even by a reference to Karl Marx. In five successive paragraphs, Marchais tells of the need for: '*Nouveaux rapports dans l'économie .... Nouveaux rapports dans la cité .... Nouveaux rapports dans la région .... Nouveaux rapports dans la nation .... Nouveaux rapports ... entre les nations ....*' (pp. 14–15). He thereby presents to the audience a libertarian vision of society and claims that the *basis* for change towards it already exists, waiting only to find expression:

quand nous parlons de socialisme démocratique, autogestionnaire, quand nous mettons l'autogestion parmi nos objectifs fondamentaux, nous ne nous livrons pas à des astuces de langage .... Nous

répondons aux besoins concrets d'une société, la France de 1979.
(p. 15)

This evocation of the future and shift back from the future to the present responds to a formal rule in Communist doctrine, namely, that reference to socialist society requires explicit discussion of the method of converting the present into the future. The rule is observed in the text, not by offering a line or a settled strategy, but by first offering, as we have seen, a vision or glimpse of a future society, relating it to contemporary events and then offering *la lutte*: *'résolue, imaginative, dynamique, puissante'* (p. 15). Without a named strategy such struggle serves a purpose similar to that of faith in confessional religions: wisdom and understanding are achieved with a combination of insight and the humility to undergo positive experience without having previously understood it. The struggle, however, at this discursive moment, is not a mythical/heroic one. The imagined future refers struggle to a *lutte quotidienne*, one which gives coherence and justification to daily life. The imagined society is therefore offered to the mind, related to the present, then withdrawn and replaced with the immediate focus of struggle and duty. The *form* of struggle thus becomes the central issue. This is, however, defined negatively: *'Lutter pour quoi? D'abord pour dire non'* (p. 15). It is a call to struggle against the status quo, against austerity, redundancies, unemployment, the ruin of businesses and the deliberate organisation of France's economic decline:

> *Nous opposons, nous communistes, un non résolu et définitif à la politique du capital, qu'elle soit conduite par Giscard d'Estaing aujourd'hui, ou par qui que ce soit d'autre demain.*

Here the *'non'*, as well as offering a libertarian future within the discipline of an organised present, is the eternal one of both the revolutionary/anti-fascist and the patriotic traditions. It is also, of course, a reference to the chances of a Mitterrand victory in the 1981 presidential elections and thus represents the first hint of a secondary focus upon the person of Mitterrand, the other main personal adversary implied in the Report. This idea of rejection of (rather than allegiance to) something, is also, apart from being the voicing of an imagined audience's feelings, an idea widely considered as a major element in voting choice in modern democracies. Finally, and perhaps most significantly, it can, without proper specification, be construed as an instruction to do nothing.

Having thus framed the notion of some form of daily activity in terms of an imagined future, Marchais goes on to name certain *objectifs*, though again the form of struggle is not elaborated. '*Nous luttons pour*' precedes twelve named objectives, including the preservation of the standard of living, the 35-hour week, a lowering of the retirement age, rights for immigrants and guaranteed food prices. He ends this list in a manner which illustrates the nature of the personalist use to which *autogestion* and *lutte quotidienne* are put. After the twelve '*nous luttons*', Marchais says: '*Nous nous prononçons pour la reconnaissance du droit à l'autodétermination des départements et territoires d'outre-mer*' (p. 17). The General Secretary thus takes on the role of French observer rather than revolutionary. The proposed solution of '*autodétermination*' will be, in nationalist manner, '*dans le cadre de la République française*' (p. 18). The barely perceptible change from '*nous luttons*' to '*nous nous prononçons*' therefore shifts through: 'You and we struggle' to: 'We, the Party say', on the basis of '*le voyage que j'ai effectué*' (p. 17).

Finishing this section of the speech, Marchais reiterates the simplicity of the moral choice with which people are confronted. Either:

l'adaptation à la crise du capitalisme dans l'intérêt des firmes multinationales, avec les conséquences désastreuses inévitables qui découlent de ce choix pour notre peuple et pour la nation.

Or:

la mise en cause effective de la domination du capital, une série de transformations démocratiques profondes permettant d'avancer, par la démocratie, vers le socialisme pour la France. (p. 19)

Communists have chosen the latter course: '*Nous voulons le changement démocratique*' (p. 19). This, the closing sentence of this section, is made without qualification, yet has a double significance. First, it means that we, as opposed to the '*grande bourgeoisie*' and the '*politiciens*' who serve its interests (p. 19), desire a change *to* democracy. Second, it means that we want change *by means of* democracy. Revolutionary and reformist registers are conflated in one expression and thereby become mutually dependent and reinforcing: the only true democratic road is a revolutionary one, the only true revolutionary road is a democratic one. And here, as in the previous extensive evocation of democracy in the Report, the term is alluded to, taken as desired, taken as presenting no confusion of ends and means in its evocation, taken as understood, charged with significance: where it does not exist it must be established; where it does, it must be extended. It is, however, never defined because it acts less as a doctrinal reference point than as a discursive medium through which, by virtue of its universal acceptance and lack of specificity, other ideas can flow.

Throughout his exposition of the choice between *voies*, Marchais is, in effect, asking the congress to embark upon a difficult and unpredictable course of action even though it proceeds from a simple ethical choice. Moreover, the party is to do this without its former ally – towards the end of the section, the *Parti socialiste* is mentioned once, François Mitterrand twice (p. 19), as having preferred capitalism to democracy – and without a defined strategy. The assurance offered, moreover, is a personal one: through the Report's exposition Marchais is asking the party to trust in his understanding of society, politics and theory, his judgement on when to change direction, his Communist credentials and his moral sense and vision. In so doing, he reminds his audience that they share the added security of a common tradition which acts as a qualification to the libertarianism and nascent populism signified in this first section.

Part II

The second major section of the Report is entitled: '*Notre stratégie internationale*' and is presented through two very different forms of argument. One form explains the ultimate triumph of socialism in terms of general historical trends within a simplified though grand sequence of events. The second stresses the complexity of the current phase of those trends. The connection between the two is assumed though not described. And it is the speaker who, by offering his own judgement and interpretations, renders intelligible a difficult reality and thus epitomises the application of scientific thought to historical processes and the relation of a refined socialist consciousness to the flux of events.

The discussion begins with the assertion of the need to pass from the old to the new, from oppression and violence to liberty and peace (p. 22). It is cast at such a high level of generality that it cannot of itself serve as a guideline for action. The resolution of this problem involves the application of the considered judgement of the speaker which will combine an understanding both of reality and of the perspective of that reality embodied in the party's tradition (and manifest in this symbolic moment of delivery). The traditional perspective is itself personalised before the subject itself is elaborated so that the ensuing interpretation of a complex reality is 'given' by the speaker:

> *Il n'est pas inutile de prendre une certaine hauteur pour saisir les lignes de force de l'évolution du monde d'aujourd'hui.* (p. 22)

A mutation of the '*genre humain*' (p. 22) – and by implication of hitherto accepted modes of thought – is said to be under way.[6] A brake is put upon immediate activity in that the delicate balance involved in the organisation of the forces of progress is such that those involved must know how to '*intervenir avec justesse et efficacité*' (p. 22).

The struggle for liberation here, therefore, is akin, not to the local struggles, but to the great historical upheavals like the transition out of the Dark Ages or the eighteenth-century Enlightenment. The struggle is presented, not as those struggles referred to in the previous section, but as a '*lutte au niveau planétaire*' (p. 22). The counterpoint to these allusions to vague historical themes and moments which precede major historical events is the unambiguously confident statements on the part of the speaker as independent person (as, for example, when he speaks of China thus: '*Je veux m'arrêter un instant sur cette question*' (p. 25)) and as *interlocuteur valable* of the party (as, for example, in the many uses of *nous* and *notre* in this section signifying the party as a whole).

In this way enormous responsibilities are placed upon the activist who does not accept guidance. This guidance takes the form in the Report of a precise telling of the socialist tale – and the dissociation of the Communist from the Socialist movement in that telling – in order that the strategy followed be the historically correct one.

In this historical review, the Second International is recognised as authentic though inadequate because it was scientifically impoverished: '*la force . . . du mouvement ouvrier français et international . . . insuffisants . . . pour . . . utiliser crises et contradictions . . .*' (p. 23). From a Communist perspective such inadequacy is recognised as understandable. What is more significant here is that the identification of nineteenth-century history with the Second International is a prelude to the identification of the twentieth century with the Third. The Revolution in 1917 thus becomes the century's focus. Moreover, not only is the October Revolution seen as the realisation of socialism, it also signalled the decisive development of socialism on a world-wide scale. The ambiguity of the phrase 'signalled' ('*a été le signal'* (p. 23)) conflates without discussion the voluntarism and the determinism present in Marxism–Leninism. This conflation is reinforced by the assertion that such a revolution has held and is holding the line for other movements while they develop and mature. Thanks to it, therefore, dramatic changes for France are '*à l'ordre du jour*' (p. 24).

We can see from this that international affairs are being handled in a ritualistic way, but the emphasis upon international affairs underlines the ordinary party activists' lack of direct experience of the issues being discussed, while offering a macrocosmic view of what they may have direct experience of, *la lutte quotidienne* referred to in the previous section. In this section, therefore, the General Secretary not only underlines the party's orthodoxy, he is also like the interpreter of a morality play, the intermediary between the Soviet Union (and historically, the Comintern) on the one hand and the PCF and its activists on the other. However, the functional role of the Soviet Union in PCF discourse is not always the same.

Traditionally, the Soviet Union, as the site of the original realisation of socialism, has existed as an unquestioned truth within Communism. As such, moreover, Communist discourse often portrays the Soviet Union as in need of protection: in the 1920s against the Western allies and the forces of counter-revolution within; in the thirties against Fascism as an international force; in the forties against the USA and its allies. In the 1960s and 1970s, however, mediation becomes more difficult, partly because the Soviet Union's foreign policies become more complicated and partly because of the increasing autonomy claimed by or imposed upon national Communist parties. This involved more than a change in the degree of mediation by the party leadership. It now had to reconcile established mythology about the transition from capitalism to Communism on a global scale with a bewildering series of discrete responses to individual issues.

The present foreign policy of the party is then elaborated: '*sur la base de quatre grands objectifs, étroitement liés entre eux*' (p. 28): the independence of nations; peaceful coexistence, disarmament and the emancipation of nations; a new international order; and a democratic Europe. The first three issues are elaborated in a complex though traditional way, thus emphasising the orthodoxy of the speaker as interpreter. It is on the discussion of the last point that we see the reappearance of an explicitly personal dimension: '*Moi . . . je fais . . . je suis . . .* (p. 32); *je veux dire . . . je n'hésite pas . . .*' (p. 33) which, as we have seen in the emerging pattern of collusion, distancing and dissociation, is reinforced by : '*nous* ... (p. 32); *notre parti* ... *notre attitude* ... *Nous sommes* ... *nous agissons* ... *Nous savons* ... *Nous ne sommes pas* ... *Nous disons* ... *nous récusons* ...' (p. 33), and reimposes the presence of the speaker as personal voice as well as privileged interpreter of a historic truth. The focus of the argument then becomes specific to the point of banality as the speaker refers to the first elections to the European parliament:

> *C'est sur ces bases claires, solides, que nous appelons les Français et les Françaises à se rassembler et a nous exprimer leur soutien lors des élections européennes du 10 juin prochain.* (p. 34)

The familiar topic of the European elections brings once more into relief the true subject of the Report: the relationship between the audience/activists and the leadership/speaker. The reference to the elections is not an example of bathos after the exposition of the forces at work in world history. On the contrary, it is the focussing of a transcendentalism. The elections are to the international order what the *lutte quotidienne* is to the *lutte au niveau planétaire*. In this way the June elections and the activism that will accompany them are the crystallisation of the myths hitherto expounded; the myth as daily lived experience and future orientated activity.

Part III

The subject of this section is the nature of the relationship between the PCF and the socialist countries. It combines insistence upon the practical achievements of '*le socialisme existant*' (p. 40) in raising economic living standards with the affirmation of various principles such as the absence of a single model of socialist society and the quintessentially democratic nature of socialism. With reference to this latter point, the Report asserts the party's own commitment to a plurality of parties and to elections. These points qualify the general argument which is that, both practically and morally, the socialist countries are superior to their capitalist counterparts.

The central metaphor in this argument is that of a *bilan* which is sustained throughout the section:

> *Comme l'écrit notre projet de résolution: 'à la question de savoir quel est aujourd'hui l'apport du socialisme au mouvement histori-que des pays concernés et à l'humanité dans son ensemble, nous répondons; le bilan des pays socialistes est globalement positif'.* (p. 40)

The expression '*bilan globalement positif*' was a contentious one even – perhaps especially – within the party itself.[7] The speaker, by addressing himself to the issue, thus enters the discussion both as *rapporteur* (the term *bilan* is in the draft resolution as well as in the Report) and as arbitrator:

> *Je passe rapidement sur les querelles de mots qu'a pu susciter, ici ou là, le terme 'bilan'. Quelques camarades ont fait l'analogie avec un bilan comptable, comportant une colonne pour l'actif, une colonne pour le passif . . . et ils en ont conclu à l'impossibilité d'effectuer de tels bilans 'en matière de réalisations humaines'! Mais voyons: qui va s'imaginer, si je parle du 'bilan catastrophique' de cinq années de pouvoir de M. Giscard d'Estaing, que je suis un expert comptable?* (p. 40)

This scathing dismissal of criticism both discredits external enemies and associates internal dissidence with them.

What the above quotation actually does is to admit that the term '*bilan*' is a metaphor and imply that it was always recognised as such. What it does not argue is whether it is an appropriate metaphor. Given this, Marchais can shift attention to the main element of the argument, which is that it is '*positif*':

> *Or, je l'ai montré, un examen portant sur l'ensemble de la période historique que nous vivons montre que le sens des évolutions qui modifient notre monde en profondeur est sans équivoque: ce qui avance, c'est le socialisme; ce qui perd du terrain, c'est le capitalisme.* (p. 40)

The Report itself here is used to legitimate the argument. The '*examen*' that the speaker points out he has demonstrated in fact refers, not to a previous document or established party position, but to a previous section (pp. 22–4) of this speech. The *bilan* metaphor is thus deemed appropriate because it adequately describes an earlier established position within the speech which involved a historico-ethical justification of the Soviet Union. It is the argument concerning the notion of historical advance as ethical justification which would undermine the speaker's argument, but this lies outside its established terms of reference. In the absence of such a challenge, that which is positive is that which advances. Within limits, therefore, a debate about the appropriateness of the *bilan* metaphor legitimates – and masks – the metaphor of (military) movement which lies behind it.

The speaker then defends the whole expression '*bilan globalement positif* – and thereby instigates another censorship of disagreement – by arguing that it possesses a dialectical truth, in that the adversary and its media make daily play with an imagined negative *bilan*. Thus the more its antithesis is argued (and the verbs used to describe capitalisms methods here are: '*endiguer*', '*détourner*' and '*ruiner*' (p. 40)), the more such a struggle in its defence will point to a transcendent truth. Partial understanding, therefore, or puzzlement on the part of the activist, is, paradoxically – or rather, dialectically – an indication of the truth of the argument. Doubt is thus seen as acceptable, even constructive, continuing doubt as subversive and an indication that the dissidents are the victims of the wider capitalist conspiracy:

> *comment expliquer que les militants d'un parti d'avant-garde en viennent à préconiser, comme position révolutionnaire, que nous nous cantonnions dans une prudente neutralité face à cette campagne de tous les instants? Comment l'expliquer, sinon parce que, peu ou prou, ils cèdent eux-mêmes à la pression énorme de cette campagne?* (p. 41)

The point is reinforced by a reminder that the party must not desert the class struggle: '*nous ne pouvons déserter ce terrain essentiel du combat de classe, et nous ne le ferons pas*' (p. 41).

The objections to the use of the term '*bilan globalement positif*' have therefore been attributed to: (i) a misunderstanding of its metaphorical sense; (ii) the failure to see it as an antithetical moment of a transcendent truth; and (iii), if (i) and (ii) are not accepted, the dissident's lack of faith and his/her abandonment of the class struggle. Internal disagreement – in conjunction with the strong and parallel desire for unanimity – is not a disadvantage to this form of leadership, but a necessary feature of it because it sufficiently distances the speaker from a perceived lack of harmony within the party for him to assert and reassert authority within the Report.

This kind of political argument involves the displacing of guilt on to the listener. Although it is the speaker who has initiated the shift in discourse from the particular to the general, and from the concrete to the theoretical (here, from struggle to reflection upon it), it is the listener who is accused of converting simple truths into complex mystifications. The implicit allegation is that the listener, aided by the very nature of discourse, has created the conditions for misconstruction in thought and for deviance in action:

> *Dans ce domaine, aucune astuce de langage, aucune finasserie tacticienne, qui permettraient tout à la fois d'esquiver la difficulté et d'escamoter le problème, ne peuvent être de mise.* (p. 41)

Refusing, therefore, others' readiness to do this or their desire that he do it for them, Marchais faces the consequences of his position head-on. Given this courageous stand on the part of the speaker, all hesitation or qualification on the part of the audience becomes equally unacceptable. All doubt must be cast aside as a prerequisite to advance. The argument then focusses upon two alternatives only concerning the *voies* to be chosen. And the choice is simple and offered with demagogic force:

> *donner une réponse simple et claire à la seule question qui importe en définitive: oui ou non, est-ce une bonne chose que les peuples concernés aient construit le socialisme, ou aurait-il mieux valu qu'ils ne le fassent pas? Notre réponse à cette question est offensive et sans ambigüité: oui, c'est une bonne chose, pour eux et pour nous.* (p. 41)

From this example and from several before and after it in the section and speech as a whole, we can see that a rhythmical pattern of collusive advance towards the audience and profitable retreat from it is established. A problem is raised, its simplicity or complexity stressed. If the problem is defined as simple, nuances are added, and, if complex, a categorical response cuts into the apparent complexity. Then categorical agreement from the audience is implicitly made a condition of the problem's resolution. It is after this that qualification is made, but now it is given exclusively by the speaker, the imagined audience/interlocutor having agreed a moment earlier that the point discussed is resolved. In this case, for example, after the '*réponse sans ambigüité*', which, as we can see from the way the argument has developed so far in this section, is given in the form of a fundamental and unavoidable moral choice, the speaker continues: '*Naturellement, nous devons nous expliquer sur cette réponse*' (p. 41).

And so the argument continues upon the diversity of situations, the individual histories of socialist countries, their historical reference points, national diversity, and this at precisely the point where the problem had been answered and its possibilities ostensibly exhausted.

It is in this context that Marchais mentions the need to formulate '*une appréciation*' (p. 41). In the light of the perpetually renewed complexity of issues, it is clear that the *appréciation* will be the speaker's own and will be revealed to the audience rather than be presented as the reflection of its own deliberations. Let us look first, for a moment, at how, from the beginning of the section, such an approach was built in to the argument.

The section begins with Marchais naming the subject of the section: '*l'appréciation que nous portons sur le socialisme existant . . . . C'est la troisième question que je veux traiter*' (p. 40). Not only is the CPSU/PCF connection posited in a conversational manner but there is even, at this level, a priority of '*nous*' over '*les pays socialistes*': our appraisal of them rather than our relationship to them. Moreover, the suggestion of urgency and risk is introduced because the speaker is broaching a subject as contentious and ethical as human rights, a point which becomes explicit later on in the section. Being prepared to discuss this topic, the speaker is in this way portrayed as giving voice to the unspoken preoccupations of a diffident audience. The speaker is thus – simply through the nature of the subject addressed – presented as both honest and courageous, as well as sensitively aware of anxieties which both exist within the party and are used by its enemies to undermine its faith in itself.

In spite of the fearlessness of the discussion, however, the speaker has guarded against his own deviationism by making 1917 the last sacred-historical reference point before the immediate 1976–9 period, in the previous section. There is, therefore, an underlying reassurance that '*nous*' (a non-socialist country) must, in the final analysis, aspire to and become '*un pays socialiste*'.

The true subject of this section, therefore, is not the traditional one of the PCF/CPSU connection but the speaker's assessment of the Soviet Union, which will involve criticism but only upon condition that the speaker alone undertakes it. The speaker's own standing is reinforced because the contentious issues discussed are moral ones. Marchais is therefore seen as a thinker capable of addressing the problem of and passing judgement upon the Soviet Union and its socialist and humanitarian status. And of course such a discussion will, by definition, involve, on the part of the listener, subjective agreement – or disagreement – with the speaker.

In this way, when the speaker comes on to the question of formulating '*une appréciation*', he need do so by referring only to the argument so far developed within the Report. Having made, in the discussion so far, '*les pays socialistes*' synonymous with '*bilan positif*', the '*appréciation*' can be made and the Soviet Union judged, not in terms of its internal conditions, but purely by demonstrating that the '*bilan*' of the capitalist countries is a negative one. This is done in four stages.

First, the socialist countries are praised for overcoming hunger, misery, illiteracy, under-development and social inequalities. The implication is that these forms of oppression not only existed in these countries before socialism and have been removed, but still do exist in capitalism. Second, the speaker points out the better *rate* of growth in socialist countries, thus showing that even in capitalist terms socialism is successful. Third, the speaker makes a reference to the *tribune de discussion*, here from the federation of *ouvriers spécialisés* at Peugeot–Sochaux,[8] thus allowing the archetypal victim of capitalism to illustrate the point:

> '*Nous qui travaillons en usine, à la chaîne, derrière un four ou une presse ... nous échangerions volontiers nos cadences, nos conditions de travail, notre système d'exploitation de l'individu contre celles de nos camarades des pays socialistes.*' (p. 42)

Fourth, Marchais points out that capitalism often needs to operate through dictatorships. Here he lists South Africa, Uruguay, South Korea, Argentina (before the fall of the Junta), Nicaragua (before the revolution), Haiti (before the overthrow of Duvalier), Namibia, Rhodesia (before Zimbabwe), Chile, Colombia, Guatemala, Zaire, and finally Indonesia, and ends: '*Je pourrais, hélas, continuer l'énumération*' (p. 43). We may note here the sweep of countries mentioned. The *énumération* goes from Africa to South America, to Asia, back again to South America, to Africa, to South America again, to Africa and finally again to Asia. In this way, the speaker assumes the global moral indignation at the tortures and institutionalised murders in these countries and makes them synonymous – because of their joint connection to capitalism – with the parliamentary democracies. By extension, the notion '*globalement*' in the expression '*bilan globalement positif*' is itself modified. Not only does it now mean globally in terms of its overall positive and negative value and its relation to its own past, but global in the sense of socialism being the only alternative and acceptable system on the globe.

Having thus described capitalism and explained socialism's practical and moral superiority in terms of the deficiencies of its opposite, and having seemingly reduced the problem once more to one of stark choice, Marchais then mentions the crimes of the '*époque de Staline*' and '*les écarts*' (p. 43) between what does and what should exist under socialism. Thus once again the persona of the speaker reappears to pass comment at a point in the argument where moral certainty was assured and is now questioned:

> *Vous le voyez donc, camarades ... notre souci est de parvenir à une appréciation lucide, équilibrée, le plus près possible de la vérité.* (p. 44)

In this way, Marchais dissociates himself from both capitalism and Stalinism by naming them. He must, however, justify this distance from the latter if he is not to be implicated. This he does by recourse to thinly-veiled fury:

> *Voyez-vous, je tiens à garder une expression mesurée dans le cadre de ce rapport. J'aurais beaucoup à dire à ce communiste qui s'abaisse, au détour d'une phrase et pour les besoins de sa démonstration, à assimiler les dirigeants de son parti aux responsables de crimes dont, nous, communistes, sans doute plus que tous autres, nous portons l'horreur en nous. C'est ignoble.* (p. 45)

Thus, only unjust accusation is seen as capable of moving the speaker to (just) anger.

Immediately before this near-outburst, moreover, a certain guilt, which involves the party as a whole, is implied by the affirmation that, because of the '*nouveau rapport de forces mondial*' (p. 44), the road to socialism in France is now possible and will be '*moins coûteuse*' (p. 44). The implication is that a measure of guilt must be assumed by those now willing to profit from the consequences of the struggle which gave rise to it. Given the logic of the Marxian interpretation of history – that society develops from lower to higher forms of social organisation – the future is irrevocably implicated in the past.

The speaker, if he is to offer an image of the party as guiltless and thereby be seen to release the audience from such responsibility, must simultaneously show that, through his argument, the party itself need not be implicated. This is done by emphasising, in order to stress the Frenchness of French socialism, the Russianness of Soviet socialism: that the specificities of it stem, in part, from its own Tsarist (pre)history and that this modified the essential characteristic of socialism, its universal democratic impulse. The argument is strengthened, and the Soviet Union protected, by the assertion that the 20th Congress of the CPSU in 1956 recognised this in its denunciation of Stalin. In this way, and in the context of the implicit defence of the Soviet Union, difference, even dissidence, on the part of a sister party can be recognised, in that diversity itself – as in democracy – is an indication of a higher level of unity.

Eurocommunism is therefore justified (and named here) and a French road both endorsed and, because of the underlying teleology, seen as the only strategically justified road. Reassurance of this truth – and an indication of the leadership's paternalism – is given:

> *Les camarades qui, ici et là, manifestent à cet égard des craintes n'ont pas de raisons de s'inquiéter.* (p. 48)

In conclusion, then, we can see that the underlying method of argument in this section is to present the speaker's personal assessment of the Soviet Union as an analysis of the PCF's relationship to it and to appropriate, through a series of alternatingly simplified and sophisticated ethical arguments, the sole position from which to judge the issue and thereby impose a new perspective – or reimpose an old one.

Let us look at the key words and expressions which appear throughout this section and which facilitate this personal appropriation. The problem centres upon the interpretation of reality and the manner in which such interpretation is to be made. The method for doing this is to *faire un bilan*: making a reckoning, balancing the good against the bad. This, however, is coupled with the notion that this needs delicate and sensitive interpretation. Such a *bilan* consequentially leads to the need to *tirer les enseignements* and *tirer les leçons* (pp. 45–6 and 49). It is from these that one must *porter* or *formuler une appréciation* (pp. 41, 45 and 49). This idea of *appréciation* is the crucial one. And '*Nous voulons nous garder, et définitivement, de toute appréciation outrancière*' (p. 44). The activist, therefore, may identify the method of enquiry but not draw conclusions from it. However, *appréciation* itself is linked here to an older notion in Communist discourse, that of *réflexion* (pp. 45, 46, 48 and 49). *Réflexion* is the right and duty of the activist (though we may point out that it is subordinated later in the Report to activism). *Appréciation* is the conclusion of *réflexion* and remains the domain of the speaker. If this is done, utopianism, flights of fancy on the part of the unskilled activist, can be avoided (though we may note the manner of the *professeur* in the way ('*disons un peu*') it is condoned):

*il ne faut pas cacher que l'expérience et la réflexion nous ont permis
. . . de dépasser une vision, disons un peu utopique et abstraite, du
socialisme.* (p. 46)

If we now move in closer to the text and see the linking words and
expressions behind these key terms of *bilan*, *réflexion* and *appréciation*, we can see the structure and dynamics of the argument as very
complex, and see how impossible it would be for an activist to know
the way forward without guidance. These expressions describe what
the leadership has had to do in order to know the correct strategy
(which will be the subject of the following section). This, then, is
what the activist or dissident would need to do:

faire le bilan (p. 40); *ne pas déserter le terrain du combat de classe,
ne pas cultiver des illusions, donner une réponse* (p. 41); *prendre en
compte, constater, ne pas ignorer* (p. 42); *répondre* (p. 43); *examin-
er, parvenir à une appréciation, se garder de, prendre en compte*
(p. 44); *ne pas atténuer, ne pas modifier, prendre une position,
réaffirmer, ne pas céder* (p. 45); *définir le socialisme, repousser des
idées, dépasser une vision abstraite* (p. 46); *ne pas tomber dans
l'erreur, repousser l'idée, proposer, attacher d'intérêt, ne pas se
tromper, prendre en compte* (p. 47); *parcourir un chemin, adopter
la démarche créatrice, considérer, trouver le chemin, avoir une
vision* (p. 48); *avoir la volonté, tirer les lecons, porter une
appréciation, veiller* (p. 49).

Then, and only then, can the party (*'nous'*) *'mettre en oeuvre la ligne
politique'* (p. 49).

In these conceptual circumstances, the leader becomes the interpreter of a complex reality for an unsure audience. Marchais becomes
a persona who can think the unthinkable while displaying unwavering
faith. He acknowledges and deplores the crimes of certain forms of
socialism and admits the distance between ideal and real socialist
forms. He thus presents a material order in moral terms and –
drawing upon the *tribunes de discussion*, which here operate as fables
illustrating the myth of a new socialism which is taking shape – offers
himself as having understood it. In this capacity he inducts the
listeners into the art of formulating *une appréciation*, while simultaneously asserting that acceptance of himself is the condition of its
success.

Part IV

The presentation of the next two sections of the Report is the most problematic for the speaker. They are concerned with party strategy and party organisation. The problems at issue here, being more immediate and observable, are more explicitly traceable to leadership responsibility for both past and present decisions. Lines of enquiry on strategy and organisation converge, in fact, upon the office and role of the General Secretary and, in the field of leadership action, upon the initiatives taken by Marchais himself, identified as the advocate of the now rejected Common Programme strategy. Marchais must, therefore, project his own persona while avoiding blame for the recent past. It is therefore significant in this section of the Report, where guilt will be dealt with and justification sought, that *nous*, said or understood, shifts, more than elsewhere in the Report, between a *nous/moi*, a *nous/nous tous*, a *nous/direction collective* and a *nous* associated with *ceux qui sont anonymes mais qui n'ont jamais douté*.

The explicit theme and title of the fourth section is: '*L'Union pour le changement démocratique*'. The dominant implicit preoccupation, therefore, is the development of a social and political strategy and the justification of future action which will not involve an alliance with the Socialists.

The section begins with a review of the period 1972–8 (pp. 52–5), that is to say, the period of the Common Programme; then points to the lessons to be drawn from that experience (pp. 55–8); and lastly offers a new strategy based upon a new party offensive, itself based upon mass support (pp. 58–66).

Within this framework the argument in the section as a whole is as follows: in the post-1978 period, the past does not provide a sufficient guide to action because: (a) it differs from the conditions obtaining at the time of the Popular Front (p. 57); (b) the imminent revolutionary break is not comparable to that of 1917 (p. 61); (c) there can be no return to the pattern of union with the PS on the basis of the Common Programme (p. 63); and (d) the 22nd Congress has excluded the dictatorship of the proletariat. The new strategy, therefore, will take the form of a vigorous activism which will produce a '*rassemblement majoritaire*' (pp. 58–9) and initiate the decisive movement towards socialism. This will need leadership and guidance with scope for immediate judgement and tactical adjustments. These themselves involve asking the correct questions and deciphering appropriate responses and their implications for action (p. 61). The activists themselves, however, need only act, struggle and fight without *réflexion* (actions which now surpass the *réflexion* discussed and defined by Marchais in the previous section). The two essential requirements for the success of this overall enterprise are (i) a strong party and (ii) the taking of measures to prevent the masses from being duped by social democracy (p. 63).

As this section is introduced, immediate and direct connection is made between the speaker and the party *réel* or *profond*. Simultaneously, Marchais presents himself as sensitive to what is perhaps the major area of anxiety within the party:

> *J'en viens maintenant à la quatrième grande question, qui a occupé la place essentielle dans la discussion préparatoire, et dont un camarade a pu écrire, à juste raison, dans la tribune de discussion, qu'elle était la 'question clé du congrès' lui-même.* (p. 52)

The key question itself involves how the party is to go forward. Clearly, such an issue involves historical justification. This takes the form here of a very recent historical focus which is made possible by the earlier mythification both of the party's history and the previous congress in particular. For (self-)justification to be effected, Marchais needs to demonstrate: (i) that his vision of the past and in the past was correct; this is facilitated by allusion to an underlying, determining social process similar to that used at the beginning of the Report to distinguish (infrastructural) *crise* and (superstructural) elections; (ii) that the failure of 1978 was due, not to a deficiency of this vision, nor to the nature of the events and issues within it, but to an unforeseeable degree of treachery in a partner (albeit always more or less perceived as opportunist) which deformed or arrested the teleology itself; (iii) that the possible accusation of guilt for such a situation can be displaced from the PCF leadership; and (iv) that the future orientation of the party is perceived as a continuation, and therefore justification, of the past – but also one born of the wisdom of experience (or rather, the leader's reflection upon experience). In these circumstances there is a further level of significance to the argument: an implicit distinction between two forms of wisdom: the wisdom of the party and that of Marchais. The party's wisdom is real though recent, but that of Marchais predates this, given the authoritative and knowledgeable tone. The General Secretary implies that the party's past strategy (which involved a belief in the Socialists as a sure ally) was, in part, a necessary demonstration by the leader to his party that the Socialists were devious beyond the ordinary party activist's comprehension. In this way, guilt for the failure of the Common Programme strategy shifts away from the leader rather than towards him, while lending him the quality of a man not only acutely aware of the Socialists' faithlessness but also one prepared to deal with the consequences of this.

The justification of the leadership position is that: (a) the Common Programme was itself the product of years of previous struggle (there is a suggestion here that, as such, it is not only morally defensible but that, organisationally, it was not the responsibility of the present leadership) and (b) the six years (1972–8) did at least act as a means of bringing the economic crisis to the political consciousness of the public while also acting as a holding operation in the face of the capitalist onslaught against the working class:

> *L'examen lucide des faits le montre donc: en signant le Programme commun, nous avons pris – dans les conditions de l'époque – la seule décision juste et réaliste.* (p. 53)

Having offered this interpretation, the speaker now must anticipate and dispel criticism from two areas, the ideological 'right' and 'left' within the party.[9] This he must do, not by allowing for the arguments of dissidence, but by demonstrating that alternative interpretations stem from a lack of information, foresight, intellectual authority and, perhaps, integrity. The two identified oppositions within the party are characterised as: (a) that which sees the error of the party in its adoption of the Common Programme strategy in 1972 (the left) and (b) that which sees party error in the abandonment of the strategy in 1977/8 (the right). The leadership's position is maintained by offering the *same* defence to both, radically divergent, criticisms thereby denuding them of their originality and value.

As in the argument concerning *les pays socialistes*, the defence of the party is made in terms of the opposition it must counter, and concerns only the question of who was loyal to the Common Programme (the PCF) and who renounced it (the PS) (p. 53). This approach to the argument is given strength, moreover, by the avoidance of any reference to the notion of strategy and emphasis upon the theme of trust betrayed. Citing the opportunism of the *ligne d'Epinay* (a veiled personal attack upon Mitterrand) and Mitterrand's own assertion at the time that the Socialists' strategy was to capture the ground occupied by the PCF,[10] Marchais asserts, with supporting reference to the draft resolution, that the PS carries the entire responsibility for the failure of 1978. The principle that social democracy betrays revolutions or progressive advance is a basic one in Communist philosophy. In the French case, such betrayals are always seen as prefacing, and putting a brake upon, a potentially revolutionary moment. The SFIO National Assembly votes of 1914, 1940 and 1958 are common examples of social democracy's lack of revolutionary integrity. In the Report this question of entire guilt is an intriguing one. The logic of it here is this: the refusal of the PCF to accept any responsibility for the Left alliance's failure not only justifies a particular tactical decision (successful or unsuccessful) but also indicates that, not least because it is a difficult assertion to assimilate intellectually, an act of faith is involved, along with a mental accommodation to the PCF's being a party on a different level from others (repeatedly shown by history as being such), particularly at a moment of PCF unpopularity in the country.

In order to maintain or attain this level of difference, the party itself must undergo a *réflexion approfondie* (p. 55). In the Report this consists of an explanation by the leader of the facts to those who failed (and fail) to see the true nature of the PS. And there were many (*l'idée s'est répandue'* (p. 56)) who were deluded. Having previously, therefore, put all ascribable blame elsewhere, Marchais then projects on to the party itself a mitigated guilt for which *réflexion approfondie* is a kind of penance. The focussing of guilt is then sharpened even further:

> *Pour autant, cette activité* [and, significantly, what *activité* refers to here is not clear] *a-t-elle été dépourvue de tout défaut, de toute insuffisance? Non, nous l'avons dit. Nous ne prétendons pas à la perfection. Le parti tout entier pouvait sans doute faire preuve d'encore plus d'esprit d'initiative, de détermination dans les efforts visant à développer l'action des travailleurs et des masses populaires, en écartant des tendances opportunistes dont nous avions constaté publiquement l'existence au lendemain des élections de 1973.* (p. 56)

From this we can see that a party guilt has in fact been identified: that of a lack of vigilance. The implication is that certain forms or deformations of *réflexion* are implicated in the party's misfortunes. This is an early indication of the leadership attack upon the dissident intellectuals which is developed at greater length in the next section of the Report. Suggesting that it would be possible to identify the guilty – by saying that it is dangerous to seek perpetually to cast blame – Marchais develops further this indirect inquisition. It is necessary to '*comprendre pourquoi ces illusions qui se nourrissaient de l'union autour du programme commun étaient si fortes*' (p. 56). The implication is not that it will be necessary in the future to identify these illusions, but that it is necessary for the speaker to identify them in the Report. Explanation therefore is held, and held back, by the speaker.

First, (and again) '*il faut dépasser le simple constat pour aller plus au fond des choses*'. And here the blaming of actors, emphasis upon will or lack of it, preparedness or lack of it, are now superseded – but, having been named and commented upon, are not negated – by a structural explanation in which actors and their desires (and their alternative suggestions) are only surface phenomena.

The structural (deeper) explanation for the PCF's tribulations is, quite straightforwardly, the global crisis. This in turn necessitates '*un changement de société*' (p. 56). Both diagnosis and remedy point away from immediate issues and, having already been elaborated ('*je l'ai montré dans la première partie de ce rapport*' (p. 56)), are legitimated without discussion. Marchais only needs then to assert the uniqueness of the present situation and its differences from the Popular Front and the Liberation (both named). This last assertion of distance emphasises, of course, not only the difference between 1936/1944 and 1979 but also the fact that they are actually forms of the same phenomenon and therefore different expressions of a higher unity. It is as if a nostalgia is surreptitiously allowed and pushed aside: '*Mais poussons plus loin le raisonnement*' (p. 57).

It is at this stage of the argument that Marchais begins to refer to the '*masses populaires*' (p. 57), '*mouvement populaire*' (p. 58), '*mouvement majoritaire*' and '*forces populaires*' (p. 59). These references are an indication that strategy will be developed without reference to party political alliances (though the implication is that these will be consequential). The dominant idea here is that the party must link up with its heritage, the working class/people (here, as at many moments throughout the Report, the two terms are interchangeable), both to serve them and enlighten them. The argument (pp. 57–8) centres upon the idea that the fear of crisis expressed by the masses has allowed social democracy to exploit this area of uncertainty by simultaneously offering an unrigorous version of socialism and a set of quasi-revolutionary illusions. In this way, the earlier optimism of the Left political class is reflected in the naivety of the less politically conscious masses. The argument, as well as offering the leadership the opportunity to redevelop strategy within a Leninist view of the masses, provides reassurance to party members in that it suggests that party truth and historical justification exist in inverse proportion to success. The strategy – we could in fact talk here of a counter-strategy – therefore takes on the form of a perhaps costly but worthwhile crusade for the reconquest of a deluded proletariat. Before elaborating upon the form of this strategy/crusade, Marchais asks if such a strategy means renouncing the orientation defined by the 22nd Congress:

> *Absolument pas. C'est l'inverse qui est vrai.* (p. 58)

Three textual references are then made: one to the draft resolution of the 23rd Congress concerning the willing adoption of the 22nd's orientations; one to the 22nd Congress itself and its commitment to '*la voie démocratique à un socialisme aux couleurs de la France*'; and one to a quotation by Waldeck Rochet (pp. 58–9). It is, therefore, a question of reinterpreting, reading again, finding the true meaning of the old formulations. Union remains the objective, but it will be a different kind of union, and a real one:

> *l'union populaire, l'union de toutes les victimes de la politique du capital, dans leur diversité sociale, politique, spirituelle, idéologique.* (p. 59)

The long argument in this section has the specific effect of illustrating the point that complexity of argumentation is reflected in a complexity of tactics and strategy. Here the first person singular and personal address reappear: '*Je veux insister sur cette question*' (p. 59), '*j'insiste*', '*Je viens de le noter*', '*Ainsi, camarades*' (p. 60), thus underlining the leadership's privileged relationship to the subject being addressed: '*la lutte en bas*' (p. 60).

The strategy itself takes the form of a call to '*l'union dans l'action*' (p. 59) which is '*la seule voie possible*' (p. 59). The term '*voie*' appears several times at this point, as do a collection of words – '*priorité absolue*', '*lutte*', '*action*'(p. 59) – indicating activity and urgency. The tasks for the activists here are seen as simple: the encouragement of '*revendications*' and the extension of democracy at all levels (p. 59). An impression of animated, busy, forthright and dedicated activity is thereby evoked. Union of and with the workers is of course an undeniable and (when not taken as given) always sought-after objective for the party, both for its own sake and as a universally perceived prerequisite for the taking of power and its effective and uncorrupted exercise. The first glimpse of a concrete set of activities is therefore presented in terms of one of the strongest and most fundamental Communist myths.

In this myth (which contains within it a duality ever-present in Marxist parties, given that they are both of the working class and, through scientific socialism, ahead of the working class) lies the irresistible Leftist argument and lesson, namely, that the party must get back to its roots, must recognise that without its base and proletarian contacts it is nothing. It must return to its source in order to bathe again in its real strength before embarking once more on the (final) crusade. This act of renewal and penance is deemed all the more urgent as Marchais points out a little later on, because the social democrats, the eternal traitors, will steal the PCF's source of strength with their lies and promises of paradise (p. 62).

It is in this context, and with this revised image of social flux, rather than the traditional tableau of predetermined, relatively predictable social groups (which is itself revived in the next section of the Report), that Marchais defends the rejection of an initiative such as '*une rupture de ce type de celle de la révolution d'octobre*' and the 22nd Congress's rejection of the notion of the dictatorship of the proletariat (p. 61). It is worth noting, however, that an uncompromising commitment to insurrection has not been replaced by another with equivalent organising power, and that the explanations of the party's relationship to other parties and to its social base are confused and incomplete. The reasoning adopted is that of the party as being capable of mobilising the people in general, and that the occasions for concerted action cannot be predicted in advance with any certainty. The populist approach therefore implies a strategic opportunism defined by the speaker.

Marchais offers a solution to these problems which comes as a reminder of the party's own decision:

C'est sur ces bases – et parce qu'il s'agit d'un document de congrès traitant de stratégie – que nous proposons dans le projet de résolution non pas un programme mais un certain nombre d'objectifs de lutte. (p. 61)

In the guise of dismissing a programme, Marchais then offers to the audience the idea that there need be no defined or named strategy at all:

Mais, dans l'esprit de ce que je viens de dire, nous n'avons pas voulu décider à l'avance de la capacité du mouvement populaire à se déployer, à s'amplifier et à imposer telle ou telle revendication à tel ou tel moment. Nous n'avons pas voulu corseter ce mouvement dans un programme et un échéancier stricte que nous aurions définis pour lui. (p. 61)

There is, then, in the name of the urgency of the task, an almost total absence of doctrinal reference. This does not weaken the call to action but strengthens it:

Partout où se trouvent des femmes et des hommes communistes, nous les appelons à prendre en charge toutes les aspirations populaires dans leur diversité, à animer et à soutenir les luttes appropriées à chaque situation. (pp. 61–2)

Given the argument so far, it would still be quite impossible for the activist to know the form of '*luttes appropriées*' without guidance. The notion of doctrine in fact is everywhere replaced with that of the imminence of dramatic social events and therefore of the need for preparedness. Specific instructions are not given, whereas *un appel* to specific areas within the party as a whole is made in what is both a symbolic (though, as we shall see, only momentary) general mobilisation and an offer of sudden total freedom of action and the negation of the leadership control thus exercised in the Report:

Nous appelons les militants, les cellules, les sections, les fédérations à faire preuve d'audace, d'imagination, d'esprit créateur pour prendre les initiatives . . .
Oui, sans attendre et partout, luttons, camarades . . . . (p. 62)

Here Leninism and council communism coincide. The party itself, within this imagined explosion of creativity, is accorded the task of '*mener le débat politique pour que les travailleurs, les forces populaires non seulement s'engagent dans l'action, mais tirent tout le fruit de l'expérience des luttes*' (p. 62). This statement is an indication of how party authority (and therefore authority within the party) maintains its vanguard position. In that which concerns the '*débat politique*' itself, Marchais affirms that the party's own contribution will not consist of a mere hurling of insults. And against media pretence that Communist leaders are '*des gens peu recommendables*' (p. 62), the speaker points to the total absence of invective and insult in Communist Party debate. The focus of this '*débat*' is the General Secretary himself who, as virtually the only well-known party figure in this period at the level of national public debate, takes upon himself the attacks made indirectly upon the whole party. Concomitantly, he draws to himself the sympathy and protectiveness of the activists and party that he is himself shielding from attack.

The party leadership's political prerogative is then re-established as an explicit brake upon the enthusiasm evoked by the Report itself, and by the presentation of the leader as the personification of the party. The leader's position is enhanced still further by the discursive reconciliation of the speaker ('*je*') with the notion of collective leadership ('*nous*'), in the context of a veiled warning that party action must not involve a recreation of the spirit of Left union:

> *Je comprends que cette idée* [contact with the PS] *soit mise en avant, car l'aspiration à l'union et au changement est vive et légitime. Mais est-ce la bonne voie, la voie réaliste et efficace? Nous ne le pensons pas.* (p. 63)

The libertarian strain, after being released, is therefore domesticated through allusion to the superior wisdom of a united party apparatus.

The main role of the PCF, therefore – a role deliberately presented as imposed upon the audience by Marchais himself – is the struggle, less against capitalism than against the siren qualities of the PS, especially its Leftist, even ultra-Leftist, language, its '*multiples langages*' which only mask its '*pratique de droite*' (p. 63) and its leader, who is named three times here and accused of deviousness. The PCF's willingness, on the other hand, to contribute to '*tout pas en avant réel*' (p. 64) is stressed also with examples.

The true focus of this section, therefore, is the status of the party itself as, in the first place, the only true guardian and political expression of socialism and, in the second, the only guarantee against its being abused if the Left gains power. The PCF is therefore presented as a party both of struggle and of government (p. 65) and it is this dual mission which gives rise to the complexity of its strategy. This means that the party itself is implicitly being warned that, in public, it must show itself as disciplined and resolute. In this way, the unstated conclusion here which will become the main topic of the next section is that internal dissidence is both ill-informed and nefarious. Given the manner in which this section is delivered, moreover, such dissidence is being made doctrinally synonymous with heresy and organisationally synonymous with mutiny.

Part V

The final section of the Report concerns the problem of party organisation. *'Quelques aspects de développement du parti et de son activité'* not only follows on logically and traditionally from the discussion of strategy, but here becomes the focus of the whole speech – the last word. Moreover, organisation, traditionally a rather dry subject, will be dealt with in the Report in the context of the perpetual reappearance of the previous, now legitimated, themes and theses.

This section does not – as the nature of its subject might lead one to expect – lose the transcendentalism or the personalism contained within the Report as a whole. The continuing context of the sense of urgency and therefore the need for enlightened guidance is set by Marchais' confirming the seriousness of the external situation and of internal subversion, so that the section as a whole sustains the impression of crisis. Such a discursive register enables the speaker to raise again issues of faith and doctrine as well as those concerning practical issues of organisation. And, as the argument of this part of the Report develops, the ostensible subject, the review of party machinery is subordinated to the actual subject, the status of the intellectuals in party life. Gradually, partly by denying their effectiveness and loyalty, partly by offering them sanctuary, Marchais presents himself as able to take over their roles within the party and become the sole initiator of both official and critical discourse.

Party organisation as part of a wider task is immediately stressed:

> *Comment faire grandir le Parti communiste français, accroitre ses capacités d'analyse, d'initiative, de rassemblement, développer sa présence et son activité dans toute la vie nationale? Comment lui permettre de mieux en mieux d'assumer cette influence dirigeante qui est une clé de l'avancée démocratique vers le socialisme à la française?* (p. 68)

The form of delivery here imposes a question and thereby anticipates an answer: *'Telle est la dernière des grandes questions que j'aborde maintenant'* (p. 68). In this way Marchais has access to, and will personally communicate, solutions that others can only wonder at, indeed, no longer have the authority to dare to answer prematurely. Moreover we can see from the rhetorical character of the questions that organisation as such will not be questioned. Discussion of organisation will in fact only involve discussion of how to strengthen it.

The section itself, however, assumes a traditional format. Initially it locates the present (and, by implication, future) party position in a direct line stemming from 1920. This claim to orthodoxy through legitimacy buttresses a further claim to doctrinal and theoretical exclusiveness which is used to justify and enhance the party's relation to the working class. And it is from this privileged position that other groups are addressed: '*employés*' (p. 73), '*syndicats*' (p. 74), '*intellectuels*' (pp. 75–7), '*croyants*' (p. 80), '*femmes*' (pp. 80–1), and '*jeunesse*' (pp. 81–2).

At this point Marchais returns to the intellectuals and juxtaposes a discussion of them with further reference to the masses and the need to increase party membership and to reject the social democratic party model and strengthen democratic centralism (pp. 83–6).

The traditional format of the Report is modified throughout the section by reference to three ideas which develop in a particular manner three earlier themes in the Report – activism, strategy and reflection.

Marchais returns constantly in this section to the idea that concerted activism is necessary and good. The central notion entailed is that of *lutte*, which itself draws upon a scientific justification and provides opportunities within a pattern of continuous combat rather than a predetermined plan. Struggle and knowledge, practice and theory, are coextensive: '*la connaissance est un mouvement ininterrompu*' (p. 71). In terms of this appeal to a dialectic of action and knowledge, activism *in practice* is now unequivocally posited as taking precedence over *réflexion*.

Réflexion, therefore, in the speech has become a means of understanding both activism and party strategy, but *a posteriori*. In this sense only are activism and strategy dependent on and subordinate to *réflexion*. The *réflexion* of the activist is in this way seen as that which retrospectively makes action (and strategy) intelligible. That of the leader, however, predates *both* of these and qualitatively differentiates leadership *réflexion* from activist *réflexion*. It is the former which dominates three ideas in the first part of the section (pp. 68–71): *critique*; the study of history; the study of theory. In each case, the speaker indicates first what each entails and second what each does not. Each is then offered to the audience as the subject of the speaker's privileged interpretation.

The acknowledgement of the need for criticism ('*la critique nous est nécessaire pour progresser .... Nous sommes ouverts à la critique*' (p. 68)), is joined to the declaration that it will not entail '*une sorte de jeu de société, coupé de l'action'* (p. 68). Marchais then goes on to assert that *'nous'* (speaker?/party?/leadership?) were the first to undertake this critique – here of the *'retard de 1956'* (the party's slowness of response to destalinisation) (p. 68). Critique is controlled in this manner because what is criticised is not Stalinism but the party's slowness of response to the new situation. In this way, the Soviet Union (through its 20th Congress) is implicitly praised, the leader who failed to dissociate himself quickly enough (Thorez) implicitly condemned. The Marchais leadership is further distanced from its predecessors in a statement which makes 1976 the founding moment of a new myth:

> *depuis cette époque, nous avons accompli un travail d'analyse et de réflexion, une véritable recherche théorique et politique, aboutissant, par étapes successives, aux conclusions du XXIIᵉ Congrès.* (p. 69)

The same pattern of exposition (definition, qualification, and exclusive explanation) is repeated when the speaker refers to the task of preparing a new history of the party, entailing *'des méthodes rigoureuses'* but not *'schématisme ni simplification d'aucune sorte'* (p. 69). This proposal for a new enquiry into the party's past is then offered as a gift: *'Nous proposons au Congrès de décider la création d'une commission qui serait chargée d'animer ce travail, afin de préparer dans cet esprit la rédaction d'une histoire du parti'* (p. 69). This emphasis upon the party's history, moreover, accredits to the party's present activity – and leader – the quality of historical fulfilment.

When Marchais turns to the study of theory, he places most stress on explanation, and in so doing ascribes to himself the role and style of the intellectual. Theory will rest upon philosophical foundations, but will not be *'un corps de doctrine achevé'* (p. 69), nor *'un dogmatisme fermé et scolastique'* (p. 70), neither will it rest upon *'une conception desséchée'* (p. 70). It will in fact be built upon the work of Marx, Engels and Lenin (p. 70). This appeal to theory has a triple significance: (i) it is based upon orthodoxy but will go beyond it as logically – and therefore as uncontentiously – as the present and future follow on from the past; (ii) it suggests that, while a critical approach is acceptable within the party, it is subversive when undertaken outside its formal institutions; (iii) it puts forward the present thinkers in the party – under the guidance of its leadership – as having equal status with the great thinkers of the past. This is reinforced, and an indication given that the new theoretical perspective has already been developed:

C'est ce développement vivant, enrichissant, dans le temps et dans l'espace, que nous proposons de prendre en compte en substituant, pour désigner notre théorie, l'expression de 'socialisme scientifique' à celle de 'marxisme–léninisme'. (p. 70)

This change fulfils the requirements of a new orientation while reaffirming older notions. The reason given for the change is the new circumstances, in particular the ideological war, itself the subject of much Marxian enquiry in the 1960s and 1970s. The term 'scientific socialism' is, moreover, a very old one – it is much older, for example, than 'Marxism–Leninism' – and therefore beyond challenge. The implicit message is that changes in party strategy require theoretical justification, that the leaders are equal to this task, but that the party's theoreticians and activists have not yet fully understood or grappled with the abstract issues involved. The congress itself is then consecrated, with deceptive humility, as a moment in Marxism's dialectical/theoretical journey:

*Friedrich Engels mettait en évidence le mouvement, la conquête nécessaires dans la pensée et dans l'action, en donnant à l'édition allemande de son livre **Socialisme utopique et socialisme scientifique** ce titre plus dialectique: **Le développement du socialisme de l'utopie à la science**.*

N'est-ce pas à ce cheminement scientifique que s'efforcent les documents soumis au présent Congrès? (p. 70)

This statement, furthermore, has three other effects: it implies that the recent past, as theorised by the intellectuals, was characterised by a utopianism which the 'new' theory can dispel; it focusses interest upon Engels, thus opening up new areas of enquiry into the thought of the man who outlived Marx and who, towards the end of his life, moved nearer than ever to an electoralist position; lastly, it emphasises that what may appear to be simple terms and slogans in fact stand for complex theoretical formulations.

The theoretical discussion is then focussed categorically upon the speaker as theorist in a phrase spoken with conscious under-emphasis:

Je voudrais ajouter quelques mots sur la question du matérialisme. (p. 70)

There then follows a five-line sentence containing twelve words around which, both in orthodox Marxian and in libertarian discourse, cluster a myriad of connotations: '*théorie*', '*scientifique*', '*philosophie*', '*matérialiste*', '*dialectique*', '*sensibilité*', '*émotions*', '*sentiments*', '*spiritualité*', '*inquiétudes*', '*espoir humain*' (p. 70). This short, explicitly personal contribution, underlines Marchais' own competence. He follows this with the affirmation that the party needs this kind of research: '*audacieuse et féconde*' (p. 70). In this way he narrows the focus on to the leader as the one able to undertake specific forms of *réflexion*, implicitly offering his own contribution as exemplary.

In terms of party organisation, therefore, the greatest part of this section of the Report has been devoted to the subject of *réflexion*, which is threatened, not only by dissidents amongst the intellectuals, but by intellectuals as a category. It is they who point to the alternative theoretical considerations and perspectives which inform alternative strategies and organisational processes. And it is the status of the intellectuals that Marchais then considers.

He mentions the Vitry meeting with the intellectuals (December 1978) as an example of the leadership's good faith. This reference is also an indication that the act of meeting is itself a resolution of the problems which gave rise to it, thus allowing subsequent dissent to be seen as rebellion. Marchais then abruptly moves, for a time, to a quite different subject; the problem of the party and the working class and their joint socialist task. The intellectuals are thereby mentioned, then subordinated to what are perceived as the real issues and the *raison d'être* of the PCF. The intellectuals' ideal role is, therefore, indirectly defined (simply by the juxtaposition of discussion of intellectuals with that of the party's real task) as one of discovering and expressing concern for the working class and the poor, with the aim of defending them, organising them, and leading them to and in struggle (p. 71) in an enterprise that is like an act of self-negation:

> *Grandir, pour notre parti, cela signifie être toujours mieux le parti de la classe ouvrière.* (p. 71)

The role of the party and its class is then developed over the next four pages of the speech. The inference here is that what the General Secretary is having to do himself is what the intellectuals *should be* doing. This part of the argument ends on a call for a specific target for party activity vis-à-vis its base:

> *C'est pourquoi nous proposons au Congrès de fixer pour objectif au parti: 12 000 cellules d'entreprises!* (p. 74)[11]

In this way Marchais demonstrates his ability to speak at the same intellectual level as intellectuals themselves while, unlike them, never losing sight of the party's true vocation.

Having outlined the party's specific collective task, he shifts the focus just as abruptly back again to the question of the intellectuals. They are, therefore, not only subordinated to a specific task but are indirectly held responsible for its success (or for its past deficiencies). Indeed, the text implies that intellectuals are alien to the essential party; that the best interpretation that can be placed on their behaviour is that they fail to understand what is expected of them, the worst, that they are in fact subverting the party and endangering those it protects. As aliens, almost historical anomalies, they constitute something akin to an antithesis (or necessary evil) in the movement towards a higher social form:

> *Certes, les évolutions dont il s'agit comportent de nombreuses contradictions. La société actuelle est encore très éloignée de la convergence complète entre travail manuel et travail intellectuel.* (p. 75)

Having singled out the intellectuals, and equated dissidence with intellectualism, Marchais comes close to asserting that such dissidence is unmotivated and that it is virtually a product of impersonal forces. However, the total effect of this treatment is a depiction of the intellectuals as an anomalous and marginal group within the party, their claims to pre-eminence and legitimacy seriously questioned.

Shifting attention to the implied consequent question, that of whether the intellectuals even have a role to play in the party, Marchais adopts a conciliatory approach, asserting in effect that the party should provide a place for them – if only to avoid their being taken up by social democracy and the Right (p. 76). Moreover, he continues, the party ('*nous*') must study the critiques, correct the faults, remedy the insufficiencies of '*notre*' activity (p. 76). This is seen as having been done at the Vitry meeting and here Marchais quotes himself at that meeting and promises a Central Committee special session on intellectuals, thus according to them the status of problem to be solved: '*Je propose au XXIIIe Congrès de faire siennes ces décisions*' (p. 76). In this way the intellectuals are trapped by the goodwill and open-mindedness of the General Secretary, the Central Committee and the Congress itself.

The discursive rehabilitation of the intellectuals comes in the form of a criticism of those activists who are worried about the role of the intellectuals in the party. Here Marchais stands as a protector, shielding the intellectuals from the hostility of the rest of the party. Explicitly, Marchais also addresses non-party intellectuals. Unity, he says, does not mean uniformity. Joining the party does not mean the abandonment of individual personality. Being an intellectual does not prevent a person from becoming a Communist (p. 77). Thus the intellectuals are retained in the fold under the General Secretary's protection.

This preoccupation with the party intellectual underlines the fact that, at a time of redefinition of the moral and social vision of the party, the function of the intellectual, the theorisation of optimism, must be maintained. Marchais himself can now define the role of the intellectual in this critical phase of the ideological war:

> *Or, si le socialisme est un mythe à abandonner, que reste-t-il aux peuples, hormis l'acceptation du capitalisme?* (p. 78)

The role of the intellectual is thus defined in the perspective of both the party organisation and its new, more generalised, inspirational basis. The PCF intellectual is to articulate, rather than enquire into, the natural optimism of the working class (p. 78), deviation from this vocation being tantamount to collaboration with the enemy. This role is alluded to and qualified in two closely related passages which all but name the intellectual's prescribed role as that of mythmaker:

> *Notre classe ouvrière, notre peuple, notre jeunesse, ont besoin d'espérances, de perspective, d'idéal. Nous leur en proposons.*
>
> *Non pas une espérance abstraite, mais un but et un chemin fondés sur l'analyse du réel, et donc réalisables: ceux qu'a définis, pour la France, le XXIIe Congrès et que le projet de résolution confirme et précise.* (p. 78)

and:

> *Notre évaluation du bilan réel du socialisme dans le monde écarte l'utopisme. Et l'espoir que nous proposons de faire entrer dans la réalité française ne peut résulter que d'une lutte compliquée. Mais rien ne nous fait renoncer, à cet espoir, à l'utopie en tant qu'anticipation nécessaire pour déchiffrer le sens des événements et pour éclairer l'action des masses.* (p. 78)

The possible accusation of utopianism is thus overcome both by the speaker's refusal of it and by his demonstration that the transcenden-

tal and the experiential can be one and the same thing: that dreams
are commendable if they can be realised.

He then makes his *appel* to the intellectuals and accords to them in
their new role the sacred status conferred by *la lutte*:

> *C'est pourquoi nous appelons les intellectuels français à ne pas
> céder aux naufrageurs de l'espérance. Nous les convions à lutter.*
> (p. 79)

The transcendentalism of this part of the Report has three effects: (i)
it projects the speaker as visionary; (ii) it makes optimism and
agreement with the speaker, struggle and obedience, synonymous
and thereby puts constraints upon deviation from leadership authority; (iii) it presents the ideal intellectual as a generalised case of the
speaker himself.

After a series of brief and traditional rallying appeals to believers,
women and the young, Marchais turns only in the last moments of
the Report to organisation proper and the brief justification of
democratic centralism (pp. 83–5).

Our analysis of this section of the Report gives an indication that,
for the personal leader, the intellectual mode of discourse is a
necessary one. Rival modes (and, paradoxically, intellectualism
itself) become a threat, a serious discursive rival, which needs to be
overcome, though not simply by the imposition of *ouvriérisme*. The
speaker must dominate the congress without trivialising the intellectual mode completely. (This is facilitated partly by the traditional
Communist party belief that the good intellectual is the *technicien* and
the *ingénieur*, the suspect one, the *universitaire*.) It is for these
reasons that a gradual undermining of the intellectuals as a party
within the party takes place, while a gradual taking over of the
intellectual's position occurs – and here allusions to *ouvriérisme* can
be functional (pp. 71–2) – until the only acceptable discursive mode
is either the speaker's or else official party research or propaganda.
Therefore, when democratic centralism (perhaps the most contentious issue within the party, certainly between the leadership and the
dissidents) is justified (pp. 83–5), the suggestion that the party is not
democratic can be dealt with by moral outrage rather than by
argument:

> *Que nos adversaires nous attaquent de cette façon, même en sachant
> pertinemment qu'ils nous calomnient, cela ne nous étonne pas. Que
> les Français qui ne nous connaissent que par ouï-dire se fassent une*

idée fausse de notre vie intérieure, cela se conçoit. Mais que des adhérents, de notre parti, parfois fort anciens, propagent les mêmes choses, cela me paraît parfaitement déplacé de leur part et en tout cas injustifiable. (p. 85)

In the concluding moments of the speech Marchais refers once again to the idea of novelty. First, he tells his audience that, given the influx of new members (p. 85), intra-party communication must be facilitated. The (new) party is also reminded that *l'Humanité* ('*fondée par Jaurès*' (p. 85)) is the daily means of intra-party communication. Next, he points out that hundreds of thousands of people are potential members of the party and that, therefore, the party must prepare and work for this growth. It is in this context of novelty that the *projet de modification des statuts* (whose essential features are the ratification of the rejection of the term 'dictatorship of the proletariat', the entry into the statutes of the term '*autogestion*' and the abandonment of the requirement of the belief in materialism as a condition of membership of the party) becomes significant: it is the organisational reference point for a symbolically renewed party. Now with modified statutes and, though not explicitly stated, much more besides, all that is needed if one is to be a part of this new political movement is: '*tout simplement vouloir lutter pour changer la société*' (p. 86).

In the closing lines of the Report all domination, all sanctions and threats, all leadership personalism – though not personal presence – disappear as the speaker reverts to his official function:

Telles sont, camarades, les principales idées, qui se dégagent du débat qui vient d'avoir lieu au sein de notre parti et de nos propres réflexions, que j'avais pour tâche de vous faire part à l'ouverture de notre congrès. (p. 87)

The speech ends with a final reference to the task ahead: the detonation of the complex rally within a rally, the mechanism that will set socialism in motion and realise the dream of which the present moment, the congress, is the focus and the prelude:

Durant ces trois derniers mois, les 700 000 communistes ont effectué un important travail de réflexion, de discussion et d'élaboration collective de la politique de notre parti. J'en suis persuadé, la tenue de notre XXIIIᵉ Congrès lui-même va apporter des enrichissements supplémentaires à tout ce mouvement. Il permettra de donner de nouveaux moyens à notre parti pour contribuer à construire dans les luttes pour le progrès social, le plein emploi, les libertés et l'indépendance nationale, le mouvement populaire uni indispensable pour ouvrir une issue positive à la crise. Il permettra à notre parti de mieux faire face à la responsabilité historique qui est la sienne: aider notre peuple à avancer, par la démocratie, jusqu'au socialisme – le socialisme pour la France. (p. 87)

5 Tradition and Innovation: The Communists

We have seen from our analysis of Georges Marchais' Report to the 23rd Congress that one of the main effects of the text is to deflect Communist discourse from the inherited doctrinal control of party discourse and direct it towards that of a personalised populism. It was vital to the doctrinal legitimacy of such a shift that it take place within an elaborate and important ritual moment of party life, the party congress, such doctrinal legitimacy being a prerequisite to such changes becoming 'official' discourse. This, nevertheless, brought with it constraints. The form of a congress Report had to be maintained, as well as its strict relation to the draft resolution and to the established discursive conventions of French Communism. However, despite these constraints the shift in the 1979 Report remains considerable, the most important element in it being the discursive invention of the leader/speaker as visionary. The 'vision', however, is still that of a recognisable French Communism. There remains the discursive centrality of the party as organisation, which is maintained in the Report through reference to the party, through the use of the term '*nous*' throughout the text, through the organisational context of the speech, and through its references to the party's intentions when in power, and to its being a party of government.

In the text that we shall analyse in the present chapter, the constraints mentioned above: doctrinal, contextual (organisational and ritual), and rhetorical practically disappear. This has major effects upon the discourse, and upon its doctrinal and mythical reference points, as well as upon the centrality and status of the author.

The text is the book, *L'Espoir au présent* by Georges Marchais, which was published at the end of 1980, and which served as Marchais' testament in the presidential election campaign in April/May 1981, when he stood as the Communist Party's candidate for the presidency of the Republic.[1] The effect of the text is to create a new relation in Communist discourse between a Communist leader and an imagined national constituency, and thereby the modification of the status, communicative scope, and symbolic relation of the leader to the party itself.

The book, and the presidential candidacy of a Communist leader in 1981, are a logical consequence of the 1979 Report. The 1980 text heightens and increases the innovative thematic tendencies of the 1979 Report to the point where the modifications we have identified to the status, communicative scope and the symbolic relation of leader to organisation create a new set of relations. There are, then, two features to note here. First, there is a discursive movement away from constraints, in terms of both the form of the telling – the book does not, nor does it need to, follow the classic divisions of a General Secretary's Report to congress (we shall see below the form it does assume) – and the implications of this for what was hitherto considered as being the necessary relation of Communist discourse to organisational cycles, and to the political and social realities that both official discourse and its cyclical contexts reflected. Second, and consequentially, there is a dramatic increase in the discursive deployment of a new relation, the description and analysis of which constitutes the body of the present chapter.

The new relation involves (1) the creation, through the portrayal of psychological depth, presence and centrality, of the persona of Georges Marchais, a persona sketched in the 1979 Report and (2) the concomitant elaboration of a new relation between this persona and the party, Communist doctrine, and the French nation as a whole, and, by extension, of the interrelationships between the last three.

The initial establishing of this persona is facilitated by four obvious factors: (1) the context of a presidential election campaign where single individuals stand for election; (2) the ascribing of authorship of the book to Marchais himself; (3) the absence of organisational constraints, as we have discussed; and (4) the previous encouragement of such a tendency in the discursive and doctrinal orientations of the 22nd and 23rd Congresses.

The text is book length, about 50 000 words, almost twice as long as the Report. It is divided into nine chapters, within which there are seventy-seven sub-sections. The chapter headings, which themselves indicate the mixture of a traditional style and the new personalism, are entitled: *Pas de fatalité du malheur; Le monde va de l'avant; Nous crions justice; Nous crions liberté; Oui, la révolution; Diversité et solidarité du mouvement révolutionnaire: quelques réflexions; La France, j'y crois; Edifier un monde nouveau,* and *Le Parti communiste: clé de l'avenir.* In outline, the sequence of topics can be seen as: the crisis; the struggle; employment; liberty; the planned economy; diversity within Communism; France; France and the world; the party. Each chapter and sub-section is presented as a structured argument, and, indeed, as part of a wider structured argument, that is to say, an argument taking place 'outside'. As we shall demonstrate, each chapter is also the elaboration and verbalisation of a series of consequential ideas and a cumulative body of personal insights on various topics.

We should, then, consider the reason or reasons for the public expression of such insights. Given French Communism's ambivalence, if not cynicism, concerning capitalist representative democracy – in this case the presidential election and its claim to self-evident sanctity as an end-in-itself consecration of democracy – the actual reason for the discursive entry of Marchais' persona into the major cyclical processes of Fifth Republican democracy must be presented as lying elsewhere. It is for this reason that the untitled 1000 word Foreword of the text is of such significance, as it will both justify the discursive entry of the author's persona into the campaign and create the stylistic and rhetorical conditions of the subsequent text, that is to say, its highly personalised and moral tone and content. Let us then examine the Foreword.

The first sentence of the Foreword is: '*Curieusement, au moment où je commence ce livre, une image s'impose à ma mémoire*' (p. 9). The place of writing is indeterminate, but the first thought of the book, given as '*une image*' which comes to the mind of the author at the moment he begins the book, is significant. Simply by its being the first expressed idea of the book, either as the trigger of the writing or else as an image which intrudes imperatively upon the writing of the book, it possesses a privileged status. A first point to make here is that it is a personal memory, the significance of which we shall return to below. Just as important, of course, is the content of the '*image*' itself. The author remembers returning by plane from La Réunion where he had '*témoigné*' (p. 9) the solidarity of French Communism with a people in struggle. The plane touched down in '*une capitale africaine*', whereupon a group of loud and vulgar Parisian tourists boarded the hitherto almost empty plane. This group, realising who their travelling companion was, could barely disguise their hate and spite (p. 9). The author then juxtaposes this image with reflection upon an opposite one: the crisis of the '*millions de travailleuses et de travailleurs*' who ask themselves each day how they are going to cope with the difficulties in their lives. And their questionings are given an immediacy by their being presented as direct quotations (p. 9). The author then asserts that he, like them, is a worker ('*Moi qui suis un ouvrier'* (p. 10)) engaged in a chance encounter with the rich. Moreover, he states that he has not only seen them on the plane, but also in Acapulco, Mexico, in the corridors of the National Assembly, and in the Elysée Palace (p. 10).

These first two paragraphs – *'une image'* – involve four crucially related points: the writing of the book; the image of the rich; the image of the poor; the social class of the author. All four are revealing of the essential thrust of the rest of the book. In the first place, the incident of the arrival of the pleasure-seeking Parisians on the plane is juxtaposed with the immediate memory of the other France, that of the desperate, toiling poor. More importantly, however, the agency of the juxtaposition of these two categories is the memory of the author and his personal experience which are in a relation to both categories, to the first a contingent one, to the second an original one. And it is only the author who has seen both sides of French social reality: *'Nous n'avons pas idée de la vie réelle ... des milliardaires'* (p. 10). The rich are unaware of the desperate, the latter unaware of the rich, even though their respective conditions are mutually dependent. This juxtaposition: virtue-lacking rich/virtue-possessing poor will inform much of the argument of the book. These claims to exclusive experiencings of discrete aspects of French society as forms of political self-legitimation are a commonplace in French political discourse (a classic example is the first page of Mendès-France's *La République moderne*). Here, however, there is an inversion wherein a 'leader' is not going down to his/her 'sources' to renew legitimacy, but already possesses such legitimacy, and because of this can move uncompromised into the experiencing of a higher social class and a comparative judgement of its moral standing. The notion of a politician having secret knowledge is thus maintained or redeployed, but in this case the author is (a) seen to be of the masses and (b) the possessor of an insight which they have not experienced. Such exclusiveness is enhanced by the intercontinental context of the plane scene, while this context is itself irreproachable: the reason for the journey being to offer solidarity with a people in struggle.

The author's claims to exclusiveness and legitimacy are further reinforced in the fourth paragraph, where he quotes a despairing and touching letter he received *'En rentrant à Paris'* (p. 10) from a Sarthe worker; *'Des lettres comme celle-là, j'en reçois des milliers'* (p. 10). Through the sequence of remembered incidents, therefore, the author displays simultaneously a relationship to the workers (paragraph two) and the quoted worker (paragraph four), and a privileged distance from them due to his much greater knowledge. In this way he becomes a unifying focus for their separate experiences and partial perceptions. The experience of both facets of social reality (wealth and poverty) enables the author to perceive the causes underlying the lived experience of oppression; that is to say, he is able, through his dual experience, to abstract truths from the articulated though barely-understood oppression of the oppressed. Thus, the indication of the author's dual experience is immediately followed by '*Cette société capitaliste ne se contente pas d'épuiser* ...': the capitalists also seek to make the poor feel guilty for their own situation (p. 10). The implication here is that the author can expose the true nature of social relations and thus lift this false but politically functional imposition of guilt.

The author then (paragraph six, p. 10) links the experience on the plane to an experience of social reality in France itself: the seeing '*quelque temps après*' of mile upon mile of closed factories in the Nord department. This bringing together of the personally and emotionally experienced with the ability to abstract and evaluate: '*Cette exploitation, ces inégalités, ces injustices me révoltent*' becomes the trigger of the book: '*C'est pour ça que j'écris ce livre*' (p. 10) and also, of course, an indication of the author's personality and his sense of mission.

The justificatory contexts of the book, therefore, are that the author (a) possesses authentic credentials both socially and emotionally, (b) has experienced the other side of exploitation as a privileged observer and (c), and most importantly, enjoys a unique status through the duality of his experience.

By thus establishing these themes at such an early stage the author ensures that the elaboration of the rest of the book will be in terms which are at once highly moral and exclusively personalised. The moral indignation will be that of any decent man or woman, but the perception of injustice and, by extension, the moral vision of deliverance will be a personal one. Significantly, the Foreword continues: '*Mon coeur se serre quand, dans mes réunions, je vois* ...'. What he sees is tiredness, worry, and hope on the faces of young workers (p. 10). What is striking about this image in the context of what we have said above is not only its political legitimacy (it is a meeting of workers), nor even the emotional expression contained in far] *que je parle* (p. 11). (This raises ambiguities concerning the emotions of weariness and hope, but, once again, the exclusive nature of such experience: only he can see the faces which all face him. The hope, moreover, is focussed upon the person on the platform, the author.

The author, having given, in the context of the reconciliation of experience and reflection upon it, the reason which created the book, goes on to say why, to what purpose, he writes. He states, '*C'est avant tout à eux*' [the workers in the various forms presented so far] *que je parle* (p. 11). (This raises ambiguities concerning the nature and status of the audience or readership of the book, and we shall come back to this below.) There then follows a quotation within the text: ' "*Tu as des devoirs envers ces travailleuses et ces travailleurs, tu n'as pas le droit de les décevoir, c'est pour ça que tu es communiste.*" ' (p.11). Although such a declaration acts as an example to others, it is highly personal. It is the conscience of the author himself as the focus of the meetings mentioned above. And the moral obligation not to '*décevoir*' carries within it the promise of hope fulfilled. The prerequisite of fulfilment is not, initially, the action of the people, nor that of the working class, but the discursive act of the author: '*Et je me bats. Ce livre d'espoir est un livre de lutte*' (p. 11). In this way the movement from the image of the oppressors, through the evocation(s) of the oppressed, towards hope and struggle remains tied to the author's persona. It should be remembered here that 'struggle' in Marxian discourse is a theoretically informed concrete phenomenon with scientific status contributive to revolutionary change. And it is the notion of 'change' which dominates the rest of the Foreword. In the next 300 words after the citing of the words of the author's own conscience, the word '*changer*' appears 15 times (pp. 11 and 12). The significance of this is heightened by its appearance at the beginning of nine paragraphs. Change involves change for workers, '*employés*', families, young people, senior citizens, agricultural workers, technicians, engineers and cadres, teachers, and for France itself. The specifics of these changes are not named. The adverse and inhibiting nature of prevailing conditions is. '*Changer*' thus acts rhetorically as a release mechanism, from oppression to liberation.

This sequence of relations between progressive social categories is standard in Communist and liberationist discourse. Here, however, the agency of change and of vision of the conditions for its realisation is strictly dependent upon the persona of the author. This means that although the traditional Communist Party appeals to various socio-professional categories are deployed here, it is the author who is offered as the key to this long striven for ideal of change. There is also the implicit assumption that political change is possible because the author has presented his insight into the hedonism of the rich and the oppression of the oppressed as the contrasting elements of a single moral vision.

The Foreword ends on the assertion that the hope of deliverance – initially a hope on the faces of tired young workers, now transformed through the author's insight and moral inspiration into hope for change – will be expressed by the book in order that hope may be realised – 'in the present' (p. 12). The creation of the conditions of such realisation is the aim of the book which follows: the establishing, through discourse, of a privileged relation between the author and an imagined readership. The Foreword's ending prefigures the creation of this relation: '*Alors, voulez-vous, parlons-en ensemble*' (p. 12).

Before proceeding to an analysis of the text proper I should like to make a methodological point. We have established that the central concern of the book is the presentation of the persona of Georges Marchais. There is a distinction to be made here between the book and the 1979 Report: the discursive deployment of '*je*' in the 1979 Report is used, as we have seen, to impinge upon and reorientate the traditional conventions and intentions of a congress Report and channel allegiance to the persona of '*je*'; in *L'Espoir*, the essential characteristic of the book is not simply the functional using of '*je*' to reorientate allegiance (the legitimacy of a '*je*' has been justified by the Report itself, and in the book the formal constraints do not exist) but the presentation and elaboration of the character of the author. Our analysis will concentrate upon this particular and central aspect of the book.

A second distinguishing feature concerns the medium of communication in the two texts. The Report involves the presence of the speaker and a continuous rendering, and therefore the analysis of it as oratory. It is for this reason that the analysis of the Report involves our following 'the contours' of the text. In the analysis of the present text what is crucial is character analysis itself, which is not tied to chronology. In a sense, our character analysis is not even restricted to *L'Espoir* itself. The character in *L'Espoir* would have himself, hence the book itself, the central character of hero within another story, that of the myth of the reconciliation of the visionary and the people. For these reasons, the text of *L'Espoir* is not temporally constrained as is that of the Report.

Furthermore, we are concerned here with a text in which the condition of acceptance of and allegiance to the character of the book is not necessarily dependent upon a reading at one sitting. In fact it is unlikely that a single entire reading would be the experience of most readers. Indeed it is likely – and this is encouraged by the many sub-sections of the book – that such a book would be read intermittently and not necessarily in a complete or linear fashion. Mindful of these considerations, our analysis will concentrate upon the evocation of the character of the author. Given that this is no ordinary character invented by the book alone, but a character who also designates a real person (hence my use of the term 'author' rather than 'narrator'), we need to make three readings of the text, readings which will in places overlap, but which, in the interests of clarity, will follow, as far as possible, the chronology of the book. The first involves the relation of the character to the preceding organisational conditions of his discursive deployment, that is to say, to the form, style and influence of the 23rd Congress. The second involves the relation of the character to French Communism at the time of writing, that is to say, to the doctrinal reference points of Communism, themselves modified through the 1979 Report. The third will involve the identification and analysis of the deployed character, and his relation to and effect upon French Communism at the beginning of the 1980s.

1   THE PROTAGONIST OF *L'ESPOIR* AND THE 23RD CONGRESS

In *L'Espoir*, reference to the 22nd and 23rd Congresses is fleeting (see pp. 33, 51, 118, 135, and 168). In only one of the references is a 23rd Congress text quoted (p. 168 on nationhood). This contrasts sharply with the 23rd Congress's constant reference to the 22nd as a source of its own justification and legitimation. The sources of *L'Espoir*'s legitimacy lie elsewhere.

A relation does exist between *L'Espoir* and the 1979 Report at the level of the vocabulary. Much of the Report's vocabulary remains: '*fatalité*, '*crise*', '*lutte*', '*réflexion approfondie*'. And this vocabulary maintains the modified meanings imposed upon it by the Report concerning its relation both to '*je*' and to Communist doctrine. Moreover, some of the central claims of the Report are repeated: the betrayal of the Left by the Socialists (pp. 51, 162, 200) and the justification of the party's form, specifically democratic centralism (pp. 191–5). Chapter Two, '*Le monde va de l'avant*', in particular, is similar to the 1979 Report both in its style of argument – essentially that of dismantling adversarial argument by means of painstaking rectifications, and revelations of dissimulation on the part of the adversary, and by plain scorn – and in its content.

Overall, however, both direct reference and stylistic similarities to the preceding congresses are limited. What is of significance is the way in which the Report's personalised emphasis is developed. To take one example, we saw in the Report how topics discussed were often linked to one another by a personified intervention. In *L'Espoir*, this device is accentuated to the point where the whole text resembles a logically-constructed personal argument which flows as a kind of stream of consciousness. Sub-sections are linked like this:

> *J'aimerais avoir la place de parler plus longuement de ce sujet crucial. Tout comme j'aimerais pouvoir réfléchir avec vous sur cette autre inégalité: celle du logement* (p. 68);

or:

> *un problème particulier s'impose à ma pensée: la région parisienne* (p. 70);

or:

> *Je voudrais encore vous livrer ma pensée sur une question préoccupante: l'école* (p. 71);

or again:

> *Faisons donc, voulez-vous, l'effort d'étudier ensemble les principaux aspects* ... (p. 162).

We can see from these few examples, not only that each topic addressed is linked by the author's own process of thought, but that this process is the organising principle of a discourse freed from the formal constraints imposed by the Report. Subjects of '*réflexion*' are always presented as the product of the author's mind rather than as those of collective deliberation.

It is in this context that one of the characteristics of the Report, its conflation of the idea of struggle with the verbalising of the idea through the General Secretary's Report, has particular significance in *L'Espoir*. We have already seen how this idea of struggle and the writing of the book as a moment of struggle is affirmed in the

Foreword. This idea of struggle and '*combat*' is developed through-out the text (see, in particular, pp. 23–30). Given this emphasis in Communist discourse, and given *L'Espoir*'s emphasis upon the author's recounting struggle in personal terms and prescribing it in personal terms, the book, as the verbalisation of the struggle itself, is enhanced, as is the implication that the reading of it and the reader's acceptance of it or allegiance to its author are a contribution to that struggle. The '*combat*', moreover, is attractively described in the closing lines of Chapter Two as '*Le combat du bonheur*' (p. 30). In the 1979 text also, there is emphasis upon the idea that to agree with the speaker/author is itself to contribute to the struggle (and not to, to betray it). In the 1980 text, however, given that the book itself is presented, as we have seen from our discussion of the Foreword, as a concrete example of the struggle, and is consciously written as a contribution to the struggle, the imperative nature of agreement with the text, with the ideas therein and with the author presented by it, is further enhanced. The idea of struggle as verbal – and the subsequent enhancement of the sayings of the leader of the party of struggle – is well-illustrated by the following example, where even the *signifié* 'action' is subordinated to its verbalisation:

> *Quand on dit: 'L'exploitation est infâme', il faut dire: 'Luttons jusqu'au bout pour la supprimer.' C'est cela être communiste: **dire** l'un et l'autre.* (p. 119; my emphasis)

Another example of the heightening of a rhetorical quality in the Report, which we shall examine in more detail in the last section of this chapter, is the use of the word '*je*'. Here we can just mention that in the 1979 Report, the purely instrumental function of expressions such as '*J'y reviendrai*', '*Je vais y revenir*' – which is the only use of '*je*' in a text such as the 21st Report of 1974 where '*J'y reviendrai*' means exactly what it says and nothing more – is overlaid, as we have seen in the previous chapter, with uses of the first person singular pronoun where the function is that of focussing attention upon the speaker, or else facilitating the depiction of his centrality in French Communism. In the 1980 text, the instrumental style of the type '*J'y reviendrai*' (p. 35), '*Je vais y revenir*' (p. 38) abounds. There is, however, in the context of a text in which '*je*' is ever-present (see final section of this chapter), a qualitative change even here, whereby instrumental references will focus attention upon '*je*', rather than upon the returning, as in the previous examples given, thus offering the image of an intellectual author able to categorise and classify ideas according to their priority, to mention them and return them where appropriate. And, as we shall see throughout our analysis of *L'Espoir*, the 'signifying' uses of '*je*' are so numerous that they constitute the very framework within which the ideas in the text are elaborated.

There is also the intellectual style of *L'Espoir*, now commonplace in French political discourse, and which we identified in our analysis of the Report, and which here elevates the status of the author even more. This intellectual style informs particularly the way in which problems are analysed or else solutions to them offered. Some examples (note also the personalisation present in each):

> *Ce que nous avons dit, je le résume en trois observations.*
> *En premier lieu* .... (p. 40)

> *On peut la définir* [a new economic policy], *à mon avis, par deux orientations principales.* (p. 76)

> *J'y vois pour notre pays trois sortes d'avantages.*
> *Tout d'abord* .... (p. 175)

There are, however, three other areas of reference concerning the 1979 Report, which we analysed in detail and illustrated the significance of in the previous chapter, and which, therefore, we should analyse here in order to see what has become of them. They are (a) the role and status of the audience; (b) the use of fables; and (c) the question of the intellectuals.

(a) The Audience

The imagined audience is clearly wider in *L'Espoir* than in the Report. In the latter, the actual audience were conference delegates. In *L'Espoir*, the audience is not so specific. Here, the tendency to refer to other historical figures, which is always very revealing of assumed or intended audiences, is minimal. Reference to Marx and Lenin is almost non-existent (and, when the author does refer, he points out, in passing, that Marx wrote in the nineteenth century (p. 118), and that Lenin was an intellectual (p. 190), as if unconfident of the readership's knowledge). We might also add that the potted history of Communism (pp. 188–9) can only be described as directed at the uninitiated. There is, moreover, affectionate reference to French and non- (or pre-)Communist figures such as Stendhal (p. 96), Hugo (p. 117), and Jaurès (p. 123), for example, or else to Communist figures known for activities other than party membership: Joliot-Curie (p. 29), Aragon (p. 159), and Barbusse (p. 162). There is even one sympathetic reference to the Pope (p. 178), another to de Gaulle (p. 180). Each of these citings indicates the widening of reference within Communism and the cultural ties it has with French society. The essential indicator of the relationship of author to reader is, however, as we have seen in the previous chapter concerning the relationship of speaker to audience, that which arises from the play of personal pronouns. In *L'Espoir*, '*je*' is ever-present. The '*nous*', however, which was highly significant in the Report, and which designated a series of relations involving the speaker and the party, party leadership, party members and wider public, takes on a far less significant role.

> *On nous ressasse ...*
> *On nous rabâche ...*
> *On nous sermonne ...* (pp. 96–7)

are rare examples from *L'Espoir* of a characteristic feature of the Report. What distinguishes *L'Espoir* is the assumption of a privileged, even intimate, relationship between the author and the reader. There is even the idea that this relationship has been interrupted by the author's opponents:

> *Cette accusation* [that the Communists will nationalise even hairdressers and restaurants] *de ... café de commerce est si grotesque que je ne ferai pas perdre le temps de nos lecteurs en y insistant.* (p. 115)

Even though is is not quite clear where the reader is situated – who is the author talking to if he is talking about the reader? – what is clear is that the reader is not diminished, nor is his/her status threatened, as is often the case in the Report. The apparent complexity of an issue only once informs the author/reader relation to the point where the reader's intellectual inferiority is clearly stated:

> *Je me vois donc, ici, obligé de demander à la lectrice et au lecteur de bien vouloir faire l'effort nécessaire pour me suivre dans l'examen de ces questions capitales.* (p. 161)

And even this distance is removed immediately by the proposal of a collective study:

> *Faisons-donc, voulez-vous, l'effort d'en étudier ensemble les principaux aspects.* (p. 162)

Reader status, moreover, is raised here, given that the examination of the '*questions capitales*' is very straightforward and easy to follow. In places, reader status is maintained by the introduction of a third character. A good example is the following:

> *Certains m'objecteront: 'Tout ça, c'est beau, mais utopique ...' Je parle clair.* (p. 76)

This question of the reader's status brings us to the equally intriguing question of the reader's identity. Here it is not clear that the '*certains*' include the imagined reader or those to whom the reader will speak. Whichever is the case, the reader is either addressed conversationally or unthreateningly or else is not one of the '*certains*'. It is not clear, given the complete absence in *L'Espoir*, unlike the Report, of coercion in the author/reader relationship, who '*nous*' refers to in the following quotation:

> *Cette lutte* [for change], *nous voulons la pousser jusqu'au bout, jusqu'à notre idéal, le socialisme.* (p. 10)

Nevertheless, '*nous*' is rarely multi-connotative as it is in the Report, and the essential relation is between '*je*' and a '*vous*' (understood). In the above quotation, one might argue that '*nous*' is the workers and the Communists together. If that is the case, then the reader is the workers. We have already seen from our examination of the Foreword that the reader could be one of the young tired workers at meetings organised by the party (pp. 10–11), or another '*vous*' (p. 12). There is, moreover, a logical inconsistency on p. 11 between the expression: '*c'est ... à eux que je parle*', and the '*Je vais ... vous ... montrer*' which immediately follows it. And we have already seen from the analysis of the Foreword that the moral motive for writing the book was to help the extremely poor, those asking themselves: '*Vais-je tenir?*' (p. 9). And later in the book (p. 112) the workers are referred to as '*ils*', the reader here being either a wider voting public or Communist activists themselves. And there are other examples of this confusion in the text.

We have seen in our analysis of the '*je*'/'*vous*' and '*je*'/'*nous*' relation in the Report that the shifting status of the audience is functional to the domination of '*vous*' by '*je*'. The identity (or identities) of the audience is, however mutable, always clear. In *L'Espoir*, the opposite is the case: the status of the reader remains continuously privileged and unthreatened, but the identity of the reader is constantly ambivalent, if not unstable. To what purpose? In order to answer this question, we need only return our attention to the main character, the author/narrator. The essential aim of *L'Espoir* is the deployment in discourse of the character of the author. The audience does not need to be discursively created – the audience is the reader – only appealed to. The puzzle of the reader's character is solved when we realise that in each case: reader as poor; as tired young worker; as party member; as affluent worker; or as member of a wider public, the aim of the passages where those identities – and confusions – occur, is to highlight a further aspect of the character of the author: in the first and second cases, aware and morally outraged; in the second, inspired by devotion; in the third, both of the party and of the people; in the fourth, as reassuring, patient and ready to explain or to set the record straight. We can see, therefore, that there is a qualitative and functional change in the relation of the author to the receiver between the Report of 1979 and *L'Espoir* of 1980–1.

(b)   The Use of Fables

We have seen, in the preceding chapter, the use of fables to illustrate myths: small illustrations which domesticate and 'reveal' wider persuasive truths concerning the mindless cruelty of the powerful; the enduring goodness of the poor, and so on. These stories, usually concerning ordinary people, were used in the Report to legitimate the speaker's arguments and justify the orientations within the Report. In *L'Espoir* they go beyond this. Each is infused with an emotional intensity which not only illustrates the myths of Communism, and legitimates the author's arguments, but also reveals his personality.

The '*image [qui] s'impose à ma mémoire*', concerning the plane incident, is a fable of this kind. The appearance and behaviour of those who represent capital, their mindlessness and the petty hatred they exhibit illustrate the myth of the system they support. What makes this fable doubly significant is that it is this incident (and the '*image*' of the worried exemplary poor – which involves their ignorance of the world represented by the people on the plane) which is the moral trigger of the author's action-in-discourse.

A second fable is that of Aurélie (p. 121), a Catholic CGT activist and semi-skilled worker. Only her forename is given. Just before her death she is visited by Henri Krasucki, '*mon camarade*'. His recounting of the struggle and his part in it filled Aurélie with the pride and inner strength of those who have dedicated themselves to create '*un monde des travailleurs*'. The telling of this story is prefaced with: '*J'ai lu avec une émotion indicible le témoignage de cette militante*'. The '*indicible*' quality of the emotion is as revealing of the character of the teller as it is of the tale he recounts.

One of the qualities of the two illustrations given, and indeed of all of the fables used in the text, is their profoundly religious character. In the final chapter the illustrative fable and its religious character are developed further to a 'Lives of the Saints' register and, like the illustrations already given, cast further light upon the character and emotional sensitivity of the author. The final chapter is essentially concerned with the Communist Party itself, but is introduced thus:

J'étais, le 24 mai dernier, à Thionville en Lorraine. (p. 183)

The personal insight nature of the description of the people there at Thionville with the author is reinforced by the description's being a quotation of what the author himself said at the time. The author describes the five activists there with him. The passage, therefore, is quite long and involves the apparent self-effacement of the author. We should remember, however, that the passage is, first, a quotation from a speech made by the author himself, second, a moment of self-effacing generosity on the part of the principal person on the platform and in the book, and third, begins with an imperative where the speaker invites his audience to look away from himself to the others with him. The description of the first of the five is illustrative of the whole passage:

'*Regardez les camarades qui sont ici avec vous aujourd'hui. Arthur Buchman, c'est le dirigeant des communistes de Moselle. Il a commencé à travailler à quatorze ans, il est devenu chaudronnier à l'usine et, au contact des métallos, il est devenu communiste à vingt ans. Il a laissé une partie de sa main dans un accident du travail. Arthur a été le principal responsable de la CGT du département. Et c'est cet ouvrier qui est traîné auhjourd'hui devant le tribunal pour avoir manifesté avec les mineurs sur le carreau de la mine de Falquemont afin qu'elle ne meure pas!*' (p. 183)

After the five people with him have been introduced in a similar way, recounting their struggle and commitment, the introduction ends:

'*Alors quand on viendra vous dire: "Tous les mêmes, ceux qui s'occupent de la politique", vous penserez à ces femmes, à ces*

hommes, chaudronniers, électriciens, institutrices, médecins'.
(pp. 184–5)

Given the emphasis upon the author throughout the book, and his own emphasis upon politics as a moral means to a moral end (cf: *'Non, il faut lutter, lutter pour changer vraiment. Pour moi, faire de la politique, c'est cela'* (p. 53)), we can see that a story which has apparently demystified political activity has, in fact, reinforced the myth of moral commitment which informs it. The author demonstrates his own realisation of this when he explains the reason for quoting his Thionville introduction of the five:

> *J'ai rappelé cette déclaration, parce que je pense qu'elle a valeur d'exemple.* (p. 185)

And all parables or fables illustrate the character of the parable-teller in that the selectivity and telling of such stories underline and illustrate the moral principles that the parable-teller is communicating.

(c) The Intellectuals

One of the striking features of *L'Espoir*, given that our analysis of the Report revealed that one of its main aims was the concerted and prolonged undermining of the intellectuals within the party, is the virtual absence of the party intellectuals as characters or points of reference in the text. The dissidents, indeed dissidence, are nowhere referred to in the text. In the introduction of the five party members (see previous section), two of the five, a primary schoolteacher and a medical practitioner, are described as intellectuals. When intellectuals as a category are briefly discussed (pp. 189–90), they are praised, and, as we have seen, Lenin is referred to as an intellectual (p. 190). There is one example of the scornful style used in 1979 to attack intellectuals (p. 29), but the scorn is directed not at them, but at those opposed to nuclear power – and, in fact, this style, so prominent in 1979, is itself almost entirely absent from the text as a whole. There is an oblique critical reference to dissidents, though even here it is not clear that the author is referring to them, nor is it rhetorically significant if he is, when he states:

> *En exposant cette conclusion du Parti communiste français, j'ai bien conscience d'aller à contre-courant de certaines idées reçues* [concerning the Union of the Left]. (p. 123)

The author refers to the notion of the party as a collective intellectual (p. 190). The point for our analysis, however, is rather that, after the appropriation of the intellectual's register and the intellectual's position, which we identified in our analysis of the Report, the author does not need to argue a case, only deploy a register.

In *L'Espoir*, through the discursive invocation of a harmonious Communist Party, he can posit the party as a collective intellectual, given that the 'voice' of the party is, in *L'Espoir*, the inellectual, fable-telling, insightful and moral voice of the text's author. We shall return to the discursive status of the party in the final section of this chapter.

Certain characteristics of the Report, therefore, several of them innovative in 1979, in their substance or their use: vocabulary, personalised style, fables, and the intellectual status of the speaker, are redeployed in *L'Espoir*. Here, however, unrestricted by concern with the nature of the audience, by the exigency of replying directly to internal criticism, and by the formal constraints of a party congress, they are extended and used to contribute to the elaboration of the character of the author, and further channel the discourse and doctrine of the party towards the notion of Communism as personal revelation. Let us now consider how Communist doctrine, modified in 1979 by the Report, is further developed and modified by *L'Espoir*.

2   COMMUNIST DOCTRINE AND *L'ESPOIR*

There are three doctrinally-related themes which inform the text of *L'Espoir*. Given the fact that the audience is no longer the assembled party, more esoteric doctrinal issues are absent. The three which remain, moreover, are elaborated, as are the dominant themes in the Report, within a populist framework. In *L'Espoir*, however, the populist orientation is geared more than ever to personalism, given the centrality of the author and the strict subordination of the party to his persona in the text. The three dominant and logically consequential themes are: the theme of waste; the theme of change; and the theme of France.

(a)   The Theme of Waste

The idea of waste, and the associated ideas of selfishness, of the squandering of wealth, of corruption, of deliberate and disorganised decline, and the perversion of progress, are invariably linked to ideas concerning the personality of the owners and representatives of capital. The initial example of the travellers on the plane and what they represent is the first indication of this.

Much of the first chapter is concerned with the detailing of examples of the squandering of assets and progress. Practical examples of waste (and possibilities for its avoidance) are given one after another (pp. 14–18), concerning atomic research, technological innovation, agriculture, and medicine, among others. The wastage element is reinforced by the initial assertion that these areas are themselves unequivocal indices of social progress (p. 14). Each is then described as a potential progress impeded by '*L'aristocratie de l'Argent*' (p. 19). Each of the issues discussed is invariably prefaced by a personal observation which brings them into the discussion. Some examples:

> *Je comprends les raisons de ces inquiétudes.* (p. 15)
> *J'ai vu, par exemple, à l'usine Renault.* (p. 16)
> *Autre exemple auquel j'ai été conduit à m'intéresser.* (p. 17)
> *Voici encore un exemple que m'a cité un agriculteur.* (p. 17)
> *Voyez ce qui se passe pour la santé. Je suis d'autant plus sensible à cette question que* . . . (p. 17)
> *Je ne veux pas terminer cette énumération sans* . . . (p. 18)

The notion of waste is treated as central to the author's argument, moreover. To be aware of it and what it does to man and nature '*nous touchons au fond de ce qui va mal aujourd'hui*' (p. 18). The reason for this '*perversion de la science*' (p. 18) is also revealing of the personality of the oppressors. (This is a partial inversion of Leftist interpretation. In traditional Leftist political analyses, it is the system which engenders the greed. Here it is the human greed which creates the system.) Their reasons are the following:

> *du profit, du profit, le plus gros possible et le plus vite possible.* (pp. 16–17)
> *la course au profit.* (twice on p. 17)
> *un formidable affrontement entre la loi bestiale du profit et l'homme.* (p. 23)
> *les hôtels de luxe et les palais dorés.* (p. 22)

The inevitable concomitant of these desires on the part of the rich is the attempt to culpabilise the oppressed and dissimulate guilt. The following part of the argument (pp. 19–24), therefore, allows the author to identify such dissimulation:

Les apprentis sorciers. (p. 19)
On nous dit et redit. (p. 20)
Le tapage orchestré par le gouvernement. (p. 22)
jeter un brouillard sur les causes. (p. 22)
supercherie. (pp. 21 and 23)

and to expose it:

En réalité ... (p. 20)
La démonstration que j'ai faite [three years before]. (p. 21)
Qui peut contester ...? (twice on p. 21)
Si le gouvernement veut chasser le 'gaspi', qu'il aille donc à Neuilly où la consommation d'énergie par habitant est le double de celle des villes ouvrières. (p. 22)
Ce que je démontre ... vaut aussi pour ... (p. 22)
Ce sont les deux faces d'un seul et même piège qui vise à détourner les travailleuses et les travailleurs .... (p. 24)

The centrality of authorial tone and the simplification of the nature of oppression allows for far-reaching claims to be made on the basis of an apparently simple cause/effect relation:

faire sauter le carcan du profit ... la modification des rapports des hommes ... le progrès scientifique ... la libération de l'être humain ... pour l'épanouissement de chaque personnalité. (p. 26)

One of the main features of the opening pages of Chapter One, however, apart from the elaboration of the author's debating style and the positing of liberation as being both dependent upon and the consequence of the destruction of the profit system, is the reification of progress. It is interesting to note in this context (a) that all the named areas of waste (see above) are areas of potential progress, (b) that the author makes personal observations concerning these areas (see above), and (c) that liberation and progress are made synonymous in these pages.

In the remaining pages of this chapter (pp. 24–30), the conflation liberation/progress is developed into an apologia of modernisation itself (particularly concerning the development of nuclear power). In this context it is also revealing that the examples of waste and the *'perversion de la science'* given all involve areas where *scientific* progress is possible (and desirable. At several points the author emphasises that the view that scientific progress is itself wrong is a mistaken one (pp. 15, 16, 23, 24, 25, 28, 29, 30)). As we shall see, the waste theme is carried forward to support the two other dominant themes in the text, but as the second theme is developed in Chapter Two, the notion of historical change rests upon the basis of Chapter One's conflation of progress/liberation which was itself posited as the antithesis of capitalism/oppression.

(b)   The Theme of Change

The elaboration of the notion that change (as social progress/ liberation) is self-evidently progressive and desirable means that, as in the 1979 Report, the rhetorical task is to legitimate the Communist Party and the author by associating them with the notion of change-as-historical-movement. Most of the second chapter of *L'Espoir* involves the elaboration of a classic Marxian argument: that the release from oppression and the overcoming of the crisis is possible because that is the way historical forces are moving. (And, much later, this argument reappears as a personally demonstrated truth: *'Le monde va de l'avant: je l'ai montré'* (p. 161).) The adversity created by the crisis is proof, therefore, that change/progress will happen, and that the political analysis of the author is accurate. In the distinctly Marxian affirmation:

> *cette crise est à la fois décadence d'un système périmé et naissance d'un monde nouveau.* (p. 33)

the author's claim is also a characteristic of the visionary: prophecy as justification of the claim to an accurate view of present reality, a claim which can often be 'proved' by showing the realisation of past prophecies. We shall return to this point in the final section of this chapter.

The status of author as visionary is enhanced in this chapter of the book by reference to the first theme of waste and its consequence, the wilful scheming of the oppressors:

> *Alors ils mentent, déforment, insultent, menacent. Ils font tout pour cacher la vérité aux travailleurs, pour ruiner leur espoir d'une société plus juste.* (p. 40. See also p. 119)

The implication in this assertion – and again there is the undertone of the Christian prophet revealing the sins of the wicked to the just – is that the role of Communism, and of the authorial voice, is to reveal this process of lies and deformations. Given that this is done in the context of the major elaboration of the theme of change, the prophetic aspect of mendacity as proof of an old society pregnant with the new is reinforced.

The third theme, that of France, is also linked to the progress theme in Chapter Two (and will be developed much further in Chapter Four) when the author points out that the French working class has always been part of the historical and historic progressive movement, the emotive example here being its opposition to the Nazis (p. 45). In parenthesis, we should note here that an interesting link is made at this point which relates historical movement to personality. On the question of 1968, the author presents the party's anticipation and interpretation of the events as being the product of the perception of the *'sensible et humain'* Waldeck Rochet. By implication, the author's own claim to prophecy and interpretation concerning the present is reinforced (see p. 50).

There is a large gap in the reference to these themes – Chapter Three is concerned essentially with a detailed examination of work, housing and education (we shall return to the significance of this chapter in the final section). Although, again in parenthesis, it is interesting to note that one of the rhetorical linkages, here between the experiential and the transcendental, takes place in the context of a direct and amicable address to the reader: *'Tout cela, me direz-vous, revient à un changement de société. Bien sûr!'* (p. 64). Concerning the interdependency of the three themes, the first two (waste/oppression, progress/liberation) are picked up again just before the major elaboration of the third. Towards the end of Chapter Three, the author refers again to waste in the context of the need for *'une nouvelle politique économique'* (p. 76), which is introduced and elaborated (pp. 76–80) as an idea of the author, rather than of the party:

> *Certains m'objecteront: 'Tout ça, c'est beau, mais utopique. Où prendrez-vous les moyens, où prendrez-vous l'argent?' Je parle clair.* (p. 76)

He also refers to the idea of waste here (*'gaspiller'*/*'gaspillages'* is used five times in one paragraph (p. 78)) and again in the main chapter on France (p. 101). The term *'produire français'* (p. 78) is offered here as an innovative form of release from waste/oppression at the end of Chapter Three, thus linking the three themes: waste as an indication of oppression, change as progress, 'France' as the means of eliminating the one and introducing the other.

(c)   The Theme of France

References to France abound throughout the book, but the discussion in which 'France' is seen as the key to liberation is developed in Chapter Four of *L'Espoir*, where the development of the theme involves a highly personalised exposition of (a) how the 'real' France has been suppressed, and (b) how a liberated France will take its place and inscribe itself automatically into the historical movement. The France that has been suppressed is synonymous with Liberty (arguably, a French invention). The major reference point for this is the *Déclaration des droits de l'homme et du citoyen*:

> *Comparons la Déclaration ... avec la réalité actuelle.* (p. 81)

The argument that follows involves the demonstration of the gulf that exists between '*les mots et les choses*' (p. 81):

> *Mais que de confusions! Que d'hypocrisies, et même que de crimes commis au nom de la liberté!*
> *Essayons d'y voir clair.* (p. 81)

The way in which the betrayal of the Declaration is elaborated – four examples concerning abuses end: '*C'est ça la liberté?*' (pp. 81–2), thus inviting the obvious answer – means that the Declaration itself is posited as an original and sacred entity, the abuse of which is sacrilegious. And in terms of taking names in vain, the author also points out that lip-service to liberty, in the context of its abuse, has never been greater than at the present time (p. 83).

It is interesting to note here that the exclusive focus upon the sacred text of the Declaration places unusual emphasis upon 1789 as the founding moment or Myth of the Origin. Nor is it without significance that the '*crimes*' phrase of the above quotation is a paraphrase of the dying words attributed to the Girondin, Madame Roland. What is to be re-enacted, therefore, is 1789. We are then in 1788. '*L'Etat–Giscard*' (p. 83), therefore, is by implication, that of absolutism, waste and frivolity, the domain of the late eighteenth-century aristocracy. Other nineteenth- and twentieth-century dates are mentioned, but, significantly, none is given the prominence of 1789. The focus upon 1789 is an appropriate one, not simply because within French political culture it is subscribed to almost universally, but because its essential emphasis is upon libertarianism. The role of the author of *L'Espoir* in 1981 is to lead the French to liberty through the overthrow of oppression, out of, as it were, the house of bondage.

To this end, pp. 81–6 are concerned with showing the oppressors' stifling and abuse of both liberties and '*Liberté*', essentially through callous dissimulation and a veiling of the truth through lies. Pages 86–107 are devoted therefore, not surprisingly, to a personalised demonstration of the author's struggle to re-establish those liberties and Liberty. Let us examine this in more detail.

It is significant that on this question exclusive emphasis is placed upon the Committee for the Defence of Liberties and the Rights of Man in France and in the World, '*Comité que je préside*' (pp. 87 and 88), and not upon the French Communist Party, as if an organised moral conscience has transcended the party as the defender of liberty. The party will itself be brought back later in the text as just such an organisational expression of moral concerns. However, this will be done in the context of the enhanced importance of the author, to which the emphasis upon the Committee for the Defence of Liberties is a contribution.

The central focus of the Committee is the author, the Committee being presented as a moral, even chivalric rally around him:

> *Mes amis Aragon et Georges Séguy en assument la direction à mes côtés.* (p. 86)

The moral origin of the Committee is '*cet amour de la liberté*' (p. 86), its purpose to help apply the United Nations Declaration of Rights. Each of the Committee's initiatives is presented as a personal initiative:

> *la demande que j'ai présentée à Mme Simone Veil.* (p. 87)
> *J'ai rendu publique* [in Geneva] *une liste de treize femmes et hommes injustement emprisonnés dans douze pays.* (p. 88)
> *j'avais fait remettre au président de la Tunisie un message personnel ...* (p. 88)

Moreover, the names of the thirteen imprisoned people on the list are introduced in a personal manner and in a moral/emotional way:

> *J'ai à coeur de rappeler ici ces treize noms.* [Two are from the Eastern bloc] (p. 88)

The emotional involvement of the author is then underlined: since the publication of the list: '*j'ai eu la joie intense d'apprendre que l'un de ces treize détenus ... avait été enfin libéré*' (p. 88).

The clear implication of all this is that doctrine, or Communism generally, proceeds from a moral commitment to liberty, and it is this which is the spring of the author's action. His leadership of the French Communist Party, and indeed the Party itself, through the focus here upon the Committee, are consequences of this and not causes of it. By implication, the morality which the author insists upon here precedes organisation and links him personally with the moral drive which created the Revolution. The passage concerning the Committee ends incontestably on a moral note (a quotation from Eluard):

'*Le bonheur et rien d'autre*'. (p. 89)

The notion of the betrayal of 1789 is returned to specifically a little later on with the reference to a leading banker's assertion that monarchical rule in business was necessary:

La monarchie dans la république, voilà bien l'entreprise aujour-d'hui: une société en retard de deux siècles. (p. 98)

This (re)making of the revolution is, therefore, given added impact by the idea of having to defend it against the forces that would return France to the *ancien régime*. Such a play between making and defending the revolution is possible because the author has previous-ly made the recapitulation of 1789 (a revolution which has already taken place) the aim of a personally-led socialist undertaking. This reconciled duality reappears over the question of institutional change itself. Still on the question of liberties and 1789, the author remarks that freedom of expression '*est acquise sur le papier depuis 1789*' (p. 90), but that this has been violated by '*la nature et le fonctionnement du système économique et politique*' (p. 90). Such a situation therefore requires '*la création d'institutions nouvelles, de méthodes et de mentalités nouvelles*' (91). When the author then comes on to the question of what these institutions would be, the desired system is that which, though added to since, was created in . . . 1789 (see pp. 100–3).

The following chapter is entitled '*Oui, la révolution*' (pp. 109–25), and it is here that more specific statements are made concerning the content of the revolution. The 'revolutionary' character of these statements is, however, domesticated by the fact that the revolution to be made has, as we have seen, already taken place 200 years before. The chapter begins with an appeal to the reader not to put off till later '*Tout ce que je viens d'esquisser*' (p. 109), and goes on to call for major changes in industrial and local democracy, State owner-ship, and economic planning (pp. 110–17), while warning the reader that this will involve struggle, commitment and effort. This implies an immediate question concerning the focus of the class struggle. The author affirms:

Longtemps les ouvriers ont cru possible de confier leurs intérêts à des 'personnalités' venues d'autres milieux. (p. 120)

This is a traditional historical reference to the betrayal of the workers' interests by bourgeois politicians, and a more oblique contemporary reference to the failed alliance with the Socialists in the 1970s. Several other references are made here concerning the need for the workers to liberate themselves (see in particular pp. 118–25). Nevertheless, the immediate context of struggle, in fact the only clear focus for it, even though they are not named, are the 1981 presidential elections themselves. We can see in this a major reorientation of the focus of traditional Communist discourse. In the above quotation, the apparent, and conventional, doctrinal reference is to *'autres milieux'*, and the long-established notion of class treachery. There is an equally strong implied reference to the untrustworthiness of the *'personnalités'* from other *'milieux'*, and therefore to the trustworthiness of those from the same milieu, in this case, the Communist Party candidate for the presidential elections of 1981. And this conflation of socialism/author is underlined in the closing words of the chapter: '*La révolution socialiste. J'y crois*', that is to say that the new society (*'notre idéal, le socialisme'* (p. 110), *'vie nouvelle'* (p. 111, twice), *'autre vie, plus libre, plus sûre ... autre société, plus juste, plus transparente'* (p. 112), *'République nouvelle'* (p. 116)) has been 'seen' by the author, and that he believes in it (confessionally), and knows how to realise it (practically). In the context of the theme of Chapter Four, the model for the new revolution, through its Frenchness, the institutions it advocates, the appeal to certain key concepts, and specific references to the period, is that of 1789. Given the exclusive appropriation, by the author, of interpretation and of the envisioned society, and given the impending elections as the focus of political action, the vehicle for the realisation of a re-enacted 1789 is allegiance to the author of the text.

Chapter Six is concerned with the diversity of world socialism, and therefore reaffirms, by reference to non-French examples, the French quality of French socialism. The ideas in this chapter are elaborated as the communication of further personal insight – the chapter's sub-title is *'quelques réflexions'*. The stressing of the diversity of world socialism serves to distance the author from the founding myth of 1917, thus reinforcing further the myth of 1789.

In Chapter Seven, the elaboration of what socialism in France itself will mean is expressed as an idyll (c.f. the Eluard quotation given earlier) through the invocation of the desire for simple happiness (here presented as an insight gained through personal contact):

> *Je me suis rendu dans toutes les régions françaises. Je peux témoigner que l'aspiration première des femmes et des hommes de notre pays est de vivre libres et heureux chez eux.* (p. 143)

This idyll, which underpins the second central theme of the book (change), precedes restatement of the first theme (waste) in the context of the third (France). Pages 143–50 stress the idea of France's heritage, and refer several times to the '*nation*' while listing the '*gâchis*' of the '*gouvernants actuels*' (p. 150) and, referring to the capitalists who '*stérilisent*', '*lésinent*', '*compriment*', and '*s'attaquent à*' the '*trésors*' of the French nation, the author states:

> *Bref, ils diminuent la France. Ils ont programmé son déclin.* (p. 151)

Towards the end of the book, the author will come back to what is one of the major implications of these interlocking themes: that, in some sense, the rulers since the Revolution have stolen France, and that the task of Communists and the author is to restore France to itself, as it were, to render to France, in the chivalric tradition, its true self, its honour:

> *La préoccupation des communistes, c'est de mettre en valeur tout ce qui peut assurer aux yeux des peuples la continuité entre la France de la Renaissance, la France du siècle des Lumières, la France révolutionnaire, la France des Droits de l'homme et du citoyen et la France d'aujourd'hui. C'est pourquoi je n'hésite jamais, pour ma part, à relever publiquement et à faire connaître au monde, tout acte positif qui puisse être de nature à restaurer l'image de la France dans le monde, image défigurée par le capitalisme.* (pp. 180–1)

The above three doctrinally-based themes, drawn upon by the author, all inform the idea of a crusade: the abuses, distortions and squanderings of the present system; the idea of progress as an ideal; the notion of the recapitulation of the Revolution as the way in which France will be drawn into such a process and find itself once again. The question remains as to how the initial negation, the orchestrated denial of release, is to be overcome, how progress/liberation is to be effected, and how France is to be (re)created. The implicit answer here is that these things will come to pass through allegiance to the author, the character of whom is elaborated throughout the telling of *L'Espoir* and which we shall now analyse, in order to demonstrate its functional significance, and the overall significance of the book.

3 THE CHARACTER OF THE AUTHOR

In our analysis of the Foreword of *L'Espoir*, we saw the sketching in of certain key qualities possessed by the author: perception, an emotional sensitivity, a moral sense, working-class credentials (*'Moi, je suis un ouvrier'* (p. 10)), and commitment. These qualities, characteristic of the authorial voice, inform the whole of the rest of the text. But from the Foreword, two other *exclusive* and related qualities created by the author's *situation* are equally important and informative of the rest of the text: a connection to, and therefore separation from, both posited social levels of French society; and an ability to walk among the corrupt and remain uncorrupted.

It is on the basis of these personal and circumstantial qualities that the character of the author is developed. The first thing to mention here is the sheer textual pressure of the author's persona throughout the book. We have already seen many examples of the intrusion of this persona into the issues discussed in the text. It is, however, difficult here to reproduce the extent of the intrusion. From our analysis of the 1979 Report, we mentioned the occurrence of the word *'je'* 72 times (in contrast, for example, to the dozen or so occurrences in the 1974 Report). In *L'Espoir*, which is less than twice the length of the 1979 Report, the first person singular pronoun occurs more than 350 times. Moreover, given the character traits of the author elaborated in *L'Espoir*, the occurrence of *'je'* invariably denotes two other characteristics. One of the first occurrences is: *'Je suis avec un intérêt passioné . . .'* (p. 13). And a little further on: *'J'y ai beaucoup réfléchi, j'ai procédé à des consultations approfondies'* (p. 26). Given the conversational style of the text and the fact that the author is a worker, such statements indicate the enthusiasm of the autodidact. The *'je'* denoted is, therefore, in part, an ordinary person. Given the other qualities sketched, the insight, the separateness, and the fact that the issues, followed with passionate interest or deeply reflected upon, will all be significant issues, the same statements will denote the selective judgement of the savant. This latter quality is often backed up by reference to other – often bourgeois – sources of knowledge. For example: '*Les rapports des organismes officiels les plus divers, en France et dans le monde, confirment mes arguments*' (p. 21). This interplay of ordinariness and wisdom runs throughout the text.

Another quality is elaborated, moreover, which will elevate the character of the author closer to that of the visionary. Early in the text, the author's knowledge is not only seen as pre-dating the text – the visionary's knowledge is always temporally indeterminate (or else gained on the road to Damascus) – but is also portrayed as an *unheeded* voice from the past:

> *J'ai moi-même, il y a neuf ans ... publié ... un article .... 'Vous inventez' m'a-t-on dit .... Aujourd'hui personne ne nie plus la crise.* (pp. 18–19)

The author goes on to say that the party saw clearly also. The impression remains, however, one of the party's subordination to his personalised knowledge, given the stress upon his authorship of the article itself. A little later, the validity of previous personal knowledge is emphasised again: '*La démonstration que j'ai faite alors* [during a TV debate in 1977] *reste valable mot pour mot*' (p. 22). And later: '*J'ai proposé de mettre en oeuvre* [a plan for making gas from coal] *... dès 1976. Je me heurtai alors au scepticisme de bon ton en haut lieu*' (p. 148. For another example see p. 172). This prophetic quality also indicates a further quality of the author, manifest from the very beginning when the new passengers entered the plane: the ability to carry *for the oppressed* the culumny directed at him.

One of the logical consequences of the author's claimed prophetic status, a consequence which contributes further to that status, is that the information he gives is invariably offered in revelatory form. We saw this quality of the revelation of disguised or suppressed truth in the previous section (for example, '*la vérité sur ... On nous dit ... en réalité ...* (p. 20); *Les deux faces d'un seul et même piège ... En vérité*' (p. 24)). The characteristics: foresight, unheeded foresight, and the power of revelation, all enhance the notion of the insight of the author and link up with a further characteristic: his crusading spirit.

The crusade itself is, as we have seen, that of liberating France through social progress. To this end, the notion of the author as an advocate of modernisation, the bringer of the new, is functional in the development of his character. And the author as advocate of modernisation is presented early on in the text, as we have seen, where his major examples are those of science, technology, industry, and nuclear power (pp. 14–30).

In his advocacy of modernisation, moreover, the author is presented as possessing two further qualities: the self-certainty that he is correct in his analyses; and the ability to argue persuasively. Many explanations are prefaced with sentences similar to the following: '*Pour comprendre il faut aller au fond des choses*' (p. 16). And many arguments are structured, as we have seen, either through phrases like: '*Je le résume en trois observations . . . En premier lieu . . .*' (p. 40), or else through markers which thread through the text: '*Mais*', '*Donc*', '*Or*', '*Alors*', '*Voilà*', and so on. Many of these certainties are tempered by an apparent modesty which reflects the 'ordinary' quality mentioned above: '*à mes yeux*' (p. 58), '*je ne crois pas*' (p. 59), '*mais à mon sens*' (p. 63) and the many '*je pense*'.

Aphoristic illustrations too are given to reinforce arguments. In the case of the degree of scientific progress, for example, the author states: '*Comme si la dynamo utilisée pour la torture condamnait l'électricité!*' (p. 24). Such statements invite unequivocal agreement while underlining the author's control of his subject, and his ability to summarise them in epigrammatic form.

The duality of the author as ordinary person / author as savant, is further brought to bear on the change / progress theme and lifts the status of the author even further. On the question of scientific progress, the author asserts:

> *Fertiliser les déserts, agir sur les climats, explorer et exploiter les immenses ressources des océans: ce ne sont plus des rêves, on apprend maintenant à le faire.* (p. 25)

The author is here extrapolating from the present to see into the future. He is therefore a kind of common sense visionary. (Given the concerted opposition to the liberating change the author can 'see' and argues for, the above *are*, in fact, dreams, but dreams which, through acceptance of his vision, can be realised.) Paradoxically, the notion that the author possesses exceptional perception is enhanced here by his not being a specialist. His certainty concerning science is unswerving: '*Je dis oui au progrès scientifique et technique. Un oui clair et résolu*' (p. 26). Such resolution can only proceed from a transcendent knowledge of the place of scientific progress in a wider scheme of things, given that the author is not himself a specialist. The *negative* 'wider scheme of things', the present, is detailed throughout the text: a world of oppressed workers, the squandering rich, empty factories, the shameless dissimulations of the powerful, the enormous waste of talent and resources, the rat race, the threat of war, and so on. The *potential* wider scheme of things is only given abstractly: '*l'épanouissement de chaque personnalité*' (p. 26), '*du temps pour vivre*' (p. 57), '*l'annonce d'une nouvelle civilisation*' (p. 80), '*la liberté*', '*le bonheur et rien d'autre*' (p. 89), '*notre idéal, le socialisme*' (p. 110), '*édifier un monde nouveau*' (p. 161), and so on. It is a characteristic of visionary political discourse that attention is shifted from the envisaged to the envisaging. And throughout the text the notion of a harmonious and happy society is presented as the vision of the author which he would share, though does not describe. The logical consequence of this is that allegiance to him is the precondition of the realisation of his vision born of historical perception. He asserts that the twentieth century will be remember-ed: '*j'en suis convaincu – comme un grand siècle de l'histoire*' (p. 31); '*une transformation profonde*' (p. 31); [1968] '*Une phase historique qui n'est pas achevée. Je m'explique*' (p. 49); '*Que conclure de ce tour d'horizon? Nous vivons une période historique passionnante*' (p. 52); '*Le monde va de l'avant. Nous aussi. Avançons ensemble*' (p. 53). These few examples, typical illustrations of a tendency which runs throughout the book, are an invitation to the reader, from the author, to be part of a great historical moment that has been 'seen' and understood by the author, but which, like all visions, is incommunicable outside ideal-ised generalisations, generalisations which themselves act as evidence of the author's vision and mission.

It is curious at first sight that the chapter most revealing of the author's character is not a chapter filled with such idealised generalisations, but the most substantive chapter, Chapter Three, which is concerned essentially with the question of employment and, to a lesser extent, housing, leisure and education. The first thing to say here is that each of these issues is treated from a moral perspective. The chapter begins: '*Si je suis communiste, c'est d'abord pour la justice*' (p. 55). And when the author comes on to the question of employment, he refers to the morally-charged issue of life expectancy and its relation to social class:

> *Je ne peux évoquer ce sujet sans donner mon sentiment sur une injustice qui me révolte particulièrement.* (p. 61)

The issues addressed: employment, housing, leisure and education, all involve questions (as is indicated in the above quotation) concerning the process of alienation from happiness and well-being. The first sentence of the chapter acts, therefore, as a portal into this personalised ethical discussion of the practical. If it is injustice which has made Marchais a communist, his recognition of injustice must have come before his specifically political choice, a choice involving a quintessentially moral choice. He is, therefore, by extension, the leader of a rally of morally inspired people whose organisation is simply the collective expression of their individual moral choices. It is true that '*je*' has chosen for the political expression of such a moral undertaking the organisational depository of wisdom which historically precedes '*je*', but, like a church, the significance of the organisation is presented as depending upon the individual conscience of its adherents. This double focus: individual moral imperative/ organisational agency is the real basis of the argument of this chapter. Their interrelation, and the relation of '*je*' to the party and to the issues, is well illustrated by one of the most significant passages of the book. Immediately following the author's claim that the awareness of injustice is the spring of his political commitment, he states:

> *Je ne vais pas, dans ces quelques pages, exposer un programme. Simplement, je propose quelques orientations qui me tiennent à coeur. Elles découlent de l'expérience et de la réflexion collectives du Parti communiste français, de mon expérience et de ma réflexion. Celles qui proviennent de mes rencontres, de mes voyages, de mon courrier. Celles qu'ont enrichies ou précisées les études conduites avec des syndicalistes, des techniciens, des économistes.* (p. 55)

The essential quality of this quotation is the idea that the orientations which follow will be the personal prescriptions of the author. In fact what follows is a quite detailed series of measures concerning, for example, coal production (p. 61), the SMIC (minimum wage) (p. 65), and HLMs (council flats) (p. 67). Nor is the distinction between orientations and a programme anywhere clearly made. The true distinction, therefore, is not between the orientation and the possible programme of the author. The implicit distinction is that between the Common Programme (1972–7) and the verbalisation of a range of moral issues. Whether or not the orientations are any less the property of the party rather than of the author, the point is that they are being portrayed as imperatives which proceed from personal insight and moral sense.

We are beginning here to see the relation in the text of the author to the party. He does not replace the party, but is the inspired leader of a moral community whose mission proceeds from his vision, which is itself deeply moral:

> *Quels que soient les arguments qu'on cherche à m'opposer, rien ne peut me faire démordre de cette idée simple: chacune, chacun de ceux qui veulent travailler doit avoir un emploi.* (p. 57)

And again:

> *Je considère comme une mesure de moralisation la suppression des entreprises privées de travail temporaire.* (p. 57)

The knowledge of how such morally inspired political commitment should be applied is, however, exclusive. In one of the few direct references to the reader, the author reaffirms the hierarchy between himself and the reader, a hierarchy implied by his greater insight, a hierarchy threatened, in fact, by the notion of a moral community (egalitarian by definition) which would include the reader:

> '*C'est la quadrature du cercle*', *pensez-vous peut-être. Je ne crois pas. De la réflexion et de l'étude, de l'imagination, beaucoup de concertation avec les intéressés permettront de trouver des solutions pratiques pour que toutes les travailleuses et tous les travailleurs puissent jouir d'une retraite vraiment humaine.* (p. 59)

What is being reasserted here is the status of the leader of a moral community, a leadership which is based not only upon his moral insight but also upon his experience, both practical and intellectual. That which distinguishes the author from the reader, his experiential privilege and intellect, is also that which has made him the leader of the Communist Party. What the author must do, therefore, is distinguish himself from the party as well as from the reader. He cannot do this organisationally – we have seen that the party is essentially a moral community, not an organisational entity concerned with power. The distinguishing must therefore take the form of the personal appropriation, as we have seen in previous examples, of doctrine. The point here is that it is not necessary to change or inform traditional Communist doctrine and ideas, but to present these as originating in the author, or else as being so closely associated with him that the synonymity of his and the party's ideas does not give the latter precedence over him. A few examples are appropriate here.
On employment:

> *Je ne me fais aucune illusion, ni moi, ni mes camarades. Je sais qu'une lutte acharnée sera nécessaire.* (p. 64)

On education:

> *Je voudrais encore vous livrer ma pensée sur une question préoccupante: l'école.* (p. 71)

And again:

> *Je ne peux, dans ces quelques pages, vous faire part de l'ensemble des questions que je me pose sur la formation.* (p. 72)

And, stated very close to one another:

> *Je préciserai plus loin ce que j'entends par là ...*
> *J'aurai également l'occasion, plus loin, d'approfondir cette question ...*
> *Le développement que je propose ...*
> *Je ne veux pas d'un productivisme aveugle. Ce que je veux ...* (p. 79)

And in the form of a résumé of the chapter, the simplifying of complex personal reflection:

> *Ce nouveau type de développement, pour simplifier par les mots: justice, qualification, science, indépendance nationale, démocratie ...* (p. 80)

We can see from our examination of Chapter Three of *L'Espoir* that the party is being introduced discursively into a prominent position in the text, but in a very specific relation to the author. This has effects upon the perceived role of Communism in modern politics. The author's ideas are not placed in opposition to it in order that new ideas and specific orientations are introduced, as they were in the 1979 Report. Rather, they are presented as uncontentiously his ideas. This new characteristic resolves, for example, the party's ambivalent attitude towards '*alternance*', because the question raises itself not in Leninist but in millenarian terms: if Communism brings the new society and is so certain it will do so, '*alternance*' is no longer even an issue. The democratic caution and the transcendental nature of Communism are now both possible because of the channelling of wisdom and certainty into the author's persona. He can remain right even if the people make the 'wrong' decision. Even though right, the personal leader must step down if rejected, as his power, though not

his authority, comes from the people. Commitment to *'alternance'*
and to transcendentalism can both be maintained, therefore, because
the party is using here what is essentially the Gaullist myth.

The appropriation and personal transcendence of organisational
ideas is well illustrated by the author's treatment of women's rights
(pp. 93–6). The historic significance of the movement, like social
progress generally, is first personally stressed:

> *Je l'ai dit: leur combat pour leur libération est l'un des faits les plus
> importants du XXe siècle.* (p. 93)

and then the combat itself seen in personal terms:

> *Rien ne me tient plus à coeur* (p. 94)
> *Toutes les mesures de justice et de liberté que je mentionne dans ce
> livre tendent à libérer les femmes.* (p. 94)
> *C'est pourquoi j'ai tenu à appuyer personnellement la demande*
> [concerning family allowances] ... *C'est pourquoi également, j'ai
> attaché un prix particulier à apposer ma signature* [concerning
> women's rights in marriage] ... (pp. 94–5)
> *Je défends cette liberté* [abortion] ...
> *Avec les députées et les députés communistes, j'ai combattu et je
> combats* [for sex education] .... (p. 95)

One of the added consequences of the author's appropriation of
areas traditionally portrayed as originally or primarily residing in the
party itself is the emergence of the character trait of indefatigability.
The author is portrayed as having knowledge, conviction, prescriptions and emotions on a very wide range of issues and, given that
writing about them is portrayed in this book as itself part of the
struggle, and that the references to the author's struggle and calls to
struggle are numerous, there is evoked the image of a man never
resting, tireless and continuously engaged in a crusade. His energy,
like his knowledge, therefore, is not that of ordinary people.

This notion of action is reinforced by the frequent references to
foreign travel, and to all of it as being part of the struggle, to none of
it as leisure. Moscow, Acapulco, Budapest, la Réunion (*'où je me suis
rendu ... pour mesurer la détresse matérielle et morale'* (p. 106)),
Africa, Asia, Latin America, Algeria, the Middle-East, Luxem-
bourg, Berlin are all mentioned as places that have affected the
author emotionally (see in particular p. 170), have given him
experience (see in particular p. 134), or where he has worked (see in
particular p. 181), or has contributed to the struggle (see in

particular p. 171). As well as conveying the notion of the indefatig-
able crusader, the references to foreign travel have three other
functions. First they restate that the author has had experience of the
world that is beyond the experience of most people. Secondly, they
imply that his view of the world is likely to be more accurate than
most people's because he has had more experience of it. Thirdly,
such travel enhances the author's status through the naming of the
people he has worked with abroad, such as Edward Gierek (p. 138)
and Houari Boumedienne (p. 181) (both of whose first names are
given). Here are just two examples of the role of travel in the shaping
of wisdom:

> *Les voyages que j'ai pu faire dans de nombreux pays m'ont*
> *encouragé à m'en tenir à une grande prudence de jugement.* (p. 134)
> *Mais je les ai vus, ceux qu'on appelle les pauvres absolus ... il faut*
> *tout faire pour que cela cesse ... Tout faire.* (p. 170)

Travel within France and contact with all areas of France (see, for
example, p. 143) is also stressed throughout the text. There are not
only the many letters received from ordinary working people (p. 10),
but also personal contact with them which gives the author a
legitimacy, and his ideas the quality of truth:

> *un exemple que m'a cité un agriculteur ...* (p. 17)
> *Un ami breton m'a rapporté ...* (p. 27)
> *J'ai lu avec une émotion indicible le témoignage de cette militante*
> *...* (p. 121)
> *J'ai constaté combien les Françaises et les Français ont la passion de*
> *l'histoire de France.* (p. 144)
> *J'étais ... à Thionville en Lorraine.* (p. 183)

And throughout the text a score of French towns and regions are
mentioned, including '*ma Normandie natale*' (p. 27).

This multiplicity of contacts within France itself not only indicates
authorial contact with a Leftist version of '*La France profonde*' but is
an indication of the author's own continuing simplicity and lack of
corruption, in spite of his exclusive experience of the wider world.

His contacts with the towns and regions of France are also linked
to his worker status. There are, as we have seen, many references to
his class origins. The following is a good example of the way origins,
geography, elevated status and crusading mission are mixed.

> *Je connais la réalité. Je vis avec les travailleuses et les travailleurs.*
> *Je suis député d'une banlieue ouvrière. La majorité d'adhérents – et*

des dirigeants – de mon parti sont des travailleuses et des travailleurs. Bon nombre d'entre eux éprouvent dans leur vie personnelle les injustices contre lesquelles, avec eux, je m'insurge et me bats. (p. 75)

As a worker, the author exhibits the idealised worker's respect for culture and participatory activities: science (p. 13), sport (p. 37 and pp. 73–4), education (p. 71), literature (pp. 117 and 159). This kind of workerist humility in the author's character, coupled with his manifest experience, also lends itself to the further portrayal of the author as possessing the humility of the humble worker's opposite, the sage:

Etre révolutionnaire aujourd'hui, c'est aussi apprendre à lire avec une certaine humilité dans le grand livre du monde. (p. 134)

Two other rhetorically persuasive traits are given a prominence in *L'Espoir* through the personification of official discourse, traits precluded from the impersonal conventional rhetoric of Communism: humour and emotion.

The author refers with humour to traffic jams in Budapest as a sign of progress in a Communist country (p. 36). There is a light Shakespearian reference: '*Une région parisienne pour les privilégiés ou pour les travailleurs: voilà la question*' (p. 70). There is even the humour of understatement concerning the organisation which replaced the Comintern:

En 1947 a été créé entre neuf partis communistes d'Europe un Bureau d'information dont le moins qu'on puisse dire est que toutes ses initiatives ne furent pas des réussites. (p. 136)

And concerning the working-class origins of party leaders, the author states:

Soixante-deux [ouvriers] dans son Comité central, onze sur vingt et un dans son Bureau politique, et . . . son secrétaire général. (p. 185)

And finally, there is a play on words concerning the permanent officials:

Ils s'occupent en permanence . . . de la révolution! (p. 186)

These lightnesses of touch, made possible by the personalisation of official discourse, are indications both of the author's urbanity and of his humanity.

This latter quality is heightened still further by the deep emotionalism of the text. We have already seen several examples of outrage and just anger concerning injustice, and appeals to the reader concerning the elevated moral status of political commitment. This emotionalism, apparent from the Foreword onwards, is underpinned by the deployment in the text of the extreme emotional vulnerability of the author in matters which touch upon either injustice or else microcosmic illustrations of the moral values that will inform socialist society, a vulnerability which is presented as an unmediated emotional demonstration to the reader of the man that lies beneath the office of Communist Party General Secretary:

On the Olympics:

Je suis encore sous le coup des émotions que j'ai éprouvées aux Jeux Olympiques de Moscou, (p. 73)

On freedom:

En écrivant ces pages sur la liberté, je pense à l'émotion que suscitent en moi... (p. 107)

And, after quoting a revolutionary song, the author concludes:

Justice, liberté, fraternité, oui, c'est ce que je veux, avec tous mes camarades. Quel beau combat! (p. 107)

On patriotism and the struggle against the Nazis, a quotation from Aragon:

*"Patrie également à la colombe ou l'aigle
De l'audace et du chant doublement habitée
Je vous salue ma France où les blés et les seigles
Mûrissent au soleil de la diversité."* (p. 159)

On the question of world peace:

Elle me tient à coeur. Si j'ose dire, viscéralement. (p. 161)

In all of the above examples, as in the previously mentioned examples concerning emotions, or even the *'émotion indicible'* concerning Aurélie (p. 121), the 'virtue' possessed by the author which is being added to those other personal qualities possessed and demonstrated by him, and universally held as exemplary (charity, faith, prudence, hope, humility, honesty, fortitude) is that of solidarity. It is this quality, born of a deep moral sense (rather than, say, scientific analysis) which lifts the character of the author to a status higher than other national figures, and which is the foundation of his political commitment and therefore of the doctrine to which he professes faith and of the party to which he belongs. What is particularly significant here, both for our understanding of him as a persona and for our understanding of his party, is that it is through him that the party itself is justified and discursively mobilised as morally exemplary and politically efficacious. Let us examine how this leader/party relation operates in the text.

The party as organisation only begins to become discursively prominent from about half-way through the text (p. 109). Before this, the persona of the author is the almost exclusive protagonist against injustice and wrong. When the party is brought prominently into the text, moreover, it is usually depicted as a grouping of comrades, or else as a moral community, as we have seen. The author's early established conflation within his own persona of ordinariness and wider vision are themselves the justification of the party: that which is of and yet which transcends its origins:

> *Mais il faut aux travailleurs un parti qui analyse la situation, lutte sur tous les terrains, formule des propositions nationales, relie entre elles les luttes des différentes catégories exploitées pour les rassembler, élabore et défende des solutions politiques pour le changement, un parti–digue, un partie–charrue, un parti–phare. C'est le rôle que nous nous attachons à assumer.* (p. 198)

This quotation is from the final chapter of the book. What is striking about this chapter, in the context of a book almost exclusively devoted to the presentation of one character, is that, in it, the persona of Marchais retreats, and the near-exclusive focus is upon the party. The pronoun *'nous'*, the use of which, compared to the 1979 Report, is hitherto restrained, informs almost every paragraph of the concluding chapter. The party is presented as historically indispensable to social and political change in 1936, 1940–4, 1945–7 (see p. 196) and, today, as the only alternative to crisis (the Right) and fiasco (the non-Communist Left): *'il faut le parti communiste'* (p. 200). It is as if the party is, in the final chapter, being recuperated by the text. Two points need to be made here. First, in the text as a whole the prominence of the author by far outweighs that of the party. And when the party is prominent in the text (Chapter Nine), its prominence takes the form of its justification by the author: he defends it, its structure, mode of operation, and political role.

Secondly, the party, as the organisational expression of ethico-political commitment, is justified throughout the text through the agency of reference to the author's personal experience and views.

We can conclude, therefore, that there is a change in the function of leadership persona between the 1979 Report and *L'Espoir* which is that, in the former, it is used essentially to dominate the party and constrain dissidence; in the latter, it is used to transform the presentation of the French Communist Party itself.

In the 1980 text, the party is being presented as an element of French society, a politically organised moral expression, completely understood by and loyal to its leader, and the politico-cultural precondition to a transformational change by means of which France will create a new future for itself while remaining France. And it is the confidence of the author which is the assurance of this in the last sentence of the book:

La France s'ouvrira un nouvel avenir. J'ai confiance. (p. 201)

The closing line is, therefore, an implicit appeal to the reader to place his or her confidence in the author on the basis of the author's claim to vision.

6 Discourse and Organisation: The Socialists

The impact of personalism in the case of the French Communist Party is perpetually refracted by its organisational and doctrinal traditions. In the case of the *Parti socialiste* (PS) the impact is more dramatic and has radical organisational effects. From 1971 one of the strongest organising principles within the PS was that presidential power could provide the essential conditions for power in the legislature, regions, localities and administration, and therefore that the party's purpose was to stimulate and sustain a campaign for the presidency of France.

This principle and purpose were to express themselves in a commitment to the rally politics organised around the personality and leadership of François Mitterrand, the First Secretary of the party. It was a commitment which contradicted many of the declared principles – doctrinal and organisational – upon which both the party's immediate and its more distant predecessors had been built. During the Third and Fourth Republics, the *Parti socialiste (Section française de l'internationale ouvrière)* (SFIO) had been organised around the generally accepted principle that the party maintain and be sustained by the routines of parliamentary affairs, party alliances, cycles of municipal, cantonal and parliamentary elections and inter- and intra-party negotiations. From 1971 the PS, though not abandoning this principle, was also organised around the idea of a rapid ascent to the commanding heights of Fifth Republican politics. Its doctrines and its policies were therefore formulated within the context of a rally for the presidency as the most likely prelude to the application of socialist programmes. The party administration also functioned within this context even though it was directed to immediate and 'lesser' electoral and other tasks.

This lack of correspondence between the co-existing personalism, sectionalism in organisation and a long doctrinally-informed organisational history created the conditions of conflict within the party. One of the effects of personalism on Socialist politics was to accentuate and intensify certain of the organisational and doctrinal

126

tensions which the party had inherited from pre-existing organisations.

These tensions were expressed in the public discourse of party occasions, as the traditional themes were overlaid with new ones. Doctrinally, the result was the emergence of a dominant mode in party discourse within which the strongest theme was that the party could transcend its historical origins and lead a great national awakening. In earlier decades, Socialists had generally accepted that their first loyalty was to the preservation and maintenance of the party itself. Throughout the 1970s, however, they came to treat their party in a different way, and to transfer their loyalty in two quite different directions – at one level, towards Mitterrand and to others who might succeed him, such as Michel Rocard who left the *Parti socialiste unifié* (PSU) in 1974 to join the PS, and at another level, to an idea that Socialism would become something akin to a great moral movement, capable of breaking out of organisational confines.

In order to examine this hypothesis, I have chosen to analyse two documents: the integral texts of the *Assises du socialisme* of October 1974 and the motion submitted by Rocard and others at the party's Metz Congress in April 1979.[1] In Chapter 7 we shall analyse a text which demonstrates what happens to Socialist discourse after the party takes power.

The *Assises du socialisme* were deliberately framed as a symbolic moment in the life of the party and of the non-Communist Left as a whole and were intended to give ceremonial and doctrinal meaning to the incorporation into the party of elements from the PSU and the *Confédération française démocratique du travail* (CFDT). They were intended to mark the almost complete reunion of the various groups which had separated from the SFIO in the 1950s and an extension of the process of political 'mobilisation' inspired by Mitterrand's near-victory in the presidential elections held earlier in 1974. Although their symbolic unifying significance was modified by a certain animosity towards them from sections within and outside the PS – notably the *Centre d'études, de recherche et d'education socialistes* (CERES) and other elements within the PS and CFDT – they took place in an atmosphere of optimism and celebration by a Left which confidently expected to form a government in the ensuing period. By contrast, the party's congress at Metz in April 1979 was a statutory party congress, the first to take place after the 'historic' defeat in the 1978 legislative elections. Their contrasting contexts colour the two texts in predictable ways. However, the texts share a preoccupation with the problem of expressing and preserving a particular vision of a future socialist society in France, while overtly resisting the pressures of tradition and organisational habit. Both record attempts to glorify and realise a socialist rally of the French people and both have as their implicit focus – the first in the form of confirmation, the second in the form of contestation – the personalism of the new party.

1   THE *ASSISES DU SOCIALISME*

(a)   The Political Context

The *Assises* of October 1974 stand out as one of the central events in the history of the PS. They were held at a time when the victory of the Left appeared, for the first time in many years, to be a tangible possibility following the co-operation between groups which had accompanied Mitterrand's campaign for the presidential election in May. Mitterrand was the principal candidate of the Left: neither the PCF nor the PSU had fielded a candidate and both these parties lent him their support. Even the politically independent CFDT campaigned both in its own name and on behalf of Mitterrand. The organisational reunification of the non-Communist Left was seen by many as a logical conclusion to this strategic convergence.

The objective of unity, in contradistinction to the fragmentation of the 1950s and the loose and ultimately ineffective federation of the 1960s, had been seriously pursued since 1971. In order to give personal public approval to this movement towards unity, Mitterrand made an *appel* on 25 May 1974, immediately after the second round of the elections: '*Je souhaite que soit fixé au plus tôt le lieu de recontre où les socialistes se retrouveront avant de repartir ensemble vers l'étape nouvelle*'.[2] The response was immediate. The PSU on 26 May issued this statement: '*Il est nécessaire de créer les conditions d'une force politique puissante et crédible avec l'appui des forces aujourd'hui dispersées au sein de la CFDT, du PSU et de divers groupes et mouvements*'.[3] The following day the national bureau of the CFDT issued a statement affirming that the CFDT would consider '*comme un élément positif l'appel lancé par François Mitterrand et noter avec intérêt les positions voisines prises par le PSU*'.[4] On 11 June another *appel* was made, this time by a hundred or so activists and others from the CFDT, the CGT, the FEN (*Fédération d'éducation nationale*) and the GAM (*Groupes d'action municipale*).[5] This last 'call' was not only an appeal to rank-and-file syndicalists but also a response to Mitterrand's call of 25 May, thus supporting the idea that the two were connected and that a complex chain reaction had been set in motion by the initial *appel*. Even though a unitarist 'wave' was underway, the central role of individual leadership thus remained evident. In this context it is interesting to note the personalised quality of Mitterrand's call of 25 May. It began like this:

> Les Français cependant m'ont interrogé sur l'avenir plus lointain, sur le type de société que nous entendons construire.
> Une réponse commune à cette question sera de plus en plus nécessaire; elle est esquissée dans le programme du Parti socialiste.[6]

However, only a moment's reflection was needed to see that the movement for unity would, paradoxically, heighten lines of tension and conflict within the non-Communist Left. In the first place, an inflow of new members into the PS could be expected to alter the balance between the different *courants*. In the second place, the arrival of new leaders with new styles of leadership and rhetoric could be expected to affect the party's hierarchy in unexpected ways. The question of whether Mitterrand would admit Rocard to his inner circle was an early indication of the potential importance of individual figures.

On 15 June the PS held a national convention at the Porte Maillot in Paris. The main topic for discussion was the approaching *Assises*. Mitterrand, as if fully aware that a considerable rally was being generated which might overtake the party itself, commented: '*Bien sûr, ni notre titre, ni nos structures, ni notre stratégie ne peuvent être remis en cause*'.[7] Jean Poperen, leader of one of the *courants* in the party, made a severe attack upon Rocard, likening him to Giscard d'Estaing (an allusion to the way the latter had used the Gaullists as a vehicle to power).[8] CERES members also put the party on guard against potential newcomers and, at a colloquium at the end of June, argued that the new momentum was in danger of splitting the Socialist movement between radical *autogestionnaires* and others. Jean-Pierre Chevènement (a CERES leader) had himself advocated the inclusion of *autogestion* in the Common Programme: the CERES objection was not to *autogestion* itself but to those who claimed to represent it. Some of Mitterrand's close associates, particularly Pierre Joxe, also made outspoken speeches. Mitterrand's action to overrule his own supporters softened the attack upon the newcomers while underlining his overall control. Those opposed to or apprehensive about the PSU and CFDT were afraid that, as both groups had opposed the Common Programme, this latter would be placed in jeopardy. What was being recognised, however, as a potential, though not explicitly stated, danger to the leadership was the person of Rocard.

No sooner, then, had the unitarist movement gained momentum than a series of constraints indicated the organisational and doctrinal problems which it posed. Hence the wish to try and control its effects and give the approaching *Assises* a functional, inter-congress role.

The reaction of the PS, as was manifested at its national convention, was an attempt to protect what was now a complex organisation from the unpredictable effects of rallyism. At the end of June, after meetings between official PS representatives and delegations from the PSU and CFDT, organising committees were set up to clarify the purpose of the *Assises* and their agenda. On 8 July, it was decided that the meeting would be presented with a *projet de société* (Project). There was also to be a series of discussion groups, *carrefours* (crossroads or meeting points), which would explore the theme: '*Militer pour le socialisme*' and report back to the plenary session. The organisation committees, which contained about sixty people in total, worked throughout the summer.

The Project itself was partly inspired by the PSU's Toulouse Manifesto which had been drafted for adoption at the 8th Congress of the party in December 1972. The draft of the Project was drawn up by Gilles Martinet (PS, ex-PSU) and Jacques Julliard (CFDT). On 16 September, the Project was submitted to the Executive Bureau of the PS. Mitterrand approved the text, objecting only to one phrase which advocated '*la liaison permanente entre la mobilisation des masses et la lutte politique*'.[9] On 25 September the Project was made public.

The *Assises* comprised fifteen hundred delegates drawn from the PS, a second *composante* (PSU) and a third *composante* (ostensibly the *syndicats* and other action groups but almost totally comprised of CFDT members). Also present were invited observers including several Left-wing Gaullists.

The *Assises* took place at the Hotel PLM Saint-Jacques on 12 and 13 October 1974. They had no constituent or statutory power, nor were they the occasion for formal recruitment of new PS members. The meeting therefore stood outside the formal structures of the party and was treated as existing outside the routine timetable of organisational life.

(b)   The Significance of the *Assises*: Egalitarianism and Personalism

Michel Rocard: '*Mes chers camarades . . .*'
Une voix dans la salle: 'Au nom de qui parles-tu?'
Michel Rocard: '*Il sera répondu à cette question dans un mois, lors d'un congrès. Pour le moment, je n'engage que moi.*' (56/38–57/2)

I have described above something of the political manoeuvring of the several political groups involved. It is true to say that the press took the view that the *Assises* were a political operation rather than the orchestration of an irresistible rally. The following are some typical press comments. Michèle Cotta stated in *L'Express* '*Le projet est étonnement proudhonien. Mais l'objet réel des assises est beaucoup plus politique.: M. Mitterrand recrute*'.[10] More ironically, *Le Quotidien de Paris* wrote: '*Comme dans les ballets classiques le processus devant mener à la constitution d'une grande force socialiste se déroule apparemment de façon bien réglée*'.[11] Recognising the symbolism of the operation Colette Ysmal concluded that the PS wanted only '*ralliements symboliques mais spectaculaires tel celui de Michel Rocard*'.[12] To admit that the above points are true does not, however, explain the significance of the *Assises* as collective ritual, nor the role of symbolism or discourse, nor the reasons why the 'spectacular' is desirable, nor the method whereby it is accommodated to the organisation as a whole. By the same token it is also true that the participants were themselves well aware of the symbolic importance of the meeting. One of the characteristic features of the *Assises* was the extreme self-awareness of those taking part and a general sensitivity to the symbolic nature of this ritual occasion. Let us then examine how the participants themselves perceived both their own role and the significance of the meeting itself.

On the second day of the *Assises*, J–P. Cot declared: '*Jamais jusqu'à présent, on n'avait procédé à une exploration préalable aussi poussée pour s'assurer que le contrat serait solide*' (127/28–30). This declaration gives an indication that the exceptional nature of the occasion involved the notion of an intangible contract.

The *Assises* were understood to fulfil four possible functions. Firstly, they seemed to make the radical restructuring of the Socialist movement possible – as indicated by the attempts to stop this happening. Secondly, they marked the 'coming home' of the prodigals and the rediscovery of community. Thirdly, they were seen as a necessary moment of interpretation and activity in the socio-political crisis of capitalism – hence in part the justification of the sense of urgency and the radical tone of the Project. And fourthly, they were the symbolic occasion of a gathering of forces in preparation for a call to government within the institutions and practices of the Fifth Republic.

Given that the *Assises* were an unusual event and therefore a relatively unpredictable one for leadership, it was imperative that Mitterrand should 'appropriate' the meeting, without dominating it. The key to this problem was the fact that the *Assises* were the willing response to the 'call' that Mitterrand had made five months previously. After Jeanson, whose speech opened the *Assises*, Mitterrand was the first speaker. Characteristically, he gave advice to the assembled, but this was an apparently uncontentious call to '*réévaluation doctrinale*'. His speech was relatively short. In this way Mitterrand's restraint made him the director rather than the principal actor, as he had been at Epinay in 1971. The personalist leader in this context, therefore, has several unnamed functions. He must be seen to: (i) allow the meeting; (ii) welcome it; (iii) subordinate it to his own leadership status; (iv) be part of it; and (v) make it the ritual confirmation of socialist egalitarianism while not allowing such egalitarianism to take on the significance of a myth subversive of personal leadership. How then did the other political actors and the text of the Project itself relate to these pressures?

What is surprising about the *Assises* when one considers the usual historical precursors of any 'historic' banding together of the French Left (the formation of the SFIO in 1905, the Popular Front of 1935–6, the Resistance alliance in 1944–5, for example) is the assumed immediacy of the causes of the *Assises*. Mitterrand's *appel* has already been mentioned, but the only two historical events referred to throughout the *Assises* that act as mythical source are those of May 1968 and May 1974. It is as if French Socialism had no history prior to the Fifth Republic. Gilles Martinet, co-author of the Project, declared that the '*premier héritage*' was no more than a decade old:

> *Le projet de société comporte des idées neuves. Mais on y retrouve aussi des avancées plus anciennes: la planification démocratique, les formes nouvelles que revêtiront les nationalisations, la décentral-isation régionale, l'Union de la gauche, la nécessaire indépendance*

de l'Europe à l'égard des impérialismes, tout cela avait déjà été proposé, dans les années 60, à l'occasion des multiples rencontres, congrès et colloques. (47/5–13)

We shall discuss later the significance of the events of 1968 and 1974 for the *Assises*, but it should be noted here that this sense of a recent origin was linked both to the *Assises* as a whole and to the Project, the document which became the explicit focus of the gathering.

The idea that the Project had achieved a synthesis in doctrine was consistent with the notion that the *Assises* represented the moment of fusion between the libertarianism represented by 1968 and the discipline represented by May 1974 (which were two of the symbolic moments of legitimation for, respectively, Rocard and Mitterrand). In its opening paragraphs the Project asserts:

Mai 1968, c'était l'éclatement spontané de tout un possible long-temps réprimé. Mai 74, la démonstration que l'union politique des forces populaires est là, prête à assumer la responsabilité qui lui incombe. (13/35–14/3)

To appeal to the spirit of 1968 is to appeal to the notion of direct action as a method of redefining a society. In that it idealises the explosion of popular feeling, however, the appeal to 1968 is an appeal not to a specific kind of socialist strategy but to a specific kind of libertarianism.

The reference to 1974 brings to this libertarian tradition another Leftist tradition with no less an emotional appeal. The sense of unity generated on the Left by the presidential elections of May is reminiscent of the long-suppressed dream of '*la gauche au pouvoir*' exemplified by the early period of the Popular Front and the anticipated social revolution of 1944–5.

In this context, even though the strategy advocated in the Project was ill-defined, it implied previous socialist traditions and therefore served as a link between socialist feeling and political action. The *Assises* themselves, by means of the Project on the one hand and the *carrefours* on the other, establish a symbolic connection between faith and action, between doctrine and activism.

The *carrefours* were workshops intended to theorise the daily action of activists, or else lend theoretical justification to activity By condemning the parochialism of the politics of '*la petite semaine*' (127/38), the *Assises* elucidate the idea that all Socialist action is an integral part and significant moment of the overall struggle. The *carrefours*, therefore, act as agencies linking the particular to the general. They thus complement the Project's statement of principle, reinforcing the necessarily muted references to pragmatism, policy decisions and short-term aims made in the Project. The twelve *carrefours* comprising delegates from each of the *composantes* were: *Agriculture; Armée-défense; Cadre de vie; Consommation et modèle de développement; Education, formation permanente, culture; Entreprises; Information; Justice et libertés publiques; Régions et collectivités locales; Santé; Femmes; Immigrés.* On the first day of the *Assises*, questionnaires were presented to the *carrefours* concerning methods of activism. The questionnaires harmonised the work of the *carrefours* to some extent, though they were regarded only as guidelines to them. On the second afternoon, after a morning's discussions, their results were presented to the full *Assises* in summary form.

The underlying political theme of the *Assises* was therefore the traditional one: that theory was a prerequisite for action and action the necessary consequence of theory. If this is true, the historical reference slight, and the ritualised preparation for the future marked, it is clear that, either as a founding or as an eschatological myth, the *Assises* are implying not only 1968, 1971 and 1974 but also themselves as a major future doctrinal/mythical reference point.

The *Assises* have two essential characteristics. The Project corresponds to traditional socialist egalitarianism while stressing the novelty of the discovery, as do the reports from the different areas of interest at grassroots level. However, these are juxtaposed throughout the *Assises* with the essentially anti-Left notion of the leader as central to the process of social or political change. Reference to this commitment is indirect. Virtually every speaker refers to Mitterrand's *appel* of 25 May. Neither Jaurès nor Blum, and certainly not Mollet, attracted such ritual verbal homage.

In this way the *Assises* of 1974 are an unprecedented occasion in the development of Socialist mythology because they attempt to rationalise definitively two competing traditions. Although Mitterrand had demonstrated the possibility of a Left-based campaign for the presidency as early as 1965, it was only on this occasion that a Left-wing organisation vindicated personalism in the context of and by means of the egalitarianism within Left-wing doctrine and rhetoric. Let us now examine what happens to Socialist discourse in order that this adaptation be achieved.

We have seen that in one sense the Project fulfils the role of prophecy in that it symbolically offers that which is enacted by the *carrefours*. It also serves a multiplicity of other purposes. Jeanson says, for example, at the opening of the *Assises*:

> *Il n'y a pas de modèle qui puisse nous renseigner sur ce que pourrait être cet autre socialisme. Mais il est désormais possible d'en établir le projet sur des bases solides et crédibles.* (28/36–9)

For him, therefore, the Project and the *Assises* as a whole are only reference points from which a doctrine, which will help build an as yet undiscovered socialist society, can be imagined. For Mitterrand, however, speaking directly after Jeanson, the role of the *Assises* is to '*défendre*' the Project (54/4). Even if we bear in mind that the word '*défendre*' carries with it the nuance of 'critically support', it is clear that the Project and therefore the *Assises*, are offered by different people as signifying different things. Throughout the *Assises*, references are made to the Project none of which points towards a definitive explanation of its role or purpose. How then does the Project fit as a whole into the mythology upon which the *Assises* are based, for although it is necessary for the participants to demand that the Project be discussed, discussion is in fact out of the question because the *Assises* are the symbolic negation of the congress (where policy and orientation are debated) and are themselves the site where faith is renewed or created?

The word '*socialisme*' in the title of the occasion has special significance here. It is not a truism to say that socialism is a central concept at the *Assises*. One of the functions of the *Assises* was to save the non-Communist Left from being lured into overtly Centrist alliances at a time of transition within the party system. The word '*socialisme*', therefore, offers socialism as something to be aspired to and preserved as well as being a quality that all the participants at the *Assises* mutually agree to recognise in one another (as they would at, say, a party congress), and this prior to the PSU and CFDT members joining the PS. The PS itself, therefore, becomes no longer simply the site where Socialists are formed but the point at which socialisms meet. Thus, through the *Assises*, the PS projects itself as a rally in spite of its retention of its original organisational form. The word '*socialisme*', therefore, though lacking precision, serves to define those who took part in the *Assises* in relation to 'outsiders', to one another, and to the new party.

This modification of a political party's standard vocabulary has certain consequences. In many respects, the *Assises* contradicted the idea of the Socialist Party. They were organised in a way which was obviously intended to contrast with a party congress, offering spontaneity instead of deliberation, great principles instead of mundane issues, an assembly of a communitarian type rather than a gathering of delegates and party officials, and vibrant faith instead of determined hope. At the *Assises* faith is prior to all other considerations. Once this is recognised, we can see the necessity for a series of implicit ideological compromises within the *Assises* which have been made necessary by the explicit notion that the Project and the *Assises* are not doctrinal *compromise* but the expression of an original truth. The result is that, not doctrine, but the appeal to faith is reinforced. At this point, the logic of personalism and rally discourse comes explicitly to the fore, replacing discussion of doctrine and of strategy with an accentuated reference to myth.

Within Socialism there are competing myths which must be reconciled if a rally leader's claim to have offered a form of allegiance which transcends discrete allegiance is to be credible. One of the ways of arriving at this reconciliation discursively is to create the illusion that one is the cause of the other or else its logical consequence. Let us look at an example to which reference has already been made, that of the juxtaposition of May 1968 and May 1974.

These events are constantly referred to as the 'sources' of the *Assises*. It could be very easily argued, however, that the two events represent irreconcilably contradictory responses: the one insurrectionary and anti-bureaucratic, the other participatory and institutionally directed to the Republic and to the regime of organised parties. In this light, 1968 is the negation of 1974. In a very obvious way, these two sources of instant mythology fulfil distinct functions which are, though in opposition to one another, both attractive to the socialist imagination. The 'spirit' of 1968 is not future-orientated but timeless, idealistic, highly moral and individualistic. 1974 is future-orientated, practical, disciplined and collective. Thus, by discursively joining these two moments together, the contradiction between spontaneity and organisation is partly resolved.

(c) The Project and the Speeches: Mediations

It would have been possible to hold the *Assises* without the Project. The influence of the leader would even have been enhanced, as his own speech would have been the meeting's reference point. However, the meeting would have been less predictable, less easy to regulate, and less able to conflate personalist claims with socialist discourse. To understand why and how the Project has this limiting and steadying effect, let us look at its contents in more detail.

The Project (*autogestion*, democratic planning, the transformation of the State, and a strong Socialist Party) is constructed around a central notion of capitalism which is described in the following terms:

> *L'histoire du capitalisme est traversée de nombreuses crises. Il les a surmontées en se modifiant, tout en conservant sa logique essentielle. Notamment sous la poussée des luttes sociales, le capitalisme est constamment obligé de déplacer le lieu des contradictions qu'il secrète, par une sorte de fuite en avant qui ne lui permet pas de les régler sans en faire naître d'autres.* (17/11–18)

The most striking theme in this passage is the representation of capitalism as a corporate entity, responding to challenges in a rational way, and attempting to adapt itself to changing circumstances. Equally arresting is the confidence with which this interpretation is advanced with nothing in the way of qualification, and alternative explanations of capitalist development excluded, including those within socialism which perceive capitalist development differently. The essential quality of the description of capitalism is not that it is simple, but that it is exclusive and asserted as self-evident.

In terms of other aspects of social theory also, there are several assumptions made within the Project which, as far as is possible and desirable, reduce, by exclusion, fundamental disagreements. It is beyond dispute here, for example, that the goal of political action is control of a unitary State and not the winning of elections or the presidency or a series of institutional practices. The Project urges '*un combat politique global qui vise la conquête de l'Etat, sa transformation et, à terme, le renversement du pouvoir de la classe dominante*' (24/5–8). It is worth noting here that, even though exclusive of certain perspectives, such a declaration nevertheless accommodates, by the unspecific use of '*combat*', '*conquête*' and '*renversement*', to several different and opposing socialist interpretations of both the modern State and the aims of political action. What we have here then are polyvalent terms being used as if they were uncontentious. Just as the Project sustains a particular view of capitalism by excluding other possible views, so its claims about the inevitability of a social transformation are advanced with complete certainty, as if no

other ideas are worth consideration. On the first page of the Project
two classical socialist models and their theories are touched upon
before being rejected:

> *D'où partira le nouveau cours?*
> *Des tentatives ont déjà eu lieu: soit parce qu'elles menacent l'homme*
> *d'une soumission totale à un Etat tout-puissant* [USSR model and
> orthodox Marxism], *soit parce qu'elles n'ont pas su proposer une*
> *alternative suffisante aux défaillances économiques et sociales de la*
> *croissance capitaliste* [Social-Democratic model and revisionism],
> *elles ne constituent pas aujourd'hui une référence accept-*
> *able pour la construction du socialisme.*(13/11–19)

There remains in socialist theory one other alternative which must be
dealt with. The passage continues:

> *D'autres expériences se cherchent dans le tiers monde. Elles*
> *requièrent notre attention et notre solidarité. Mais c'est d'abord là où*
> *il a posé les fondations de son pouvoir que le capitalisme doit être*
> *mis en cause.* (13/20–4)

Third-world Marxism, subscribed to in the West by parts of the ultra-
Left, is respectfully noted and then rejected. The way is then open for
a justification of the party as the proper expression of Western
socialist traditions. We can note from the second quotation that there
is an assumption that simply being in the continent where capitalism
began justifies the party's claim to a kind of fundamental authenticity. The discussion of alternative ideal social models concludes
confidently:

> *Il n'y a plus de solution que dans l'audace d'une expérience*
> *nouvelle.*
> *Par les atouts qu'elle possède aujourd'hui, la France peut*
> *répondre à l'attente.* (13/25–8)

In this way, not only does late twentieth-century Western Socialism
find itself in a uniquely favourable moment in history, but is also in
the chosen country, France, the historic land of revolution. The
implication is that membership of an enlarged French Socialist Party
is itself the point at which individual and collective destinies coincide.

Many problems, however, remain. The area of agreement is only
sketched by the Project. Within the socialist movement, irreconcilable differences are of long standing, and the Project must, by
circumspection, be made acceptable to everyone present: the

libertarians and the disciplinarians, the party of order and the party of movement. Although the socialist intellectual tradition approves of synthesis and doctrinal confidence, it needs, nevertheless, to acknowledge the existence of contradictory theories and the necessity for compromise and philosophical accommodation. The Project, despite its synthetic and exclusive qualities, reflects this tradition innovatively. Opposites are not presented simply as a series of compromises but are combined positively with one another. In the light of what we said above concerning the presentation of May 1968 and May 1974 as logically linked rather than as irreconcilably opposed to one another, let us look at a few examples of how opposing political sentiments are presented:

[1] *Un but lointain clairement défini, mais trop de flou quant aux périodes intermédiaires nécessaires pour l'atteindre: tel est, pendant longtemps, apparu le projet socialiste.*

[2] *Le but lointain: la fin de l'exploitation de l'homme par l'homme et la disparition du salariat, c'est-à-dire une société où sera abolie la division entre tâches de direction et tâches d'exécution, entre travail manuel et travail intellectuel; où la diversité des talents ne sera plus hiérarchie des talents; où s'effaceront les rapports marchands; où le calcul monétaire fera place à un calcul social fondé sur la quantité de travail dépensé; où, enfin, l'Etat dépérira jusqu'à disparaître complètement.*

[3] *Ces objectifs, formulés dans la deuxième moitié du XIXe siècle, expriment encore aujourd'hui – et justement – des aspirations profondes qui s'opposent de façon radicale à l'idéologie des classes dominantes. Ils font apparaître le caractère relatif et transitoire des conceptions que ces classes considèrent comme naturelles et éternelles.*

[4] *Mais on ne peut se contenter d'un but lointain: nous savons d'expérience qu'il est impossible de supprimer dans un court délai historique tous les mécanismes économiques et toutes les structures mentales que nous lègue le capitalisme.*
Le socialisme de demain restera longtemps tributaire de l'héritage du passé. (24/28–25/21)

What is happening here under the guise of a mature acceptance of difficult political realities is that the socialist dream (para. 2) is presented and then withdrawn (para. 4). Even though the ideal is being presented here as an act of faith, if not as a chimera, a sense of its immediacy is nevertheless being evoked for emotional effect.

Paragraphs 1 and 3 are references to the shortcomings of utopian socialism (Proudhon) and an implicit reference to outdated Marxian socialism (the PCF). A causal link between two ideas is created ('here is what we want but we must be practical'), yet, in fact, two opposing socialist sentiments concerning utopian thought are being evoked.

The next example follows exactly the same pattern: two ideas about capitalism are presented yet distinguished, justified and 'reconciled' by a causal link:

> *Cet héritage nous offre, sur le plan scientifique, technique et culturel, une base de départ infiniment plus favorable que celle qu'ont connue les précédentes tentatives.*
> *Mais il n'a pas que des côtés positifs. Adapté au système capitaliste, il continuera d'en porter les caractéristiques au-delà de l'abolition du système d'appropriation privée des principaux moyens de production et d'échange. Il est impossible d'agir comme si la technique était neutre et pouvait être indifféremment mise au service du socialisme et du capitalisme. La machine peut être libératrice, mais elle peut être aussi aliénatrice.* (25/23–36)

We are again presented with two ideas, both of which find a response within the socialist consciousness: (1) the link with capitalist technology will be maintained, and (2) the link with capitalist technology will be broken.

The same format is identifiable in the ostensibly straightforward passage on education. In this passage, two ideas, both with a socialist pedigree (education is liberating, education is constraining), are presented in one paragraph. The two are linked by the conjunction '*Mais*':

> *Tout aussi ambigu est l'héritage culturel. Le niveau d'enseignement et de culture auquel est déjà parvenu l'ensemble de la population est un atout considérable pour une expérience socialiste. Mais le système éducatif a trop souvent abouti à développer la compétition, le sens de la hiérarchie et de la soumission. Bien des habitudes mentales qui sont à transformer profondément resteront ancrées, et pour longtemps, dans les comportements individuels et collectifs.* (26/26–35)

The final example concerns the Left's preoccupation with the idea of the extension of democracy and popular control. Once again the sequence of ideas is presented as following a logic. In the first paragraph due homage is paid to the notion of democratic control. In the second it is subverted:

> *La règle générale sera bien l'extension du principe démocratique à l'ensemble des activités économiques et sociales.*
> *Mais l'élection, c'est-à-dire la délégation du pouvoir ne résout pas tous les problèmes. Le rapport mandant–mandataire tend, d'une certaine manière, à reconstituer le rapport dirigeant–dirigé.* (29/19–27)

These examples all indicate an attempt to present as axioms contrasting ideas which, if questioned, would endanger the contrived synthesis between the revolutionary and the reformist strains within the socialist tradition.

What then is the significance of the Project? It displaces to the level of accepted historical tradition and myth topics which should be the subject of strategy, policy, social theory and doctrinal discussion. The new constraints imposed by the Project-as-charter involve the rejection of many of the assumptions that influenced the SFIO in its sixty-four years of existence. There is virtually no mention of the Communist Party, no discussion of the problems for Socialist theory of an exclusive party political strategy, nor of the manner in which the Fifth Republic's institutions will be converted to a socialist purpose, nor a considered recognition of the political/historical role of the *syndicats*. The overall effect of the Project is to strengthen the references to myth in Socialist discourse and to divert attention from strategy, social theory and policy, even at the moment it refers to them or evokes the seriousness of the issues they raise. This approach completely redefines the role of the individual within the party and within Socialist ritual. Let us look then at the way particular speakers at the *Assises* adapt to this new phenomenon.

An examination of the content of the speeches reveals that they have much in common with the Project, not only in style but in structure, especially in the way in which they also link contradictory axioms as if they were causally related. At the same time a comparison of the speeches indicates a subtle interplay of roles, such as those, for example, played by François Mitterrand and Régis Debray.

Mitterrand opens the debate on the first day, speaking after the welcoming remarks by André Jeanson, and Debray opens the proceedings of the second day. The difference in quality between the two occasions is significant. Through his address Mitterrand legitimates the gathering. He had characterised the *Assises* as a moment of doctrinal re-evaluation. As such, they provide an occasion for relaxation, reassurance and a sense of purpose. Debray, on the other hand, creates a sense of urgency and offers the threat of real danger and, thereby, confirmation of belief. As Guevara's comrade-in-arms and a political figure who has truly fought and suffered, Debray speaks words which cannot easily be contested. Evoking the 'lessons of Chile', Debray, speaking on the second day, brings a sense of vigilance to Mitterrand's sense of doctrinal re-evaluation, as well as a sense of the exotic: '*Ceux qui ont assassiné Salvador Allende . . . sont prêts à intervenir aussi chez nous*' (125/11–14). Debray, by superimposing the idea of immediate danger upon Mitterrand's encouragement to doctrinal exploration, ensures that dual and contradictory states of mind are exploited: that which sees socialism as an imposed solution fighting against great odds (Debray) and that which conceives it as the product of a reflective historical development (Mitterrand).

For their part, the third *composante* representatives collectively serve a dual function: the delegates are reassured of the rightness of their position because there are, at the *Assises*, unequivocally genuine representatives of working people. Many of the third *composante* delegates, however, stress that the realities of socialist struggle lie not in such gatherings as the *Assises* but on the shop or office floor. The delegates' status – as in the Mitterrand/Debray example given above – is therefore both confirmed and undermined. The role of individuals at the *Assises* is therefore complex and subtle.

The key speakers operate by appeasing each other for the most part. They do this by expressing, not their own ideas, but those of their potential critics. Mitterrand speaks respectfully of *autogestion*, the direct negation of personal leadership. Rocard speaks favourably of the Communist Party. The *syndicats* speak of positive co-operation with the political party. Mauroy, whose action in encouraging Rocard to attend and in stressing the importance of the *Assises* could be represented as threatening Mitterrand's position, makes a low bow to the king at the end of the *Assises*:

> *à cette réunion, il fallait un catalyseur, il fallait qu'un rassembleur se levât: ce fut la campagne présidentielle et ce fut François Mitterrand.* (173/8–11)

By such mutual accommodation a strong sense of collusion is created. In this setting, it is significant that Rocard, the major potential rival, is the one person who is directly criticised. We have already indicated that Debray furnishes the *Assises* with 'the Word' from the outside (revolutionary struggle in South America). Rocard's significance has several facets. He is, above all, the one figure who is suspect. All the attacks are made in the context of socialist doctrine and yet he takes on, because of the attacks, the mythic significance of the Stranger who stands at the edge of the encampment.

In fact there are three attacks upon him, all of which occur within a short space of time and thus reinforce each other. Claude Germon refers to Rocard by name and reprimands him for having suggested to the press (betrayed trust) that there is a deep division between CGT and CFDT ideas. Significantly, his criticism is pitched at the level of social vision. He says that to hold Rocard's views '*ne reposerait sur aucune réalité idéologique*' (130/32–3). In the context of the *Assises*, this is tantamount to the accusation of a heterodoxy that borders on heresy. Jean Poperen's attack is indirect and is a warning to those who might wish to undermine the Common Programme (pp. 133–7). The third and most severe attack is made by Lionel Jospin. He accuses Rocard of a strictly non-socialist weakness, pessimism (144/ 16). Rocard, in his speech, for rhetorical effect, had stressed that time was running out for socialist action.[13] Jospin selects this rhetorical device and, like Germon, both names Rocard and attacks him from a position of orthodoxy, accusing him of having misinterpreted history: '*Une telle constatation* [that the world is in crisis] *ne justifie pas, pourtant, le pessimisme dont faisait preuve hier Michel Rocard. Non, la France n'est pas condamnée à une expérience solitaire*' (144/15–18). Rocard's opponents, however, have an insurmountable task. Even if Rocard is condemned as a false prophet, he is, in the context of a personalist party, simultaneously both focused upon as a potential rival to Mitterrand and invested with the potential qualities of the future leader, scorned in the past. This is inevitable in the context of a party which practises, though cannot name, its own personalist orientation.

A further function of these rare personal comments is that they reinforce the idea that the *Assises* are a genuine demonstration of open discussion and the exchange of ideas. Restrained comments within and even upon the *Assises* reinforce their symbolic significance. The example of Debray's near scolding of the delegates has been mentioned. When Georges Sarre, a CERES member who was concerned that a change in the leadership was in prospect, attacks the false oecumenical character of the *Assises* (71/5), he in fact strengthens the philosophical unity which he wanted to question. It is extremely difficult to extract for criticism those myths which form a basis for ritual demonstrations of allegiance. Let us look at two examples of declarations which ostensibly attempt to expose the mythology of the *Assises*.

The first is part of a speech by J–P. Cot. For him, the Project itself is too ambiguous and needs to be analysed and opened up in order to be useful:

> *Tout texte est passible de plusieurs lectures, le projet de société comme les autres. Les militants aujourd'hui réunis dans les Assises doivent donc avoir une lecture responsable du projet et ne pas céder à la tentation de l'ambiguïté, du double langage. Au contraire, ils doivent s'attacher, dans les mois qui viennent, à préciser encore leur langage et leurs options, à parler haut et clair, entre eux d'abord, mais aussi pour les millions d'hommes et de femmes qui espèrent dans la gauche unie et dans le socialisme. Ainsi pourront-ils accélérer le puissant mouvement qui se dessine dans le pays. Un rendez-vous avec l'histoire les attend sous peu. Ce jour-là, il faudra être prêts.* (128/25–39)

The result of this *mise en garde*, particularly as it concludes with an avowed declaration of belief that, after examination, the Project will prove to be the expected charter of a chosen people, is that the Project is thus remythologised. What Cot is subscribing to is the principle that the believer's faith is strengthened, not by a re-examination of the source of inspiration, but by the self-awareness of examination-as-process.

Another example of this belief is Héritier's (third *composante*) volley of questions towards the end of the final day:

> *Que signifie exactement la formule 'contrôler aujourd'hui pour décider demain'? Que veut-on dire lorsque l'on parle de 'politisation des luttes'? Quels types de rapports faut-il établir entre partis et syndicats? Comment donner la priorité à l'implantation du parti dans les entreprises? Enfin, comment articuler l'action d'un gouvernement de gauche et la mobilisation populaire?* (159/17–25)

These very relevant questions *must* be asked. What is also clear, however, is that it is not the role of the *Assises* to answer them. Throughout the two days questions are raised, but it is the process of questioning which is important and not the possible solutions. Perhaps the only effective undermining of myth is the contribution of one speaker, Irène Charamande, who deplored the implicit anti-feminism of the *Assises* where women were under-represented as they were in society in general and the issues specific to them not taken seriously enough (158/14–32). This assertion, though isolated, is a demonstration of the successful subversion of a prevailing myth, in this case the myth of community, because the idea that communion has taken place is itself questioned.

In general, the crucial relations: electors/elected, *syndicat/* political party, leader/people, party/regime, party/people are never clearly examined. Many of the statements of certainty are akin to the expected, though spiritually reinforcing, certainties of religious ceremony. In fact the actual role of the *Assises* and the Project is to unite, as we have seen, through selection, contrast and mutual recognition. They also unite through ambiguity. It is the role of ambiguity that we shall examine next.

(d) *Autogestion* and the Function of Ambiguity

The *Assises* present, as we have seen, an identifiable set of ideas by both exclusion and mediation. Within this, ambiguity and allusion further reinforce the *Assises* as collective ritual and, more prosaically, act as an aid to the formulation of a common area of agreement. The best illustration of this functional ambiguity is the word 'autogestion'.

The doctrine that underpins this idea is relatively new in the social theories of organised Socialist parties, and the attention it has received is extensive. The nearest English equivalent of the word is 'workers' control' or 'self-management' (and there is a similar lack of clarity in the French as to whether this involves ownership). In the French, however, the word has a far greater evocative value and suggests a way of conducting one's whole life as well as one's relations in the workplace. Apart from the ambiguity of its meaning, therefore, *autogestion* explicitly signifies a radical reform of capitalist relations, but implicitly signifies a revision of the doctrinal reference points of modern socialism. It is, as the *Assises* demonstrate, very difficult, and fortuitously so, to define *autogestion*. Let us look at several references to it before suggesting an explanation for its central significance.

In the Project *autogestion* as a strategy, is described thus:

Cette forme d'organisation de la vie sociale est la seule qui, aujourd'hui, puisse prendre en charge le besoin de responsabilité et de création que le capitalisme refrène si puissamment. (31/3–6)

Two paragraphs further on, *autogestion*, as an immediately realisable social goal and, therefore, desirable political strategy, is withdrawn and is presented as an ideal to be striven for:

Il faut redire: l'autogestion n'est compatible qu'avec une société très égalitaire. La longue période de sa mise en place exige donc une lutte constante pour diminuer les inégalités héritées du capitalisme. (31/34–8)

In the Project *autogestion* is presented as both desirable strategy and ultimate goal. It resembles, therefore, a norm and an ideal. In the text which precedes the discussion on the *carrefours*, '*Militer pour le socialisme*', social life is considered as ideally organised when it is viewed in a '*perspective autogestionnaire*' (90/18). *Autogestion*, then, is given no single structural or other definition. For Jean Poperen, it is the '*rêve de toujours: que les producteurs maîtrisent leur destin en devenant maîtres de leur outil de travail et maîtres aussi des institutions qu'ils se sont données*' (135/10–14). Jacques Chérèque, the representative of syndicalism and, as such, a speaker with a 'legitimate' claim to speak on the subject, gives an ostensibly more down-to-earth explanation:

Je vous parle ici en militant syndical attentif à ce qui mobilise les masses. On peut débattre sans fin et théoriquement de l'autogestion. L'autogestion, pour nous, c'est le développement de l'intervention réelle et efficace, de tous ceux qui ont intérêt à une rupture définitive avec la société capitaliste. (64/5–11)

For Robert de Caumont (also third *composante*), *autogestion* is that which the working class searches for, as a plant seeks out the light, without ever having heard the word pronounced: '*le droit de contrôler réellement ce que l'on fait de leur argent, puis le droit de décider eux-mêmes, c'est-à-dire, sans que le mot soit prononcé, l'autogestion*' (138/16–19). The fact remains that, in spite of Chérèque's and de Caumont's wish to cut through sophistication, if these explanations are anything more than politically conscious trade unionism, then *autogestion* is ineffable and remains an integral part of 'the vision', which, as was said earlier, is experienced and not described.

There are two characteristics which reduce the ambiguity: *autogestion* is seen as both morally right and fundamentally natural. Gilles

Martinet calls *autogestion 'l'élection plus le contrôle'* (147/32–3). This definition is perhaps the nearest one gets to a clear idea of *autogestion* but, by the same token, falls far short of the powerful image of the control of one's destiny. Jacques Julliard (third *composante*) conflates the idea of *autogestion* as source of inspiration with that of *autogestion* as praxis: *'l'autogestion, c'est le socialisme en marche'* (164/26–7). The idea of *autogestion* is, then, central, polyvalent and novel. André Jeanson, when opening the *Assises*, describes *autogestion as la clé voûte de la future société socialiste'* (49/27). This phrase, when seen in the context of all the references which follow Jeanson's assertion and which we have examined above, is illuminating: *autogestion* is not the keystone of socialism, as Jeanson declares, but of the *Assises* themselves. *Autogestion* is the mythical referent through which the participants in the ritual obtain a more fundamental sense of union. Furthermore, *autogestion* evokes social and cultural, rather than economic, considerations in the search for a solution to socio-economic problems and is therefore a quasi-religious rejection of materialist solutions to the problems posed by capitalism. In this way *autogestion*, by referring to total solutions, refers to a mythic order.

The centrality of an area such as *autogestion* is an indication that myth plays an essential part in the creation of a framework for this evolving socialist discourse. Myth has, perhaps, an immediate and dramatic effect upon thinking *because* it refers to a timeless condition and thereby eternalises and mythologises aspects of the present, especially ritual occasions. *Autogestion*, therefore, as a declaration of that which will come to pass, provides, along with its sense of morality and its sense of naturalness, a sense of immediacy. At the *Assises* at least, *'autogestion'* has virtually supplanted certain of the functions of the term 'socialism' which, as we have seen, is definitive rather than evocative here. The use of this new term is further evidence of how the *Assises* were taken to mark the creation of an essentially new kind of socialism capable of inspiring an essentially new kind of person. Ritual acceptance of *autogestion* symbolically wipes out the past, thereby allowing a traditional organisation and its members to be treated as new or spiritually renewed.

Another example of the way in which the role of ambiguity is fulfilled by certain 'appeal' words is the expression *'lutte des classes'*. Unlike *'autogestion'*, *'lutte des classes'* is ambiguous, not because it is a new expression in socialist theory, but because it is a very old one.

It does not need to be defined and refined, only referred to, and thereby acts as proof of a speaker's socialist credentials.

The first reference to the class struggle as self-evident truth is made in the Introduction of the Project, *'Les socialistes n'ont pas inventé la lutte des classes: elle est un fait'* (14/14–15). In the *Assises*, however, the way in which this providential fact is used is problematic. The *Assises*, as we have said earlier, have, as one of their most important ideas, the connection between doctrine and action. Through the presence of the *carrefours*, this idea is 'applied', and here we can see the danger which the *Assises* as ritual must face if they are to demonstrate what an emotive idea such as class struggle might involve in the daily life of the Socialist activist. In the *carrefour* on *Consommation et modèle de développement*, for example, one of the primary methods advocated of Socialist intervention in the class struggle is to compare prices and goods in different shops and so outwit capitalism by buying cheap (92/18–19).

Autogestion too fares badly when applied to the *carrefours* on *Education, Armée–défense* and *Entreprises*. These three *carrefours* in particular might have offered very good indications of what an *autogestionnaire* society would be like. However, because of the fundamental incompatibility between what is an essentially anarchist idea and the idea of a rationally governed but still essentially centralised France, it was virtually impossible to use these fields of policy to illustrate how an implicitly uncontested centralised polity and society could be reconciled with the organisational implications of *autogestion*. The *Education carrefour* presents no theory of education or of culture and restricts itself to a few remarks about the struggle against graduate unemployment and about continuing education, and calls for the education system's mandarins to *'sortir du ghetto scolaire'* (96/10–11). The *Armée-défense carrefour*, for its part, makes no mention whatever of the possibilities of creating a socialistic militia, for example, or a nation-in-arms which would protect the Socialist *patrie en danger*, and it fails to draw any conclusions from the contemporaneous Portuguese experience. It is true that a few serving officers and some pacifists were present at the *Assises*. Their discussions however, involved the temporary patching-up of irreconcilable differences for the sake of unity. The *carrefour* concluded with the defensive hope that the Armed Forces would not intervene to bring down a Socialist government.

The *Entreprises carrefour* provides the best example of the difficulties presented by the attempt to represent simultaneously both doctrine and strategy. It is worth noting that this *carrefour* is one at which Mitterrand, Mauroy, and Rocard spent most of their time. The crucial questions, of course, are the discussion of the relationship between *syndicat* and political party both in and out of government, the presence of the party on the shop floor, and *autogestion* as a mode of production or as an industrial strategy. No mention is made of the way in which the *syndicat* in the Fifth Republic, notably since 1963, had entered into corporatist relations with government. None of these issues is raised and the *carrefour* contents itself with a call for the longed-for increase of Socialist Party presence on the shop floor. Whether as discussion groups or as sites of policy formulation, it is clear that the *carrefours* are not very successful. Their significance in fact lies elsewhere. Let us now examine how they, the Project and the speeches fit into the *Assises* as a whole.

(e)   Representation and Significance of the Whole

The *Assises*, in order to repair the division of the past (1958) and prepare for the future (1978 and the years following), create a sense of the epic, which serves the dual function of reducing disagreement and providing inspiration. One of the difficulties faced by non-Communist French Socialism, however, is that it had always defined itself negatively, usually with reference to capitalism or else to Marxism or, more specifically, Marxism–Leninism. Yet the point of the *Assises* is not to depict and criticise bourgeois or Soviet society but to evoke the paradisal qualities of Western European socialism. In the absence of models, it is the *Assises* themselves which serve the function of transmitting the image of a just and harmonious society.

Firstly, they represent tolerance. The *Assises* arguably demonstrate an over-representation, in terms of preparatory committees, delegates and speeches, of the second and third *composantes*.[14] The PS, proportionate to its influence in national and local politics and within the organised Left, is significantly under-represented. At traditional gatherings these proportions of representation would be unacceptable. In this way, the *Assises* represent a type of Saturnalia and the symbolic enactment of a unification congress even though no such fusion had taken place in formal terms.

The *Assises* also provide a sense of completeness. Drama, folk tales and adventure stories are often characterised by the sense of movement, which has been generated by an initial feeling of lack or motivated by an act of villainy.[15] The trials of the hero then follow, wherein the hero creates or is subject to this necessary sense of movement. Finally, the hero triumphs because of his suffering, and plenitude is attained. A similar pattern is discernible at the *Assises*:

	Lack/Villainy	*Trials*	*Plenitude/Triumph*
Level 1	Capitalism	Speeches, reflection, debates, *carrefours*	Vision of socialist society
Level 2	Absence of accord between socialists	Speeches, reflection, debates, *carrefours*	Sense of communion
Level 3	No one leader	Testing of leader's faith and credentials	One heroic leader

The idea of trial is linked to the notion of the return to the source of inspiration. In practice, the activists are allowed to bring the voice of uncorrupted authenticity to that of wisdom. There is evidence here, well understood in epic poetry, for example, that a sense of downward movement will lead to, or create the illusion of leading to, truth. The opposite idea – that upward movement will lead to revelation – is also present. Both kinds of 'quest' are operative. After the downward movement has been made (doctrinal re-evaluation), the attempts at synthesising experience and theory correspond to the upward movement which attains plenitude and a state of grace. In this way toleration and completeness are mutually dependent.

There is an implicit assumption in socialist theory, particularly that which distinguishes itself from the consciously imposed solutions of state socialism, that socialism is fundamentally natural and that capitalism is a distortion of a Rousseauist social ideal. It is in this context that the *carrefours* acquire their significance.

Robert Chapuis, on the second afternoon, declared:

> Le grand risque d'une organisation socialiste, c'est de se prendre elle-même pour la société, de chercher en elle-même sa propre finalité. (168/36–8)

This, however, is precisely what the *Assises* set about doing.

Before the *carrefours* debated and reported back to the plenum, they were given a set of guideline questionnaires concerning what forms of struggle should be employed or reflected upon by the different sections of interest. In this way the *carrefours* as the place where doctrine and theory are fused is suggested. Rocard saw their role like this:

> *L'objet des douze carrefours qui s'ouvriront cet après-midi sera précisément de canaliser vers l'objectif commun des forces innombrables qui agissent en ordre dispersé, à travers des luttes ponctuelles, et que nous n'avons pas toujours su utiliser pleinement parce qu'il nous manquait un instrument de coordination.* (60/31–7)

We have seen, however, in the case of 'struggle' meaning 'comparison of shop prices', that the *carrefours* are doctrinally, strategically, and even tactically, insignificant and that they must serve another role than that which they claim to serve. It is with the report back on the second day of the *Assises* that their proper significance becomes apparent. By giving a voice to the party's base, the *carrefours* symbolise, on the one hand, *cahiers de doléances*, which, by virtue of where their complaints are brought, legitimate the executive and thereby create a symmetrical, feudal pyramid-image of social harmony and control. They are, on the other hand, a dramatic representation of the elusive *société autogestionnaire*. The *carrefours* 'reveal' an idealised social structure by offering models for the unity of social organisation in socialist society. They not only discuss socialism but, in form and style, exemplify it. Socialism is both the object of discussion and speaking subject. The myth of harmony and communion not only conveys the sense of unity and coherence but also evokes the outlines of an ideal social world. By framing an imagined future which incorporates people's hopes (rationally understood society, social justice, free speech, time for reflection, significant individual and collective destiny), a socialist future is apprehended, fear of autocracy allayed and belief thereby reinforced. It is for this reason that the *carrefours* contribute to the mythic effect of the *Assises* as a whole, even though they bring with them certain problems.

As well as representing toleration, plenitude, a rationalised social structure and a commitment to idealism, the *Assises* embody a constant tension between permanence and change, between stasis and movement, between the idea that socialism is to be striven for and the idea that it only awaits implementation, that the *Assises* are themselves a moment of becoming and a moment of fulfilment. Appeals to both dispositions are made several times during the *Assises*. Poperen, Mauroy and Mitterrand all represent different traditions within Socialism, yet all stress the need to encourage that which changes and to protect that which endures. Poperen's words are characteristic of all three and are words of warning rather than words of advice: '*Il s'agit de relier ce qui dure et ce qui passe, le permanent et l'éphémère, le structurel et le conjoncturel*' (133/38–134/2). The aspect of the *Assises* as a privileged meeting-place of old and new, the place of arrival and departure '*vers l'étape nouvelle*',[16] therefore demonstrates symbolically above all else, not the warning to the new members to leave the party untouched, but the myth of reunification.

The idea of union is perhaps the strongest single theme at the *Assises*, as is underlined by such small gestures as Debray's well-timed and unscheduled reading of the telegram of greeting and encouragement sent by the Spanish Socialist Party. The telegram gives credence to the idea both that the eyes of the world are upon the participants at the *Assises* and that the delegates are part of an even greater, indeed universal, communion.

The *Assises* therefore play the symbolic role of demonstrating what appears to be collective agreement on a fundamental set of social theories and myths. By interlinking this cluster of significations the *Assises* further strengthen the idea of unity. They also reconcile the opposing drives of doctrine and action, and of millenarianism and organisation, in such a way as to offer what appears to be a new and purer form of Socialism, but one which accommodates to the new demands of a personalist undertaking. Discursively – and therefore by extension, doctrinally – the *Assises* screen out Molletism from the history of French Socialism.

(f) The Consequences of the *Assises*

The SFIO's reluctance to abandon its attachment to exclusive parliamentarianism in the early Fifth Republic reflected its belief that the regime would ultimately revert to the model of the Fourth and not develop around the presidential principle. It was in October 1974 that the non-Communist Left tacitly but irrevocably accepted the Fifth Republic as a regime of substance, with characteristic avenues to power and associated modes of discourse.

However, this most recent act of republican faith was fundamentally different from those made by the SFIO, because it entailed acceptance that the principles of the secular republic could be combined with those of exalted and transcendent leadership. Socialist mythology had always contained the 'belief that the people were capable of uniting, despite their differences, in the name of progress, but this belief had always been tied to the conviction that the party would be the mobilising and uniting force needed to achieve this. This assumption was no longer offered unambiguously and Socialist rhetoric now suggested that progressive leadership was as important as, if not more important than, party in inducing the rally of the people. Personalism was now offered as the companion of socialist republicanism.

With the modification of the party principle, ambiguity about the proper approach to strategy, policy and doctrine was introduced along with shifts in the significance of established socialist myths. Internal party politics lost their traditional focus and factions became as much concerned with the possibilities for promoting or downgrading particular personalities as with the routine competition between *tendances* and *courants* which had absorbed so much energy in the old SFIO. The themes and modes of party discourse began to shift accordingly, and the maintenance of party institutions became increasingly a matter of ceremonial and ritual affirmations.

Even though the PS retained its local organisation in certain cities and maintained its strong support in the Pas-de-Calais, Nord and Bouches-du-Rhône federations, its discourse was not securely related to the interests of its activists and branches. The transformed PS did not encourage the kinds of analysis and strategic aims that were favoured by the Keynesians of the British Labour Party nor the pragmatic reformism of the German Social Democratic Party. Instead, the PS developed a public language which could be accommodated to two teleologies, millenarianism and personalism. In practice, the old SFIO base remained and this fundamental disharmony or lack of correspondence between leaders and organisation is one of the characteristic features of the modern party.

The relations between the various *courants* and groups in the PS were also changed. Ideologically, CERES and the *courant des Assises* (the Rocardians, essentially) were very close to one another and, after 1974, there was practically no scope for a rival group to establish a distinctive set of policies in the doctrinal territory which they occupied. It was their own efforts to differentiate themselves that set in train the internal conflicts which were to trouble the party in the mid-1970s. The split at Pau in January 1975, which saw CERES leave Mitterrand's majority, was the opening event in this new intra-party battle. Furthermore, because adherence to a particular *tendance* or *courant* had now, more than ever, acquired a strategic and tactical significance *vis-à-vis* the leadership, doctrinal debate became exclusively centred upon power relationships within the party. It was inevitable in such a situation that doctrinal attacks would take the form of accusations that a group had strayed from the true path of socialism. It is not surprising, therefore, that the aftermath of the euphoric *Assises* brought a certain sense of deception among activists, new and old.

2   THE METZ CONGRESS, APRIL 1979

The Metz Congress of the PS in April 1979 was affected both by a concern about the Left's electoral defeat in 1978 and by anticipation of the next presidential elections of 1981. The congress motions reflected the tension between these two perspectives, offering explanations for past defeats and failings while declaring confidence that the party would secure power through the presidency.

The initial intention of the Rocardians had been to challenge, even defeat, the leadership or, failing that, to bring about a change in policy which would impose Rocard as the party's presidential candidate. However, it soon became clear that the resistance to Rocard within the party was considerable. The criticisms expressed by the Rocardians were nevertheless maintained up to and during the congress. Their congress motion (motion C) and the speeches they made in its defence present a striking demonstration of the discursive possibilities of and constraints upon the attempt to promote an alternative leader or party presidential candidate.

From the moment of the Left's defeat in March 1978, the press and media considered the Mitterrand/Rocard dispute as one essentially concerned with leadership. The results of opinion polls comparing Mitterrand and Rocard appeared frequently throughout 1978 and 1979. The Metz Congress, therefore, raised two issues of leadership: one concerning actual leadership of the party, and one concerning a future bid for the presidency of the Republic and therefore notional leadership of the State.

Mitterrand asserted himself forcefully in the months preceding the congress. There were cantonal elections in the winter of 1978/9 and he toured the cantons in support of Socialist candidates, emphasising the need for unity and building up his following amongst the party's rank-and-file. On 30 January 1979 he gave his first press conference in seven months, thus using his position in the party as a means of reasserting his presidential stature. This was also the period when Mitterrand was advocating the recruitment of new and younger people into the party's hierarchy, thus making the accusations of his monopoly of power a difficult one to sustain. Rocard was at a severe disadvantage in the face of all this activity: he could not have challenged Mitterrand on a personal basis without exposing himself to the charge of disloyalty, and he acknowledged this at the congress by stating that he would not stand for the presidency if Mitterrand were a candidate.

The Rocardians had therefore to attack the leadership at two levels. Explicitly, they proposed that the issues were doctrinal, but at the same time, implicitly, they blamed the Mitterrand leadership for personal failing. Hence the persistent themes of misjudgement and betrayal, of strength diminished, of loss of contact with the true heritage of the party and of impaired vision about the nature of a future socialist society.

There were seven motions presented to the congress. Of these seven motions, only A, B, C and E were significant in terms of the final voting and therefore in the distribution of offices. All the main motions dealt with similar themes: the Union of the Left, decentralisation, Europe, capitalism, economic planning, *autogestion* and the rights of women. The motions, moreover, adopted similar approaches to nearly all of the main topics. Epinay too is mentioned in all the main motions. The most obvious policy difference was that between CERES and Mitterrand over the question of Europe. We can see, therefore, that organisational fragmentation is overlaid with a relative doctrinal coherence. Because of the leadership question, however, there also occurred, both at federal congresses and at the national congress, a bipolarisation around the Mitterrand and Rocard motions to the detriment of the Mauroy and CERES motions.[17] In the Paris federation, for example, the CERES group found that, despite its hitherto dominant position, it was unable to prevent substantial support being expressed for the Mitterrand and Rocard motions. The final Metz vote enabled Mitterrand to go into an alliance with CERES, thus putting Mauroy and Rocard into the party's minority. In this context of doctrinal coherence, internal fragmentation, bipolarisation, the organisational constraint of the traditional party congress, and the leadership perspective, let us examine one of the motions of the congress, the Rocardian motion.

Motion C   *'Redonner ses chances à la gauche'*[18]

The distinguishing themes of the Rocard motion are its stress upon the notion of power (in the first instance in the polity; in the second, the party), its denial of the need for another *rapprochement* with the PCF before rallying the people, and its insistence upon the need for links with the *forces vives* outside the party proper. The strongest emphasis in the motion is upon the need to remove impediments and to restore the party's ability to respond to the currents of sentiment and interest which presage the great rally of the people. The motion's stress upon the incrementalist aspect of Socialism is interwoven with a sense of urgency and with that of the imminence of release, reminiscent of revolutionary language. The motion argues for a realistic approach and yet its ultimate purpose and effect are transcendental. In Mitterrand's motion – as in that of CERES – the stress upon instant *rupture* implies that socialism can be rapidly implemented because it already exists (in the party). The Rocardians must point to a socialism which lies either outside the party or in a future time (and *not* in the party).

One of the fundamental problems for the Rocardians was to show that their view of socialism entitled them to challenge the doctrines of the Mitterrandists and to claim a distinctive and enduring tradition within French socialism. While accepting their part in the making of the *Parti socialiste* they had, at the same time, to demonstrate their independence from it, and their consequent ability to judge its leader severely. In this enterprise, they had to ensure that they were not identified as Centrists trying to steer a middle course between the Communists and the Right in the manner of the Fourth Republican SFIO after 1947 and of the Defferrists in 1963–5.[19]

Let us now sharpen our focus upon the Rocard motion, bearing in mind that it combines the assertion of a doctrinal and philosophical perspective with an attempt to demonstrate, while never overtly stating, that the vision represented by Rocard is superior fo that offered by Mitterrand. We should also take into account the motion's prescribed form: the fundamental difference between a text like the *projet de société* of the 1974 *Assises* and a congress motion is that the latter takes place in the main organisational moment in the life of the party and therefore needs to deal with the concrete issues of party strength, the efficacy of current policies and the assessment of past and future performance. It is, nevertheless, like a *projet de société* in that it addresses itself to party orientation and to doctrine. In this way, the Rocard motion conforms to a tradition of disputing doctrine within organisation while conveying the promise of escape from organisational constraints. To this end it combines the themes of millenarianism with the language of organisational realism, and offers the prospect of success through the familiar paths of doctrinal argument. Because of Socialist doctrine, however, it cannot – just as Mitterrand could not – refer explicitly to the need for personal or personalist leadership. In order for the motion to create its desired effect it must, in the manner of the *Assises*, move towards a rally style through its use of myth and transcendentalism in an effort to offer new reference points to the 1971–8 perspective. By the same token it must usurp the rally quality of that tradition while making the Mitterrandist perspective akin to a *pre*-1971 position, to the period 1946–71, thus symbolically re-enacting in 1979 the essential quality of 1971 and 1974, namely, the rejection of the past. In order to do this, the motion itself must elucidate the loss of faith, the site of a new faith and, only then, the necessary practical consequences of this change.

The basic thrust of the motion is anti-authoritarian. This is not the problem for the Rocardians that it is for Mitterrand because (i) at the congress, the Rocardians had virtually no record of authority to protect and (ii) the communitarian aspect of Rocardism does not need to address itself to structures or practices of domination within its own projected form of Socialism. A *notional* alternative authority is pointed to but is seen as lying outside the party and therefore potentially within the control of everyone.

The motion attempts to associate Mitterrand himself with the idea of an *équipe*, a quality which possesses little mythical legitimation on the Left, and to associate itself with a *courant*, but a *courant* in its original sense, that of a *courant d'idées* which goes out beyond or comes from beyond the party's boundaries. (In effect the motion bleaches out from Rocardism the 'team' character it had itself built up between 1974 and 1979.) This is how, in its Conclusion, the motion defines itself:

> *Une motion de Congrès n'est pas un programme de gouvernement ni un projet de société. Elle ne peut évoquer tous les aspects de la réalité politique, économique et sociale dans leurs détails . . .*

> *Elle n'a pas non plus pour objet de reprendre chacun des textes qui constituent l'acquis collectif du Parti Socialiste: elle les complète et les enrichit en abordant les problèmes qui sont ceux de notre avenir. Nous avons essayé de définir les perspectives d'un projet clair, offensif et mobilisateur. Il n'apparaîtra celui de la majorité de demain que si la vérité du langage et la rigueur des moyens accompagnent l'audace des choix qu'il propose. Les Français, à juste titre, se méfient des promesses.*

By referring to itself as not being either a governmental programme or a *projet de société*, the motion nevertheless becomes much more than a congress motion. In its own terms, it defines the perspectives of a Project. By doing this, the motion implies a Project and, by further implication, an ideal society. It also implies that the author(s) of the motion possess knowledge of this ideal society and the method for its realisation, but are constrained from expressing it fully by the formal requirements of congress motions.[20]

This pointing away from the motion and its function is anticipated in a quotation from Jaurès which serves as its preface (it is a rallying call made to '*la jeunesse*' in 1903). In literary or philosophical texts such a lead quotation is used to remind or assure the reader that the author is sensitive to and is working within a flow of ideas which have been defined by great writers and thinkers who captured in few words some form of essential truth. Its adaptation to the form of the congress motion creates similar effects. Through this device the signatories signify their awareness of the enduring concerns of socialist idealists and honour a leader and a sense of purpose more substantial, by implication, than those of 1979. Reference to Jaurès, moreover, is a reminder of the man who synthesised different intellectual traditions within French Socialism and created the unified Socialist Party of 1905. The author(s) of motion C thus pay homage to a leader revered throughout the twentieth century, both by revolutionaries and reformists, and one who combined a unifying task with a sense of mission. The principal author of the present motion is thereby implied as being another such leader.

Yet the quotation serves simply as a portal: it is not developed at any point within the text. No tradition is overtly claimed, nor is any affinity between Rocard and Jaurès explicitly stated. It nevertheless indicates that the motion claims to be something other than a motion.

The motion itself is divided into four parts, each part divided into sub-titled sections. The Introduction, about 600 words long, sets out the underlying aim of the motion, namely, the apportioning of blame, which is taken up again in the last part of the motion. Initially, a collective party disillusionment and a sense of generalised loss are evoked:

Un immense espoir a été brisé en mars 1978. (1)

At this point, the Rocardian *courant* is implicitly accepting its share of the blame, thus initially limiting possible disagreement on the part of those with whom it is trying to establish contact. Progressively the blame is shifted away from the party onto the leadership. This actual reference to the failure of 1978 points, without explicating, to another – imagined – event, the loss of nerve of the leadership and thereby the betrayal of trust. The leadership error or failing is compounded by the implication, given the failure of 1978, that this unnamed second event predates the first. The notion of the leadership's dissimulation of its failings is suggested also by explicit statements as to how the existing leadership is trying to cope with the defeat of March 1978:

Aucune astuce de présentation, par les mots ou les chiffres, ne pourra gommer ce sentiment de défaite. (2)
la tentation de l'immobilisme, de la gestion prudente d'un patrimoine électoral d'opposition en vivant sur nos acquis d'hier et sur quelques certitudes élémentaires. (7)
Certains l'ont empêché [debate] (8)
procédés plébiscitaires, qui transformaient chaque question, chaque interrogation, soit en une déviation, soit en une querelle de personnes. (8)
Aurions-nous si peu de foi en nous-mêmes pour remettre l'espoir du socialisme à une prochaine génération? (9)

When these allusive references are taken together, the idea of a party leadership which is beginning to abandon its principles through fear and opportunism is indicated. The inadequacies of the leadership, therefore, are being cited as evidence that the party is slipping back, in spite of the 1974 intake and the expected rally orientation, to its old SFIO ways. In other words, it is shifting away from its task towards a kind of Guesdism or Molletism.

To contrast with this argument – and in order to heighten the dichotomy between guilt and moral rectitude – certain other words indicating an alternative to leadership guilt and moral inadequacy are introduced. These words link up with the notion of '*forces vives*' which are mentioned in the second line and which become the extra-party site of legitimacy later on in the motion. The '*forces vives*', along with '*militants socialistes*', are depicted as being '*en souffrance*' and '*meurtris et pleins d'amertume*'. An alternative hope is then depicted in '*ne s'y résignent pas*', '*espérer*', '*créer*', '*luttes*', '*volonté*', '*nouvelle*', '*liberté*' and then '*synthèse*', '*clarté*' and '*choix*'. This cluster of words and expressions thus offers an image or promise of release. The last three words ('*synthèse*', '*clarté*' and '*choix*') are linked to the idea of '*débat*' referred to seven times in the Introduction which thus becomes the method or avenue of release from '*souffrance*' and '*amertume*'. Insistence upon the word '*débat*' refers back to the allusion to leadership refusal of debate and forward to the overcoming of this refusal as the condition of renewed hope.

There is throughout the text, in fact, a constant play upon the difference between discourse and language on the one hand and intentions or action on the other. When referring to the leadership, such a gap is presented as being evidence of the general dissimulation on the part of the guilty:

> *Aucune astuce de présentation, par les mots et par les chiffres, ne pourra gommer ce sentiment de défaite.* (2)
> *decalage entre la pratique et le discours.* (42)
> *C'est autant à la pratique qu'au discours que se jugent les volontés.* (48)
> *La liberté ... si elle ne trouve pas ... au-delà du discours.* (77)
> *Les Français ... savent trop ... combien il y a un discours pour les envolées lyriques des congrès et un autre au milieu des difficultés et des incertitudes de l'action.* (Conclusion)

The text also conveys the impression that the party's new *Projet Socialiste*[21] will be void because it will not have been properly discussed. Here too words will not have been preceded or followed by appropriate action and, by implication, the leadership is again to blame.

The discussion called for by the motion itself, however, offers the party an opportunity to atone for its past mistakes and engage in a sincere and open debate, both to pave the way for effective action and to develop an appropriate political ethic. The process of debate (with the PCF, between members of the party, and with the people) is presented not so much as an exchange of views as a process of enlightenment from one source which stands at the edge of the party proper and which will enable it to develop a *rassemblement*. It is in this sense that debate is confidently assumed to constitute a prelude to successful action, and the motion itself is portrayed as the legitimate discursive prelude to such a rally.

In this way, the position of the writer(s) is established as one of opposition to the leadership and of readiness to make contact with – and knowledge of how to make contact with – the *forces vives*. In this context, debate does not represent the desire for an actual exchange of views – the challenge to leadership is too outspoken for that – but is instanced as proof that motion C reflects honesty, openness and correctness. This debate becomes synonymous with liberty, the pursuit of the one, debate, synonymous with the achievement of the other, liberty.

The underlying myth in motion C, therefore, despite the apparently reasonable demand for the recognition of failure and the call for rational debate, is one concerning a gathering of forces and a migration away from both disillusionment and forms of oppression to the realisation of hopes. The writer(s) of the motion situate themselves away from the centre, on the party boundary, at the point where the party interacts with those social forces which represent the hope of progress. The unseen destination is not described but it is evoked (by reference to the National Plan, discussed below) and implied (by constant contrasting reference to either the regime or the party leadership's refusal of liberty).

In order to present itself as the site of a new rally, the motion must treat the original rally (around Mitterrand) as a kind of false start or necessary prelude to the rally proper. This is done in two necessarily subtle stages (the motion can attack neither the party nor Mitterrand at this stage). First, it reaffirms socialism as lying partly outside the party by referring to the fortitude of socialists after the failure ('*l'insuccès*') of the 1974 presidential elections, that is to say, it focuses upon those non-PS socialists who were willing to join the party and prepare for the successful rally. Second, it reaffirms allegiance to the party but actually diminishes it by doing so:

De 1971 à 1978, porté par les choix d'avenir faits à Epinay, le Parti Socialiste s'est affirmé comme le parti de l'union et du renouveau. (4)

On the surface this statement seems complimentary to the party in general. However, not only is 1971 seen as the beginning of a process which ends in failure (the legislative elections of 1978), this apparent homage to 1971 is a reminder that the *choice* that ended in the 1978 defeat was made before the Rocardians entered the party. By implication the party is being asked to make another choice in 1979.

Again in the Introduction reference to the party is used to reinforce the idea that the source of socialism lies outside the boundaries of the party. When the motion states that year after year the party was joined by waves of recruits '*qui avaient reconnu dans le message "Changer la vie" l'expression de leurs luttes et de leur volonté*' (4)[22] not only is the sense of disillusioned hope reinforced but '*leurs luttes*' and '*leur volonté*' strengthens the idea that socialism existed as much outside the party as inside it.

All the main features of the Introduction of motion C: a series of disillusionments, deviation from the true path, the refusal by others of open debate, affirmation of an alternative source of socialism, indicate the need for a doctrinal *mise au point*, an ideological and ethical revision which in its turn must inform action in order that the party:

reprenne l'initiative et la gauche le chemin de la victoire (8)

The party is thus enjoined to resume the initiative once possessed and the way now lost. The reference points for such revision are '*volonté autogestionnaire*' and '*socialisme autogestionnaire*'.

Towards the end of the Introduction comes the affirmation:

Nous avons la conviction . . . qu'il n'y a pas de fatalité à l'échec de la gauche. (9)

Thus what follows will be the exposition of an effort of intellect, faith and will which combats the fatalism to which others have succumbed, which contributed to defeat and which, by implication, can be overcome by a rally around a new leader or presidential candidate.

The first main part of the motion: '*A problèmes nouveaux, réponses nouvelles*', serves the purpose of setting up the parameters of reference to which the later parts of the text will offer a solution. The tone of this part is both scientific and authoritative. It uses figures and percentages to reinforce standard Leftist arguments, namely, that the economic growth rate has been broken, inflation is dominating capitalism itself, that uncontrolled money circulates and subverts the banking systems, that the crisis is comparable to that of 1929, and that France's internal consumption and production are becoming more than ever dependent upon international economic relations. In this way, the credentials of the author(s) for discoursing upon the texture of the real world – and all of it – are established.

It will be remembered that the fatalism (of the Left) has already been referred to and rejected. A method for overcoming capitalism will also be elaborated in an anti-fatalistic, voluntarist manner now that the extent of the problems has been revealed. First, the motion makes the point that:

> *les contraintes, c'est-à-dire les faits, sont têtues. Elles ne sont ni de droite, ni de gauche.* (20)[23]

Later – in the same part – capitalism is described as an economic regime which cannot find solutions to its problems and not as one which has formulated its own crisis strategy – a much more common representation in Leftist writings. By representing the problems of capitalism as those of bad management, the motion implicitly contends that its author(s) have the solutions and are good managers, in a holistic, Saint-Simonian sense.

The implicit claim to a rational and comprehensive grasp of reality and the unparochial nature of Rocardism is reinforced by the assurance with which the text offers solutions to the problems raised by such international issues as the nuclear industry, hunger, human rights, and even the survival of the human species (21–23). The ability of France to pursue such goals will be linked to its moral stature, and is offered as a prize:

> *le peuple qui sera capable de bâtir le grand projet du socialisme autogestionnaire aura certainement une influence dépassant celle qui résulterait de sa propre puissance.* (23)

Here, the use of the word '*projet*' has a specific function. First, it lends an existential quality to the idea of a political undertaking, giving it the connotation of a Sartrean project. Secondly, it diminishes the actual *Projet Socialiste*, later to be elaborated under CERES control. The word '*projet*' is used many times in the text and always – except when it refers to the *Projet Socialiste* – refers to the notion of adventure or great task, that which breaks away from organisational constraint.

In this part of the motion, and in several other places in the text, the author(s) refer to processes which lie outside the organisational structures of the party and which precede them both in time and in status. There are also several allusions and references to the extra-institutional *Soixante-huitarde* tradition claimed by Rocardism. However, the basic ethic offered by the text is not one of revolutionary force but one of moral suasion, the object being to '*entamer un processus de rupture avec le capitalisme par les voies légales*' (36). References to violence do occur: for example, reference is made to the steel industry (violent confrontations between the police and strikers were taking place during this period in Longwy, a steel town, which is mentioned by name later (109)), and to resistance to the violence that the State exercises against the men and women '*de notre pays*' (25). '*Nouvelles formes de révolte*' (25) are developing in response to this – and here there is some ambiguity as to whether these involve violence. However, these instances are given as consequences of failure, explicitly that of the regime to respond to just demands, implicitly that of Socialism to inspire and provide leadership.

By referring to forces outside the party, the text draws attention to them and both underscores the party's failure to take them into account and implies that it is the failure to recognise them which has led the country towards violence and strife. It is interesting to note in this context that the image of a future society which the text goes on to elaborate, and which we shall examine below, is profoundly pacifist.

In terms of this ideal society, the motion first effects the rejection of alternative socialist models, thus creating a *tabula rasa* for the exposition of its own *autogestionnaire* socialism in the next section. All the models are rejected on the basis of their denial of liberty. The Soviet model is depicted as being no model at all: '*Le Goulag a fait de l'Union Soviétique un anti-modèle*' (34). Cuba and Cambodia are named as unacceptable variants (34). Social Democracy, as illustrated by the authoritarian style of West Germany, is also rejected (35). In this way, a doctrinal area is opened up and the description of a future socialist society becomes the domain of the text itself. One obstacle remains: the kind of society implied by the Union of the Left. This is dealt with in the last sub-section of this part of the text.

Thematic strain is imposed upon the text by the need to recognise the Union of the Left in some form. This problem is dealt with by appealing to the Leftist rally in the name of the Union of the Left (which simultaneously involves a close reading of the text, given this near-heretical claim to orthodoxy). The text places the notion of the Union of the Left at two levels: one which belongs to an apparently real world, the alliance between the PS and the PCF, '*la forme qu'elle a connue depuis 1972*' (37), broken in 1977; and another belonging to an imagined world of union between the Communist and Socialist movements (38) and in fact referring to myth. The party leadership is preoccupied with the first, those represented by the motion, with the second. The first main section of the motion therefore presents the party with an image of itself as having laid down the conditions of the rally of the people incompletely. The motion presents itself as providing the missing elements in the next three sections and thereby implies that Rocard is the focal point of the new rally.

The next part of the motion, called '*Les réponses du socialisme autogestionnaire*', involves the further criticism of leadership and the development of the implied myth of migration away from bondage through the evocation of an ideal society. The criticism takes the form of the rejection of the Jacobin tradition (the traditional Left) and the monarchical (the Right), both interpreted as aspects of the same phenomenon (49). The leadership of the PS and the old SFIO are, furthermore, simultaneously implicated in the wrongs which stem from these centralising traditions by a brief reference to the Algerian crisis: '*ce noir hiver du socialisme*' (42). This is a reference to the Mollet government of 1956–7 and its allegedly repressive Algerian policies. It is also an allusive reminder of the ministerial career of the young François Mitterrand.

One of the characteristic features, moreover, of the shameful Algerian episode in the history of the French Left is identified by '*ce décalage entre la pratique et le discours*': '*rupture*', '*classe ouvrière*' and '*révolution*', masking '*torture*', '*guerre*', and '*répression*' (42). This '*décalage*' between what is said and what is done is the most dramatic example of the consequences of the non-correspondence between practice and discourse but offers a general warning of what it can ultimately lead to. Here its purpose is to preface the presentation of what purports to be the true reflection in discourse (the motion) of an imagined future practice. The bulk of this second part involves the description of an ideal society and the method of its attainment. In order to avoid the accusation of a naive utopianism and the actual description of an envisaged society, and to maintain the realism projected in the Introduction and first section, a singular form of inversion takes place: the *socialisme autogestionnaire*, normally the aim, becomes the method; the Plan, normally a strategy, evokes an ideally structured society.

The pattern of future events described in this section is straightforward: first comes the formation of a Socialist government whose initial task will be to carry out reforms of structure which will effectively decentralise the State through a series of regulated '*ruptures*' and the mobilisation of popular support through democratic consultation; second, the organisation of a reformed economy will be necessary to facilitate and maintain decentralisation, participatory democracy and a transformed market. Various claims are made concerning the effectiveness of these proposed arrangements; one being that a transformed France will, in its turn, transform Europe and the Third World.

Autogestion in this context is offered as the true means of realising such a society in that it moves the argument away from purely economic considerations (which by implication constitute the traditional Left's inadequate formula), to what the motion considers to be other structures of domination. The reforms of structure are portrayed as a kind of release mechanism which will enable people to see more clearly in order to act in a more rational and social manner. It is significant that this section occasionally associates practices of domination within the party with those of the regime, thereby introducing a theme which will dominate the last main section of the motion. Culture will no longer be considered as it has been, even by Socialists '*et non les moindres*' as '*beaux arts*' and '*belles lettres*' (56). This reference to culture is an indication of what *autogestion* is meant to signify here: a total response to life that involves the transformation of the way the world is perceived and its cultural rewards valued. The logical political changes envisaged indicate a spiritual contagion. This is why the *autogestionnaire* society in France will transform the EEC and then the Third World, just as it will initially transform the regions and their culture in France. On the one hand, therefore, *autogestion* will mean a world where '*chacun pourra prendre en mains son épanouissement personnel*' (58). On the other hand, it will transform whole communities as it floods through existing structures, such as the EEC, creating, as it does so, a community '*pour que l'Europe existe enfin*' (68), and will ultimately '*déplacer en faveur du socialisme les grands équilibres mondiaux actuels*' (76). In the local, the European and the world context, brief examples are given of this process to lend a rationality to the argument. In the local case, the example is a *proposition de loi* giving Corsica a particular status (51). The European example is the emergence of the new forms of syndicalist struggle in Germany and Spain (67). The global examples are the signing of collective agreements and a co-ordinated resistance to the multi-nationals (75). These several practical examples serve two functions. Firstly, they are practical evidence that an *autogestion-naire* perspective corresponds to, even inspires, new political relations. Secondly, they reassure the reader: in spite of the evocation of contagion and transformation, society will remain substantially the same. This juxtaposition of sameness and transformation is presented to the reader through the extensive description of the Plan which takes up the next five sub-sections of this part.

Just before describing the Plan, the text ridicules alternative (economistic) Leftist approaches to managing the economy ('*capitalisme plus 20 pour cent*' (81)) and in so doing claims, as part of its wider vision, an economic soundness and authority, thus masking utopianism with an authoritative and scientifically informed tone. In this way it offers its own exposition as being of a qualitatively different order from other expositions, thereby making it not only scientific and practical but transcendental also. As well as ridicule, a warning is given against alternative (impractical) approaches by citing Chile as an example of a Leftist economic disaster, however morally justified its intentions. In a clearly anti-Marxian reference, the text refers to other Leftist economic interpretations as proceeding from '*une idée du XIXe siècle*' (81).

The utopianism of this section is further heightened by the use of the term 'Plan' in a general and evocative manner. Derived from an earlier and respected Socialist discourse, in which *planification* had been placed in opposition to both the economic liberalism and protectionism of the Third Republic, the notion of planning (elaborated by the National Resistance Council from ideas which had gradually gained acceptance in the SFIO in the late 1930s) was associated with the virtues of harnessing resources and eliminating injustice through the regulation of production and distribution. The planning policies of Jean Monnet (and later, of Mendès-France) had been represented, in this discourse, as Socialist in intention, although the subsequent indicative plans under the Fifth Republic were said to have been drained of content. The term 'Plan' in the Rocard motion picks up these earlier connotations while serving as a prefiguration of future society, the promise of which, in the form of discrete motivated struggles (*les forces vives*) and (implicitly) repressed political formulations of them (Rocard as party leader or President of the Republic), already exists.

The Plan as advocated in the motion interprets a comprehensive and complex social contract which would encompass vast areas of social, political and economic life, even though a market economy would still exist (though not prevail): reduction of income differentials, national investment, research (88) *syndicat* activity (90); the socialisation of power (in production) and innovation (in industry and society) (92). The Plan is the organisational image of true democracy and therefore is (in the text) or will be (in the envisaged society) the *proof* of Socialism. The Plan, one aspect of Socialist doctrine, is therefore elevated here to a total social form which will reflect the shape, texture and depth of an as yet unrealised democratic society.

The continuing existence of a form of the market economy is an indication of the free nature of the contract. The market is no longer to be feared: it is itself presented as an ideal one, contained and regulated by free agents engaged in '*une profonde délibération collective*' (96). The text, without referring to imperative planning, portrays the Plan as indicative in form yet imperative in effect – a kind of new facilitative Plan. It is able to do this because it draws upon the myth that there is a deep-seated and repressed desire within the community for the attainment of happiness through contract rather than conflict. It thus articulates the Rousseauist notion of the General Will, and thereby avoids other issues in democratic theory such as the status of dissent, the rights of minorities and the appropriateness of forms of representation. The Plan, therefore, has the same function in the Rocardian motion C in 1979 as the *carrefours* had in the 1974 *Assises*: the symbolic representation of an ideal society.

Therefore, although the idea of '*rupture*' is maintained in the text it does not actually signify the coming to power of the proletariat or its representatives. Because of the implicit allegiance to the political practices of the Fifth Republic and the explicit elucidation of the Plan, the idea of community displaces that of class. The *autogestionnaire* society dissolves the proletariat, incorporating it into community.

The third part, '*Construire le socialisme autogestionnaire*', is a short section and outlines the bases of a strategy designed to implement the ideas outlined in the previous part. Immediate reference to the '*principaux affrontements*' (109) creates a sense of urgency and relevance while reinforcing the claim that an *autogestionnaire* society would resolve the contradictions which give rise to these. It is interesting that the text identifies these clashes as essentially those of the workplace ('*entreprises*'), itself the main arena of *autogestionnaire* politics. And '*colère*', '*situations explosives*' (109) and '*batailles*' (111) illustrate the chaos of the present.

These references to workplace violence and strife and other struggles (such as those for employment, better working conditions and a greater sensitivity to ecological questions, for example (111)), even though they refer to the deficiencies of the Giscardian regime or of capitalism in general, underline a parallel reality that at present lies beyond the actual activity of the political party. The text calls upon the party to analyse these many struggles (113) (stating that the parties have been forced into supporting them rather than doing so willingly (111)). This call not only implies that the PS has not done all it can on these issues, but also associates it with the deficiencies of all political parties by not singling it out from them.

Given this qualified attitude to the role of the party, it is here that the motion further elaborates upon the two distinct meanings signified by the Union of the Left. Using its deeper meaning, the text transforms the terms of this union into '*L'Union des forces populaires*' (120); the unification of concerted party activity with that of other groups involved in struggle. Two of the groups referred to here are women (113) and the peasants (114–116), the latter reference being a covert criticism of the fundamentally urban elitism of organised Socialism. Let us look in more detail at the case of women as illustrated in the text in order to see its function.

The feminist movement and the social and cultural oppression of women is referred to on innumerable occasions in the text. In the previous part alone, there are five substantial references. This preoccupation has a multiple significance and is an indication of the way the motion as a whole works. Firstly, the perpetual use of women as an example indicates the motion's utilisation of a now self-evident truth in Leftist discourse: that women are equal in potential and should be equal in rights, opportunities and duties to men. In this way, agreement on this issue enables the text to bring forward other ideas which might be less acceptable. Secondly, the question of women's status is now a normative one in the Left, alongside other issues like racism and capital punishment. It acts, therefore, as a constraint upon disagreement with the text. Thirdly, it indicates not only a major issue in French political life but a deficiency within the party, as the predominance of men in all areas of party life was incontestable. Fourthly, the women's movement does not fit easily into classical interpretations of social and class struggle and therefore explicitly points to deficiencies in Socialist doctrine and the need for theoretical re-examination and revision. It therefore reinforces the idea of community more than it does that of class because women are not class-specific. Fifthly, the organised women's movement is a good example of the kind of extra-party organisation with which Rocardism advocates alliance. Finally, the capture of the female vote in party political terms would constitute the kind of support enjoyed in the 1960s by de Gaulle and the Gaullists who were supported by a substantial section of the female electorate. As the motion points out, women make up 52 per cent of the population (161) – an overall majority. The references to women throughout the text, therefore, reinforce the normative, theoretical, organisational, strategic and tactical points that the motion wishes to convey. Women indeed signify a potential political reality able to '*transformer les règles du jeu politique et social*' (29).

These extra-party processes are seen as indispensable, yet neglected. In this way, this part of the text significantly shifts the (present) party's place in the topography of the overall struggle from its imagined central place to the periphery and makes the periphery (localised conflicts, extra-party groupings) the true centre. Those represented by the motion are, by implication, already on the borderline between the two (and were in fact being forced into opposition inside the party) and can therefore depict themselves as the point at which the *forces vives* will gather. Thus, the Union of Popular Forces subverts both the 'class front' thesis (elaborated by the party in the 1970s) (118) and the Union of the Left (127). The Union of the Left as constituted is, the text argues, only active at the municipal level (129). The PCF itself should be confronted and – if necessary, the implication runs – ignored. In this way the gathering/migration myth is recovered. Allegiance to the party in the past, moreover, is reaffirmed at this crucial moment of near-heretical doctrinal claims: '*Nous réaffirmons solennellement l'engagement d'Epinay*' (122). In the context of the ideas expressed, such an undertaking vindicates the motion's orthodoxy while suggesting others' deviation from the principles of the founding congress. With this combination of clairvoyance, boldness, a claim to orthodoxy and unashamedness (which, by implication, it denies the adversary), the text posits *autogestion* as the party's real mission and affirms the need to leave the citadel in order to accomplish it:

Cela suppose que nous engagions le débat avec le Parti Communiste, ses militants, son électorat, à tous les niveaux. Il ne s'agit pas d'entamer un dialogue idéologique qui stériliserait l'action commune, il s'agit de le questionner sur des points essentiels qui touchent à la nature même de notre projet: autogestion, analyse de la crise, stratégie internationale et nature des pays de l'Est. (125)

Therefore, both in terms of the overall Left union and in terms of a united party, the Union of Popular Forces is justified because, although it surpasses other forms of union, it also claims to be unafraid of engaging with them. The new union must be nurtured: '*Il faut la rassembler et l'élargir*' (120). Here the *Projet Socialiste* is referred to and a call made for its proper discussion to become the occasion for '*une vaste confrontation publique*' (121). Here too the author(s) cast doubt upon the value of the *Projet Socialiste* and claim the quality of fearless honesty needed for the formulation of a new *projet*. The last paragraph of this section calls for a resumption in the movement arrested by the breakdown of the Common Programme in September 1977 (130) and virtually attacks the present leadership of the *Parti socialiste* for its inactivity. This virtual attack opens the way to the fourth and last part of the motion which is a direct attack upon the party as it is at present led. We can see, therefore, that strategy is treated transcendentally – the strategy is the triggering of a rally – and that the description of a utopian society is treated prosaically (the Plan). In this way, transcendentalism is disguised as realism and vice versa.

With the exception of references to guilt and blame, the ideas underpinning the motion so far are very similar in content and intention to those contained in the *projet de société* written for the 1974 *Assises*. This fourth part of the motion, '*Un parti pour aujourd'hui*', transforms these fundamentally millenarian ideas by adding to them a concerted display of criticism and recrimination. In this sense, the motion finds its true expression as the attempt to impose upon the party a set of values and orientations on the basis of a thwarted millenarianism. This is done by arguing that the party is not effective because it is based upon the wrong principles and has deviated from the fundamental democratic inspiration that is an intrinsic part of Socialism.

In order to do this, the text must reverse initially the implicit and explicit denigration of the party so far exhibited in the text and displace criticism directly onto the leadership. The party has '*de grandes et légitimes ambitions'* (132); *'il prétend aussi modifier les formes mêmes du pouvoir'* (132). The text also refers to *'Un grand parti comme le PS'* (166). Having re-established the party's greatness or potential, the text can then elaborate upon the notion that it has defaulted in its task and has done so because of the corrupting effects of absolute power within it.

The simple conclusion from this is that internal democratisation of the party will remedy the party's shortcomings and misfortunes. Indeed, this is put forward as the essential, in fact the only, prerequisite for success. Just as the party is being portrayed as exhibiting many of the oppressive characteristics of the Fifth Republican State, so the same kind of solution (democracy) is offered for both State and party.

The democratisation of the party as logical and unequivocal consequence of the preceding argument is reinforced in this part by several imperative linking expressions which concern the changes proposed: *'doit'*, *'il faut que'*, *'il faut'*, *'doit être'*, *'doivent être'*.[24] The steps to such democratisation, moreover, are all straightforward and all refer to a prior distortion of democratic structures and practices and the abuse of power conferred. The demands and criticisms come in such rapid succession that they constitute a list which can be represented thus:

1. Need for *ouverture* (131).
2. Need for collegial leadership (133).
3. Need to abolish leadership of an arbitrary presidentialist type (133).
4. Need to upgrade (*revaloriser*) the role of the *Comité directeur* (135).
5. Need to downgrade or reorganise the system of *délégués spécialisés* and *rapporteurs nationaux* appointed by the First Secretary (136).
6. Need to give more publicity to work and study groups (137).
7. Need for collective elaboration of propositions and decisions (138).
8. Need to decentralise the party structure and institute regional committees and co-ordination to aid research and action (148).
9. Need for better recruiting arrangements (151).
10. Need for better links with workers, the young and women (154–159).
11. Need to expand scope for activists (163–165).

12. Need to check and scrutinise party finances (166).
13. Need to put a stop to the accumulation of offices (the practice of one person holding several elected positions at once) (167).

Significantly, these criticisms and demands rest upon normative themes which are widely subscribed to within the Left. Concerning (2) and (3), the First Secretary is criticised for not expressing the party's views and for forcing it to express his own (133). The *rapporteurs nationaux* are criticised because they, being responsible only to the First Secretary, do not express the party's views. Party openness and debate are demanded in the name of previously agreed party decisions: '*Le règlement intérieur a prévu à cet effet des dispositions précises qui doivent être appliquées*' (145). And regional decentralisation has already been called for by '*les articles 22 et 23 votés en 1974*' (148).

All of these demands, therefore, are made on the basis of a quasi-ethical assumption that trust has been betrayed. The demand for openness in financial accounting is a particularly good example of this. By making apparently practical demands about organisation, the text refers to a moral sense which rejects the corrupting influences of power and politics and the restriction of moral values and faith. The party apparatus, therefore, is being accused, in both organisational and doctrinal/ethical terms, of denying the principles which call a Socialist party into existence.

In bolder type at the end of the motion there is the 450-word Conclusion which we considered at the beginning of this analysis and which, as we have seen, reasserts the modesty of the undertaking of a congress motion.

Motion C at the 1979 Metz Congress is in many respects a recapitulation of the millenarianism which characterises the texts and speeches of the 1974 *Assises*. Firstly, there is an appeal to doctrinal re-evaluation as the prelude to the creation of a popular rally which itself will create an ideal society. Secondly, in both cases, re-evaluation (commitment to personalism) has already taken place, but this is hidden by appeals to egalitarian and millenarian myths which will accommodate to this. Thirdly, both texts point, by definition, to a future society. The 1979 text, doctrinally legitimated by the 1974 text and speeches, is able to develop the implication that the path to the future has been glimpsed (1974) but lost (1978). And in the last part of the 1979 motion some of the causes are suggested: irregular money management, the concentration of power, the denial of free expression, and the devious and deliberate creation of personal rivalries. In this way a new 1974 (now with the statutory power of the 1971 change) is called for in 1979 in order that the victory denied in 1978 be at last won.

Two dominant themes in the 1979 motion – the proposed ideal society and the removal of impediments to its attainment – are implied as being causative of one another, the second being the cause of the first. The nature of connection between the two is never argued but is replaced by the myth of a mysterious migration. Although the 1979 text, like the *Assises*, does not explicitly advocate allegiance to a leader, it develops the myths of the *Assises* which make this possible and consequential.

In terms of the ideal society proposed, moreover, it is interesting to note that the link between it and the means of realising it cannot be discovered, only accepted or rejected. It forms a totality and consequently informs a way of interpreting reality. *Autogestion*, perpetually used, contributes to this process of interpretation, as well as to the imagined destination of the migration. As a noun, '*autogestion*' forms part of the totality envisaged. '*Autogestionnaire*', as an adjective or as part of an adverbial phrase, informs the mode of interpretation of that totality and the method, or route, whereby it is reached.

In the 1979 motion, the party is often conflated with the idea of present society. This means that a desire to be liberated from the one is synonymous with a desire to be liberated from the other. The 1979 motion shares with the *Assises* the assumption that a rally is needed to move away from the past and existing institutional ties towards the future and victory.

We can see that motion C at the Metz Congress of 1979 is able to maintain a certain orthodoxy because it is consistent with an accepted text and mythical moment, that of the *Assises* of 1974. The *Assises*, however, as we have seen, are the symbolic representation of a certain form of socialist community which actually runs counter to existing party practice (both in 1974 and in 1979). This enables motion C to be subversive of leadership and to develop explicit criticism of leadership because the great promise made at the *Assises* had not been fulfilled. Just as egalitarian and millenarian myths were necessary to a Socialist party accommodating itself to personalism in 1974, so they were used in the same manner by a different potential leader, Rocard, in 1979. Motion C's attitude to Mitterrand's leadership is not of itself critical of personalism (only of a

monarchical style), because it uses the style of the 1974 *Assises*, itself
a Left rally discourse adapted to personalism.

The dominant feature of Socialist discourse under earlier republics
had not been its justifications of the exercise of power – these had
always been weak and conditional – but its refusals of power within
untransformed institutions. What our analysis of the *Assises* and the
Rocardian text demonstrates is that the drive for personal power,
rather than for government in a bourgeois republic, was acceptable
to the broad mass of the rank and file, to the *courants* within the
party and to its leaders, with the result that old millenarian and
romantic themes had now acquired a new resonance. The *Assises*
reveal that the accentuation of romanticism in Socialist discourse was
linked to personalist allegiance. The Rocard motion shows that, even
when internal conflict develops, opposition to leadership is still
expressed in these terms. In other words, the essential references of
Socialist discourse and their implications for and within party
organisation were transformed in the space of a decade. We shall
return to these points in the conclusion. Let us first examine what
happens to Socialist discourse after victory has been won.

7 Organisation and Modernisation: The Socialists

Mitterrand's public decision to seek the PS's nomination as the party's candidate in the 1981 presidential elections ended all internal party criticism, and directed party attention and effort to the presidential and the legislative election campaign. The reassertion of unquestioning allegiance to Mitterrand was maintained and amplified by his success in the elections but, as we shall see in the present chapter, the relationship between the new President and his party became qualitatively different. Let us now examine the manner in which changes in the relationship informed French Socialism after the PS took power in 1981.

For French Socialists, François Mitterrand's victory in the 1981 presidential elections, and the party's astounding success in the ensuing legislative elections constituted a moment of historic arrival. After the early years of aimless manoeuvring in the young Fifth Republic, the rise of the Socialist Party in the 1970s offered a national image of a party destined for power. The confusion and pessimism of the 1977–81 period, after the collapse of the Socialist–Communist alliance, seriously threatened the party's self-confidence and sense of direction. And, as we have seen, the Rocard phenomenon and its notion of the promise of renewal was one of the results of this. But the 'historic' presidential and legislative victories of 1981 revived all the optimism and expectations of a party which had committed itself totally to a particular course. What was that course? What were the strategy, the policy, the aim, the effort of the party directed towards from 1971 onwards? Like Churchill's, they were one: victory. Hence the sense, in 1981, of arrival.

For French Socialists, and for the French generally, who had voted for them in their millions in that year, 1981 was also a moment of departure. The last years of the Giscard d'Estaing presidency had been marked by political scandals, acrimony within the governing majority, and a worsening economic situation. And French Socialism had offered much more than a different President and a new government. Its official discourse and that of its leaders abounded in

176

promises of a new, harmonious, and plentiful society, at last liberated from the constraints of the Giscardian years. The deluge of reforms which accompanied the taking of power were a response to, and were part of, the momentum of that *expectation*. But the price paid by the new party of government is not only to be measured in terms of a growing lack of popularity due to the government's failure to control inflation and eradicate unemployment, but in terms of the degree of *disillusionment*, given the expectation created by the Socialists' victory, a victory and an expectation which were themselves created in part by the hope and promise of significant changes at all levels of society and government.

This is the context, if not one of the causes, of the change of premier (July 1984) and the new government headed by Laurent Fabius. The previous administration, that of Pierre Mauroy, had committed itself to an interventionist approach to the new technologies in terms of investment and contractual arrangements (which were facilitated by the nationalisations of 1982). It was the Fabius administration, however, which became the symbol of this Socialist commitment, in terms of both its policies and its official self-presentation of commitment to the 'modernisation' of France above all other things. (I shall return to the significance of the inverted commas.) A cynical view would be that such a total commitment to and public involvement in technological change was an essentially public relations response to the perceived failures of the first years of the Socialists in government. There may be some, though, as I shall demonstrate, little, truth in this view. The public involvement of the Fabius administration in modernising France between 1984 and 1986 had such a high profile that all other policy issues, outside foreign policy and defence, were dwarfed in comparison. The involvement was such that, by contrast, the liberal, technocratic years of the Giscard presidency seemed old-fashioned, in spite of the fact that Giscard's image had been built originally around just such a commitment to a streamlining, modernist political undertaking. As a political strategy for victory or success, there is no evidence to indicate that a commitment to 'modernisation' would be a successful one. The fruits, if there were any, of government investment would not be borne until after the elections of March 1986, and in previous regimes commitment to 'modernisation' had never been a recipe for unequivocal political success.

The question therefore arises: Why this total commitment to 'modernisation'? Our analysis will reveal that the search for an answer to that question is both complex and revealing of the nature of Socialism's adaptation to the Fifth Republic. For it is not true that 'modernisation' as a governmental effort was the only course open to the Socialists in power. Nor is it usual for such a commitment to be so total and all-consuming. Why was 'conservationism' not developed into a national programme? Or 'decentralisation'? Or 'industrial renovation'? Or a neo-Keynesian social project for the productive redistribution of power and wealth? All of these have a significant mobilising capacity within the party and, potentially, in the country at large, and furthermore could be elaborated into a national effort, or *projet de société* which would touch all levels of society. 'Modernisation', moreover, not only took on a startling centrality in both governmental and party discourse, it captured the attention and the approval of all strands within the party, from 'social-democrats' across to the CERES group.

We have raised several questions: Why was 'modernisation' discursively mobilised in Socialist discourse? Why did it become so central? Why did it meet with so little criticism? Is its significance to be understood in terms of the government/country relation, or in terms of the government/party relation, or in terms of intra-party factionalism? How did 'modernisation' lead to the relative eclipse of other issues in French Socialism? Why did it not lead to upheaval inside the party? There is, of course, another question which is all too seldom asked: What exactly is modernisation? We can answer these questions and elucidate the significance of 'modernisation' as a central theme in 1980s French Socialism if we answer just one question: What was it in political discourse and its relationship to political practice that allowed this phenomenon, the centrality of 'modernisation', to occur? The answer will demonstrate that there is a very real – though not necessarily consciously elaborated – rationale to this development, which has to do with the nature of Socialist discourse in the 1980s and its relation to Socialist doctrine or ideology as it has developed in the period of the Fifth Republic.

We shall answer this question by examining a contemporary corpus of Socialist discourse on 'modernisation'. First we must state briefly the doctrinally-related strategy options of Fifth Republican Socialism, in order to see how these form the conditions of and inform the doctrinally-related governmental choices in the post-1981 period. In the pre-1981 Fifth Republican mainstream Socialism we can identify four essential core strategies which overlap one another, both in content and in time. For the purposes of exposition, however, we can describe them sequentially. Their respective rises to prominence within the party did, in fact, follow one another more or less chronologically, although this was due more to the holders of power and influence within the party at a given moment than to any one strategy logically implying another and calling it into being.

The first core strategy was Guy Mollet's and the SFIO's – not unquestioned – commitment to de Gaulle's new Republic, which would involve the party in the party-of-government role it had enjoyed (or suffered) during the Fourth Republic, but which attempted to treat the Fifth Republic as essentially parliamentary rather than presidential. Significantly, perhaps, at the level of discourse and rhetoric, the Marxist orientation remained as the intended point of reconciliation between the tendencies within the party, and as the point of contact between the party and its apparent constituency and the ever-potential constituency of traditional Communist voters.

The second strategy involved bringing the party far closer to the developing normative practices (bipolarisation, presidentialism) of the regime, and a concomitant attempt to 'modernise' or rejuvenate the party. Defferre's extra-party support, his attempt to gain the party's 1965 presidential nomination, and the developing significance of the political clubs, were the most prominent examples of this strategy. Whether by design or not, these developments seriously questioned many of the traditional tenets of Mollet's Socialism, not least its anti-presidential emphasis and its stress upon a Leftist/ Marxian discourse.

The third core strategy, which had been followed in different forms and to differing degrees from the beginning of the Fifth Republic, was that which culminated in the Union of the Left with the French Communist Party and the Common Programme, launched in 1972. One of the most enduring effects of this strategy was the anchoring of Socialist discourse (for reasons of political constituency, party cohesion and political credibility – given alliance with the Communists) well to the Left within the tradition of French Socialism. The alliance, however – and Mitterrand's leadership, which I shall come to in a moment – offered the serious possibility of electoral victory for the Left for the first time since 1958. As we have seen in the previous chapter, the cultivation of this potential increased dramatically the triumphalist, transcendental strain within Socialist discourse, albeit, because of the alliance and the balance of forces within the party, well within the referential parameters of French Socialism.

But something else, far more subtle and irreversible, was also happening. It drew, for all appearances, upon previous core strategies, the options of modern French Socialism. It would, however, as we have seen in the preceding chapter, have enduring effects which would alter party discourse, strategy, strategy options, even the doctrinal reference points of Socialism itself. It was the commitment of the party, after 1971, to a presidential endeavour within the context of the alliance. It was – and still is – argued as being the necessary tactical effect of a deeper, fundamentally Socialist, strategy. But it was always far more than that, and its effects have been multiple. As we have seen in the previous chapter, it did not involve the draining away from Socialist doctrine of its principles of egalitarianism, nor did it involve the unequivocal hero-worship characteristic of Rightist political parties. Socialism was too deep-rooted in French political culture for either of these things to happen. It is unlikely that the party would have survived such a switch, and the party's members, intellectuals and second-rank leaders, too aware of both the organisational and ethical imperatives which underpinned the party, would have combatted such 'adventurism'. And the Union with the Communists would have been impossible.

It is still the case, however, that Mitterrand was given near-unconditional support, and the fate of the party put to a large extent in his hands. He became not only the sole truly valid spokesperson of the party, but also the personification of it. The idea of Socialism-as-victory in the Fifth Republic was embodied in his political persona. The central strategic organising principle of the party in the 1970s was not how it was to cope with the Union of the Left, but how it could accommodate, doctrinally and discursively, to Mitterrand's unquestioned and exalted leadership. The two were, of course, linked, and linked by Mitterrand himself. There is, moreover, a constant slide in meaning in Socialist discourse in the expression '*la ligne d'Epinay*', between the principle of adherence to the Union of the Left and that of allegiance to Mitterrand. And union was always presented, after 1971, as 'his' strategy. The two allegiances – to him and to union – were linked but were not mutually dependent, even though they often were portrayed as being so. The taboo placed upon attacking the party leader, and the considerable constraints placed upon Michel Rocard in the context (1977–81) of a failed alliance strategy, are strong evidence of this. It was still the case that in the post-alliance period, after 1977, Mitterrand could lead the party with few constraints upon him and, in fact, rally support from past and potential critics in the face of Rocard's leadership challenge, in the name of party unity. François Mitterrand was able to do this, not simply because he embodied unity, but because he embodied the party itself.

The one constraint placed upon Mitterrand from 1971 onwards was a discursive one. His discourse and persona-in-discourse had to accommodate to a party that was accommodating to him, which itself in turn had to remain identifiably 'socialist' in order to mark itself off from Centrists and maintain the credibility of the Union of the Left. According to circumstances, he could claim greater freedom from party constraints (1974, 1981). These departures were seen as acceptable because of the exceptional circumstances of a presidential election. On condition that he did not openly repudiate party policy, these occasions in fact enhanced his status within the party.

There would have been, given the investment made by the party in Mitterrand as the bringer of victory, major discursive and ultimately, perhaps, doctrinal reorientations, and probably a change of leadership, if Mitterrand had not won the presidency in 1981. But he did win and, in the legislative elections (because of his victory), the PS won – and in fact without the Communists. The President's party was now the party of government. Here we come back to our initial point concerning disillusionment. It was not that the party had no policies, but these were, in the first place, severely constrained by – indeed to a great degree were merely a function of – presidentialism, and, in the second, were of far less significance as a mobilising force, both within the party and, after 1981, in the country at large, than the triumphalism and transcendentalism which had developed in party discourse, and which were themselves a function of the reconciliation of personalism with the continuing Leftism which had held the party on its troubled, though ultimately successful, course after 1971.

What, then, had facilitated the discursive reconciliation of these apparently mutually exclusive doctrines? We have already seen that personalism had not taken place through the emptying of party discourse of its doctrine. And Mitterrand was, and still is, seen as being in a line stemming from Jaurès through Blum. But a change did take place, and one which would accommodate to personalism, would lead to victory and, as we have argued, to disillusionment. There was, after 1971, a diminution of several strains and emphases within Socialist discourse and the heightening of another, a strain which could be intertwined with allegiance to a personal leader, a leader who was the bringer of Socialism as victory – in short, a leader who was a Socialist version of the visionary. The Marxian strain in Socialist discourse, the province of CERES, was seen to be too close to the Communist Party and too difficult to accommodate to the notion of inspired leadership. Socialist incrementalism was pitched too far to the Right within Socialist discourse. Even the social-democratic distinctions of Blum's Socialism, between the conquest and the exercise of power, were inappropriate in a party which needed to present itself as storming the gates of capitalism and 25 years of Rightist dominance. There is one other strain within Socialism which informs most aspects of Socialist doctrine, accords perfectly with the triumphalism of 1970s Socialism, which does not repudiate other, more explicit forms of Socialist discourse, has a legitimacy in the movement and, above all, accords with the personalisation of Socialism; that is to say, the millenarianism which we identified in the previous chapter.

The discourse of Socialism in the 1970s is imbued with millenarianism, and the visionary, the carrier of the unexplained promise contained within millenarianism, was François Mitterrand. The contradictions between Leftism and overt personal leadership are reconciled in millenarianism. Such a development within Socialist discourse, such single dominance within Socialist discourse's competing strains will have strong effects, not only upon strategy and upon internal party activity, as we have seen, but also upon the elaboration of policy. In fact, it implicitly undermines policy-making in the name of deliverance as an end in itself. It was this discourse which, in part, generated the rally of opinion around Mitterrand and the Socialists in 1981. The strategy was, after only a decade, successful. The problem with millenarian discourse is that in order to be, or to remain successful, the millenium should not arrive. And it did, in 1981.

As we stated earlier, victory was the essential policy and strategy of the party, and total allegiance to Mitterrand, and all that that entailed at the level of discursive accommodation, was the precondition of it. The focus upon victory-as-liberation was so strongly stressed – and this in a party which had not experienced political power in the Fifth Republic and would have to face the hostility of both capital and other vested interests – that generalised disillusionment was very likely to occur at the slightest mistake, let alone a series of them.

After the 1981 elections the party's symbolic relationship to the

President had to be maintained through its relation to his government and its policy. Its *raison d'être* and discursive orientation, and the continuity of its political purpose, was intimately linked with the activity, and fate, of the government. A party of victory whose discourse developed a transcendentalism and single practical focus over a decade will have considerable difficulty in a period such as that of 1981–4, when the government's early reforms and popularity were transformed into an embattled unpopularity. Moreover, the organisational cycles of a party which comprises several currents of opinion (and several potential and rival leaders) will ensure, indeed it is the hallmark of democratic integrity, that reorientation will in any event be slow. Given the fulfilled purpose of a ten-year strategy, the 'lead' and stimulus to reorientation had to come from government itself, rather than from within the party.

The first three years of the Socialist government (the Mauroy administrations) saw the party offering solidarity with a government whose popularity declined inexorably, while containing its own internal dissensions. Two imperatives, therefore, present themselves to a party locked into such constraining conditions. The first is the creation of a focus for party allegiance. This refocussing was facilitated by the nomination of the new Prime Minister, Laurent Fabius, in July 1984. The second was the need to find a doctrinal/ discursive focus which would offer to the party a sense of direction, self-confidence, cohesion and purpose. Given what I have said above, this had to involve a coincidence of party orientation and government policy initiatives. It had also, however, to replace or reinforce, complement or revive millenarianism. In other words, it had to fill the crucial discursive space created by Mitterrand's victory and the Mauroy government's unpopularity, a space brought into being in part by the necessary commitment to millenarianism itself.

In this situation, it is clear that the party would be responsive to a transcendental endeavour – in the form of a governmental policy – which for both party and government would take the form of a *projet de société*, and which would offer once again the promise of total social transformation, experienced as liberation by every citizen. Such a discursive reorientation had therefore to come *from* government *into* the party; be compatible with the discursive conditions of Socialism in the 1980s and the doctrinal reference points of Socialism generally; conflate policy and '*projet*'; leave enough potential for other leaders to appropriate it; and offer a universalist (governmental), rather than a more narrow (party), focus.

One immediately identifiable and measurable transformation, and one which could be experienced by every individual simultaneously, is the computer in every home and in every school classroom, which, ostensibly, would direct the lives of those individuals towards an egalitarian life of effortless and co-operative intercommunication: the technological revolution transformed through discourse into '*la révolution politique et sociale*'. A claim on the part of any other political party to be the carriers of technological innovation/ modernisation, and there were others, would, therefore, *increase* Socialism's adherence to the principle of this kind of change, making its task, in part, that of ensuring that *Socialism* and 'modernisation' remained the one social project which would avoid, say, an Orwellian form of social and political change. And to shift French society as one consenting social entity, in one move, or in a series of co-ordinated moves, towards the culturally and materially rich yet equal society of the computer age is to offer the new millenium.

Our analysis so far has offered certain explanations: the reason for and role of the discursive mobilisation of 'modernisation', the degree of its importance, the abandoned terrain it occupies within French Socialism, its contribution to transcendentalism, its necessary con- nection, not only to government, but perhaps more importantly to party. We now need, in order to complete our explanation, to demonstrate *how* it accords with French Socialism, a Socialism which, as I have indicated, is still doctrinally elaborate; how modernisation was legitimated and discursively deployed; how it was accepted, democratically, into party discourse; how its transcenden- talism meshes with the transcendental liberationism of Socialist discourse; and, finally, how it can coincide with the quintessentially moral imperatives of Socialist commitment. In order to do this, I have chosen a corpus of texts which refer to the National Conven- tion, called by the executive bureau of the party following the creation of the Fabius administration, and which took place on 15 and 16 December 1984 at Evry (Essonne).[1]

The *formal* legitimation of the text is brought about by its being the text proposed to and voted on by the National Convention. The Convention is the second most important organisational moment in party life after the Congress. The text voted upon at a Convention, however, is more important, from a doctrinal point of view, than a Congress motion, the latter being the function of the play of forces within the party, rather than a pure statement of doctrine. The democratic status of the text is underlined in a 400-word preface by

the First Secretary, Lionel Jospin: 2000 sections debated and replied
to a party questionnaire on modernisation; several sessions of a
national commission, designated by the executive bureau and
chaired by the First Secretary, analysed and integrated the questionnaire replies and prepared the text of the resolution to be debated
and voted upon; the resolution was passed unanimously by the
executive bureau on 15 November. The Convention theme, therefore, is formally legitimated, both by the important occasion of a
National Convention and by the party base/party leadership interac-
tion which preceded the text of this particular Convention. It is,
therefore, the true voice of the party. Moreover, two comments by
the First Secretary encourage the legitimation of the theme and
discussion of it. These comments open and close the preface. The
first refers to the government:

> *Débattre sur ce qui constitue l'un des thèmes centraux de l'action du
> gouvernement et débattre pour agir, tels sont les objectifs que nous
> nous sommes fixés pour cette Convention 'Modernisation et progrès
> social'.* (1)

The relevance of the theme is therefore presented as being beyond
discussion. The second refers to the party's agreement with the
government's view, offers the party some discursive space and a
discursive role by referring to the short-term risks of modernisation,
but reinforces the *fait accompli* nature of the Convention's theme:

> *si le caractère impératif de la modernisation est reconnu par
> l'ensemble des militants les risques à court terme en sont bien
> soulignés. A notre Parti de ... réussir la modernisation.* (8)

The same process occurs at the beginning and the end of the
preamble to the text proper. '*Modernisation*' is given prominence by
its being the first word in the text. (The last word of the text is
'*liberté*'.) A reference is then made to those who are afraid of being
its victims (9). The role for Socialism is therefore repeated, but the
unquestionable place of modernisation is again stressed at the end of
the preamble:

> *Parce que nous sommes socialistes nous voulons la modernisation.*
> (9)

Two points can be made here concerning these two examples,
examples which reappear many times in the text. Firstly, in the text,

'modernisation' is constantly linked to 'Socialism'. The need and right of Socialists to discuss modernisation are stressed throughout, the option of refusing its relevance thereby curtailed. 'Modernisation' is given a reality within the discourse (which is encouraged both by the formal legitimation of the Convention and by Jospin's preface). Secondly, neither in the preface nor anywhere in the text proper – and this is in direct contradiction to the perceived need for discussion – is 'modernisation' defined. Hence my use of quotation marks: 'modernisation' is a word, a key word, but a word nevertheless. At no point in the text is any indication given as to what 'modernisation' is. Whatever it is, however, it is desired. What, then, is the significance of this repeatedly stressed/never defined word, for we can infer that, in rhetorical terms, there is *some* reason why 'modernisation' is not defined? The clue to this puzzle is given in the title of the Convention and resolution: '*Modernisation et progrès social*'. The latter expression, 'social progress', is also difficult to define, but it has a long pedigree in Socialist discourse. Its inclusion in the title has the initial effect of acting as a counter-balance to 'modernisation', simply by its being alongside it in the title. Modernisation without social progress will be valueless. However, given the centrality of 'modernisation', the implicit message conveyed is 'modernisation equals social progress'. The rhetorical effect is, in fact, even greater than this. The self-evidence of the meaning of 'modernisation' is such, and its dominance in the text so great, that the ultimate rhetorical effect is not that modernisation is social progress, but that the real word for social progress is modernisation. A subtle but crucial rearranging of the ontology of Socialism.

It is in the context of the exclusion of a critique of 'modernisation' that the text constitutes not simply the reconciling of 'modernisation' with Socialism, but the *inscribing* of it into Socialist discourse as a promise, as an end to be attained, as well as the method of its attainment.

This is the connotative context which will inform the three main sections of the text, sections which are classical sub-themes of the Left's discourse: (a) that the theme (here, modernisation) will be/can only be brought into being by the authors of the text: '*La modernisation est portée par les socialistes*'; (b) the theme will bring into being that which is the *raison d'être* of the authors of the discourse: '*Moderniser pour le progrès social*'; (c) the theme will reinforce democracy and will be attained through it: '*La modernisation par et pour la démocratie*'. The formal presentation of the theme will, therefore, further enhance its status as a fundamental tenet of Socialism.

The 2000-word introduction which precedes the three sections is also traditional in texts of this kind. Its *content* is also traditional. Almost. It talks of '*la crise*' (which is referred to by name nine times here), stresses the degree of the crisis, gives dates and figures. This is traditional, as we have seen from the previous chapter. However, two related shifts in traditional emphasis occur which respond to the two exigencies mentioned above: the exclusive choice of 'modernisation' as solution, and the governmental source of its inspiration. The first exigency is dealt with by the interpreting of the crisis as being one which is generated essentially by outdated international mechanisms of economic regulation (rather than by, say, the move towards monopoly capitalism). The second is dealt with by making the Socialist endeavour appear as a national one (and here, as in Section 1, the text draws upon the ever-potential nationalism in Socialist discourse, which in this text is expressed as a Eurocentric internationalism).

The development of the new technologies is causally separated from the crisis itself:

> *il ne faut pas confondre cette crise avec la mutation technologique.* (13)

and is seen as constituting not a choice in itself, but a choice of how 'modernisation' is to be harnessed and applied:

> *Les nouvelles technologies conduiront-elles demain à la déqualification accrue . . . , ou permettront-elles . . . à chacun l'accès à plus de créativité: les socialistes pensent que c'est un des enjeux du débat sur la modernisation.* (15)

The Eurocentric response is then evoked by exclusive concentration upon the United States and its economic strategy and hegemony as the source of France's suffering. And chauvinism takes the form of a challenge which, one assumes, will create a combative response:

> *Auteur exclusif de la première révolution industrielle, auteur principal de la seconde, l'Europe est en train de manquer son entrée dans la troisième révolution.* (19)

The idea of an alternative mode of modernisation is then evoked by reference to the idea, widespread in French political mythology, of the betrayal of France, here of the national bourgeoisie's willingness (and that of their counterparts in Europe) to sell out, here, to America (21).

The counterpart voluntarism which these statements imply is encouraged over the next four paragraphs (the title of the sub-section is: '*Agir et non subir*'). The implication here is that 'modernisation' is not only a form of salvation and one which presupposes a voluntarism, but that failure to support it is itself a form of betrayal. At this point in the text, where the value of 'modernisation' has been established and the choosing of it presented as the only choice possible, its fragility as an undertaking is underlined. It is here that the claim is made that there are other, false, roads to take. Within France, there is another road. It is a question of choosing between them. The text, therefore, has made 'modernisation' the only choice for the Left, and now offers its only alternative, Rightist modernisation, which would entail using the new technologies simply to lower production costs (27). In this way, Leftist 'modernisation' is enhanced, allowing the text to praise it in the context of its Rightist alternative and not, here, as an end in itself (27). It will reduce inequality, offer education and culture to all (29), transform power relations (30), involve the participation of working people (31). In spite of this relative demystifying of modernisation by naming what it will do, it is still preserved as the only instrument of social change; it is accorded privileged status, and is legitimated further by its integration into a '*projet social*'. Within the text, however, as we have seen, and shall demonstrate in our analysis of the text's main sections, it is *de facto* the '*projet social*' itself.

In Section 1, Socialism, as the only fully moral and responsible agent of modernisation, is elaborated. This section takes the traditional format of emphasising what the Right's version of such an undertaking would involve. We should note here, however, that, rhetorically, and irrespective of the named deficiencies and deviations, the Right is, at the outset, excluded from offering a way forward, not so much because of such deficiencies and deviations, but because, hitherto in the text, modernisation is *itself* endowed with a quality which non-Socialists could not attain. The first sub-section of Section 1 is entitled '*La droite française ne peut plus moderniser*'. In the circumstances of the rhetoric of this text, it *could* not. This duality is carried through Section 1: the Right did modernise, but only the productive apparatus ('*appareil de production*') (34); and '*le chômage d'aujourd'hui est l'héritage de l'absence de modernisation d'hier*' (36). There are, then, two 'modernisations', one real, the other false. The dualism in this attack upon the Right (it modernises in a different way/it cannot modernise) is reconciled in the following sub-section, and the nationalism, touched upon earlier, renewed, by elaborating upon the duality of meaning which exists in the idea of falseness itself: 'false modernisation equals no modernisation; false modernisation equals modernisation as betrayal':

> *Aujourd'hui la droite ne peut plus moderniser. Elle ne peut qu'aller chercher à l'étranger un modèle qui n'est pas transposable à la France.* (42)

Criticisms are made one after another of US, UK and Japanese 'modernisations' (sub-sections 1.2.1, 1.2.2 and 1.2.3 (pp. 9–11)), and that it is these the Right wishes to 'transplant' (43) into France. The ten-paragraph rejection of these three alternative models is in effect an unusual application of a rhetorical technique often used in Socialist discourse, by which a choice is justified, not by an analysis of its implications, but by systematic dismissal of alternatives. Traditionally, Socialist discourse's emphasis upon Socialism itself is made, as we have seen in the preceding chapter, by references to and rejections of other forms: Soviet, social-democratic, labourist. Here, the same process of naming and rejection is effected, but here 'modernisation' replaces Socialism, and US, UK and Japanese modernisations replace alternative Socialisms. And, significantly, it is here – because the question *could* pose itself at this point: Is modernisation itself not nefarious if the above three examples are so awful? – that the other Leftist alternative in France, the French Communist Party, is cursorily rejected. The Communist Party, the ally of five years in opposition and three years in government, has to be excluded from the text, or dealt with in this cursory manner as an irrelevance (59–61). The effect of this is to imply that the Socialist discourse elaborated in this *text* reflects a *new* Socialism. And it is not without significance that the rejection of French Communism (and with it those within the party who are cautious of the new direction) is made on patriotic grounds which also reinforces the 'governmental' emphasis of the discourse:

> *Ce refus d'accepter dans ses termes réels le processus de la modernisation est incohérent. Il conduirait immanquablement à un recul de la France sur la scène internationale et une baisse du niveau de vie.* (61)

The national effort implied above and elsewhere in the text as we have seen, serves to displace party identity towards identification with the government. This also facilitates the transition from such identification to identification with the State itself. This sub-theme will be elaborated even more in Section 3 of the resolution. The idea of the State has a long lineage in French Leftism. It is, of course, Jacobin in origin and needs little justification in Socialist discourse (particularly as the image of Giscardianism and neo-Gaullism is that of dismantling the State in favour of 'pluralism' or neo-liberalism), and can be presented as the necessary territory from which to effect change (nationalisations, for example) in an economy that is, in spite of political power, in the hands of the adversary. Another strain within Socialist discourse, however, and one which influenced the millenarianism of the 1970s, as we saw in the preceding chapter, also needs to be discursively appropriated, appeased or neutralised. The following sub-section, 1.4: '*Conduite par les socialistes, la modernisa-tion constitue une chance pour la France*', therefore, must begin the discursive reconciliation/conflation of the Jacobin and anti-Jacobin tendencies in French Socialism. This it does here by presenting decentralisation and modernisation as part of the same process (62–63 and 71). This preliminary conflation, elaborated in Section 3 in the form of modernisation of the State apparatus as release mechanism for the blossoming of a decentralised interactive society, allows this first section to end on the idea that 'modernisa-tion' is not only synonymous with social progress but with Socialism itself. It is modernisation which will bring the new society, and the whole of society which will be modernised. The closing lines of the first section are:

> *C'est donc bien une modernisation de l'ensemble de la société qu'il s'agit d'entreprendre, elle ne saurait se limiter à l'appareil de production.* (83)

The discursive register of Section 2 changes markedly from that of Sec-tion 1. Much of the transcendentalism, epigrams and '*petites phrases*' disappears, and the text addresses itself to Socialism's *actual* constituency: trade unions, social-democrats, incrementalist local politics. The first step back from the notion of 'modernisation equals Socialism', which the Introduction and Section 1 created, is apparent in the title of the section: '*Moderniser pour le progrès social*'. Here 'modernisation' *is* presented as a function, an instrument. And sub-section by sub-section, modernisation is justified rationally as a *means* to a higher social form. This section deals with modernisation as an aid to employment, as the proper way of responding to the problems of education (sub-section 2.1), of reducing working hours (and a lot is made here of co-operation with the trade unions) (sub-section 2.2), of responding to the problems of the exclusion of social groups in a period of social transition, of increasing social security (*'protection sociale'*) (sub-section 2.3.2), of increasing Socialist support in Socialism's traditional constituency: salaried workers, small and middle agricultural producers. It goes on to call for the continuation of the ideological struggle against the Right, the struggle for effective social integration which will include the unemployed, the young, immigrants and undefended workers (sub-section 2.4). The traditional political strategy, moreover, *'le front de classe'*, elaborated in the 1970s, is named three times in this section.

The section serves to remind Socialism's Fifth Republican constituency that, in a sense, nothing has changed. Significantly, Mitterrand is mentioned twice in this section.

What, then, is the rhetorical status of 'modernisation' at the beginning of Section 3, the final section? Through the two previous sections, 'modernisation' has been presented in a transcendental (Section 1) and in a rational form (Section 2). In the first, social progress *is* modernisation, in the second modernisation will *bring* social progress. The two fundamental strains in Socialist discourse, the transcendental and the experiential have both been presented. And there is bathos in the movement from the one to the other. The second threatens, as it were, the millenarianism of the first – even the *'pour'* of *'Moderniser pour le progrès social'*, the title of Section 2, is a denial of the first section's implication that the two are one, indeed implies that modernisation is itself subordinate to social progress. The rationale of the text is this: the final section will rehabilitate 'modernisation' *as* Socialist society in the context of the social-democratic caution, and the former will be reintroduced as the result of the latter: the promise of 'modernisation' as Socialism becomes dependent upon the social-democratic strategy, that is to say, the conquest of institutional power and the exercise of government. And it is here that the Jacobinism introduced at the end of Section 1 will be demonstrated as the political precondition of the non- or anti-Jacobinism in Socialist thought. Thus the two will be reconciled and depicted as interdependent preconditions of Socialism.

In Section 3, *'La modernisation par et pour la démocratie'*, the focus of the reconciliation of the millenarian and the experiential is the State. This emphasis not only strengthens the position of the Socialist government as the site or instrument of the Socialist effort, it puts a brake upon the potential rhetorical enhancement of other forms of Socialist action that millenarianism encourages (the ultra-Left republicanism of Third Republicanism, for example, or anarcho-syndicalism. It is significant that all references to the trade unions in Sections 2 and 3 depict them and their vision as restricted to the protection of the workforce in the period of transition, or else to the facilitating of the mechanisms of Socialist government. No reference is made to the very strong element of transcendentalism in French syndicalism itself).

Control of the State apparatus ('*Etat*' and '*Administration*') is the key to social transformation. The word '*Etat*' is mentioned 12 times in the first sub-section: '*Affirmer l'Etat et rénover l'administration*'. All major social advances since the war and in the Fifth Republic are seen as having been dependent upon State intervention (124). What remains to be done is to modernise the State itself (126), and the rest of the sub-section re-emphasises this notion of modernising the administration in order to create the necessary conditions of transformation. This emphasis has two other functions, apart from that of legitimating Socialist strategy as governmental support: it offers Socialism a further task within the institutional parameters of the Fifth Republic; and it explains why the State has hitherto not brought the transformations which Socialism now claims it can bring. Allegiance to the Jacobin (and Gaullist) idea of a strong State is thereby seen as the unequivocal, though complex, and therefore not to be compromised, strategy for Socialism. The exclusive nature of this form of Socialism as the only form is underlined by reference to its being the expression of the '*projet socialiste*', a key term in 1970s Socialism, as we have seen, whose meaning shifts between '*projet*' as an elaborated, explicit, usually written strategy and text, and '*projet*' as a morally-based sense of direction. The '*projet socialiste*' is referred to once before in the text in a similar manner, where it is seen as the indispensable context into which technological change must be integrated and once later, where it is itself subordinated to the Plan.

It is at this point in the text (sub-section 3.2) that the next mechanism, which is rhetorically dependent upon the conquest of the State as the exclusive Socialist strategy, and which will reconcile discursively – by integrating politically – decentralisation and centralisation, is named: the Plan.

As we saw in detail in the preceding chapter, the Plan, as an ideal image, both of the means to and the depiction of Socialist society, is central to Fifth Republican Socialism – though it is not, as we also indicated, of Socialist origin. It serves as a compelling metaphor because it responds better than any other metaphor or image in French Socialism to both the transcendental (it depicts the working of an ideal society), and the experiential (it is a logical, efficient and just allocation and deployment of resources). Furthermore, and perhaps crucially in this text, discussion of the Plan is the means whereby the centripetal (*'Etat'*) (sub-section 3.1) and the centrifugal (decentralisation) (sub-sections 3.3 and 3.4) ideas of political organisation are further reconciled and between which it is textually situated. Momentarily, even *'modernisation'* (135) and the *'projet socialiste'* (136) are subordinated to it. The emphasis on the Plan is a recapitulation of one of the central themes of Socialist discourse in the pre-1981 period. As an image, it remains, however, rhetorically rich and evocative of social transformation because the Plan was not given a central role in the post-1981 government, and the text points this out (136). The Plan, therefore, maintains its quality of promise. The notion of the Plan (as yet unfulfilled) not only offers the image of that which will reconcile the competing drives (centripetal/centrifugal), it also offers an explanation of and solution to the problem, real enough after 1981 and ever-threatening in Socialist thought, of the inexorable distancing of government from people in the period of disenchantment which follows a Leftist victory. Sub-sections 3.3 and 3.4: *'Favoriser la démocratie dans l'entreprise'* and *'Développer une dynamique locale'*, extend the idea that the systematisation of the consultative process will complete, and in fact justify, the consolidation and reform of the State.

The following sub-section: *'Faciliter l'initiative culturelle'* is a traditional addendum in Socialist texts to discussion of the Plan. Discussion of the Plan, essentially economic, must always include consideration of 'culture', in order to emphasise its *'projet social'* origins and distinguish it from Rightist economic planning. And here, as in motion C at Metz, the claim is made that an authentic culture, or multiplicity of cultures – given the context of decentralisation – will arise from the consultative process and devolution of decision-making. The final sub-section of section 3: *'Aller vers de nouvelles solidarités'* is also traditional, and underlines the positive European consequences of France's social transformation. Given, however, that the central theme of the text is that of 'modernisation', the text is able to reintroduce in this sub-section the idea of threat from without, the threat named earlier, that of American hegemony (and we can see from this example and our earlier one that one of the ways in which French Socialism avoids the direct accusation of nationalism is by displacing the idea of threat from the national to the continental context). Here, the danger is presented as that of '*la chute lente vers la vassalisation*' (154).

The three main sections of the text, therefore, present an apparently logical series of choices, all of which both depend upon one another and exclude alternatives: (American-inspired) crisis; the Socialist response – modernisation; modernisation as end; modernisation as means; State reform; and reconciliation of competing drives within Socialism through a Plan for modernisation. Solidarity with this series of ideas is the only possible choice, the alternative being, as the text reminds, a return to the initial premise: American domination.

The Conclusion of the resolution is a 1000-word or so, barely disguised, party autocritique. The fact that the self-criticism is barely disguised is the clue that the Conclusion's real function lies elsewhere. The Conclusion refers to the post-1981 period – and it is significant here that the pronoun '*nous*' dominates the section but does not differentiate between a '*nous*'/government and a '*nous*'/ party. The guilt and future duties, therefore, are shared.

The Conclusion begins by affirming that on 10 May 1981, the Socialists inherited (the words used are '*ont trouvé*' (158), which apart from offering justification, imply that government is a political site where secrets are revealed. (Socialist) government is thereby posited as indispensable) '*une société française*' (158) in complete social, ideological, even moral disarray (158). The productive apparatus (*appareil de production*) was obsolete, and so the first task was to ensure the working of a machine in disrepair (159), while trying simultaneously to respond to some of the more striking inequalities: '*En un mot, il a fallu tenir les deux bouts de la chaîne*' (161). The responsibility for these failures is directed at the post-Gaullist Right (whether this refers to the 1969–81 period or the 1974–81 period is not clear). The Right is then accused of having attacked education ('*base pourtant de toute modernisation*' (164)), research, industry, employment, and of aggravating inequalities, while submitting to the '*grands intérêts privés*' (164). This relatively long series of accusations/self-justifications (167), not only underlines the Socialists' difficult inheritance, it *implies* the, however justified, insufficiencies of the 1981–4 period:

Aujourd'hui, malgré nombre d'insuffisances ... il est certain que bien des avancées ont été faites ... depuis 1981. (166)

The overall impression of this, irrespective of responsibility, is one of lack of fulfilment. When the text goes on to stress what has been achieved (28/38–29/1), the achievements too underline the sense of lack. And, significantly, the list begins with a question:

N'avons-nous pas réussi, tout de même, à ... (167)

Even the '*tout de même*' devalues the list, before it is given. The list comprises bettering the lot of the underprivileged, giving dignity back to the workers, industrial reforms of structure, decentralisation, restarting scientific research, slowing down inflation and the rise of unemployment, and contributing to the construction of Europe ('*la construction européenne*') and to the establishment of a new world economic order and to human rights. All of these issues are presented as partial achievements or else the foundations upon which real achievements can be established. The effort, therefore, is seen as a real but an incomplete one. The clue to the significance of all this lies in the emphasis, not so much upon the injustices, but upon the oldness, the inappropriateness, of previous administrations. If the previous period had been a modernising one, runs the logic of the argument, then the post-1981 period would have fulfilled the promise of social transformation. Social transformation has not taken place, it is only that the ground has been prepared. This is reinforced by the desultory appraisal of Socialist achievements: there is no mention of the historic abolition of the death penalty, the central integration of women's affairs into government policy, or the government's addressing of the question of legal/structural racial discrimination. The rhetorical effect of this is that both the pre- and the post-1981 periods are unfulfilled moments: the first was a period of neglect; the second one of preparation. The promise, therefore, is yet to be fulfilled:

il nous faut assurer solidement les bases de l'essor du pays en modernisant ses structures économiques comme son organisation sociale. (168)

The text continues in an even more self-critical tone, not in terms of wrong decisions taken, but, again, in terms of 'yes, but not enough': has the rhythm of reforms been properly co-ordinated? have

priorities been properly worked out? have enough efforts been made
to modernise the administration? (169), and so on. The self-criticism
here, like that above, underlines the incompleteness (and the
unquestioned imperative nature) of the policy/project, and again the
Right is blamed for the present 'difficult' climate it has stirred up,
now as always, when the Left is in power (171). The allusion here, an
allusion which connotes one of the strongest myths in French
Leftism, is that a modernising Socialist government will build upon a
collective enthusiasm and thus succeed where the Popular Front had
failed.

The divergent focuses of this Conclusion, part self-justifying, part
accusing, or self-accusing, are then brought together, and the
underlying role of the text made clear:

> *Légitimement fiers de l'oeuvre qui a été accomplie, nous sommes à*
> *la fois lucides devant nos insuffisances et décidés à continuer dans*
> *la voie de la modernisation et du progrès social.* (172)

Here, as we have seen before, modernisation and social progress are
brought together and presented as interdependent entities, rather
than the one the means of attaining the other. Furthermore, the
'*voie*' of modernisation and social progress is presented as the task
begun in 1981, and as the undisputed '*voie*' to follow. The '*nous*
sommes ... décidés à continuer' further links the party to a
governmental undertaking, making intra-party deviation from such a
'*voie*' difficult. Many other '*voies*', which would be represented
textually as themes, have also been closed off, in particular those
which would develop the portmanteau expressions of '*crise*' or
'*classe*' in a direction which would question, not only the post-1981
period, but Fifth Republican Socialism itself. The following sentence
further reinforces 'modernisation' as both the means and the aim of
Socialism, while implying that the real values and ideal have as yet
not been realised:

> *Obligés parfois de changer de rythme devant les difficultés du*
> *moment, nous n'avons pas pour autant abandonné nos valeurs ni*
> *notre idéal.* (172)

What, therefore, does '*idéal*' refer to here? In the context of the
foregoing, it refers to 'modernisation' itself.

The final paragraphs of the Conclusion list some of the failures of
capitalism on a global scale, and reaffirm the Socialist principles of

realism and idealism, and the quest for the realisation of progress, justice, fraternity and liberty (173–182).

Our analysis of the National Convention resolution of the PS, *'Modernisation et progrès social'*, indicates how a lacuna, which appeared in Socialist discourse after 1981, was filled, and that this was not simply a response to the disenchantment that most governments face after taking office. The cause and degree of the *'écart entre le discours et la réalité'*, as French politicians so often say, are to be found in the pre-1981 period. An established political party, with a long organisational and doctrinal tradition, found itself able to strike at power via the institutions and normative practices of the Fifth Republic. The prerequisite of this was its reorientation to allegiance to a personal leader, and the highlighting of his singular status. The highlighting of the millenarianism in Socialist discourse was the method whereby such reorientation could take place without placing intolerable strain upon that discourse and eventually upon organisation. In the post-1981 period, the concept of 'modernisation' had the effect of filling the lacuna occasioned by the experience of government. And the particular rhetorical treatment of 'modernisation' facilitated its integration into Socialist discourse to the point where it was able to offer itself as the new crusade. The difference between the two periods in the life of French Socialism is that in the 1971–81 period a discourse which was not originally personalist was orientated towards the leader via millenarianism. In the post-1981 period, 'modernisation' allowed for the renewal of millenarianism in the context of a political party whose transcendentalism had been tested by both the experience of power and the developing uncertainty concerning the party/leadership relation in the post-victory period and the forms of leadership renewal.

8 Conclusion: The Left and the Republic

The foregoing analysis of the public discourse of the Communist and Socialist parties in the Fifth Republic during the 1970s and 1980s has demonstrated that the politics of party leadership and changes in the significance of leadership are both more subtle and more consequential than has hitherto been argued or assumed. Our analysis has further indicated that the nature of party organisation and of change within it are in a complex relation to leadership, and that discourse is itself a formative condition of this relation. Furthermore, political personalism, which, as we have argued in Chapter 2, is both a discursive and an organisational phenomenon, is related to three factors involved in the political parties' response to a presidential republic: leadership, organisation and discourse.

Two initial points concerning personalism can therefore be made: firstly, it is a major political phenomenon, the complexity of which is not reducible to the notion of hero-worship, nor even to the more sophisticated notion of charismatic authority. Nor are its elements in any strict relationship to those ideas and assumptions which are taken to be part of the science or practice of the political 'marketing' or calculated presentation of presidential candidates; secondly, and consequently, personalism is not used by parties merely as a means of competing for presidential power, but is a complicated response to the institutional changes effected in the Fifth Republic, is a response which has enduring effects upon organisation and upon party identity. Four essential characteristics of this response can be identified.

The first is that each of the two political parties incorporates personalism into – or educes it from – its own variant of the republican tradition. Thus, while enhancing the overall significance of the republican ideal, the use of personalism implicitly challenges specific aspects of it. Such a challenge highlights the problematic nature of political representation in polities endowed with democratic institutions.

The second characteristic is that each party's future-orientated self-identity is accentuated and modified through the use of personalism.

The party's traditional presentation of itself as the path to, or as the symbolic representation of, a desired future society is given a discursive prominence which affects the traditional maintenance of equilibrium between activity and party orientation. This accentuated future-orientation (and the enhancement of the present as historic prelude) is further modified in that it is displaced explicitly or implicitly towards the persona of the leader who tends to be represented as the personification of the party, and the only valid interpreter of its tradition, identity and aims.

Thirdly, the two parties come more and more to present themselves as the bearers of a perpetually renewed vocation for the country and/or the parties' actual or potential constituencies. This constrains them to refer constantly to a ritual and a discourse appropriate to such renewal.

Lastly, the personalist response of each of the two political parties extends the means of resolving the tension between the contradictory drives within political organisation – towards, on the one hand, specialisation, internal differentiation and the doctrinally esoteric and, on the other, towards generalisation and responsiveness to the party's constituency and potential constituency. This tension is partially resolved by each of the parties' offering to itself an image of itself as a rally on the eve of the triumph of the party's ideals and efforts.

The characteristics referred to above serve to shape the responses of the two parties of the Left. However, each retains its own traditions, organisational methods and practices, and these inform the manner in which personalism is manifested within them. The two parties offer, therefore, two distinct styles of political discourse. Both, however, incorporate or undergo the prodigious intrusion of myths and discursive claims of imminent release from existing circumstances. These myths and claims had hitherto either lain outside the traditional discourse of the respective parties or else existed within them in different forms or had a different status or function. We can illustrate this point if we look briefly at the idea of the rally itself.

There exists within Left-wing discourse an ancient and venerated idea of the rally which has no personalist connotation but which (i) is traditionally associated with the idea of a rising and is therefore in some form of relation to violence; and (ii) offers little or no indication of its transitional and transformational forms of organisation. Because of the political conditions which were predominant throughout the Third and Fourth Republics and which encouraged incremental approaches to Left-wing politics and concomitant claims of allegiance to the institutions and practices of the two regimes, the notion of the rally as a gathering together of the people and as a prelude to the sudden and total abolition of oppression lost much of its rhetorical value. Within the context of a presidential regime, the idea of a rally can be effectively revived and its violent and destructive connotations displaced onto a symbolic level by linking it to a different rally tradition, but one which accommodates easily to a presidential republic: namely, the rally around a personal leader. Little change in terminology is involved, and the connotations and respectability of the earlier notion justify or mask the reality of personalist allegiance in the later one.

This kind of discursive innovation happens at all levels of party discourse. In this way, doctrinal reference itself is changed. Personalism therefore has the effect of changing the political party's history, aims and orientations, doing so surreptitiously and without the overt repudiation of past allegiances. The different, and often ritually maintained – or excluded – traditions, myths and taboos of the two parties will affect these changes in different ways and thus influence the manner in which each party comes to accept personalism and the deployment of a personalist discourse. Thus in the PCF, the doctrinal rigour of Leninism and the experience and repudiation of the cult of personality determine the need for caution, and the claim to special insight and the capacity for judgement has to be stripped of explicit claims for personal power and uncritical adulation. In the PS, the existence of *courants*, the subsequent emergence of rival leaders, a looser doctrine than that of the PCF, and the greater expectation of gaining the presidency will involve the concerted evocation of the traditional notion of an impersonal rally, and its subsequent adaptation to a personalised rally. The pedigree of the traditional idea, however, will leave more open and less conclusive the question of which leader is the best instrument of that rally, and which *courant* might embody the rally in essence.

There are, therefore, two identifiable orders of political change: that which affects the parties as a result of their acceptance of new forms of representation; that which affects interpretations of politics in general and the relationship of political discourse to political action. In order to comment upon these orders of change we shall divide the remainder of this discussion into two general areas. The first will examine the effects of change upon the two parties, the second indicate what the study of discourse in the context of ritual, doctrine and leadership reveals of the nature of politics in general.

1.1 *LE PARTI COMMUNISTE FRANÇAIS*

Through personalism, the PCF found, for the first time since its creation in 1920, a doctrinal justification for contingent action, rather than a purely tactical one. From our study in Chapters 4 and 5 we can see that such a discursive shift in the justification of party action is dependent upon the way the office of the General Secretary is treated. The change towards a personalist treatment of the office and of the person of the General Secretary was accompanied by a partial or apparent liberalisation of the party between 1972 and 1976–7. The emergent personalism in the party was, as we have seen, related to – though subsequently not dependent upon – this image or process of liberalisation. It is clear that the liberalisation of the party facilitated the emergence of personalism partly because it presented the image of a party undergoing not only doctrinal revision, but also modernisation and adaptation to a Left alliance within the framework of the Fifth Republic. For as long as this process continued (until the breakdown of the Common Programme alliance and its aftermath), personalism within the party went relatively unquestioned. When concerted criticism did emerge, leadership authority – the right of a leader to speak on behalf of a harmonious party – proved difficult to undermine. The reasons for this inability to provide effective criticism were: first, that allegiance to the leader had been presented as normative rather than tactical – and this not least because it was implicit rather than declared; and second, that, in spite of the abandonment of key Marxian terms such as the (revolutionary) dictatorship of the proletariat, leadership discourse remained substantially an identifiably Communist Party discourse, and one located within the traditional parameters of the discourse of Marxism and Marxism-Leninism, the myths which gave rise to them, and to the myths they enhance in their turn.

This brings us onto a related point which is that Marxism and Marxism–Leninism reveal themselves to be far more ambiguous and connotative than is often assumed. And it is, in part, these qualities which facilitate the orientation of French Communism towards a personalist enterprise. Changes within discursive representations arise not only from circumstances and external political influence, but also from the multiplicity of potential meanings within Marxism itself. And it is this kind of polyvalence of reference which allows certain aspects of and connotations within Marxism to become appropriate and formative according to circumstance. There is no real dichotomy, within the bounds of an accepted social vision, between ideological coherence and deviationism. Marxism is less a method of enquiry, or a social theory, than it is a discourse. And it is this which allows the French Communist Party to move from the strategic positions and declared sentiment adopted and expressed by the 22nd Congress to those of the 23rd and after.

From our analysis, what emerges as being as politically important as principle and doctrinal reference is literary form and its effects within ritual occasions. It is, for example, largely because of the status of the General Secretary's Report and the style of its delivery at the 1979 congress that what are arguably incompatible ideas – such as the call for both State control and *autogestion*, the status of the party as both vanguard and rally, the leader as both servant and inspiration – can be presented as compatible. It is also largely because of the status and style of the Report that these ideas, both explicitly stated and inferred, serve the claim to personalism within it, and prepare for the even greater transcendentalism of *L'Espoir*.

The range of possibilities within Communist rhetoric is extremely wide, although there are certain exigencies and constraints upon it, irrespective of those imposed by organisation. The party must, for example, always make some form of claim to revolutionary status. Within a representative process it can maintain this claim by, for example, transforming the idea of the party as vanguard into that of the party as mobilising framework, or by displacing the notion and the value of the term 'proletariat' onto that of 'people', or again, that of class-consciousness onto that of the party as the articulation of an aggregate of discontent. It must, however, always avoid – or try to avoid – overt accusations of 'Right' deviationism, that is to say, deviation from a revolutionary integrity towards reformism, just as it must avoid accusations of adventurism, Bonapartism, economism and Stalinism. A discursive shift leftwards, however, is possible: towards Trotskyism, Luxemburgism, council communism, or anarchism – on condition that these alternative allegiances are not named – thereby reinforcing the symbolic representations of a spontaneous (and therefore natural) rising or of permanent (and therefore authentic) revolution, and so on.

Such a radicalisation within discourse must also, however, be

accompanied by the avoidance of the specific naming of forms of
political action or desired forms of power, such as those suggested by
the dictatorship of the proletariat. This is because the function of a
symbolic revolutionism is to evoke the immanence or reality of the
rally and to represent it as an effect of personalist leadership. And,
as we have seen, the personalist leader is always portrayed as
possessing a vision, but rarely engages in expounding it or in
elaborating the structures of authority within a future society.

1.2 LE PARTI SOCIALISTE

The organisational context of personalism in the case of the PS
differs from that of the PCF because in the former the principle of
presidentialism is more strategically explicit. Allegiance to Mitterrand after 1971, first as the leader of the party, and then as the
party's presidential candidate in 1974, was an explicit rejection by
the PS of the ambivalent SFIO attitude to presidentialism and an
implicit rejection of Molletism. Therefore, in spite of the maintenance of the essential characteristics of the SFIO's organisational
structure and dependence upon its constituency, the strategic shift
towards presidentialism and the discursive shift towards personalism
are more concerted and pervasive than in the PCF. Given the
organisational structure of the PS, personalist discourse and a
personalist orientation spread easily throughout the party, thereby
imposing new tensions upon traditional lines of divergence or
convergence.

The principal problem raised by the party's commitment to the
attainment of presidential power by and through its leader is that the
personalised, transcendental register of Socialist discourse in the
1970s and 1980s needs to be constantly maintained. This involves a
diminution of traditional references to that which changes or that
which endures within both the movement and the republican
tradition as a whole (traditionally, such references distinguished the
Socialist Party from the parties on both its Right and its Left while
facilitating a broadly social democratic approach to politics). These
references within French Socialism are displaced after 1971 because
of changes in the party's interpretation of the republic and in its
interpretation of the possibilities for limited action within it. In this
way, the nature of the relationship between Socialism and republicanism is itself changed. During the 1970s the conquest of

presidential power was portrayed as the moment of the great awakening of the people and the moment of a transformation of the republic's identity. This change was to have major effects upon the aims, strategy, policies and performance of the Socialists once they attained power in 1981. The result of the discursive conflation of reformist and transformational registers in PS discourse was the abolition of the traditional distinction in Socialist thought between the 'conquest' and the 'exercise' of power. The ambivalent register of revolutionism in Socialist discourse is thereby replaced in the 1970s by a millenarian one which will itself place further stress upon both discourse and organisation once political power has been attained.

Because of the resulting discrepancies between organisational form and leadership status, and between policy aims and discourse, the myth which resolves the tensions between these and justifies party activity both in traditional doctrinal and in personalist terms is one of migration: the idea that a form of gathering is taking place, with the party as its locus, which will transform itself at a given moment into a migration to a socialist world, the norms and institutions of which will be constructed rapidly and effortlessly, and will involve the active participation of the French nation. The prerequisite to the success of this migration is inspired leadership. The dependence upon personalism is exacerbated because such a myth contains only one major event within it: the migration itself. The reduced prominence in Socialist discourse of appeals to incrementalist strategies and policy initiatives, and the concomitant focus upon the transition to socialism as one event increases still further the dependence upon leadership and upon transcendental discourse.

Because of the organisational structure of the PS, the traditional *courants* within the party take upon themselves the role of creating and promoting second-rank leaders who have a claim to vision. The most prominent of these throughout the 1970s and 1980s was the leader of the *courant des Assises*, Michel Rocard. Contesting the party leadership, therefore, involves, essentially and necessarily, not a new strategy or different policies, in the first instance, but all the characteristics of the dominant mode: the claim to vision, an assertion of the actual leader's loss of direction or vision, a myth of migration in some form, millenarian ideas of transformation, and the symbolic re-enactment of renewal, rejection of the past, and the imminence of victory.

In this way, personalism ceases to be a simple strategic commitment of the party or even an instrument of internal control, and becomes the major discursive resource within organisation and the central feature of party identity and activity.

2.1 RITUAL AND DISCOURSE

The fundamental point which arises from our study of texts in their ritual context is that a proper understanding of their significance and effects is dependent upon an understanding of the role served by ritual in party affairs.

Traditionally, ritual at a conference or other major gathering of the members of a political party served as a reminder of the continuity of organisation, and as reassurance that there was an overall purpose to disparate or individual activities. Along with the meeting's practical role ('party business'), there was a certain stress upon ritual as confirmation or renewal of faith. From our analysis of party ritual in Chapters 4, 6 and 7 it is clear that these functions have been modified by the amplification of certain of them, in particular that of ritual as renewal of faith into the ritual of revelation. The PCF congress was traditionally a ritual of the renewal of faith through the justification of local effort and the exemplification of the wider context of party activity. This remains a strong element in the PCF example we have studied. We have also seen, however, how this ritual occasion lends itself to a form of ritual as revelation, in this case of the General Secretary's wisdom. And it is the character of the visionary leader that *L'Espoir* develops and portrays. Similarly, it is implicit in the Rocard motion of 1979 that the Mitterrandists were trying to impose the ritual of purely cyclical renewal once again upon a party which had developed and accepted the ritual of revelation. The *débat* called for by the Rocard motion is, in part, a call to the party to move back to the ritual of revelation. By 1984 the party as a whole is able to do this, re-appropriating to itself the discourse usurped by the Rocard motion of 1979.

We have also seen how ritual is in a very close relationship to discourse and, in the case of the expressions of it studied in this book, gives it its public character. We can say, moreover, that attention to such a relationship has indicated that ritual not only serves as the site of the mediation of tension or of spiritual renewal through collective experience, but is also the site of change.

Given the role that is traditionally ascribed to ritual, this is significant. Ritual is ostensibly the method whereby change is arrested or impeded: prescribed roles and rules for participants, accepted symbolism, recognition of the public and formal or ceremonial character of occasions. However, because of ritual's close relationship to discourse, it can – and does, in the political circumstances appropriate to personalist claims for new forms of allegiance – become the instrument of major political reorientations. Moreover, major party ceremonials and rituals are 'natural' occasions for the deployment of leadership discourse. This appositeness of leadership discourse makes the move towards personalist allegiance easier because the ostensible context in which personalism attempts to legitimate itself is that of the ritual declaration of allegiance to party myths and traditions many of which, as we have seen, are essential to the deployment of personalism.

Ritual therefore facilitates doctrinal change because it is both an accepted and a finely regulated process, the essential, though variable, elements of which may be characterised thus:

1. Recollection of previous gathering(s).
2. Honouring of previous gathering(s).
3. Enunciation of fundamental common beliefs.
4. Allusion to accepted mythic referents.
5. Affirmation of the practical political context of the present gathering.
6. Affirmation of the symbolic significance of the present gathering.
7. Identification of specific approved sources of doctrinal reference.
8. Identification of specific problems.
9. Identification of enemies.
10. Acknowledgement and encouragement of members engaged in day-to-day tasks.
11. Evocation and promise of total social transformation and/or political victory.
12. Elaboration of the method of attainment of short-term and/or long-term aims.
13. Celebration of the audience as the embryonic form of a transformed future society.

The role of the leader in relation to these elements of political ritual is, of course, variable. The point here is that, through discourse, change can be effected by the exploitation of or emphasis upon some or all of these events. The PCF in 1979 effects change by great stress upon nearly all of these, especially upon the recollection and honouring of a previous gathering (1 and 2) and upon the identification of problems and enemies (8 and 9), in the context of the encouragement of daily tasks (10). The elaboration of the method of attainment of long-term aims (12) is understressed in the Report, overtly stressed in *L'Espoir*. With the *Assises* there is no recalling of a previous gathering (1 and 2) (hence the great stress upon two other occasions: the 1968 uprising and the presidential election of 1974), no enunciation of fundamental, shared beliefs (3), but great stress upon allusion to accepted myths (4) and upon the evocation of total social transformation (11). As regards the method of attainment (12), the winning of the presidency of the Republic, the *Assises* themselves are part of the process of party adaptation to it. The 1984 text is, therefore, in certain key respects, a symbolic recapitulation of the trend begun at the *Assises* and a restatement of allegiance to its transcendentalism.

Ritual, therefore, gives a symmetry to the unpredictable consequences of unregulated personalist allegiance while allowing it a forum and the possibility of being sustained over time, that is, within the formal cycles of associational politics. It therefore allows personalism to find accommodation both with associational politics and with party myths and traditions which do not have a personalist provenance.

2.2 DOCTRINE AND DISCOURSE

As we indicated in the previous section of this chapter, ritual and discourse work in a close relationship to one another. We can characterise this relationship metaphorically by depicting ritual as 'hard' and discourse as 'soft': it is the relative rigidity and consciously prescribed elaborateness of ritual which establish the conditions upon which a personalist claim can be made within the plastic, mutable context of discourse.

Such a metaphor implies another, that of 'social structure' and its relationship to discourse. While this relationship has not been the subject of this study, some remarks on it are appropriate here. Our analysis does not demonstrate that discourse is or is not related to social structure, nor that discourses do or do not reflect the interests of various social groups, classes or categories within class. It does, however, demonstrate that there exists a claim to the reality of a particular kind of socio-political association, and an appeal to a particular kind of allegiance to the political expression of such an association. This expression is the rally, transformed, as we have seen, into a personalist rally. The rally as a transcendental political relation may or may not indicate that there is no necessary relation between class and the articulation of class interest. We can say, however: firstly, that claims to the immanence of a rally, and appeals for its realisation do affect the range of possible conceptualisations or depictions of socio-political relations; secondly, that there is little doubt, from our analysis, that transformations in ideas take place within discourse and that the latter *of itself* affects political relations.

Over and above party political traditions, moreover, there is identifiable a rhetorical register or style of personalist discourse, a style which is partly fashioned by, and partly fashions, leadership discourse itself. The most striking characteristic of this style is the accentuation of transcendentalism and the diminution of reference to incrementalist approaches to politics. It is also the case that this characteristic does not need to involve any extravagance in tone, subject-matter or delivery, or any invocation of violence as a political method. Associated with transcendentalism is the promise or implication that the mode of access to power will be unusual, most probably sudden, and inevitably momentous. Another characteristic of personalist rhetoric is the perpetual use of oppositions, either to contrast or to mediate. This affects the manner in which political action is represented in discourse. The future, for example, is invariably depicted as part of a teleology and/or as confrontational at a mythic or epic level. Because of this form of depiction, the future is never seen as proceeding from the present in a variety of possible and mutable forms (as it is in, say, policy-making), but as a series of crossroads, forks or detours involving major decisions concerning direction – and implying major disasters in the event of wrong decisions. In transcendental discourse, therefore, the future is treated as certain at one level and uncertain at another.

As is the future, so is the present treated either mythically or else as a charade or mask covering true reality. Because of this, there is great scope for the use of or allusion to fables which illustrate, through their local and exceptional character, universal truths and forces, and lift the referential from its local context, making it illustrative of the great task of the political party which is itself part of a greater design.

As we have seen, the constantly signified myths offer the link between faith and uncertainty, local and universal struggles, adversity and victory. Many of these are held to be so fundamentally true that they need only be alluded to or implied to have rhetorical effect. For example, the myths of migration to a better world, of a popular rising, of an original, lost truth, and of a utopian society are central to political discourse. And the myth of the visionary leader, which de Gaulle's life exemplified, is so complete, incorporating as it does myth, fable, moral tale and the depiction of an exemplary life, that it becomes the legend which dominates all aspects of Fifth Republican political discourse. However, apart from the central role of this exemplary 'life', there exists a range of precisely or vaguely apprehended traditions and conventions which inform, reinforce or modify the more elaborate and rational discourses of doctrine, strategy and policy.

2.3 PERSONALISM AND DISCOURSE

Finally, and perhaps most importantly of all, our study modifies interpretations of political leadership in general, and of party leadership in the Fifth Republic in particular, by its identification of two interacting political levels or phenomena: presidentialism in the context of the Fifth Republic's institutions, and personalism in the context of the rally myths which refer back to 1789 and beyond. Personalism, moreover, exploits the features pertaining to representation within the republican tradition, making the republican tradition itself more ambiguous (or else making its inherent ambiguities more salient). This extension of the ideas of leadership and of representation has, in its turn, extended the idea of party within the republican tradition, making permanent and continuous the party's claim to be the core of a more extended rally of the people.

As the parties offer themselves as rallies they also shed certain aspects of their history: the PCF its Stalinist period; the PS its Molletism. The effect of this is to make the political party timeless or part of a teleology, and thereby uncorrupted. The definition of time – and, by extension, strategy, tactics and programmes – becomes a function of leadership discourse. And we have described in Chapter 7 some of the effects of this phenomenon upon a party which subsequently becomes a *governing* party (that is to say a party operating in real time). The discursive manipulation of time allows the party to perceive itself as having been brought into existence as the response to a mythical moment rather than as a straightforward organisational imperative: the PCF's founding date is no longer 1920, but a combination of 1917 and 1976; the PS's, not 1905, but a combination of 1968 and 1971. The role of the party in these circumstances becomes that of maintaining the promise of release or victory foreshadowed by these historic moments by means of the continuous deployment of certain discursive resources.

Personalist leadership, therefore, breaks into the party's traditional interpretation of its past, partly because it requires historical interpretations appropriate to a rally, partly because it requires the rejection or the transcendence of party allegiance to past leaders. It thus modifies the party idea of the collective derivation of knowledge and offers in its place, or else in association with it, the themes of revelation, transcendental community, nostalgia, spectacle, hope and reassurance, all adapted to the party's own traditions.

Our study has revealed that the appeal for allegiance to a personal leader in politics is a highly complex phenomenon. In the first place, it is not something that is simply accepted or rejected but, because of its context in discourse, has a variety of qualities and effects, many of which protect it from choices as stark as explicit acceptance or rejection. It has little in common with the psychology of hero-worship and involves neither the abandonment by the parties of their traditions and organisational rationale, nor total surrender to a leader. Personalism is in a varying and elaborate relation to the parties and their traditions, and is based upon ideas immanent in them, such as those connected with previously accepted rally appeals, or those concerning the delegation of authority to *hommes de confiance*.

At the level of electoral politics, personalism does not simply have the effect of going for 'the middle ground' or the 'floating voter', but involves the investment of party members with a certain privileged status and the discursive invention of a new electorate – and a set of adversaries – who are defined in relation to the leader and the reorientations of the party.

At the level of the polity itself, the generalised acceptance of the presidential republic by the Left in France has shown that the conditions of, possibility for, and constraints upon party political allegiance to the presidential principle are cultural and discursive as well as constitutional; that these conditions and constraints have forced party leadership and (potential) national leadership into a new form of relation; and that this new relation throws new light, not only upon the way ideas about government and about party doctrines are to be interpreted, but also upon ideas related to the notion of political representation itself.

Appendix 1: 'Redonner ses chances à la gauche'; Motion C to Metz Congress of the Parti Socialiste: April 1979

'Envers une idée audacieuse qui doit ébranler tant d'intérêts et tant d'habitudes, et qui prétend renouveler le fond même de la vie, vous avez le droit d'être exigeants. Vous avez le droit de lui demander de faire ses preuves, c'est-à-dire d'établir avec précision comment elle se rattache à toute l'évolution politique et sociale, et comment elle peut s'y insérer. Vous avez le droit de lui demander par quelle série de formes juridiques et économiques elle assurera le passage de l'ordre existant à l'ordre nouveau. Vous avez le droit d'exiger d'elle que les premières applications qui en peuvent être faites ajoutent à la vitalité économique et morale de la nation. Et il faut qu'elle prouve, en se montrant capable de défendre ce qu'il y a déjà de noble et de bon dans le patrimoine humain, qu'elle ne vient pas le gaspiller, mais l'agrandir. Elle aurait bien peu de foi en elle-même si elle n'acceptait pas ces conditions.'

Jean Jaurès, *Discours à la Jeunesse (1903)*

INTRODUCTION

1. *Un immense espoir a été brisé en mars 1978. Les aspirations de millions de Français, représentant les forces vives du pays, sont restées en souffrance. La droite a-t-elle été trop forte, la gauche trop faible?*

2. *Les militants socialistes, qui ne s'étaient pas démobilisés au lendemain de l'insuccès de mai 1974, sont restés meurtris et pleins d'amertume après l'échec des élections législatives. Aucune astuce de présentation, par les mots ou les chiffres, ne pourra gommer ce sentiment de défaite.*

3. *Nous nous adressons à tous ceux qui ne s'y résignent pas. Nous appelons tous ceux qui veulent retrouver des raisons d'espérer la victoire de la gauche à en créer à nouveau les conditions, à en définir les objectifs et les moyens. Ce doit être le seul objet du débat, ce doit être le seul enjeu du congrès.*

4. *Le parti ferait un choix funeste s'il décidait de refaire les batailles du passé. De 1971 à 1978, porté par les choix d'avenir faits à Epinay, le Parti Socialiste s'est affirmé comme le parti de l'union et du renouveau. Année après année, se sont retrouvés au PS tous ceux qui vivent l'espérance socialiste, dans leurs combats syndicaux, municipaux, associatifs, dans le mouvement des femmes, tous ceux qui avaient reconnu dans le message 'Changer la vie' l'expression de leurs luttes et de leur volonté.*

UNE NOUVELLE ETAPE

5. *Une nouvelle étape s'ouvre aujourd'hui devant nous.*

6. *L'offensive du capitalisme, en France et dans le monde, crée des problèmes différents de ceux d'hier. La lourde inquiétude qui monte des régions sinistrées par la politique brutale et cynique du pouvoir, le redéploiement sauvage du capitalisme multinational, la domination accentuée de la droite sur l'appareil d'Etat et les moyens d'information, les dangers plus lourds qui pèsent sur le monde du fait de la multiplication des conflits, de la dissémination de l'arme atomique, de la modification des équilibres instaurés à Yalta, voilà autant de données nouvelles qu'il nous faut prendre en compte.*

7. *Plus que jamais, le monde d'aujourd'hui a besoin du socialisme dans la liberté. Et nous n'avons plus ni le temps d'attendre, ni le droit d'échouer. Seul le débat de tous les militants socialistes peut nous permettre de résister à la tentation de l'immobilisme, de la gestion prudente d'un patrimoine électoral d'opposition en vivant sur nos acquis d'hier et sur quelques certitudes élémentaires.*

8. *Ce débat a été long à s'ouvrir au sein du Parti socialiste. Nous avons tout fait pour qu'il soit pris en charge par l'ensemble de la direction qui, autour de François Mitterrand, a eu depuis quatre ans la responsabilité de la conduite de l'action. Certains l'ont empêché, tantôt en employant la 'stratégie du soupçon', tantôt par des procédés plébiscitaires, qui transformaient chaque question, chaque interrogation, soit en une déviation, soit en une querelle de personnes. Nous avons donc, avec Pierre Mauroy et bien d'autres, présenté une contribution destinée à nourrir ce débat sur la situation résultant de l'échec de la gauche en mars 1978. Cela n'a pas suffi. Parce que nous pensons que la synthèse nécessaire à l'unité du parti ne peut plus maintenant venir que de la clarté du débat politique et des choix que feront les militants, nous leur présentons aujourd'hui dans cette motion les réponses que nous croyons nécessaires, pour que le parti socialiste reprenne l'initiative et la gauche le chemin de la victoire.*

9. *Nous avons la conviction, qui fonde notre espérance socialiste, qu'il n'y a pas de fatalité à l'échec de la gauche. Qu'il est possible de définir un*

projet offensif et mobilisateur pour faire face à la situation des années 80. Comment pourrions-nous prétendre convaincre et rassembler notre peuple autour de cette volonté autogestionnaire de prendre en main son destin, si nous nous abandonnions nous-mêmes à l'idée que de toute façon, le socialisme viendra bien un jour, porté par quelque sens de l'Histoire? Aurions-nous si peu de foi en nous-mêmes pour remettre l'espoir du socialisme à une prochaine génération?

10. *Pour répondre à la confiance profonde et tenace que les Français conservent au Parti Socialiste et à la gauche, nous avons la responsabilité de définir les objectifs, de préciser les moyens qui permettront au socialisme autogestionnaire d'affronter les conditions nouvelles de la prochaine décennie. Il nous faut aussi faire de notre Parti un instrument de réflexion et d'action adapté au monde d'aujourd'hui.*

11. *Cette confiance nous engage, et nous ne formulons qu'un seul voeu: que notre débat et notre Congrès en soient dignes.*

1ere PARTIE: A PROBLEMES NOUVEAUX, REPONSES NOUVELLES

1   Crise ou Mutation du Capitalisme?

12. *Au début des années 1970, la France se trouvait dans une situation de plein emploi relatif, aspirait à une forte croissance et se contentait encore d'un taux d'inflation à un chiffre. L'impérialisme américain se dégageait à grand-peine du bourbier indochinois et reprenait son souffle en organisant la détente stratégique et idéologique avec l'Union Soviétique.*

13. *Aujourd'hui, les données économiques internationales ont changé et ont considérablement aggravé les conditions dans lesquelles une expérience de gauche pourrait répondre aux problèmes de la société française.*

14. *La croissance a été partout cassée et le monde industrialisé compte 17 à 18 millions de chômeurs. Comme la productivité des outillages augmente plus vite que la demande, comme on n'a plus inventé, après l'automobile et l'électro-ménager, de nouveaux biens mécaniques appelant beaucoup de travail et que les consommateurs exigent aujourd'hui plus de qualité des services que de produits fabriqués, le retour au plein emploi n'est plus possible dans les règles du jeu actuelles. Il y faut une autre orientation de l'économie et un autre partage du travail.*

15. *Cet affaiblissement de la croissance n'a pas tué l'inflation. Il n'est pratiquement plus un pays occidental qui arrive à préserver la valeur de sa monnaie. Stabilisée mais non réduite, et toujours menaçante, l'inflation traduit l'incapacité des pays capitalistes à établir un partage*

accepté de la richesse collective. La fragilité de nos sociétés s'en trouve accrue.

16. *720 milliards de dollars sont en errance incontrôlée dans le monde, sans que les banques centrales soient en mesure d'intervenir: une telle instabilité monétaire internationale est une lourde menace pour le monde entier.*

17. *Une catastrophe au moins aussi considérable que celle de 1929 peut dépendre de l'ampleur des soubresauts spéculatifs ou des accidents stratégiques de la politique des firmes multinationales. Ce ne sont plus seulement des produits finis que les pays sous-développés nous achètent aujourd'hui mais surtout des usines clés en mains ou des technologies, c'est-à-dire les moyens industriels et commerciaux de concurrencer l'industrie européenne. Déjà la sidérurgie est durement frappée par le développement de la production au Japon et dans bien des pays du Tiers-Monde, l'industrie textile par l'importation massive à bas prix des produits venus de Hong-Kong, de Corée ou de Taïwan. L'augmentation du coût des matières premières, et notamment de l'énergie, à la fois en raison de la stratégie de développement des pays du Tiers-Monde et de la prise de conscience d'une rareté relative, ne peut qu'aggraver la situation.*

18. *Notre civilisation se rend lentement compte qu'elle entre dans un monde et une époque dominés par la rareté: trois richesses essentielles, les matières premières, l'emploi, la liberté, sont en train de devenir des biens rares à la surface de la planète.*

19. *Ces conditions plus difficiles représentent pour la gauche française une contrainte supplémentaire extrêmement forte. Le maintien d'une économie ouverte sur le monde est en effet une nécessité absolue pour la survie et la possibilité d'une expérience de transformation sociale dans notre pays. 20 pour cent du PIB (produit intérieur brut), 40 pour cent de notre production dépendent de nos échanges économiques internationaux. L'interdépendance technologique et commerciale de notre économie, qui résulte à la fois de conditions historiques, géographiques particulières et de l'actuelle division internationale du travail, est trop forte pour que l'on puisse s'en abstraire, à moins de faire délibérément le choix de l'austérité et de la pénurie.*

20. *Mais reconnaître cette contrainte ne signifie nullement s'y soumettre. C'est au contraire la seule façon de trouver les moyens de la surmonter sans s'y briser. Car les contraintes, c'est-à-dire les faits, sont têtues. Elles ne sont ni de droite, ni de gauche. Et si la politique de la droite consiste à dire qu'elles sont insurmontables, celle de la gauche consiste à les analyser dans toute leur ampleur pour les dépasser.*

2 Les Enjeux des Années 1980

21. *Les rapports de force diplomatiques et stratégiques se sont eux aussi*

bouleversés: les menaces qui pèsent sur l'équilibre planétaire et sur la paix sont incontestablement plus lourdes qu'il y a dix ans. La Chine s'ouvre au monde, avec ses immenses besoins, et s'affirme de plus en plus comme une grande puissance, avec les moyens militaires et diplomatiques que cela implique. L'Union Soviétique, incapable d'assurer la succession d'une équipe dirigeante vieillie et à bout de souffle, se sent encerclée à la fois par les initiatives chinoises (accord sino-japonais, établissement de relations diplomatiques avec les Etats-Unis), et par les brèches que crée dans son glacis d'Europe l'exigence montante du respect des droits de l'homme.

22. *Les conflits localisés se sont multipliés, et si le cynisme diplomatique les faisait apparaître hier comme un substitut limité à l'affrontement des deux superpuissances, la dissémination de l'arme atomique ne permettra plus de lâche soulagement dans l'acceptation de cette situation: d'ici dix ans, Israël et l'Egypte, le Brésil et l'Afrique du Sud, l'Iran, parmi d'autres, peuvent devenir des puissances nucléaires. Les nouvelles révoltes du Tiers-Monde ont fait éclater le bloc des pays non-alignés: la Chine et Cuba ont perdu leur ascendant et au Proche-Orient, en Indochine, dans le Golfe Persique des revendications nationales originales apparaissent, et secouent le joug des puissances tutélaires. Un milliard et demi d'êtres humains n'ont aujourd'hui d'autre destin que la faim: laisserons-nous encore s'écouler une décennie sans poser au monde ce problème?*

23. *Pour le désarmement, le respect des droits d'l'homme et du droit des peuples à disposer d'eux-mêmes, le soutien aux luttes de libération nationale, la France a devant elle un champ d'initiative immense, et le peuple qui sera capable de bâtir le grand projet du socialisme autogestionnaire aura certainement une influence dépassant celle qui résulterait de sa propre puissance. Sachons simplement que l'enjeu d'une réponse socialiste à ces questions concerne désormais la survie même de l'espèce humaine.*

Les Problemes de la France

24. *Dans les dix prochaines années, vont se poser à la France des problèmes non moins graves et nouveaux. L'existence d'un chômage massif, dont les effets frappent brutalement des régions entières, n'est pas près de disparaître si se poursuit la politique actuelle. Il frappe durement les femmes, qui représentent 54 pour cent du nombre des chômeurs et dont le droit au travail, c'est-à-dire à une relative autonomie économique, apparaît moins que jamais en termes de 'libre choix'; les jeunes, dont le tiers d'une génération désormais et bientôt la moitié, sera entré dans la vie au sortir de l'école ou de l'armée en connaissant au mieux les allocations et l'assistance, au pire le rejet; les travailleurs immigrés, dont le capitalisme se débarrasse comme le citron que l'on a pressé et dont il tente de faire les boucs émissaires de la crise; les travailleurs les plus âgés, qui perdent leur emploi quelques années avant l'âge de la retraite et qui se consument lentement dans la misère morale que provoque le sentiment d'abandon et d'inutilité sociale.*

25. *Une profonde violence monte de cette violence qui est faite aux femmes et aux hommes de notre pays. La dureté de la lutte des classes, la brutalité de la répression, l'apparition de nouvelles formes de révolte et de contestation en sont autant de manifestations.*

26. *L'incapacité du système capitaliste à maîtriser l'évolution industrielle et technique ne peut qu'aggraver cette situation: des milliers d'emplois sont supprimés ou sont menacés, non seulement dans la sidérurgie, la construction navale, le textile mais aussi dans le téléphone, les banques, les assurances, les services.... Notre tissu industriel se désagrège et un emploi sur deux actuellement créé dans le secteur secondaire est un emploi de bureau: comment ne pas voir, dès aujourd'hui, sa précarité devant la généralisation des moyens informatiques?*

27. *L'agriculture, présentée hier comme le pétrole de la France par Giscard d'Estaing, n'est pas épargnée. L'exode rural se poursuit, l'incapacité à maîtriser les circuits de distribution accroît les inégalités et les gaspillages, nos échanges agro-alimentaires continuent d'être largement déficitaires.*

28. *Le système de protection sociale, conquête des travailleurs, est gravement menacé par la détérioration de la situation de l'emploi pour ce qui concerne les garanties de retraite et par les projets gouvernementaux pour ce qui est de l'assurance maladie. Le déficit non maîtrisé des finances publiques, et tout particulièrement la crise des collectivités locales, accentuent le sous-équipement de la France dans de nombreux secteurs de la vie sociale.*

29. *Un des enjeux des années 1980 est aussi la question posée par la libération des femmes. Peut-on déceler, au travers des manifestations diverses, contradictoires, parfois ambiguës du mouvement social des femmes, une force de nature à transformer les règles du jeu politique et social? Il ne s'agit rien moins que de réintroduire, dans la politique et dans l'histoire, une moitié de la population. Hommes et femmes deviennent de plus en plus solitaires et étrangers à leur milieu: parqués dans les empires du béton, isolés dans des espaces naturels gangrenés par la pollution, consommateurs d'une culture artificielle et factice, coupés de leurs racines et de leur histoire....*

30. *Des signes avant-coureurs montrent de quelle manière inquiétante les techniques peuvent échapper à la maîtrise de l'homme: la France plongée dans le noir et le froid le 19 décembre 1978 en a brutalement pris conscience. Loin d'apporter une réponse à ces questions, la fuite en avant vers le nucléaire que représente le programme énergétique du gouvernement a légitimé ces inquiétudes.*

31. *Sont en cause à la fois le développement économique et social du pays, l'absence de contrôle à grande échelle des conséquences (rejets ou retraitement), les décisions technocratiques imposées aux élus et aux*

populations, la centralisation, et la soumission aux impératifs de quelques grands groupes industriels. Comment le silence, le secret et la dépendance de forces si lointaines et si formidables n'engendreraient-ils pas la crainte?

32. *Il y a quelques mois la marée noire qui a ravagé les côtes bretonnes fournissait au lendemain d'élections législatives gagnées par la droite une occasion exemplaire au premier parti de France de souligner par une campagne d'explication et de solidarité concrètes, l'ampleur nationale, l'impuissance du système à maîtriser son propre développement et d'affirmer les réponses socialistes.*

33. *Sommes-nous vraiment prêts à prendre en charge les défis des années 80?*

3　Crise ou Mutation du Mouvement Ouvrier?

34. *Dans le même temps, le mouvement ouvrier n'a pas été en mesure, dans aucun pays, d'apporter aux mutations du capitalisme des réponses victorieuses et durables. Beaucoup de ses références traditionnelles se sont effondrées. Le Goulag a fait de l'Union Soviétique un anti-modèle: les images d'hier se sont inversées, avec la prise de conscience qu'il ne s'agissait pas seulement d'une aberration monstrueuse, d'une déviation criminelle circonscrite à un pays ou à une époque. L'évolution intérieure des pays du bloc soviétique mais aussi de Cuba, les affrontements militaires en Indochine après la découverte que le communisme pouvait aussi, au Cambodge, prendre le visage de l'autogénocide, ont souligné qu'il s'agissait là d'une tendance inévitable, d'une pente fatale sur laquelle seront inéluctablement entraînés tous ceux qui auraient oublié que les moyens de la transformation économique sont indissociables de ceux de libération sociale et culturelle. A cet égard, la crise des pays socialistes est aussi la crise du modèle de libération des femmes par le seul travail et la confirmation que la modification du régime de propriété des moyens de production ne peut pas constituer l'unique réponse capable de prendre en charge l'ensemble des aspirations de la société et de toutes les couches dominées.*

35. *La social-démocratie n'a pas été plus capable de faire face aux éléments nouveaux de la crise du capitalisme qu'à la manifestation des échecs du modèle communiste. Devant la radicalisation des difficultés, elle a même paru succomber, comme en Allemagne Fédérale, à certaines tentations d'autoritarisme social.*

Une Seule Stratégie: L'Union de la Gauche

36. *En France, l'Union réalisée autour du Programme commun de gouvernement a représenté toutes ces dernières années une tentative unique et originale pour entamer un processus de rupture avec le capitalisme par les voies légales. Elle a canalisé et porté tous les espoirs,*

y compris de ceux qui n'en étaient pas directement partie prenante: syndicats, associations, mouvements d'extrême-gauche même.

37. *L'Union de la Gauche, sous la forme qu'elle a connue depuis 1972, n'a pas résisté au refus de la direction du Parti communiste d'être distancé par le Parti Socialiste dans le rapport de forces électoral.*

38. *Pour autant, elle reste une aspiration forte et vivace, qui s'exprime à travers chaque lutte comme dans chaque élection. Dans un pays où la classe ouvrière se reconnaît pour partie dans le mouvement socialiste, pour partie dans le mouvement communiste, il est clair qu'il n'existe pas d'autre stratégie possible, d'autre alliance politique envisageable pour porter les espoirs du monde du travail. Mais il est non moins clair que l'Union de la Gauche devra prendre d'autres formes, s'appuyer sur d'autres rapports de forces, non seulement sur le plan électoral, mais sur le terrain social, dans les entreprises et les cités.*

39. *Toutes les organisations du mouvement ouvrier, tous les mouvements sociaux qui plaçaient leur espoir dans la victoire de mars 1978 sont traversés par cette interrogation. Pourquoi le Parti Socialiste aurait-il été épargné par ce débat, que connaissent aussi bien le Parti Communiste que la CFDT, l'extrême-gauche que la CGT?*

40. *Pouvons-nous là aussi nous contenter d'attendre que le Parti Communiste reprenne le chemin de l'union? Ou devons-nous avoir l'initiative d'un débat politique et social qui s'adresse à l'immense peuple de la gauche, hommes et femmes qui continuent avec une profonde fidélité à faire confiance à l'union par leurs votes, mais attendent d'elle qu'elle retrouve, dans ses objectifs et ses moyens, la crédibilité de l'espoir de vivre mieux et de vivre autrement qu'elle portait il y a encore un an?*

2ème PARTIE: LES REPONSES DU SOCIALISME AUTOGESTIONNAIRE

1   La Rupture... Avec Quoi? Comment?

41. *Les problèmes nouveaux que pose l'évolution du capitalisme ne se limitent pas au champ économique, et les réponses qu'appelle le socialisme pas davantage. C'est bien pourquoi la rupture que représente le passage d'un système à l'autre n'est pas seulement une affaire de conditions, ou de calendrier, mais aussi d'objectifs.*

42. *Faute de préciser les uns et les autres, on réduirait l'ampleur et la complexité d'un processus qui est en fait la transition au socialisme, à un débat sur les moyens. Le passé proche témoigne encore des effets destructeurs pour le parti et le pays de ce décalage entre la pratique et le*

discours. Souvenons-nous de ce noir hiver du socialisme où les slogans de Congrès: rupture, classe ouvrière, révolution, avaient pour écho dans le monde réel: torture, guerre d'Algérie, répression!

43. *Il n'y aura pas de rupture avec le capitalisme sans une transformation profonde des rapports sociaux, des structures de pouvoir et du modèle de développement et de consommation qu'il véhicule. Il n'y aura pas de transformation des rapports sociaux sans une rupture avec les rapports hiérarchiques et autoritaires, sans rupture non plus avec le patriarcat qui est sans aucun doute un des modèles les plus profondément enracinés. La mise en cause de la vieille division entre tâches d'exécution et de direction exige de mettre fin à un modèle et à un système dont les hommes ont été les agents, qui pèse sur tous les opprimés, hommes et femmes, et musèle en permanence la conquête de la liberté. Il n'y aura pas de socialisme sans libération des femmes, pas de libération des femmes sans socialisme; c'est là une rupture fondamentale.*

44. *Ces rapports hiérarchiques et autoritaires se retrouvent évidemment dans les structures de pouvoir, et se traduisent par l'exclusion de la grande majorité des intéressés de la prise de décision, que ce soit au niveau de l'entreprise, de la ville, de l'Etat. Il faut rompre avec la concentration du pouvoir, partout aux mains d'un petit groupe de responsables.*

45. *Enfin, la rupture passe par une lutte continue contre les différentes formes d'exploitation, de domination et d'aliénation, non seulement dans le domaine de la production mais aussi dans celui de la consommation.*

46. *Qui peut imaginer sérieusement qu'un projet aussi vaste puisse être l'affaire de cent jours, de trois mois? Pour n'être pas seulement le changement de quelques hommes ou de quelques lois, la rupture devra être faite d'un enchaînement de RUPTURES, portant sur tous les mécanismes qui assurent le fonctionnement du capitalisme. Ces transformations évolueront à des rythmes différents, il y aura nécessairement des seuils et des paliers. Ainsi, dès les premières semaines, un gouvernement de gauche devra mettre en oeuvre les réformes de structure qui peuvent créer les conditions de la rupture: maîtrise de l'appareil économique par la nationalisation de ses pôles dominants, lancement du Plan démocratique, nouveaux droits pour les travailleurs, décentralisation de l'Etat, transformation du système scolaire, qui devront être décidées d'autant plus rapidement que leurs effets seront longs à se faire sentir. Mais faire voter des lois ne suffit pas, il faut aussi que ces lois s'inscrivent dans les faits et toute transformation profonde se heurtera à des résistances qui ne seront pas seulement celles du capitalisme dépossédé, mais aussi celles des habitudes acquises, des petits privilèges à déraciner, des mentalités à changer.*

47. *Ces premiers acquis seront-ils irréversibles? Il n'y a que deux moyens de l'assurer: la dictature policière ou la mobilisation populaire. Pour des socialistes autogestionnaires, seuls le développement continu de la*

mobilisation populaire et la sanction permanente du peuple français, par l'expression du suffrage universel, pourront le garantir.

48. *Enfin, souvenons-nous toujours que la rupture avec le capitalisme ne commencera pas avec l'arrivée de la gauche au pouvoir, mais qu'elle est déjà inscrite dans les luttes, dans l'action que mènent les socialistes dans les entreprises sur le terrain du cadre de vie, dans les municipalités, les régions, les associations où ils ont des responsabilités. Le socialisme se définit à travers des objectifs et par une démarche: c'est autant à la pratique qu'au discours que se jugent les volontés.*

2 Transformer l'Etat

49. *C'est une grande tentation, par les temps de crise, que d'en appeler sans cesse à l'intervention de l'Etat. Comme par ailleurs les premières mesures que prendra un gouvernement de gauche auront pour effet de renforcer la capacité d'intervention de l'Etat dans le domaine économique (planification, nationalisations), il est de la première importance d'entreprendre simultanément la décentralisation d'un Etat hypertrophié et bureaucratique, hérité à la fois de la monarchie et de la tradition jacobine dans notre histoire.*

50. *La conquête du pouvoir de l'Etat devra s'accompagner simultanément d'une redistribution de ses compétences, afin que nombre de problèmes puissent être traités plus simplement, plus directement, à un niveau plus proche de la vie quotidienne des gens. Cela passe bien entendu par l'élection au suffrage universel d'Assemblées régionales aux compétences et aux moyens étendus, la suppression de la tutelle du pouvoir central sur les conseils municipaux et les conseils généraux, une véritable redéfinition des champs d'intervention et des moyens des collectivités locales.*

Les Peuples Minoritaires

51. *Si la décentralisation est la traduction politique du droit à la différence, cela implique que tous les problèmes ne soient pas traités d'une manière uniforme sur les 550 000 km^2 du territoire français, c'est-à-dire que l'on n'attende pas tout de la loi et du règlement. La montée de la revendication des peuples minoritaires à retrouver leur identité économique, sociale et culturelle montre à l'évidence que les réponses à des mêmes problèmes ne sont pas identiques en Alsace et au Pays-Basque, en Bretagne et en Occitanie, en Catalogne et en Corse. La proposition de loi du Parti portant statut particulier de la région Corse en est un exemple. Il faudra laisser aux régions une marge d'initiative, d'innovation et d'expérimentation y compris au-delà de la loi pour réellement garantir que la décentralisation ne sera pas une simple déconcentration administrative.*

52. *En effet, comme l'indique la contribution des fédérations du Finistère et*

du Morbihan, dont nous partageons les orientations, si l'on définit un peuple 'par un passé vécu en commun, qui se traduit par une culture et qui s'exprime par une langue (et généralement par un espace où le peuple a ses racines territoriales)', on est bien en France en présence de plusieurs peuples.

53. *La tenue avant l'été des Assises socialistes des peuples minoritaires, préparées de longue date, s'impose pour que la direction du Parti prenne en charge un texte de base l'engageant dans ce domaine. Cela doit permettre au Parti socialiste de proposer aux forces vives de ces peuples l'élaboration démocratique d'un projet politique pour chacun d'entre eux, conformément à la perspective du socialisme autogestionnaire.*

54. *Autogestionnaire, nous ne sommes pas anti-étatistes. Nous voulons substituer à l'Etat hiérarchique, autoritaire, patriarcal et répressif, un Etat dont la légitimité et la justice reposent sur la subordination de l'Etat à la loi et au droit. De même, l'Etat ne devra-t-il plus, sous peine de demeurer oppressif et conserver en lui les germes du totalitarisme, prétendre régenter tous les aspects de la vie sociale et de la vie privée. L'Etat, lorsqu'il intervient dans le domaine de la natalité, doit cesser de considérer la femme comme sa propriété. Il n'appartient pas au monde politique, sous quelque expression que ce soit, de prescrire aux femmes leur comportement et leur statut selon les nécessités de l'heure: les femmes doivent être seules juges du fait d'avoir ou de ne pas avoir d'enfant, sauf leur liberté d'associer leur compagnon à ce choix. C'est ce que les socialistes devront réaffirmer lorsque le Parlement discutera de la reconduction de la loi Veil, dont il faudra étendre l'application, notamment par la prise en charge de l'interruption de la grossesse par la sécurité sociale.*

55. *Et si le vieillissement de la population est un problème dont les socialistes comprennent l'importance, ce n'est pas d'abord de l'Etat qu'ils attendent des réponses mais de l'ensemble de la société. La chute de la natalité n'est-elle pas aussi le fait d'une société qui rejette l'enfant, d'une société qui n'a plus confiance en elle-même.*

La Rupture, Projet Culturel

56. *Certains s'étonneront peut-être de trouver ici une brève réflexion sur l'action culturelle. C'est que, trop souvent encore, les socialistes, et non des moindres, confondent la culture avec les 'beaux-arts' et les 'belles-lettres', l'action culturelle avec les 'colloques' académiques, et croient qu'on en a fini avec ces problèmes quand on a réglé le sort des théâtres, des bibliothèques ou des musées. Les textes officiels adoptés par le Parti depuis cinq ans ont pourtant dénoncé cette illusion.*

57. *Nous n'entendons ni laisser en friche le patrimoine national, ni priver les créateurs du soutien auquel leur situation matérielle de plus en plus difficile leur donne droit, ni de freiner en quoi que ce soit l'activité des*

institutions 'culturelles' traditionnelles, bien au contraire. Mais nous nous refusons à identifier l'action culturelle avec la seule diffusion des oeuvres consacrées: la culture à nos yeux, c'est, dans un sens beaucoup plus large, un comportement collectif, une réflexion sur le mode de vie, c'est l'accès à la conscience critique et à la capacité d'expression. Au service de cette conception, l'école dans la plus noble tradition de la laïcité, la formation permanente et l'animation culturelle doivent converger. Il nous paraît donc essentiel que le Parti soutienne les multiples initiatives par lesquelles des groupes professionnels, locaux, régionaux, s'efforcent de défendre une identité collective et d'affirmer un droit à la différence que le collectivisme de la marchandise (la même chanson jouée au même moment sur tous les juke-boxes) leur refuse. Cette observation vaut, en particulier pour les radios locales, aujourd'hui sévèrement réprimées par le pouvoir. La rupture, elle est là aussi: si nous voulons donner sa vraie dimension au projet socialiste, il est temps, grand temps, que nous prenions en charge ces problèmes et que nous comprenions que l'ensemble des organismes culturels, socio-culturels et socio-éducatifs qui sont autant de foyers d'éveil – et qui, la plupart du temps d'ailleurs, fonctionnent sur le mode associatif – doivent devenir des lieux privilégiés de la lutte pour le changement.

58. *L'Etat n'a pas pour mission d'assurer le bonheur des gens. Quelle rupture déjà si nous pouvions le transformer par assez de justice et d'égalité, par assez de démocratie et de liberté pour qu'il réalise les conditions dans lesquelles chacun pourra prendre en mains son épanouissement personnel!*

3 Rompre Avec le Capitalisme à l'Echelle Internationale

59. *L'ouverture économique de notre pays sur le monde est un fait, dont nous avons déjà indiqué combien il représentait une difficulté supplémentaire pour une expérience de gauche, compte tenu de l'aggravation des effets de la division internationale du travail.*

60. *Le premier réflexe, face à une telle situation, est alors spontanément celui du protectionnisme et du nationalisme. La tentation est grande de trouver à l'extérieur un bouc émissaire, en particulier pour tous ceux qui sont les victimes immédiates de la restructuration sauvage du capitalisme. La bourgeoisie est à cet égard partagée entre deux stratégies: celle de la grande bourgeoisie, du CNPF et des firmes multinationales, incarnée par Giscard et Barre, qui cherchent une 'sortie de crise' en laissant le capitalisme multinational restructurer librement et brutalement le capital et le travail à l'échelle mondiale. L'autre, celle de Chirac, porte-parole de la petite bourgeoisie nationaliste et populiste, veut préserver ses intérêts de classe par le repli craintif sur l'Hexagone et l'exacerbation d'un chauvinisme agressif et autoritaire.*

Deux Stratégies Inacceptables

61. *Les Socialistes ne peuvent, ni de près, ni de loin, joindre leur voix à l'une*

ou l'autre de ses stratégies. Ils doivent en particulier rejeter avec force les thèmes lancés par le RPR, et exploités par le PCF et la CGT du 'Non à l'élargissement' et du 'Non à l'Europe allemande'. Non seulement le développement du nationalisme en Europe a toujours profité à la droite la plus réactionnaire, mais une telle campagne ne peut que rejeter davantage la République fédérale allemande dans les bras des Etats-Unis, renforçant par là-même la tutelle américaine sur notre continent.

62.   *Et dans la mesure où il est aujourd'hui très clair que le marché mondial n'a rien d'un marché, qu'il est manipulé et dominé par les interventions des Etats devant le désordre du système monétaire international, et par les multinationales, mais aussi qu'aucun Etat n'a aujourd'hui la possibilité d'y résister seul, les socialistes n'ont d'autre choix pour mener à bien leur expérience nationale de transformation sociale que de renforcer au maximum les solidarités internationales. En Europe, en direction des représentants politiques et syndicaux du monde du travail des pays de la CEE, où les difficultés rencontrées sont de plus en plus semblables aux nôtres. Dans le Tiers-Monde, où nombre d'Etats ne demandent qu'à échapper à l'actuelle logique des blocs en nouant avec l'Europe un type nouveau de relations.*

Construire l'Europe des Travailleurs

63.   *L'Europe est notre premier environnement. Telle qu'elle s'est développée depuis 1959, la Communauté Economique Européenne n'a certes pas répondu aux espoirs que les socialistes avaient mis en elle. Si elle a été un facteur de paix, le développement quasi exclusif des mécanismes libéraux, au détriment des politiques communes, n'a permis ni de réduire les inégalités sociales et régionales, ni de préparer les évolutions indispensables pour sauvegarder son indépendance et maintenir le plein emploi. Bien au contraire. De plus, le 'Marché commun' s'est naturellement dilué dans une vaste zone de libre-échange atlantique, pour le plus grand bénéfice d'intérêts extérieurs à notre continent.*

64.   *L'Europe des marchands ainsi mise en place a cependant créé de telles interdépendances entre ses membres qu'il n'y a plus d'autre solution pour un gouvernement de gauche en France que de participer à la construction d'une Europe des travailleurs, c'est-à-dire à la construction européenne d'une volonté politique et économique cohérente, reposant sur une politique planifiée et sur de puissants moyens publics d'intervention. Pour bien des problèmes, la nécessaire ligne de résistance à l'impérialisme américain se trouve aujourd'hui à l'échelle continentale. Bien entendu cela suppose une France capable de maîtriser ses propres problèmes afin de peser sur cette évolution plutôt que de la subir.*

65.   *L'Europe des travailleurs, si elle veut être autre chose qu'un slogan, implique alors une stratégie de confrontation et de dialogue avec l'ensemble des forces qui représentent le monde du travail. Ce dialogue avec les social-démocraties d'Europe du Nord, au-delà des discussions*

idéologiques auxquelles on ne voit pas aujourd'hui d'issue, peut déboucher sur des points d'accord pour apporter une réponse commune aux problèmes concrets posés par la crise, le chômage et l'évolution industrielle. Il trouvera son équilibre par une démarche parallèle avec les représentants des forces non seulement socialistes mais aussi communistes d'Europe du Sud. De ce point de vue, la perspective d'adhésion à la CEE de l'Espagne, de la Grèce et du Portugal, peut se révéler une donnée nouvelle et positive.

66. *Le Parti Socialiste a défini, dans sa résolution de Montpellier et dans le rapport Sutra, les préalables économiques et sociaux nécessaires pour que ce deuxième élargissement se fasse sans aggraver pour la France les effets de la crise. Ces exigences seront d'autant plus facilement satisfaites qu'elles seront défendues au niveau international par les représentants de tous les travailleurs des pays concernés. Le Congrès devra donc donner une réponse positive au récent appel du parti communiste italien proposant un renforcement des relations entre l'ensemble des forces de gauche en Europe.*

67. *Les nouvelles revendications et formes de lutte du syndicalisme allemand, le développement au grand jour du syndicalisme espagnol, le renforcement de la Confédération européenne des syndicats viennent attester combien sont grandes les potentialités d'une stratégie européenne offensive, capable d'imposer la réorientation de la CEE actuelle.*

68. *Il reste que la construction européenne est aujourd'hui dans l'impasse, qu'elle demeure dominée par des forces capitalistes et que, dans ces conditions, tout pas en avant vers la supranationalité risque d'être un pas vers plus de libéralisme économique incontrôlé, c'est-à-dire vers plus de chômage. A ce compte-là, l'Europe deviendrait vite odieuse à ses propres travailleurs. C'est dire toute l'urgence de cette coopération active des forces de gauche, indispensable à l'édification de l'Europe des travailleurs. C'est dire aussi que dans l'ordre industriel, commercial et monétaire, une autre politique est nécessaire, bien qu'à l'évidence elle comporte des risques. Tant que le capitalisme domine l'Europe, faire naître entre les pays d'Europe des solidarités et des interdépendances capables à terme de les lier les uns aux autres plus que chacun d'entre eux ne l'est, séparément, avec les Etats-Unis, est un objectif. C'est même la condition véritable de l'autonomie technologique puis commerciale, puis financière et par là politique, de l'Europe par rapport aux Etats-Unis. C'est au fond la condition véritable pour que l'Europe existe enfin.*

69. *Encore nous faut-il réaffirmer que le Traité de Rome n'est qu'une étape et non une fin en soi. Le Traité, dans le respect de la règle actuelle de l'unanimité, peut suffire pour réaliser les propositions présentées par notre parti dans son 'Manifeste socialiste pour l'élection européenne': nouveaux droits des travailleurs, contrôle des firmes multinationales, planification européenne, etc... Il ne résume pas l'avenir que nous*

assignons à l'Europe. Celle-ci représente, entre les blocs, l'espace d'un projet de société alliant pour la première fois démocratie politique et démocratie économique, au niveau continental comme au niveau décentralisé: ce projet est celui du socialisme autogestionnaire.

De Nouveaux Rapports avec le Tiers-Monde

70. *Le Tiers-Monde représente aujourd'hui l'élément le plus explosif de notre planète. Son accession à l'indépendance politique, sa revendication de l'indépendance économique sont les faits majeurs des trois dernières décennies. La décolonisation est cependant loin d'être achevée et nous devons soutenir les luttes de libération qui se mènent aujourd'hui dans le monde, en particulier en Afrique australe.*

71. *Mais il nous faut aussi affirmer que l'on ne peut sans absurdité encourager la hausse des prix des matières premières et l'industrialisation des pays sous-développés, et demander en même temps une réduction sensible de nos échanges extérieurs ou le recours à un protectionnisme durable.*

72. *Il ne peut y avoir de nouvel ordre économique international sans redéfinition de l'actuelle division internationale du travail.*

73. *Pour contrôler les évolutions inévitables, un double processus doit s'engager: la négociation avec les pays du Tiers-Monde d'accords de co-développement pluri-annuels, incluant des engagements liés au respect des droits de l'homme – travailleurs dans leur pays d'origine et travailleurs immigrés – et la mise en oeuvre dans notre pays d'une planification démocratique.*

74. *La défense des droits de l'homme n'a de sens que si elle intègre la volonté de l'élimination de toutes les discriminations subies par les femmes, qu'il s'agisse de l'accès à la culture et de la lutte contre l'analphabétisme, du droit au travail, des libertés politiques et du respect de l'intégrité physique.*

75. *Dans le même temps, nous devons nous battre syndicalement et politiquement pour que soient prises en compte dans les pays du Tiers-Monde les normes de l'Organisation Internationale du Travail: signature de conventions collectives au niveau mondial, refus de facilités d'impôts ou d'importations aux multinationales tirant leurs profits de bas salaires ou des conditions de surexploitation maintenus par des régimes répressifs, voilà deux exemples d'actions concrètes, au niveau européen. Elles montrent justement comment l'intérêt des travailleurs français, en termes de concurrence, rejoint celui des travailleurs du Tiers-Monde.*

76. *C'est à ce niveau aussi que nous pouvons contribuer à déplacer en faveur du socialisme les grands équilibres mondiaux actuels.*

4   L'Economie au Service d'un Projet Politique

77. *L'ensemble de ces ruptures, au niveau de l'Etat et des rapports de forces internationaux, suppose que la collectivité maîtrise les instruments économiques de cette transformation. Depuis des dizaines d'années, la tradition du socialisme explique que la transformation de l'économie doit passer par son organisation démocratique. De là est née l'idée de Plan. Aujourd'hui, les leçons des multiples échecs d'expérience faites au nom du socialisme à travers le monde doivent nous conduire à affirmer un second principe: la liberté n'est jamais assurée dans une société si elle ne trouve pas son enracinement, au-delà des discours, dans les structures économiques et sociales. C'est en vertu de ce principe que nous avons déjà expliqué que les objectifs et la démarche de la rupture avec le capitalisme sont indissociables. Le contenu de la décision et la manière de la prendre sont aussi importantes; nos propositions concernant l'autogestion dans l'entreprise (les conseils d'atelier, par exemple) et dans la ville (démocratie municipale et groupes de quartier) comptent autant que le contenu de notre politique, car elles sont la garantie que le socialisme reposera sur un exercice réel du pouvoir par l'ensemble des travailleurs et des citoyens, et non par quelques technocrates ou dirigeants.*

78. *Ainsi, une infrastructure économique centralisée et bureaucratique ne peut pas produire une société libre. Encore faut-il savoir de quelle économie nous parlons: l'économie à transformer n'est pas celle du siècle dernier mais celle des vingt ans qui viennent.*

4.1   *L'Economie de la Fin du XXe Siècle*

79. *L'incapacité de la gauche française à maîtriser les problèmes économiques de son temps est un des handicaps les plus lourds qu'elle ait eu à supporter. Les classes ouvrières des pays occidentaux comparables à la France ont aujourd'hui un niveau de vie souvent nettement supérieur à celui de la classe ouvrière française (le salaire minimum est aujourd'hui proche de 3000 F aux Pays-Bas et dans les pays scandinaves, et de 2500 F en Allemagne fédérale).*

80. *C'est d'une part parce que la droite au pouvoir en France a toujours mené une politique particulièrement antisociale. C'est d'autre part parce que la gauche n'a jamais réussi à aller durablement au pouvoir et a trop rarement été capable de concilier les deux conditions indispensables du succès: la rigueur économique et l'audace politique.*

81. *L'économie n'est pas un jeu de construction pour enfants, où il suffirait de déplacer les pièces pour changer la construction, où il suffirait de vouloir changer pour que les choses changent. La croissance, le pouvoir d'achat ou le nombre d'emplois n'augmentent pas brusquement parce qu'un responsable politique aurait dit: 'Je le veux'. L'économie ne se change pas par décret. S'il suffisait d'augmenter d'un tiers le SMIC et de*

nommer les chômeurs fonctionnaires pour que tout aille bien, on se demande pourquoi la droite ne le ferait pas tout de suite: l'idée selon laquelle le socialisme, c'est le capitalisme plus 20 pour cent est une idée du XIXe siècle.

82.   *Si nous considérons que la rigueur économique est une condition décisive du succès de la gauche, ce n'est pas par amour de Comptes de la Nation bien ordonnés et bien équilibrés. C'est d'abord parce que nous savons, par l'expérience de bien des échecs du socialisme, que dès que l'on cesse de compter, c'est la peine des femmes et des hommes que l'on cesse de compter. C'est ensuite parce que nous nous adressons à un pays adulte, qui n'est pas dupe de l'accumulation des promesses si l'on n'indique pas précisément les moyens que l'on compte mettre en oeuvre pour les réaliser. En économie, la vérité ne se divise pas en parts. C'est encore parce que les expériences manquées de la gauche, à commencer par la France – mais qui oublierait le Chili? – nous enseignent qu'un taux d'inflation insupportable contribue à affaiblir le soutien populaire, à diviser la coalition des forces politiques au pouvoir, aggravant ainsi les effets des attaques conjuguées de l'intérieur et de l'extérieur.*

83.   *Quand arrive la division au milieu des difficultés, l'échec n'est pas loin.*

84.   *Ainsi il serait à la fois dangereux et injuste d'augmenter les salaires tout en maintenant la hiérarchie actuelle.*

85.   *Une augmentation importante du SMIC, correspondant aux 2400 F que le Parti demandait en mars 78, devra s'accompagner d'une forte réduction de l'éventail des salaires.*

86.   *La complexité de l'économie moderne n'est pas un prétexte pour ne rien faire. L'exigence de rigueur dans les moyens ne doit pas conduire à abdiquer l'audace de nos choix et la volonté politique de les mettre en oeuvre. Mais il est indispensable de disposer d'une stratégie capable de surmonter les contraintes économiques: c'est le rôle central du Plan socialiste.*

4.2   Le Plan, Projet Politique

87.   *Plus qu'un document économique le Plan est d'abord un projet politique. Son objet majeur est d'être la charte démocratique du développement économique et social. En ce sens, il indique les choix faits par la collectivité pour la période à venir. Ces choix définissent les domaines dans lesquels vont porter les efforts de transformation de la société et les délais dans lesquels ces transformations doivent être réalisées. Ainsi, le Plan est l'acte politique par lequel la Nation, après avoir mesuré les contraintes et les marges de manoeuvre possibles, définit les objectifs et les moyens du socialisme dans les années à venir. C'est le Plan qui indique et mesure les progrès de la rupture avec le monde ancien.*

La Logique du Plan

88. *Ces objectifs et ces moyens portent sur les aspects les plus importants de l'économie. Par exemple, la réduction de la hiérarchie des revenus, le choix des grands investissements nationaux en vue d'assurer de nouveaux emplois, de soutenir le progrès technologique et de modifier le mode de croissance, la réforme de la fiscalité, etc. L'étendue des domaines traités par le Plan et la volonté politique qui détermine ces choix montrent que la logique actuelle est inversée: ce ne sont plus quelques pôles privés dominants qui décident, c'est l'ensemble de la collectivité qui fixe ses propres choix après un grand débat démocratique. Le Plan est donc à la fois un acte et un moyen de la rupture avec le capitalisme.*

89. *La planification n'a de sens que si la Nation est à même de maîtriser les principaux pôles de la vie économique, qu'il s'agisse du crédit, de la banque ou des secteurs industriels dominants. La nationalisation n'a de sens que si elle se fait à la fois par le haut et par le bas, c'est-à-dire si le transfert de la propriété et du pouvoir dans les groupes industriels et financiers nationalisés s'accompagne d'une autre organisation du pouvoir dans les entreprises qui dépendent de ces groupes. Ce que nous avons déjà dit de l'échec des pays dits socialistes suffit à montrer que si le pouvoir peut passer par la propriété, la propriété ne saurait à elle seule résumer tous les phénomènes du pouvoir.*

Le Secteur Public

90. *Aujourd'hui, le secteur nationalisé et le secteur public reconnaissent aussi peu de pouvoir à leur travailleurs et sont autant ségrégationnistes vis-à-vis des femmes, que les entreprises capitalistes: l'exploitation et l'aliénation, la discrimination dans les responsabilités et les promotions, la dévalorisation de statut et de traitement des secteurs féminisés y sont analogues. Notre conception du secteur public est d'en faire un exemple dans la prise de responsabilité par les travailleurs et particulièrement en matière de travail des femmes: politique d'embauche, transformation des secteurs entièrement masculinisés ou féminisés, politique de formation continue. C'est également dans le secteur public que l'instauration de conseils d'atelier devra être le plus poussée: élus directement par les travailleurs de chaque atelier ou service, ils auront un pouvoir de décision sur l'organisation des conditions de travail, le choix d'équipements nouveaux, ils participeront à la définition des tâches, et en négociation avec le conseil d'administration, à l'élaboration de la politique de l'entreprise. C'est ainsi que se réduira, par la pratique, la division du travail entre dirigeants et exécutants, les effets de la hiérarchie du savoir et de l'aliénation du travail. C'est en fonction de ces perspectives que nous parlons de socialisation autant que de nationalisation.*

91. *Les techniques nécessaires à l'élargissement du secteur public sont variées, doivent tenir compte de la réalité financière et industrielle de ces*

entreprises et doivent préserver leur souplesse et leur rapidité d'action. En dehors du secteur bancaire et financier et des neuf grands groupes figurant dans le Programme commun, ce qui représente l'engagement commun à tout le Parti, il conviendra de préciser et de compléter les critères de nationalisation envisagés par le Programme du Parti 'Changer la Vie'.

92. *En dehors de quelques pôles dominants et de secteurs-clés qui seront nationalisés, l'immense majorité des entreprises restera dans le secteur privé. Les droits des travailleurs devront y être affirmés: extension des droits syndicaux et reconnaissance de la section politique d'entreprise, pouvoirs renforcés des comités d'entreprise et d'établissement notamment sur l'organisation du travail et les salaires, l'embauche et les licenciements, les cadences, l'hygiène et la sécurité, etc. La démocratie doit enfin pénétrer dans l'entreprise. Un troisième secteur, dit 'd'économie sociale', que représentent déjà en partie les mutuelles et les coopératives, doit être développé afin de favoriser la socialisation du pouvoir dans la production et l'innovation industrielle et sociale.*

Plan et Marché

93. *Comment voudrait-on en effet que le Plan puisse être démocratique si le secteur public, principal instrument de la collectivité pour orienter, impulser, coordonner les objectifs mis en avant par le Plan, est lui-même centralisé et concentré? Il n'y aura d'avancée autogestionnaire réelle et étendue que si nous savons montrer que nationaliser, c'est transférer le pouvoir et son organisation à la collectivité aux divers niveaux où elle est organisée: Etat, région, entreprise, commune, et non pas seulement diriger du sommet. Il n'y aura de croissance nouvelle que si nous savons montrer que l'autogestion, c'est l'introduction de la liberté et de la démocratie dans le domaine économique, et non pas produire comme on administre, par la loi et le règlement.*

94. *En définitive, les choix du plan orientent le développement du pays, mais ils ne se substituent pas à l'action de chaque individu ou de chaque entreprise. Cette conception du Plan est profondément antinomique de la planification bureaucratique et centralisée de type soviétique. Il ne suffit pas de déplorer les excès d'un tel système: il faut avoir conscience qu'il n'est pas d'exemple où il n'ait débouché sur le rationnement, faillite technique, et sur la dictature, faillite politique. C'est d'ailleurs normal: la conception selon laquelle un fonctionnaire de l'Etat central est capable de dire comment doit marcher une entreprise mieux que les travailleurs de cette entreprise est à l'inverse de nos conceptions autogestionnaires.*

95. *Dès lors, le Plan socialiste ne se conçoit que comme un plan contractuel, régi davantage par des contrats que par la loi, contrats entre unités de base comme entre ces unités et le ministère du Plan. Cette conception doit être étendue à l'agriculture. Et dans cette logique contractuelle, il serait absurde que ce soit le ministère du Plan qui fixe les quantités, les*

prix, les qualités de tous les produits fabriqués dans notre pays. Ce serait retomber sous la coupe d'une bureaucratie toute puissante et irresponsable, qui gère par l'arbitraire du rationnement et de la distribution administrative. L'ajustement à court terme entre l'offre et la demande continuera donc à se faire par les mécanismes du marché, pour tous les produits où il subsistera une pluralité de producteur. Ce libre choix du consommateur est la condition fondamentale, nécessaire mais non suffisante, de la liberté dans l'ordre politique. Le marché restera aussi un indicateur de performance et de résultats pour la majorité des entreprises quel que soit leur statut juridique.

96. *Le Plan fera l'objet d'une profonde délibération collective, associant les entreprises et les collectivités locales et régionales, les élus, les travailleurs et les consommateurs. L'échelon de la Région sera en particulier un lieu décisif où s'exprimeront les grands choix du développement économique et social. Canalisé par les orientations du Plan et soumis aux objectifs déterminés démocratiquement, le marché deviendra alors un auxiliaire du Plan indispensable à la décentralisation et à la démocratie économiques. On ne peut en effet prendre très au sérieux les discours qui disent à la fois que dans de nombreux secteurs, le marché a cessé d'exister, et que sa toute-puissance est une menace avec laquelle il faut rompre. Le Plan permet de rompre avec la logique du profit, ce qui est différent de la logique du marché. Que la concurrence soit aujourd'hui faussée sur le marché par les entreprises dominantes est une réalité: c'est bien pourquoi l'organisation des marchés, sans cesse menacés par la concentration capitaliste, devra faire l'objet d'une politique volontariste dans le cadre du Plan.*

97. *Enfin, la planification devra soustraire des secteurs entiers de la vie sociale, comme le sport et les loisirs, la santé et la culture, à l'empire des valeurs marchandes.*

4.3 *Une Stratégie Pour l'Emploi*

98. *L'emploi est un des principaux problèmes qui attendent du socialisme une solution neuve, et du Plan une stratégie économique et sociale.*

99. *Le chômage d'aujourd'hui n'est pas une fatalité. Il n'a cette ampleur qu'en raison du mode de développement du capitalisme contemporain. Si celui-ci n'est pas changé, la croissance actuelle, qui n'est pourtant pas négligeable (3 pour cent) par an, continuera de produire des chômeurs. En effet il substitue systématiquement le capital au travail, refuse un autre partage du temps de travail, ne conçoit la création d'emplois que par l'extension des activités marchandes. Dans une telle perspective, il est clair que le capitalisme a renoncé de manière durable au retour au plein emploi. Or, chacun des composants de ce mode de développement doit être remis en cause.*

100. *Il est possible de poursuivre la croissance en utilisant plus de travail qu'on ne le fait aujourd'hui. Favoriser la création de petites entreprises*

industrielles ou artisanales, réduire la hiérarchie des revenus, c'est-à-dire les inégalités, pour alléger le coût du travail, encourager l'innovation et la recherche, supprimer les cumuls, transférer à la charge du contribuable une partie des charges sociales qui incombent aujourd'hui aux entreprises de main d'oeuvre, voilà quelques mesures qui vont de ce sens.

101. *Il en va de même pour le partage du temps de travail. La semaine de 35 heures est un objectif essentiel des socialistes. Elle doit être négociée avec les organisations syndicales et réalisée sans perte de salaire pour les basses et moyennes catégories. Elle doit être accompagnée d'une réduction importante de la hiérarchie des revenus. Elle sera d'autant plus facile à mettre en oeuvre que sa réalisation sera menée parallèlement dans d'autres pays européens.*

102. *La récente grève des sidérurgistes de la Ruhr est un pas important dans ce sens pour l'Europe des travailleurs.*

103. *Par ailleurs, la revendication de la diminution du temps ne vaut pas seulement pour les emplois qu'elle peut libérer, elle s'inscrit dans la volonté d'assurer un réel droit au travail pour les femmes, une plus juste répartition des emplois existants, et une meilleure utilisation individuelle et collective de chacun. Le travail tel qu'il est organisé aujourd'hui n'est libérateur ni pour les hommes, ni pour les femmes: il est essentiellement le moyen d'acquérir une relative autonomie économique. Davantage de temps libre signifiera pour les travailleurs davantage de temps à consacrer à sa famille, à des activités collectives dans son quartier, son syndicat, son parti, davantage de temps pour les loisirs ou simplement pour profiter de la vie. Que signifie en effet 'prendre son destin en main' pour celui ou celle qui fait les 3 × 8, passe des heures interminables dans les transports en commun des conglomérats urbains, qui aperçoit conjoint et enfants dans l'escalier au petit matin ou le soir à la nuit? Davantage de temps libre pour tous est une des conditions de l'autogestion et donc un objectif prioritaire. Lutter dès aujourd'hui pour qu la société conçoive le travail de la même manière pour les hommes et pour les femmes, s'attaquer aux fausses théories d'un prétendu libre-choix de travailler réservé aux femmes, c'est contribuer à préparer une société plus égalitaire où hommes et femmes ne seront plus contraints de travailler autant que la tradition les y a contraint.*

104. *C'est enfin une des conditions du développement social, dans la mesure où la rareté de l'emploi développe le besoin de la sécurité à tout prix: une société qui se replierait sur les situations acquises, qui perdrait le sens de l'initiative et de la responsabilité, qui n'assumerait plus le risque, serait une société en déclin.*

4.4 Une Nouvelle Croissance

105. *Améliorer la situation de l'emploi appelle enfin un autre contenu de la notion de croissance. Le monde capitaliste se divise à cet égard en deux*

catégories de pays. Les uns, peu nombreux (Norvège et Suède, notamment), ont mis en place une organisation économique et sociale décentralisée et dans laquelle les activités non marchandes tiennent une grande place. En d'autres termes, ces pays considèrent que l'économique et le social – au sens large du terme – sont l'envers et l'endroit d'une même réalité. La situation de l'emploi y est meilleure que partout ailleurs.

106. *Les autres pays, les plus nombreux, connaissent une organisation économique centrée exclusivement sur les activités marchandes. Ces pays connaissent aujourd'hui un fort taux de chômage, y compris ceux qui, comme l'Allemagne fédérale, sont considérés par certains comme des modèles. Ainsi, l'argent est de droite non seulement parce qu'il fausse les rapports sociaux, mais aussi parce que le type d'économie dont il est le centre exclusif ne permet pas de procurer à tous le plus indispensable des biens sociaux: le travail.*

107. *Une nouvelle croissance ne peut s'envisager sans une autre politique de l'énergie. Afin d'assurer une diversification des approvisionnements, comme des usages, de mieux utiliser les ressources locales, d'économiser l'énergie, de développer la recherche des sources nouvelles d'énergie, permettre un contrôle populaire des installations nucléaires existantes: telles étaient les orientations indiquées par le Parti Socialiste en octobre 1977. Il conviendra de les préciser et de les actualiser.*

108. *Autrement dit, il ne peut y avoir pour un socialiste d'opposition entre vivre mieux et changer la vie, entre les objectifs qualitatifs et quantitatifs pourvu qu'on en assure les moyens. Et le droit au travail pour les hommes et les femmes de notre pays ne sera assuré que si la stratégie économique du socialisme est porteuse à la fois des moyens économiques et financiers du 'vivre mieux' et d'un autre mode de vie qui réduise la prééminence de l'argent dans les rapports sociaux.*

3ᵉᵐᵉ PARTIE: CONSTRUIRE LE SOCIALISME AUTOGESTIONNAIRE

1   Les Mouvements Sociaux

109. *Les principaux affrontements sociaux qui se déroulent aujourd'hui dans le pays ont pour théâtre les entreprises menacées de fermeture ou frappées par les licenciements. Dans la région de Longwy, dans le Valenciennois, à St-Etienne, à La Rochelle et dans bien d'autres villes, la colère s'accumule et fait naître des situations explosives.*

110. *La tâche du parti socialiste est de combattre jour après jour aux côtés de ceux qui ont perdu ou qui risquent de perdre leur emploi mais elle est aussi de leur ouvrir des perspectives et, ce qui est sans doute plus*

difficile, d'établir un lien entre la lutte immédiate et les objectifs d'une nouvelle politique économique et sociale. C'est ainsi que dans le cas de la sidérurgie, il ne s'agit pas seulement de dire que les emplois actuels doivent être préservés et d'ajouter qu'à moyen terme la solution ne peut être trouvée que dans le cadre d'une stratégie globale. Il faut encore indiquer comment on pourrait gagner le temps nécessaire pour que puissent s'opérer les inévitables reconversions et que se constitue un nouveau tissu industriel. Cela implique aussi bien la création de la 5ᵉ équipe, le passage aux trente-cinq heures que l'exigence d'une relance rapide de l'industrie du bâtiment et des travaux publics, grosse consommatrice de produits sidérurgiques.

111. *Mais les batailles pour l'emploi ne doivent pas nous faire oublier celles qui ont pour objectif le maintien du pouvoir d'achat et la transformation des conditions de travail. Elles ne doivent pas davantage nous conduire à sous-estimer les nouveaux problèmes qui ont été posés à la société française depuis un certain nombre d'années, et surtout depuis mai 1968, qu'il s'agisse des peuples minoritaires, de l'écologie, de la lutte des femmes, des mouvements de consommateurs ou de l'apparition d'expressions culturelles nouvelles. Parce que ces revendications ont été souvent posées en dehors des partis politiques, on a eu tendance à les juger marginales. Mais peu à peu les partis ont dû en tenir compte et tenter de les prendre en charge.*

112. *Nous n'échapperons pas à une analyse sérieuse de ces mouvements qui donnent une nouvelle dimension à la lutte des classes. Sans doute n'ont-ils pas tous un caractère anti-capitaliste et beaucoup sont loin d'être parvenus à leur pleine expression politique. Mais nous aurions le plus grand tort de sous-estimer le rôle qu'ils peuvent jouer dans la transformation de la société.*

113. *C'est ainsi que l'analyse des rapports de domination mis en lumière par le mouvement des femmes ne permet pas seulement d'expliquer les rapports de domination homme–femme. Elle permet de mieux comprendre l'ensemble des phénomènes de pouvoir et de dépendance. En saisissant dans toute sa dimension le problème du féminisme on parvient à mieux définir la nature de notre projet autogestionnaire.*

114. *Dans le monde rural aussi, le développement du mouvement paysan sous ses formes les plus actives a contribué à poser le problème des rapports du paysan à sa terre en tant qu'outil de travail plus qu'en termes de propriété. A cet égard, il est pour le moins contradictoire avec les proclamations si généreusement affichées d'une volonté de rupture avec le capitalisme, que la première concession faite au Parti communiste lors des négociations d'actualisation du programme commun ait porté sur les Offices fonciers.*

115. *Si la défense de la propriété familiale contre les mécanismes de concentration capitaliste garde toute son importance, il n'en est pas*

moins nécessaire de faire progresser la proposition des socialistes de créer des Offices fonciers. Différents des SAFER actuelles, trop centralisées et peu démocratiques, ils permettront d'assurer à de nombreux paysans par un bail à vie, éventuellement transmissible à leurs descendants, la terre dont ils n'auront plus dès lors à assurer les charges foncières en tant que propriété. Tous les travailleurs de l'agriculture devront bien entendu trouver leur place dans la gestion de ces Offices.

116. *Une autre revendication s'est fait jour à travers le mouvement paysan: celle de las garantie d'un revenu suffisant dans le respect des caractères propres au travail de la terre et à la liberté d'initiative et d'organisation. Pour y parvenir, plusieurs mesures doivent se conjuguer: des offices par produit pour garantir des prix minimum aux producteurs, dans une négociation où les représentants des consommateurs et des autres travailleurs de l'agriculture doivent avoir leur place; décentralisation et démocratisation du statut des coopératives; conventions collectives entre producteurs agricoles et industries agro-alimentaires; indépendance du système de distribution à l'égard des banques d'affaires qui jouent des importations et des exportations contre les producteurs français; contrôle effectif des agriculteurs sur le Crédit Agricole, afin de permettre de limiter l'endettement des jeunes agriculteurs, les aider à se maintenir à la terre ou à créer de nouvelles exploitations. Il n'y a pas de possibilité d'aménager le territoire français sans une relance de la politique agricole sous toutes ses formes.*

2 L'Union des Forces Populaires

117. *Il nous faut donc tenir compte à la fois du développement des batailles ouvrières et des potentialités offertes par ces nouvelles formes de lutte qualifiées trop hâtivement de 'secondaires'. C'est à partir de là que peut se construire l'union des forces populaires. Il ne s'agit pas de faire de cette formule un substitut à l'union de la gauche. C'est indiscutablement à travers les partis politiques que continuent à s'exprimer la nécessité et la possibilité du changement politique. Mais ceci ne doit pas nous empêcher de chercher à rassembler toutes les forces sociales dont la logique de développement est une logique anti-capitaliste. Nous sommes ainsi conduits à nous tourner vers les syndicats, les associations et les mouvements sociaux.*

118. *Pour définir la base sociale du projet politique dont ils sont porteurs, les socialistes ont évoqué la notion de front de classe. Ils entendaient souligner par là qu'ils ne voulaient ni d'un regroupement des masses populaires sous la conduite éclairée de quelques théoriciens ou chefs historiques qui posséderaient les clés de l'avenir, ni d'un rassemblement des mécontents que ne viendrait souder aucun projet politique.*

119. *Il apparaît aujourd'hui qu'une conception trop statique, ou trop statistique, du front de classe, se limitant aux facteurs économiques et sociaux de l'exploitation, et ignorant les phénomènes d'aliénation et de domination, appauvrit en fait notre démarche.*

120. *L'Union des forces populaires n'est ni donnée, ni immuable, ni déjà constituée: il faut la rassembler et l'élargir, à la fois par des initiatives concrètes, sur le terrain, et par un grand débat qui puisse faire apparaître des convergences sur des objectifs d'action et de transformation sociale.*

121. *Dans cette perspective, nous proposons que le Projet de société socialiste, auquel les militants ont déjà largement contribué, fasse l'objet avant son adoption définitive par le Parti d'une vaste confrontation publique avec l'ensemble des partis, syndicats, associations, mouvements sociaux, qui doivent être partie prenante de l'Union des forces populaires, et cela aussi bien au niveau national que régional et local.*

3 L'Union de la Gauche

122. *Nous réaffirmons solennellement l'engagement d'Epinay: 'Il est clair qu'une majorité existe dans le Parti pour mener à bien la rénovation de l'action politique en France et pour exclure toute stratégie de troisième force'.*

123. *Nul ne songe à substituer à l'union de la gauche une autre stratégie. Nul ne doit songer non plus à s'enfermer dans une quelconque tour d'ivoire en attendant que la direction du Parti Communiste revienne à de meilleurs sentiments unitaires.*

124. *Pour peser sur le Parti Communiste, il est illusoire de croire qu'il suffirait de tenir bon, maintenir le cap, se draper dans la fidélité et la justesse de nos thèses. Il faut reprendre l'initiative.*

125. *Cela suppose que nous engagions le débat avec le Parti Communiste, ses militants, son électorat, à tous les niveaux. Il ne s'agit pas d'entamer un dialogue idéologique qui stériliserait l'action commune, il s'agit de le questionner sur des points essentiels qui touchent à la nature même de notre projet: autogestion, analyse de la crise, stratégie internationale et nature des pays de l'Est.*

126. *Dans le même sens, il faudra mieux apprécier la réalité des différentes forces politiques sur le terrain: cela implique par exemple de reconnaître la responsabilité des fédérations dans l'application locale des accords qui nous lient au Mouvement des Radicaux de Gauche.*

127. *L'Union de la Gauche ne peut plus à l'heure actuelle s'exprimer ni à travers des accords de sommet, ni en se limitant au dialogue exclusif entre les partis. C'est l'ensemble des éléments susceptibles de constituer l'Union des forces populaires qu'il faut saisir de ce débat, de façon à ce qu'une pesée effective du corps social du pays ramène la direction du Parti Communiste à accepter l'Union de la Gauche.*

128. *Une telle démarche ne jaillit pas du néant: elle peut être mise en oeuvre à l'occasion des actions ou des luttes menées dans les entreprises ou les*

localités. Il faut prendre des initiatives avec les partis, syndicats, associations, mouvements sociaux, qu'il s'agisse de l'emploi à défendre, du cadre de vie à protéger, de meilleures conditions de vie et de travail à conquérir.

129. *L'Union de la Gauche est préservée grâce à l'enracinement acquis en 1977 dans de très nombreuses municipalités. Pour l'essentiel, les accords passés il y a deux ans ont été honorés. Il sera utile que le Congrès mandate le Comité Directeur et la Fédération des Elus pour dresser un bilan approfondi de l'application des accords de 1977 sur les difficultés rencontrées, les progrès de la pratique de l'union et les avancées qui doivent encore être faites.*

130. *Recréer la dynamique brisée le 22 septembre sera un processus long. Mais nous croyons fermement qu'il n'y a pas de fatalité à la désunion de la gauche. Nous entendons en tout état de cause que le Parti Socialiste ait un comportement irréprochable dans la discipline unitaire, prenne l'initiative du dialogue et de l'action commune. Ces initiatives doivent préparer avec toutes les forces politiques prêtes à envisager un gouvernement commun de la gauche la négociation d'un contrat commun de gouvernement, défini par l'énoncé d'objectifs, de seuils et de rythmes de mise en oeuvre des réformes de structures et des grands choix proposés au pays.*

4ᵉᵐᵉ PARTIE: UN PARTI POUR AUJOURD'HUI

131. *Le parti d'Epinay est passé de 80 000 à 180 000 membres en quelques années. C'est beaucoup, et c'est peu. Face aux sept millions d'électeurs qui nous font aujourd'hui confiance, il faut franchir une nouvelle étape, afin que notre capacité de mobilisation soit à la hauteur de nos succès électoraux. Nous devons prendre conscience que ce qui se débat à l'intérieur du parti concerne aussi ces millions d'électeurs ou de sympathisants qui s'interrogent sur nos orientations, sur notre démarche et sur nos projets. Si nous voulons les attirer vers nous, notre mot d'ordre doit être l'ouverture sur tous les fronts de la vie sociale et culturelle.*

132. *Le PS, d'autre part, a de grandes et légitimes ambitions. Il prétend accéder demain au pouvoir, porté par l'Union et les forces populaires et dans le cadre de l'Union de la Gauche. Mais il prétend aussi modifier profondément les formes mêmes du pouvoir. Comment pourrait-il y parvenir si, dès aujourd'hui, il n'adaptait pas ses structures à cette volonté? La convention du 25 novembre sur le règlement intérieur a marqué un progrès dans ce sens. Il faut aller plus loin. C'est l'objet des propositions qui suivent.*

1 Des Structures Démocratiques

1.1 La Collégialité

133. *Il n'y a pas de parti démocratique sans collégialité. C'est aussi la condition de l'unité. Depuis Epinay, le Parti, constitué par les apports successifs de différents courants, a fonctionné comme une confédération de groupes qui avaient tendance à rester fermés sur eux-mêmes. Il a eu la chance d'avoir à sa tête un fédérateur qui a su maintenir l'attelage, mais qui se trouvait par là même investi d'une autorité quasi-discrétionnaire. Cette situation a considérablement nui à la vie démocratique de l'organisation en favorisant une direction de type présidentialiste. Le parti dont la gauche a besoin ne doit plus désormais se contenter d'exprimer le discours de son Premier Secrétaire. C'est au Premier Secrétaire qu'il appartiendra d'exprimer le discours du parti.*

134. *Développer la collégialité veut dire notamment:*

135. **Revaloriser le rôle du Comité Directeur en lui permettant de travailler sur un ordre du jour précis et préparé par des rapports qui seraient envoyés à l'avance à tous ses membres.*

136. **Mettre fin au système actuel des délégués ou rapporteurs nationaux nommés par le Premier Secrétaire et ne dépendant que de lui. Si des délégués spécialisés doivent être maintenus pour assurer la présence du Parti dans tel ou tel secteur, ils devront recevoir leur mandat du Bureau Exécutif ou du Comité Directeur, l'exercer sous leur contrôle et répondre régulièrement de son exécution devant eux.*

137. **Donner aux travaux des commissions d'études, trop souvent ignorés des militants (voire santé, presse, nationalisations, informatique), la publicité qu'ils méritent et soumettre leurs conclusions au Parti.*

1.2 Une Elaboration Collective

138. *Un parti démocratique doit être le lieu d'une élaboration collective des propositions et des décisions.*

139. *A cet égard, nous souffrons d'un double cloisonnement:*

140. *L'information circule mal. Dans neuf cas sur dix, elle va du haut vers le bas. Encore faut-il noter que les décisions prises au sommet sont parfois transmises avec beaucoup de retard aux militants, ce qui est l'origine de flottements dommageables dans l'action quotidienne. On l'a vu par exemple à l'occasion du rapport sur l'Europe.*

141. *Un parti qui se veut 'ouvert' ne doit pas réserver les colonnes de ses organes d'information aux seuls dirigeants. Il faut que des groupes de militants puissent, s'ils le désirent, s'adresser aux autres par l'intermédiaire de notre presse interne, notamment fédérale. Il faut donner aux*

militants un droit d'initiative en décidant que, désormais, le Comité Directeur sera tenu de se saisir d'un problème, non seulement quand le Bureau Exécutif le jugera bon, mais aussi quand un nombre significatif de militants le demanderont. Il faut enfin mieux organiser nos grands débats nationaux. Chaque fois qu'un sujet important (emploi, nucléaire, écologie, santé) est soumis à l'ensemble des militants, la préparation du débat doit être assurée dans des conditions et des délais qui permettent à ceux-ci une étude sérieuse du dossier. Le Parti devra prendre aussi les dispositions nécessaires pour que les propositions qui remontent des sections soient examinées attentivement et bien utilisées.

142. *Ces procédures auraient l'avantage de mettre de temps en temps le Parti tout entier au travail, au-delà des enjeux tactiques ou électoraux immédiats.*

143. *Dans le même esprit, nous demandons qu'un compte rendu sommaire des débats du Bureau Exécutif et du Comité Directeur soit envoyé, par l'intermédiaire du Poing et la Rose–Responsables, à tous les bureaux de sections, et que l'on accélère, dès que possible, l'équipement des fédérations pour une meilleure et plus rapide communication (réseau télex).*

144. *Les études sont trop séparées des décisions. Il y a là un autre type de cloisonnement qui ne permet pas au Parti de jouer son rôle d'instrument collectif de réflexion en même temps que d'instrument d'éducation populaire. Pour que le débat prenne sa véritable dimension, il convient de veiller, dans chaque cas, à ce qu'il déborde le cercle des 'professionnels'.*

145. *Le règlement intérieur a prévu à cet effet des dispositions précises qui doivent être appliquées.*

146. *Notre réflexion collective ne devrait pas se priver non plus de l'enrichissement que peuvent lui apporter tous ceux qui, extérieurs au Parti, ont quelque chose à dire sur tels ou tels sujets et sont prêts à travailler avec nous. Dans plusieurs circonstances (sur les libertés, sur le nucléaire) nous avons fait appel à eux. Il importe de développer ce type de coopération en imaginant des procédures à la fois souples et adaptées du type ISER ou Conseil de développement culturel. Un grand parti comme le PS a tout intérêt à mobiliser autour de son projet le maximum de bonnes volontés.*

1.3 Régionaliser les Structures

147. *Nous ne pouvons pas défendre, au niveau du pouvoir, la décentralisation, la régionalisation et les refuser au niveau du Parti.*

148. *La décentralisation régionale de l'organisation du PS est absolument nécessaire si nous voulons enrichir à la fois ses effectifs et son programme. Qu'il s'agisse de l'aménagement du territoire, du développement régional, ou de la sauvegarde des cultures minoritaires*

(occitaines, bretonnes, etc.), les études et les décisions devraient être du ressort d'un échelon régional, quitte à ce qu'elles soient coordonnées au niveau national. Cela suppose que les comités régionaux de coordination prévus par les articles 22 et 23 votés en 1974, soient tous mis en place. Leur rôle n'est pas de se substituer aux fédérations, mais de permettre la décentralisation de certaines activités nationales, d'organiser l'action et la réflexion au niveau régional et d'assurer la coordination avec le groupe des élus régionaux et les représentants socialistes dans les diverses instances régionales. Ces comités, réunissant quatre délégués par fédération, désigneront un délégué régional. Ils mettront en place des commissions régionales d'études et choisiront les représentants de la région au sein des groupes de commission d'études nationaux du Parti. Chaque année une conférence nationale des régions examinera l'état de la réflexion et de l'action régionale du Parti. Enfin, un Secrétaire national chargé des questions régionales aura pour mission de coordonner l'ensemble des activités des comités régionaux.

149. *Nous avons besoin, d'autre part, de fédérations dynamiques, dotées de moyens matériels et de permanents politiques, là où les effectifs du Parti ne correspondent pas encore à sa poussée électorale. D'une manière générale, le rôle des fédérations gagnerait à être précisé pour qu'elles soient véritablement aptes à coordonner l'action des sections et à en animer les débats.*

2 Un Parti Adulte

150. *Le Parti dont nous avons besoin ne doit pas être seulement prêt à l'épreuve du pouvoir. Il faut aussi que, dans le combat quotidien de l'opposition, il puisse s'appuyer sur des bases militantes solides.*

2.1 La Formation

151. *Une véritable politique de formation est, dans cette perspective, essentielle. Elle suppose, d'abord, que l'accueil des nouveaux adhérents soit mieux organisé: trop souvent des hommes et des femmes qui seraient prêts à venir travailler avec nous sont découragés par le manque d'informations ou par la négligence dont nous faisons preuve à leur égard.*

152. *La formation doit ensuite permettre aux militants, quelle que soit leur origine, d'analyser les réalités sociales d'aujourd'hui et de les relier aux problèmes du pouvoir à tous les niveaux. Pour parvenir à ce résultat, trois conditions sont nécessaires: notre politique de formation doit être décentralisée, diversifiée et concrète.*

153. *Décentralisée: c'est la conséquence des observations qui précèdent. La formation adaptée aux situations locales doit être une des missions principales de l'échelon régional du Parti.*

154. *Diversifiée: un processus de 'politisation' unique suppose admis le schéma traditionnel selon lequel on commence par militer dans l'entreprise au niveau syndical ou dans une association (parents d'élèves,*

cadre de vie), avant de passer à l'échelon supérieur qui est le Parti. La réalité est en fait beaucoup plus complexe. L'expérience prouve, en particulier, que les femmes ne se politisent pas toujours à partir de considérations économiques et qu'à l'inverse, beaucoup d'entre elles, rebutées par le modèle masculin du militantisme, préfèrent les associations où elles sont mieux accueillies. Nous avons à tenir compte, dans notre travail de formation, de leurs aspirations propres et de leur souci d'inventer des formes d'actions, un langage politique qui y répondent.

155. *Ce qui est vrai des femmes l'est aussi des jeunes, et probablement d'autres catégories qui ne rentrent pas dans nos moules préétablis. La formation doit tenir compte de la diversité des origines et des langages de ceux à qui elle s'adresse.*

156. *Concrète: la formation n'est pas seulement idéologique. Elle ne doit pas seulement proposer aux militants une 'ligne', un 'programme', si solidement argumenté soit-il, elle a aussi un aspect pratique. On ne se forme vraiment qu'en prenant des responsabilités. Il faut donc aller vers une rotation des tâches à tous les niveaux, c'est-à-dire vers une organisation beaucoup plus collective du travail militant, qui permette à chacun de faire l'apprentissage des responsabilités, au niveau de l'organisation comme à celui de la parole.*

2.2   Les Secteurs d'Activités

157. *Le même souci de diversité doit nous conduire à respecter les particularités propres aux diverses catégories de militants.*

158. *Cela vaut d'abord, bien sûr, pour la base populaire du Parti, et tout particulièrement pour sa base ouvrière que nous voulons renforcer. Quelle est la part, dans le budget national du Parti et dans beaucoup de budgets fédéraux, consacrée aux groupes et sections d'entreprises? Combien d'ouvriers dans les instances du Parti au Parlement, dans les Conseils Généraux et Municipaux?*

159. *Pour assurer une véritable liaison entre le Parti et le monde ouvrier, il faut notamment donner aux travailleurs de la production des facilités leur permettant d'exercer des responsabilités; mettre d'urgence à l'ordre du jour le problème des permanents ouvriers dans le Parti, avec possibilités de reclassement professionnel; lutter dans le pays et au Parlement pour un véritable statut des élus locaux, qui garantissent à ceux-ci plus de temps et de libertés dans l'exercice de leur charge.*

160. *Les groupes et sections socialistes d'entreprise, dont l'importance est décisive pour la vitalité de notre projet, doivent moins être le lieu d'où l'on 'explique' aux travailleurs notre politique que celui où elle s'élabore, avec les travailleurs, notamment pour tout ce qui concerne l'entreprise et la branche d'activité données.*

161. *Cela vaut aussi pour les jeunes qui subissent souvent durement la double*

condition due à l'âge et au travail (ou au chômage!). Le problème n'est pas, comme le croient trop de dirigeants, de les contrôler, de les 'tenir en main' par crainte de leurs tendances naturelles à la 'déviation'. Ce qu'il faut, au contraire, c'est leur permettre de s'exprimer dans leur langage, à partir de leurs préoccupations. Aujourd'hui, le choix est clair; ou bien on laisse au MJS le maximum d'autonomie, et il a une chance de redémarrer. Ou bien il n'y aura pratiquement plus de jeunes socialistes. Les femmes, qui représentent 52 pour cent de la population, refusent à juste titre de poser le problème de leur participation militante en termes quantitatifs. Elles ne veulent pas non plus que ce problème soit traité comme un cas particulier parmi d'autres, sous forme traditionnelle du paragraphe: 'Le PS et les femmes'. Depuis quelques années, elles ont su mener, hors des partis traditionnels, des luttes souvent efficaces contre les conséquences de notre système patriarcal et capitaliste. Ces conséquences se font aussi sentir, qui pourrait le nier? au niveau de la vie quotidienne du Parti. Les femmes ont aujourd'hui à retrouver leur histoire, à proposer un nouveau langage et des formes différentes d'action politique. Elles veulent exister, enfin, comme sujets politiques. Cela exige une transformation profonde des mentalités. Il y faudra du temps, mais c'est, nous l'avons vu, un des enjeux essentiels de la rupture.

162. *Nous devons enfin développer d'autres secteurs que ceux qui sont traditionnellement organisés au sein du Parti. L'effort d'organisation en direction du milieu agricole doit être poursuivi et développé. Une attention nouvelle doit être portée à la réflexion et à l'action du parti en direction des secteurs professionnels d'importance croissante tels que les travailleurs sociaux et animateurs socio-culturels.*

2.3   Elargir le Militantisme

163. *Ouvrir le Parti, c'est aussi l'appeler à des tâches nouvelles correspondant à notre volonté d'être présents sur tous les terrains de la lutte sociale, non pas seulement comme des propagandistes mais comme des acteurs. Il ne s'agit pas de renoncer au travail proprement politique qui est celui d'un parti et qui exige effectivement la mobilisation permanente de ses membres pour faire connaître les objectifs qu'il s'assigne, les solutions qu'il propose.*

164. *Mais ce travail ne se résume évidemment pas aux collages d'affiches, distribution de tracts ou ventes de journaux. Il implique aussi, au niveau des sections, une réelle réflexion collective à laquelle chacun doit pouvoir apporter sa contribution en fonction de ses capacités et préoccupations particulières. Trop souvent encore, les militants ont le choix entre rester muets ou développer interminablement la ligne du parti, ou des interprétations de ce que l'on croit être la ligne à un moment donné. Les femmes ayant peu de goût pour ce genre de débats, elles ont tendance naturellement à adopter la première attitude et le parti se prive ainsi de l'enrichissement qu'elles pourraient lui apporter.*

165. *Elargir le militantisme, ce serait, au-delà des tâches pratiques tradition-*

nelles, au-delà des simples débats d'idées, faire du militant un véritable 'animateur', décidé à participer directement et dès aujourd'hui à la transformation de son milieu social et de vie, capable d'assurer, à quelque niveau qu'il se trouve et quelle que soit sa responsabilité, l'ambition autogestionnaire.

2.4   Les moyens Matériels et Financiers

166. *Un grand parti comme le PS ne peut pas fonctionner s'il ne dispose pas de moyens à la hauteur de sa tâche. Cela pose toute une série de problèmes qui ne sont certes pas faciles à résoudre et qui concernent aussi bien les locaux, où tous les dirigeants et responsables devraient pouvoir disposer de conditions de travail correctes, que le montant des cotisations demandées aux adhérents et, plus généralement, la situation financière de notre organisation. Le parti doit se décider à aborder une bonne fois cette question, qui n'est pas secondaire si l'on songe à ses ambitions et à la modicité de ses ressources actuelles. Mais surtout il est indispensable qu'à tous les échelons, national, fédéral et local, une transparence complète soit assurée. Les militants ont le droit de savoir comment notre action est financée.*

3   Un Parti Médiateur

167. *Enfin le Parti doit assurer la liaison entre ce qui se passe au niveau de l'Etat et des différents pouvoirs institutionnels et ce qui se passe au niveau de l'ensemble de la société. Cela suppose qu'il n'y ait aucune confusion entre le Parti et le pouvoir dans la société: il ne faut pas qu'une même personne cumule les fonctions de maire et de secrétaire de section locale, de président du Conseil général ou régional et de premier secrétaire fédéral, de premier secrétaire du parti et de candidat à la Présidence de la République.*

168. *Cela suppose aussi une modification dans les rapports entre les militants et les élus. Ces relations sont trop souvent présentées sous l'aspect d'un contrôle tâtillon et soupçonneux. Il s'agit plutôt de constituer autour de l'élu des 'réseaux' militants qui l'informent, le sollicitent, l'appuient, délibèrent avec lui, et, s'ils le critiquent, ne le font ainsi qu'en connaissance de cause. C'est seulement de cette manière que peut être évitée la double démission d'adhérents passifs et d'élus officiellement 'au service de tous', mais solitaires dans la décision et dans l'action.*

169. *Tout ce qui a été dit précédemment le montre: notre organisation en tant que parti, notre capacité à animer les luttes sociales et l'expérimentation de nouvelles pratiques collectives doivent exister indépendamment des structures de pouvoir dont les socialistes peuvent avoir la charge, au titre du suffrage universel. C'est une des conditions nécessaires à la victoire de la gauche, à la fois pour relancer une dynamique qui ne soit pas seulement de caractère électoral et pour faire en sorte que cette victoire soit solide et durable. Disons-le clairement: un parti pour qui la perspective d'accéder au gouvernement serait vécue comme un drame est*

un parti qui n'est pas capable de gouverner. Mais à l'inverse, un parti qui n'aurait pas, dès à présent, une attitude et un langage responsables dans l'opposition serait aussi un parti incapable d'avoir une attitude et un langage critiques quand ses représentants seront au gouvernement.

170. *Nous ne parviendrons à surmonter ces deux faiblesses complémentaires que si nous faisons du Parti Socialiste, parce qu'il sera actif aux deux bouts de la chaîne politique et sociale et rassemblé autour d'un même projet, l'instrument qui réduit la distance entre le gouvernement et le peuple: non pas pour que le peuple attende tout du gouvernement, mais pour qu'une même action de transformation sociale s'exprime à travers les changements de structures par la loi et l'institution, et à travers les initiatives populaires.*

CONCLUSION

Une motion de Congrès n'est pas un programme de gouvernement, ni un projet de société. Elle ne peut évoquer tous les aspects de la réalité politique, économique et sociale dans leurs détails. Elle propose au Parti des orientations pour les deux ans à venir.

Elle n'a pas non plus pour objet de reprendre chacun des textes qui constituent l'acquis collectif du Parti Socialiste: elle les complète et les enrichit en abordant les problèmes qui sont ceux de notre avenir.

Nous avons essayé de définir les perspectives d'un projet clair, offensif et mobilisateur. Il n'apparaîtra celui de la majorité de demain que si la vérité du langage et la rigueur des moyens accompagnent l'audace des choix qu'il propose. Les Français, à juste titre, se méfient des promesses. Ils savent trop, par expérience, combien il y a un discours pour les envolées lyriques des congrès et un autre au milieu des difficultés et des incertitudes de l'action.

Nous pensons qu'il existe une majorité dans le Parti Socialiste pour tenir ce langage et définir ce projet de société, pour vouloir renforcer l'organisation du Parti autour de ces principes. Nous souhaitons pour notre part que cette majorité soit la plus large possible, et nous travaillerons sans la moindre exclusive à toute synthèse qui se ferait sur des rapprochements clairs et positifs. Nous affaiblirions l'unité du Parti et son rayonnement par un compromis sur les principes ou un abandon sur les points essentiels.

Nous mettrons à réaliser la synthèse au congrès de Metz la même patience et la même loyauté que depuis deux mois nous avons eues pour tenter d'éviter que des clivages artificiels ne viennent briser la majorité des congrès de Pau et de Nantes.

Non que l'unité du Parti soit compromise par l'existence de divergences en son sein; mais parce que nous sommes convaincus que le parti doit se doter d'une direction cohérente appuyée sur une très large majorité pour faire face à l'aggravation prévisible des difficultés économiques, sociales et politiques de notre pays dans les années à venir.

Sur ces bases peuvent être garanties les trois conditions qui assureront la grandeur du Parti Socialiste et de son message: la clarté, parce que le choix sera celui des militants, la synthèse, parce que nous pensons possible de réunir tout le Parti dans cette volonté de franchir une nouvelle étape, l'unité, parce qu'il s'agit d'avancer dans la réalisation des objectifs qui font que nous sommes, tous ensemble, des socialistes.

Appendix 2: Convention Nationale du Parti Socialiste; 'Modernisation et Progrès Social': 15 et 16 décembre 1984 à Evry (Essonne); Textes préparatoires au débat

DEBATTRE POUR AGIR

1. *1 Débattre sur ce qui constitue l'un des thèmes centraux de l'action du gouvernement et débattre pour agir, tels sont les objectifs que nous nous sommes fixés pour cette Convention 'Modernisation et Progrès social'.*

2. *A cet égard, et bien que les délais de discussion aient parfois constitué une contrainte, le nombre des réponses au questionnaire revenues des sections – plus de 2000 – la qualité des travaux auxquels dans des assemblées générales, dans des groupes de réflexion, se sont livrés les militants et la richesse des matériaux ainsi recueillis, nous montrent à l'évidence qu'une réelle mobilisation s'est produite dans tout le Parti. C'était un de nos objectifs, il est, à cette étape, déjà en partie atteint.*

3. *2 Il nous faut maintenant poursuivre selon le processus choisi.*

4. *Comme il en avait été convenu, une Commission nationale, émanation de l'ensemble du Bureau Exécutif et que j'ai présidée, s'est réunie pour dépouiller toutes ces réponses et, en intégrant leur contenu, préparer le texte qui vous est désormais soumis pour discussion et pour vote.*

5. *La résolution présentée dans ce numéro du Poing et la Rose est le fruit de plusieurs séances de travail de cette commission au cours desquelles chacun des membres a pu apporter sa contribution orale ou écrite. Ces réunions ont été ouvertes aux responsables de commissions du Parti particulièrement concernés par le thème (économie, recherche, entreprise).*

6. *Cette résolution a été votée unanimement par le Bureau Exécutif du 15 novembre. A côté de ce texte, vous trouverez quatre amendements. C'est*

sur la résolution générale et sur les quatre amendements que vous aurez à vous prononcer ainsi que sur les amendements éventuels que vous voterez en section.

7. *Le troisième texte du Poing et la Rose est d'une autre nature. Il est une réflexion ou une tribune qui n'est pas soumise au vote des militants.*

8. *3 La nature de vos réponses aux questionnaires montre que, si le caractère impératif de la modernisation est reconnu par l'ensemble des militants, les risques à court terme en sont bien soulignés. A notre Parti de formuler (les 15 et 16 décembre) puis de promouvoir les valeurs et les moyens qui font que seule la gauche peut, au contraire de la droite, réussir la modernisation.*

PROJET DE RESOLUTION

Présenté par le Bureau Exécutif unanime (texte soumis au vote).

MODERNISATION ET PROGRES SOCIAL

9. *Modernisation: le mot résonne différemment pour celui qui la décide et celui qui la subit, pour celui qui se sent assuré d'en tirer avantage et celui qui craint d'en être victime. Cette ambigüté nous l'avons déjà rencontrée dans l'Histoire, où mutations techniques et crises de société sont toujours allées de pair. C'est à cause d'elle que les socialistes entendent aujourd'hui ouvrir un débat public sur la modernisation. Parce qu'ils ne croient ni au déterminisme inéluctable de l'Histoire ni à la solution unique aux crises, ils entendent souligner devant le pays ce qui différencie aujourd'hui la Droite et la Gauche face à ce problème. S'agit-il d'utiliser les progrès nouveaux de la technique dans un sens qui conforte les positions sociales et les positions de pouvoir des anciennes couches dominantes? S'agit-il au contraire de mettre les nouveaux outils qui apparaissent au service de la société toute entière, au service du progrès social, au service de tous? Cette différence d'objectifs implique des différences d'analyse et de moyens d'action: c'est ce que veut illustrer ce document. Parce que nous sommes socialistes nous voulons la modernisation, mais pas seulement celle de l'appareil productif, également celle des rapports sociaux et de la société elle-même, pour avancer vers plus de justice sociale, et à travers une méthode simple et sûre qui a nom: davantage de démocratie.*

INTRODUCTION
LA SOCIETE FRANCAISE EN CRISE

10. *La crise que traversent aujourd'hui la France et les autres pays industriels trouve ses origines bien avant les chocs pétroliers, dans*

l'essoufflement et le dérèglement des mécanismes qui avaient permis les trente années de croissance de l'après-guerre: essoufflement des mécanismes économiques avec la saturation progressive des marchés de consommation de masse et les limites atteintes par les concentrations d'entreprises, dérèglement des mécanismes monétaires à partir de 1967. C'est dès le début des années 70, que s'enregistrent les premières poussées d'un chômage et d'une inflation simultanés, les décisions de l'OPEP n'apparaissant que comme une réaction à la dévalorisation d'un pétrole payé en dollars et une accélération de la crise.

11. *La politique menée par les Etats-Unis pour tenter de reprendre une prééminence ébranlée par le choc politique et financier de la guerre du Viet-Nam et par la fin du système de Bretton-Woods a constitué un facteur important d'aggravation de cette crise. L'égoïsme national que les Etats-Unis ont manifesté à cette occasion n'a pas faibli depuis et contribue encore aujourd'hui aux difficultés de la situation mondiale.*

12. *Enfin, cette crise est aussi une crise des institutions et des mécanismes de régulation des rapports sociaux mis en place selon des modèles hérités du XIXᵉ siècle et qui correspondent mal à la diversité des individus et des groupes aujourd'hui.*

13. *C'est pourquoi il ne faut pas confondre cette crise avec la mutation technologique. Trop de voix s'élèvent aujourd'hui pour décrire la crise comme l'inéluctable conséquence de la modernisation. La révolution industrielle entraînerait de tels bouleversements dans la société que nous serions contraints d'accepter ces passages obligés que sont la montée du chômage, l'accroissement des inégalités sociales, la réalité d'une société duale, l'affaiblissement industriel d'une partie du monde. L'Europe et la France seraient aussi condamnées à régresser en attendant le jour où la lumière du soleil américain daignerait briller sur notre continent.*

14. *Certes, les premiers aspects de la crise ont été amplifiés par la formidable mutation technologique qui les accompagne: à travers l'informatique notamment tentent d'être mis en place à la fois de nouveaux produits de consommation (micro-ordinateurs par exemple) qui tentent de prolonger les mécanismes économiques antérieurs, et de nouvelles méthodes de production (type robotisation) qui visent à engager une nouvelle bataille entre les grands compétiteurs industriels subsistants. Mais l'introduction des nouvelles technologies dans le processus de production et dans l'ensemble de la société n'est pas la cause de la crise. Ainsi, par exemple, la substitution du capital au travail en agriculture depuis 1950 fait que ce secteur a largement rattrapé son retard technique et économique. Le problème aujourd'hui n'est pas de produire plus mais de créer plus de valeur ajoutée.*

15. *L'ensemble de cette crise et de ces mutations est en tout cas en train de remettre formidablement en cause les forces sociales et les rapports de production dans notre pays. Les premières décennies de croissance de*

l'après-guerre avaient été avant tout marquées par l'exode rural, la croissance de l'emploi industriel et de l'urbanisation. Nous connaissons depuis dix ans une phase de stagnation ou de régression de l'emploi industriel et une montée de l'emploi dans les services, où l'organisation du travail est profondément différente. Les nouvelles technologies conduiront-elles demain à la déqualification accrue d'une large part du monde des ouvriers et des employés, ou permettront-elles au contraire à chacun l'accès à plus de créativité: les socialistes pensent que c'est l'un des enjeux du débat sur la modernisation.

UNE MUTATION SANS PRECEDENT

16. *La mutation que nous traversons aujourd'hui est sans précédent, qu'il s'agisse de sa nature même ou de ses acteurs.*

17. *Les grands changements technologiques antérieurs ont été caractérisés par la substitution de l'énergie mécanique à l'énergie de l'homme, puis par l'introduction de la production et de la consommation de masse. Aujourd'hui, il s'agit d'introduire la machine dans l'élaboration et l'échange d'information, voire dans le processus de conception lui-même, et de développer ainsi, grâce aux progrès des techniques de communication, des méthodes de production et d'organisation de la société que personne ne peut encore concevoir clairement. Par ailleurs, la mutation technologique que nous vivons est beaucoup plus rapide que les précédentes: nos enfants utiliseront des biens dont la plupart n'existent pas encore.*

18. *Enfin, l'économie a achevé son internationalisation. Une issue purement française est devenue du domaine de l'illusion. Le problème du choix des partenaires internationaux est au coeur de toute stratégie.*

19. *Les acteurs eux-mêmes ont changé. Depuis les années 60, les travailleurs et leurs organisations syndicales ont pu pleinement mesurer le poids croissant des sociétés multinationales américaines et japonaises sur la vie économique et sociale. L'Europe n'a pas su s'affirmer avec assez de force. Les conséquences sont connues. Le gouvernement français dans un mémorandum de 1983 les a clairement soulignées: l'Europe n'est plus depuis quelques années la source principale du développement des innovations scientifiques et technologiques. Auteur exclusif de la première révolution industrielle, auteur principal de la seconde, l'Europe est en train de manquer son entrée dans la troisième révolution, celle de l'électronique.*

20. *L'industrie européenne des technologies de l'information ne détient que 10 pour cent du marché mondial et 40 pour cent seulement de son propre marché. Pour les robots ou les composants électroniques, le taux de pénétration du marché européen est d'environ 60 pour cent. Il est de près de 80 pour cent pour les ordinateurs personnels et de 90 pour cent pour les magnétoscopes.*

21. *Pour la première fois l'Europe subit le changement, ses bourgeoisies nationales acceptant de s'installer dans un rôle secondaire par rapport aux Etats-Unis.*

AGIR ET NON SUBIR

22. *En effet, que nous le souhaitions ou non, la mutation est en train de s'imposer chez les autres. C'est le cas dans un certain nombre de pays nouvellement industrialisés qui, accédant, voire dans certains cas dépassant, notre niveau technique avec des salaires bien moindres et une protection sociale parfois inexistante risquent de devenir des concurrents de plus en plus redoutables. C'est le cas surtout de pays comme les Etats-Unis et le Japon, où s'élaborent de nouvelles méthodes de production et de nouveaux produits.*

23. *Nous ne pouvons rester spectateurs pour trois séries de raisons:*

24. *Il nous faut non seulement résister à ces nouvelles concurrences chez nous – seul problème que considèrent les défenseurs du protectionnisme – mais être capable de les affronter dans le reste du monde: en effet, nous devons pouvoir exporter pour payer notre énergie, nos matières premières et, dans le court terme au moins, certains biens d'équipement qui nous font aujourd'hui défaut. Si nous voulons sauvegarder notre emploi et notre niveau de vie, nous ne devons donc pas nous laisser distancer.*

25. *Il nous faut préserver notre indépendance et l'indépendance de l'Europe, gage de notre liberté de bâtir entre les superpuissances le système économique et social de notre choix; accepter une domination technologique signifierait aujourd'hui accepter une domination culturelle, renoncer à assurer notre sécurité et laisser ainsi mettre en question notre identité même.*

26. *Il nous faut jeter les bases d'une nouvelle croissance permettant de lutter plus facilement contre le chômage et de reprendre la progression du pouvoir d'achat. Or la leçon de la relance de 1981 est claire à cet égard: faute de capacités de production modernisées, et à défaut d'une concertation européenne, c'est à nouveau au bénéfice du reste du monde plus qu'au nôtre que se ferait la croissance.*

A DROITE RESTRUCTURATION, A GAUCHE MODERNISATION

27. *Là est bien, en effet, le coeur du débat. Utiliser le progrès technique à la seule fin d'abaisser les coûts de production en diminuant l'emploi, telle est la rationalité de la restructuration que la droite propose.*

28. *Si la perspective de la modernisation ne saurait écarter toute idée de restructuration, si certaines de celles-ci constituent parfois des points de passage obligés, elles ne sont jamais des fins en soi: l'objectif doit être d'utiliser les mutations technologiques pour transformer la société elle-même en améliorant les conditions de vie de tous les hommes. Aux yeux des socialistes, il n'y a pas une modernisation mais des modernisations qui, au-delà de l'appareil productif, concernent l'ensemble de la vie sociale. En effet, les mutations technologiques ne prennent leur sens qu'intégrées dans un projet social, qui ne se résume pas à des mesures 'd'accompagnement' destinées à amortir la brutalité des faits mais guide l'action par les valeurs qui sont les nôtres:*

29. **lutte contre les inégalités, accès de tous à une meilleure formation et à une culture vivante.*

30. **transformation des relations de pouvoir existant tant dans l'entreprise que dans la société civile au bénéfice d'une plus grande démocratie.*

31. **utilisation de cette démocratie elle-même comme instrument de la conduite de la modernisation: le monde du travail, en particulier, doit devenir acteur du changement.*

32. *Refusant une mutation subie, les socialistes recherchent une modernisation maîtrisée.*

1   LA MODERNISATION EST PORTEE PAR LES SOCIALISTES

1.1   La droite française ne peut plus moderniser

33. *1.1.1   Le compromis social de l'après-guerre n'est plus viable*
Au cours des années 50 et 60, les classes dirigeantes de notre pays ont réussi à concilier une certaine modernisation avec la poursuite d'un conservatisme politique et social. La croissance économique rapide leur a donné la possibilité d'organiser un compromis entre les forces sociales. L'existence d'un surplus important a permis de masquer l'antagonisme du partage. Mais ce qui était possible en période de croissance forte ne l'a plus été au cours des années 70. L'arrêt de la croissance a mis en lumière les contradictions d'intérêts entre les classes dirigeantes et la collectivité, et dans une moindre mesure, au sein de ces deux ensembles. Dans le même temps apparaissait le recul relatif de la France. Des pans entiers de l'industrie française étaient abandonnés au jeu sans frein de la division internationale du travail, dans les biens de consommation (vêtements, électroménager, meubles, etc) et également dans les biens d'équipement (informatique, mécanique, etc). Depuis 1974, le phénomène s'est accéléré: près de 800 000 emplois industriels supprimés, un tissu industriel affaibli, un sous-investissement chronique.

34. *Dans de nombreux domaines, l'industrie française contrôlait beaucoup moins de 50 pour cent du marché intérieur. Mis à part quelques secteurs de pointe en meilleure santé, qui bénéficiaient souvent de fonds publics et de marchés protégés (aéronautique, télécommunication, armement), le tissu industriel français était profondément dégradé. De même, si l'agriculture contribue depuis quelques années positivement au solde du commerce extérieur, la modernisation de l'appareil de production a entraîné la concentration foncière, la diminution de moitié des exploitations sur 30 ans, l'exode rural et la désertification de certaines régions.*

35. *A côté de l'aggravation de la situation économique, la crise a également accentué les inégalites sociales. La France avant 1981 restait un pays marqué par de profondes injustices. L'existence de situations inacceptables, les cumuls de handicaps en matière d'éducation, de santé, de revenu, de travail, n'avaient pas été remis en cause. Au contraire, l'exclusion sociale s'était étendue.*

36. *A la liberté d'entreprendre, le patronat a voulu ajouter la liberté de licenciement. La flexibilité de l'emploi est sans doute une condition indispensable du progrès. Mais elle ne doit pas aboutir au développement massif d'emplois précaires et servir de prétexte aux entreprises pour liquider trente ans d'acquis sociaux. Le progrès économique ne peut se faire comme le souhaiterait la droite sur les décombres du droit social.*

1.1.2   Le chômage d'aujourd'hui, héritage de l'absence de modernisation d'hier

37. **La politique de contrôle étroit, puis de liberté surveillée des prix de M. Barre a échoué à combattre une inflation supérieure à celle de nos concurrents: +14 pour cent en 1981.*

38. **Cette inflation était le résultat d'une adaptation différée de notre économie. L'importance des coûts de production des entreprises françaises, les comportements d'endettement, un partage du revenu défavorable à l'épargne financière avaient profondément affaibli la compétitivité de l'économie française.*

39. *Ainsi, l'appareil productif français était-il, à la veille de 1981, vieilli et incapable de répondre à une concurrence internationale exacerbée. Les structures financières des entreprises qui étaient profondément dégradées, comme l'existence de sureffectifs notamment dans l'industrie (sidérurgie, automobile), constituent deux exemples notables.*

40. *A terme, cette situation rendait inévitable des choix difficiles. Le retard pris dans une gestion à courte vue a un coût: le chômage d'aujourd'hui est l'héritage de l'absence de modernisation d'hier. Les socialistes au pouvoir ont dans un premier temps sous-estimé l'importance de ce handicap.*

41. *Les modalités selon lesquelles la modernisation de la France a été engagée au cours des deux décennies de l'après-guerre ont trouvé leurs limites dès que la croissance s'est ralentie. Le pacte social a éclaté, empêchant tout progrès dans les structures industrielles comme dans les structures sociales.*

42. *Aujourd'hui, la droite ne peut plus moderniser. Elle ne peut qu'aller chercher à l'étranger un modèle qui n'est pas transposable à la France.*

1.2   Les modèles étrangers de l'opposition: de fausses solutions

43. *Le libéralisme est à la mode. Bien que parfois, sentant l'exagération de leurs discours, les leaders de la droite se défendent d'être totalement libéraux, c'est bien dans cette idéologie qui nous ramène loin en arrière que l'opposition trouve son inspiration. Elle invoque les expériences étrangères et notamment la politique de R. Reagan et celle de M. Thatcher pour valider ses thèses. L'analyse de ces politiques et de leurs résultats infirme le jugement positif fréquemment répandu; les modèles de l'opposition ne sont pas ce que l'on croit; au demeurant, leur transplantation en France n'est pas viable.*

1.2.1   La relance de l'économie américaine: qui paye?

44. *La politique de R. Reagan a connu certains succès: l'inflation a fortement reculé et, après une récession très forte en 1981 et 1982, une reprise vigoureuse de l'économie a été constatée depuis 1983. Elle s'essouffle aujourd'hui.*

45. *Quel est le revers de la médaille? N'y aurait-il aucun aspect négatif dans cette reprise, ce qui inciterait à vouloir la prendre pour modèle? La réponse est malheureusement non. Deux caractéristiques de la politique menée aux Etats-Unis la rendent inacceptable pour les socialistes.*

46. **Tout d'abord, le redémarrage de l'économie américaine laisse sur le bord de la route une partie importante du pays. Le dualisme de la société américaine s'est accentué. Plus encore qu'avant, deux Amériques apparaissent en pleine lumière, celle de la Californie dorée et celle du Bronx; il y a, selon le Bureau du recensement US, plus de 35 millions de pauvres aux Etats-Unis!*

47. **Ensuite, la relance de l'économie américaine se fait sur le dos du reste du monde. L'énormité du déficit extérieur américain est compensé par l'afflux des capitaux étrangers attirés par des taux d'intérêts élevés. Qu'en agissant ainsi les Etats-Unis assèchent l'épargne du reste du monde, qu'en maintenant des taux d'intérêt aussi élevés les Etats-Unis étranglent le Tiers-Monde, montre bien que les vertus de la reprise américaine sont bien plus limitées qu'on tente de nous le faire croire. Au demeurant, de nombreux aspects de la politique qui a été suivie sont loin de suivre la logique libérale: l'importance d'un déficit budgétaire*

(d'inspiration keynésienne), le rôle considérable joué par l'intervention de l'Etat, par l'intermédiaire des dépenses militaires et spatiales, et l'étendue du protectionnisme suffisent à le prouver.

1.2.2   La désindustrialisation et le chômage britanniques: qui en veut?

48. *Au contraire de l'exemple américain, la politique de Mme Thatcher relève d'une application rigoureuse des préceptes monétaristes.*

49. *La rente pétrolière fournie par les ressources énergétiques de la mer du Nord masque une partie des conséquences parfois dramatiques de la politique suivie:*

50. **le mouvement de restructuration industrielle se limite pour le moment à un abandon des activités les moins rentables sans que la situation du reste de l'industrie soit sensiblement améliorée;*

51. **le chômage a plus que doublé en 5 ans, atteignant désormais plus de trois millions de personnes; les inégalités et les tensions sociales s'accentuent;*

52. **malgré la rente pétrolière, les équilibres extérieurs continuent à se dégrader.*

53. *Finalement, le modèle anglais n'est rien d'autre qu'une augmentation de la productivité par la destruction du capital et la dévalorisation du travail.*

1.2.3   Le paternalisme et le dualisme japonais: qui les souhaite?

54. *Dans le dynamisme des chefs d'entreprise japonais, dans la capacité des différents agents de cette économie à se concerter il existe de nombreux points positifs qu'il ne faut pas sous-estimer. Ils ne sont pas directement transposables à la France, notre culture et notre histoire sont trop largement différentes.*

55. *Mais, plus encore, il y a de nombreux aspects de l'organisation de la société japonaise que nous ne souhaitons pas voir se développer en France. Qu'il s'agisse de la sujétion du salarié de la grande entreprise, ou de la précarité de la situation des salariés des PME sous-traitantes, comme des travailleurs des entreprises individuelles et familiales, la société japonaise est fondée sur un paternalisme d'entreprise et sur un dualisme social dont nous ne voulons pas.*

1.2.4   Ces politiques ne sont pas adaptables en France

56. *Le voudrions-nous que nous ne pourrions mettre en oeuvre la politique suivie par les Etats-Unis. Nous ne sommes pas l'économie dominante qui peut se permettre d'imposer aux autres de financer son propre redressement.*

57. *Dès lors quelles seraient les conséquences de la mise en oeuvre en France des programmes proposés par la droite?*

58. *Une plus grande insertion dans la division internationale du travail, réduisant encore notre marge de manoeuvre, la diminution du nombre des fonctionnaires, entraînant une baisse de qualité des services publics (écoles, hôpitaux), la réduction de la protection sociale remplacée par des procédures d'assurance individuelle, la limitation des garanties accordées aux travailleurs par la législation du travail, le recul de la démocratie dans l'entreprise par la remise en cause des lois Auroux, l'éclatement de la société par l'accentuation du dualisme entre ceux qui profitent de la mutation technologique et ceux qui en pâtissent, le retour en arrière sur des droits et libertés nouvelles concernant notamment l'IVG, voilà où la transposition des programmes libéraux conduirait la France.*

1.3 Les contradictions du PC

59. *Le Parti Communiste, quant à lui, développe à l'égard de la modernisation des positions parfaitement contradictoires. D'un côté il exalte le progrès technique qui pour lui serait presque automatiquement synonyme de progrès social. Mais d'un autre côté, il adopte une attitude très irréaliste, refusant toute évolution au niveau des entreprises et l'idée même que puissent y exister des sureffectifs dans certains secteurs. Ce faisant, en prétendant se battre mieux que quiconque pour l'emploi d'aujourd'hui, il sacrifie l'emploi de demain. Alors que le PC fait grand cas du développement des forces productives dans ses déclarations, lorsque le progrès est là sa mise en oeuvre semble poser des problèmes insurmontables. Le progrès est beau dans les textes mais pas dans la réalité.*

60. *La réconciliation de ces positions conduit à proposer une politique de fermeture des frontières et une prise de distance par rapport à la construction européenne. Depuis qu'il a renoncé aux responsabilités du pouvoir, le PC ne craint pas de méconnaître la réalité des contraintes du marché mondial. Dans les positions qu'il développe, soit il suppose que le problème de la croissance est résolu, soit il nie les conséquences que les solutions qu'il propose en exigeant la fermeture relative de nos frontières entraîneraient inéluctablement.*

61. *Ce refus d'accepter dans ses termes réels le processus de la modernisation est incohérent. Il conduirait immanquablement à un recul de la France sur la scène internationale et à une baisse du niveau de vie.*

1.4 Conduite par les socialistes, la modernisation constitue une chance pour la France

1.4.1 Les conditions de la modernisation ont été mises en place

62. *(a) La décentralisation engagée dès l'arrivée au pouvoir rompt avec une tradition séculaire de la France. Les difficultés que présente sa mise en oeuvre sont très grandes et de nombreuses années passeront avant que le pays puisse en tirer tout le bénéfice. Cependant, rapprochant le pouvoir de décision des citoyens, la décentralisation permet d'ores et déjà une libération des initiatives locales. Qui niera qu'il s'agit là d'une évolution majeure de la société française qui lui permettra de mieux aborder l'avenir?*

63. *(b) Les nationalisations sont intervenues dans certains secteurs industriels et ont contribué à la relance de l'investissement et au succès des restructurations sans lesquelles des dizaines de milliers d'emplois supplémentaires auraient été supprimés. Si elles n'avaient pas été nationalisées, de grandes entreprises comme Thomson, Rhône-Poulenc, auraient été démantelées, vendues à des capitaux étrangers ou auraient purement et simplement disparu. Aujourd'hui, elles sont sur la voie du redressement et connaissent des résultats industriels et financiers positifs même si elles n'ont pas encore répondu à toutes nos espérances dans le domaine économique comme dans celui de la démocratie.*

64. *Mais, surtout, les faiblesses du capitalisme français sont telles que seul l'Etat semble capable de s'engager dans des programmes préparant l'avenir. Si, grâce aux vecteurs que constituent les entreprises publiques, l'Etat n'avait pas donné les impulsions nécessaires, les succès français dans le domaine nucléaire comme dans l'aéronautique n'auraient pas été possibles.*

65. *Ainsi, la nationalisation n'est pas synonyme d'archaïsme ou de déficit. Elle garantit au contraire la mise en oeuvre et la diffusion des innovations ainsi que la prise en compte de l'intérêt collectif.*

66. *(c) La recherche scientifique est un atout majeur dans le processus de modernisation.*

67. *Convaincus que la recherche contribue à assurer à long terme notre indépendance technologique et culturelle, nous avons fait de la recherche scientifique une priorité nationale rompant avec les pratiques dévastatrices de la droite dont la politique détruisait petit à petit le tissu même de notre appareil de recherche.*

68. *Après une consultation nationale qui a mobilisé non seulement les chercheurs mais tous les acteurs sociaux et économiques de la recherche et qui a initié un dialogue que la politique de droite avait cassé, nous avons dans un premier temps accompli des réformes de structure en*

profondeur (statuts des établissements, statuts des chercheurs, décloisonnement de la fonction de recherche).

69. *Dans un second temps, et malgré des conditions économiques difficiles, la priorité budgétaire de ce secteur a été maintenue et les bases d'une politique à long terme des personnels de recherche ont été posées. Lors de la présidence française de la CEE, une politique européenne de recherche encore insuffisante et pourtant si prometteuse a été relancée.*

70. *(d) L'efficacité dans l'entreprise ne repose pas sur une organisation rigide du travail, mais sur le développement de la capacité des travailleurs à s'exprimer et à prendre des initiatives.*

71. *Les lois Auroux ne font, pour une bonne part, que permettre aux relations du travail en France de se porter au niveau des autres pays européens. Mais tout comme la démocratisation du secteur public, elles visent aussi, en accroissant les droits et libertés des travailleurs, à favoriser l'expression de leur potentiel de créativité, et leur capacité d'intervenir dans la définition et dans le déroulement du processus de production.*

72. *La droite a toujours tenu un discours hostile au syndicalisme. Ce dernier a pourtant joué dans l'histoire un rôle irremplaçable dans la progression de la législation sociale. Aujourd'hui plus que jamais, dans l'entreprise comme sur le plan national, la place du syndicalisme est déterminante. Qu'il s'agisse de la négociation des salaires, de la concertation concernant les choix de politique industrielle ou des conditions de travail et d'existence des salariés, les syndicats doivent être systématiquement associés aux décisions à prendre. Tout ce qui contribue à renforcer leur audience, à améliorer leurs moyens d'action ne peut donc que recueillir l'appui des socialistes. Le syndicalisme a un rôle spécifique et autonome à jouer dans la société, aussi doit-on veiller à la préservation de son indépendance par rapport à l'Etat, aux partis et au patronat. Il n'y a pas de démocratisation possible de la vie économique et de la vie des entreprises sans un syndicalisme fort.*

73. *(e) Une des raisons de la faiblesse des investissements dans le secteur productif découle de la rareté des capitaux qui se dirigent spontanément dans notre pays vers le financement de l'industrie comme de l'agriculture. Le capitalisme français n'aime pas prendre de risques industriels; les rentes que l'Etat peut verser lui semblent préférables, la spéculation immobilière ou foncière lui paraît moins dangereuse.,*

74. *Aussi un effort considérable a-t-il été entrepris depuis trois ans pour réorienter l'épargne vers le financement du secteur productif. Qu'il s'agisse du développement de l'intervention des banques dans l'industrie (même si elle reste encore insuffisante), de la création de nouveaux placements spécialement destinés à financer le secteur productif ou de la mise en place de nouveaux instruments d'intervention comme le Fonds*

Industriel de Modernisation, une réorientation importante de l'épargne française en faveur de l'appareil de production a été entreprise.

1.4.2   La modernisation concerne toute la société

75.   *L'Histoire montre que luttes sociales et combats politiques peuvent permettre de tirer de la modernisation ses bienfaits. Plus encore que dans le passé, une modernisation bien utilisée peut contribuer aujourd'hui à libérer l'homme:*

76.   **en permettant à chacun de disposer de davantage de temps libre, et en favorisant ainsi l'accès aux loisirs, la participation de tous à la vie de la cité, une autre organisation de la vie quotidienne fondée sur une plus juste répartition des tâches familiales entre les sexes (qu'on songe à la réduction du temps de travail déjà acquise en France par les salariés dans les cinquante années écoulées: 2319 heures annuelles effectives en 1930, 1609 en 1983!);*

77.   **en améliorant les conditions de travail, les qualifications, voire la nature même du travail (quelle différence, par exemple, entre les chaînes automobiles de l'après-guerre et les ateliers robotisés d'aujourd'hui!);*

78.   **en développant la créativité dans des entreprises à taille humaine. La modernisation n'est pas la concentration; au contraire, un renversement est en train de s'esquisser dans les économies les plus développées vers des unités plus réduites, aux spécialisations fines, permettant aux travailleurs de retrouver une vie collective et d'agir sur les conditions de production;*

79.   **en permettant d'espérer une inversion de la logique de la concentration géographique et en développant les activités des petites industries dans les campagnes grâce à l'utilisation des moyens modernes de communication, de l'informatique décentralisée et des réseaux. Grâce à l'organisation de pôles culturels dans les villes et les villages, à l'entretien des réseaux de transport et à une distribution efficace de l'énergie, une nouvelle synergie entre l'agriculture et l'industrie décentralisée pourra assurer le maintien d'un tissu rural équilibré;*

80.   **en offrant aux consommateurs, aux usagers, de nouveaux biens et services utiles (des médicaments ou des procédés qui allongent l'espérance de vie ou permettent une véritable maîtrise de la vie, des moyens de communication qui favorisent contacts et échanges. . .);*

81.   **en favorisant la lutte contre la permanence ou la renaissance de scandales comme la faim ou le sous-développement (mais cela suppose là aussi que l'appel à la modernité des techniques se fasse dans le respect des traditions et des cultures);*

82.   **en facilitant l'émergence d'une société plus démocratique, faisant davantage appel à la créativité et aux capacités de chacun (informatique*

et télécommunications pourront permettre cela aussi à travers des réseaux interactifs donnant la possibilité non seulement d'écouter mais aussi de dialoguer).

83. *C'est donc bien une modernisation de l'ensemble de la société qu'il s'agit d'entreprendre, elle ne saurait se limiter à l'appareil de production.*

2   MODERNISER POUR LE PROGRES SOCIAL

84. *Toute mutation technologique comporte des risques. Au niveau individuel, elle remet en cause les habitudes de chacun, elle crée pour beaucoup un sentiment d'insécurité et souvent une insécurité véritable.*

85. *Le sentiment d'insécurité apparaît encore plus fondé au niveau collectif. Des branches industrielles ou des régions sont aujourd'hui menacées et le risque majeur ressenti par chacun d'entre nous concerne l'emploi.*

86. *Sur le terrain de l'emploi, le gouvernement a depuis 1981 mis en place toute une série de mesures et notamment les congés de conversion visant à remplacer certains licenciements par des périodes de formation à l'exercice de nouvelles activités; l'aide au retour pour les travailleurs étrangers acceptant un départ volontaire pour leur pays d'origine; les Travaux d'Utilité Collective permettant aux jeunes à la recherche d'un premier emploi de trouver pendant cette période d'attente une garantie d'insertion sociale; l'amélioration des aides à la création de nouvelles entreprises par des chômeurs.*

87. *Il est clair que ces mesures ne peuvent être que des palliatifs. Elles marquent cependant le souci important de trouver les solutions d'attente que nécessitent les délais de mise en oeuvre de solutions plus durables.*

88. *Car pour maîtriser la mutation, il faut préparer l'emploi futur en réformant notre appareil de formation afin de l'adapter pour les travailleurs de tous âges aux métiers de demain; il faut organiser la diminution du temps de travail que les nouvelles méthodes de production autorisent; il faut, loin de réduire la protection sociale, favoriser l'émergence de nouvelles solidarités.*

2.1   L'école, la formation des hommes et l'emploi de demain

89. *Les métiers vont être soumis à des changements rapides, y compris les métiers les plus traditionnels.*

90. *La mutation technologique fait éclater le cadre de l'organisation du travail. Désormais il sera fréquent de ne plus exercer un seul métier dans sa vie, mais d'en pratiquer plusieurs successivement; les périodes de formation alterneront avec les périodes de travail.*

91. *La politique de l'emploi ne doit donc plus être uniquement défensive: il ne s'agit plus seulement d'indemniser les dégâts de la crise, mais d'inciter à la mobilité et à l'évolution des savoirs et des savoir-faire pour un meilleur emploi.*

92. *La formation constitue la clé de cette mobilité accrue. L'accélération du progrès technique doit conduire à l'élévation générale du niveau des qualifications et à leur adaptation. Il faut engager résolument la modification des structures de qualification: l'organisation du travail dans l'avenir doit comporter des travailleurs de plus en plus qualifiés, moins de travailleurs à la chaîne.*

93. *Cependant, les qualifications nouvelles, celles qui sauront le mieux s'adapter aux technologies de l'avenir ne consisteront pas seulement en une accumulation de savoirs; elles devront aussi permettre d'analyser des données plus complexes pour décider, entreprendre, et contribuer au dialogue social comme à l'exercice de la solidarité.*

94. *Comment atteindre cet objectif si la formation se conçoit et s'effectue en vase clos? Il faut, au contraire, former aux emplois futurs en instaurant de nouveaux rapports entre l'école, l'entreprise et le monde du travail, et en faisant sa place à la culture technique au sein de la culture générale.*

95. *Mais comment pourrions-nous rendre les hommes de demain plus imaginatifs, plus entreprenants, plus libres, s'ils n'y étaient préparés par l'école?*

96. *Parce que la formation des hommes est une donnée essentielle, l'école est au coeur de la modernisation; elle doit faire face aux mutations en s'y adaptant, voire en les anticipant par une mâîtrise accrue de l'évolution des connaissances, étant entendu que cette maîtrise dépend elle-même de la capacité de l'école élémentaire à assurer l'assimilation par l'enfant d'un fond de connaissances de base. Cependant, beaucoup des métiers qu'exerceront nos enfants n'existent pas encore; l'école doit être aussi un lieu où l'on apprend à apprendre. Elle doit accueillir non seulement les élèves et les étudiants en âge scolaire et universitaire, mais aussi, de plus en plus nombreux, ceux qui doivent, après être entrés dans l'activité professionnelle, apprendre ou réapprendre les nouvelles technologies et connaissances. Pour ces nouveaux élèves, doivent être mises en oeuvre des pédagogies appropriées, des contenus, des cadres et des formes d'enseignement nouveaux.*

97. *Nous devons donner au service public de l'Education nationale la mission de concilier démocratisation et qualité, grâce à suffisamment de souplesse et de variété. Il doit se fixer l'objectif de réduire au maximum un échec scolaire trop souvent lié au milieu social de l'enfant. L'école publique et ses maîtres assureront à chacun, selon ses besoins et ses capacités, l'égalité des chances devant l'éducation et l'instruction.*

2.2 Mieux répartir le temps de travail

98. *De 1900 à la deuxième Guerre mondiale, les progrès de la productivité ont permis une baisse du temps de travail de l'ordre de 30 pour cent. Depuis 1945, sur une durée analogue et avec des progrès de productivité plus rapides, la baisse n'est que de 8 pour cent. Ce phénomène touche tous les pays industrialisés. Pour éviter le chômage lorsque les gains de productivité sont supérieurs à la croissance, il faut qu'une part de ceux-ci aille à la reprise du mouvement séculaire de réduction de la durée du travail.*

99. *C'est pourquoi, lorsque les socialistes proposent le développement de toutes les formes de partage de travail, ils le font à la fois par souci de solidarité entre ceux qui ont un emploi et ceux qui n'en ont pas, et par réalisme économique. Réduire le temps de travail peut en effet coûter globalement moins cher sur le long terme que de prendre en charge socialement des centaines de milliers de chômeurs supplémentaires. 'Donner plus à ceux qui ont le moins' comme le disait le président de la République dans son discours de Figeac, 'relever le pouvoir d'achat des plus défavorisés, rechercher entre temps de travail et temps de loisir un nouvel équilibre, créer de l'emploi au lieu de le détruire...' ne sont que des formes de redistribution des gains de productivité au bénéfice des travailleurs.*

100. *La réduction de la durée du travail doit s'accompagner de mesures importantes de réorganisation visant à une meilleure utilisation des équipements. Celle-ci permet d'envisager d'une façon qui ne soit pas exclusivement comptable le problème que pose la compensation salariale, étant entendu que le pouvoir d'achat des bas salaires ne saurait être remis en question. La négociation doit être conduite de façon décentralisée entre le patronat et les syndicats, jusqu'au niveau des établissements, les travailleurs étant seuls juges en dernier ressort de l'arbitrage entre revenu, conditions de travail et emploi qu'ils acceptent pour le présent et le futur.*

101. *Cependant, même si l'autonomie de négociation entre les syndicats et le patronat doit être préservée et la politique contractuelle favorisée, l'incitation publique peut et doit être considérable en raison du coût économique et social qu'un chômeur représente pour la collectivité. Enfin, la possibilité de donner à cette action une dimension européenne est une des conditions même de son succès. Elle doit être activement recherchée notamment à la suite des positions développées par la Confédération Européenne des Syndicats.*

102. *Moyen de lutte contre le chômage, la réduction du temps de travail trace aussi la voie que les socialistes souhaitent emprunter vers une société se donnant à la fois le temps de vivre et celui de réfléchir à l'objectif et aux conditions de la production. En moins d'un siècle, nous sommes passés d'une société où le temps d'éveil des individus, au cours de leur vie, était*

consacré pour l'essentiel au travail, à une société où le temps hors travail professionnel est très largement dominant. C'est un défi considérable pour l'organisation de la vie sociale en général et pour la place du travail dans la société en particulier.

2.3 De nouvelles solidarités

103. *En période de crise, la protection sociale connaît des problèmes financiers aggravés. Sa capacité à répondre à une demande plus étendue et plus diffuse est amoindrie. Cependant, il faut en finir avec les idées fausses: on n'apportera pas de solution à la crise par une diminution de la protection sociale.*

2.3.1 Combattre l'exclusion sociale

104. *La crise amplifie des phénomènes d'exclusion qu'il nous faut combattre. Demander plus de mobilité aux travailleurs ne peut signifier plus de précarité. Sur le marché du travail de nombreuses catégories se trouvent dans une situation particulièrement difficile: jeunes, femmes, immigrés. La précarité se manifeste par une part croissante d'emplois mal rémunérés, effectués dans des conditions pénibles, au contenu peu qualifiant.*

105. *L'exclusion sociale risque d'entraîner une société à plusieurs vitesses qui tend à laisser de côté ceux qui ne peuvent s'adapter rapidement aux nouvelles conditions du marché.*

106. *Les exemples que nous donnent les Etats-Unis et le Japon sont édifiants de ce point de vue. Ainsi au Japon, on sait bien que la situation des salariés qui n'appartiennent pas aux grands groupes est souvent très difficile: salaires peu élevés, notamment ceux des femmes, absence quasi-totale de protection sociale. Voilà une bonne part de l'explication de la faiblesse des coûts de production dans ce pays.*

107. *C'est cet éclatement de la société que nous ne voulons pas. Il est contraire aux idéaux des socialistes qui souhaitent une société toujours plus solidaire. C'est cette modernisation là que nous rejettons, celle qui accepte les gâchis financiers et humains, celle qui s'organise aux dépens des travailleurs ou du moins d'une partie d'entre eux.*

2.3.2 Améliorer la protection sociale

108. *Contrairement à ce que dit la droite, c'est l'existence de garanties qui permet de prendre des risques. C'est en étant pour partie libérés de l'angoisse du lendemain que les hommes peuvent être disposés à regarder l'avenir en face. C'est ainsi que le XXe siècle a su faire progresser la société en échappant au libéralisme sauvage du XIXe siècle.*

109. *Si l'on veut que les travailleurs français puissent prendre le risque de la*

mobilité, si l'on veut que l'abandon momentané d'une activité professionnelle pour se former soit accepté, voire recherché, et non rejeté, il faut mettre en place des procédures et des moyens prenant en compte ce risque de mobilité. La recherche de plus de souplesse sur le marché du travail est sans doute souhaitable mais on voit mal pourquoi les travailleurs concernés devraient seuls en supporter le coût. C'est de plus de solidarité dans la conduite du changement dont la France a besoin.

110. *Face au thème de la charité, cher au libéralisme, nous devons au contraire affirmer le principe de solidarité. La charité consacre le maintien des inégalités. La solidarité vise à les réduire. Seul l'Etat, expression de la collectivité et garant de l'intérêt de tous les citoyens, peut et doit assurer à chaque famille un revenu minimum. Il convient de revoir l'ensemble des aides actuelles, de mieux les coordonner à tous les niveaux, et d'associer pleinement les organisations syndicales et humanitaires.*

111. *Un revenu minimum doit être garanti à tous et, de ce point de vue, des solutions doivent être apportées dans les plus brefs délais pour prévenir les situations inacceptables auxquelles se trouvent réduits les chômeurs en fin de droits.*

112. *Pas d'assistance, mais pas non plus de procédures fondées uniquement sur le système de l'assurance individuelle. Dans ce système, seuls les plus aisés pourraient se garantir contre les risques de l'avenir, les plus démunis se trouvant rejetés vers l'assistance. C'est d'une véritable solidarité dont nous avons besoin. Elle passe par un financement plus juste des organismes de protection sociale et de l'Etat. C'est pourquoi les prélèvements sociaux doivent être assis sur l'intégralité des revenus et non seulement sur les revenus du travail, c'est pourquoi nous devons poursuivre dans la voie d'une réforme fiscale qui proportionne mieux les contributions de chacun aux ressources dont il dispose. La fraude fiscale, les cumuls injustifiés, doivent être combattus avec plus de vigueur.*

113. *L'effort de réduction des inégalités n'a sans doute pas été mené aussi loin qu'il aurait dû l'être. Nous devons encore lutter pour enraciner la solidarité dans la société française.*

2.4 L'évolution du monde du travail

114. *Pour les socialistes, tout se tient: analyse sociologique, stratégie qui en découle, finalité de l'objectif.*

115. *Cela doit nous rappeler que le choix d'une politique suppose une analyse sociologique approfondie. Une telle analyse est, en effet, un préalable indispensable pour mieux garantir à moyen terme la maîtrise de la mutation, mais aussi et surtout pour mieux définir la stratégie du*

rassemblement autour de notre parti, et pour assurer la poursuite de l'oeuvre du gouvernement de la gauche.

116. *La base du Parti Socialiste composée principalement de la grande majorité des travailleurs salariés, mais aussi des petits et moyens exploitants agricoles, s'est reconnue en 1981 dans les propositions de François Mitterrand, passant, selon l'expression de ce dernier, de l'état de majorité sociologique à l'état de majorité politique. Elle constitue ce que nous avons appelé le front de classe, réponse théorique et pratique, à l'analyse des rapports de force dans notre société industrielle capitaliste.*

117. *La dynamique du front de classe exprime l'évolution, la diversification, les nouvelles aspirations de ceux qui le composent. L'homogénéisation des conditions de travail et de vie contribue à son unité même si, notamment sous le choc de la crise, des tensions et des risques de fragmentation la menacent. Il ne s'agit nullement d'additionner des intérêts corporatifs mais de rassembler dans la dynamique d'un progrès de société commun tous ceux qui contribuent par leur activité, et non par leur position de fortune, à construire la société de demain. L'effort de la droite – et notamment de V. Giscard d'Estaing durant son septennat – a toujours été d'insister au contraire sur les différences, de présenter le monde du travail comme atomisé, de faire comme si le front de classe n'existait pas, afin de l'empêcher de se rassembler. Seul le Parti Socialiste a su reconnaître son existence et s'est révélé apte à le rassembler.*

118. *Or, c'est un fait connu qu'en période de crise, la classe ouvrière au sens traditionnel du terme est soumise à des forces centrifuges, notamment par l'aggravation du chômage. A plus forte raison le front de classe. La révolution technologique vient s'ajouter par ses effets sur la formation des travailleurs, sur les conditions de travail, sur la diminution du temps de travail. Sous la conjugaison de ces deux phénomènes, le risque est plus grand de voir le monde du travail se scinder en deux dans le cadre d'un dualisme social. Mais n'existe-t-il pas plutôt un danger de coupure de part et d'autre d'un bloc central avec d'un côté les exclus de la modernisation et de l'autre ceux qui, détenant la maîtrise, et du capital et des nouveaux savoirs, y trouveraient les moyens de réaffirmer leur domination.*

119. *Telles sont les préoccupations que doit avoir aujourd'hui notre parti dans l'élaboration de sa stratégie et de ses propositions.*

120. *Mais dès maintenant la remobilisation du front de classe peut être entreprise selon plusieurs axes de lutte:*

121.   *lutte idéologique et politique intransigeante et incessante contre l'offensive menée par la droite qui pratique la lutte des classes plus vivement que jamais et sur tous les terrains;*
    lutte pour l'intégration effective non seulement de tous les éléments

souvent déjà marginalisés ou en danger d'exclusion: chômeurs, jeunes,
immigrés, travailleurs précaires;
    lutte pour le maintien et le développement de tous les droits individuels
et libertés collectives sur lesquels la droite aujourd'hui voudrait revenir,
en particulier les droits récemment conquis par les femmes.

3   LA MODERNISATION PAR ET POUR LA DEMOCRATIE

122. *Le développement de la démocratie économique et sociale est un objectif*
de société réconciliant solidarité et liberté. Il est un moyen de maîtrise
collective des orientations et des rythmes du changement en favorisant la
créativité et les initiatives.

3.1   Affirmer l'Etat et rénover l'administration

123. *Se mettant à la remorque d'une idéologie ultra-libérale, la droite*
française a repris en choeur le thème du 'moins d'Etat'.

124. *Alors que tous les grands mouvements de modernisation de la France,*
comme la mutation du monde agricole, la reconstruction après la
Libération, l'insertion dans la CEE ont tous reposé sur une action
volontaire et coordonnée sur les structures économiques, la droite
voudrait revenir en arrière et aller au rebours de ce qui fait notre culture
nationale. Si le capitalisme français était capable de se passer de l'aide de
l'Etat, il l'aurait montré au cours des 25 premières années de la Ve
République. En réalité, dans tous les domaines où la France a su
préparer l'avenir, qu'il s'agisse de l'énergie, des télécommunications ou
de l'aéronautique, c'est avec l'aide de l'Etat et des entreprises publiques
que le secteur privé a accepté de prendre des risques.

125. *Ce n'est ni d'un rejet de l'Etat dont la France a besoin, ni d'un discours*
obsolète sur les vertus du seul marché. Il ne faut pas faire moins
fonctionner l'Etat, il faut le faire fonctionner mieux. Le développement
d'une économie mixte, comprenant un fort secteur privé appuyé sur un
fort secteur public constitue, pour la France, la seule démarche
pragmatique permettant de réussir la modernisation.

126. *Il reste que depuis 25 ans, l'Etat est intervenu dans de nombreux*
domaines mais s'est peu préoccupé de moderniser l'Etat. Les textes de
réglementation et les organes administratifs, lorsqu'ils sont inutiles,
caducs et jouent un rôle paralysant dans la modernisation, devront être
supprimés ou allégés. Il ne s'agit pas, bien entendu, de céder à la mode
de la déréglementation; mais il faut désencombrer l'Etat pour libérer sa
capacité à orienter le développement économique et social.

127. *L'administration, comme le reste de la société, doit évoluer vers davantage d'efficacité, elle doit aussi être pour les citoyens une aide et non une contrainte. Réconcilier les Français avec leur administration, voilà une forme de modernisation qui doit être recherchée.*

128. *Cette modernisation de l'administration doit aussi concerner les services publics. Mais cette notion ne saurait se réduire à l'intervention de l'Etat. En effet, de nombreuses collectivités qui ne sont pas publiques (tout particulièrement des associations) remplissent des missions de service public notamment dans les domaines de l'action sociale et de l'éducation populaire.*

129. *Enfin, le rôle de l'Etat dans la défense des libertés doit être pleinement réaffirmé. L'Etat doit faire respecter les libertés de la personne comme la sécurité des citoyens.*

130. *Il faut reconnaître que le sentiment d'insécurité ressenti par beaucoup n'est pas illégitime: la crise inquiète la société, la mutation technologique ébranle l'appareil productif, les valeurs sociales mêmes sont questionnées. C'est le prix que toutes les sociétés industrielles payent aujourd'hui face au gigantesque changement qui s'opère dans notre civilisation. L'exclusion sociale qui peut l'accompagner constitue une des principales causes de la délinquance.*

131. *Ce phénomène de société, qui prend souvent à l'étranger des proportions encore plus dramatiques qu'en France, est souvent utilisé par la droite pour attiser l'angoisse collective.*

132. *Les socialistes, conscients de l'importance du débat, n'entendent cependant pas 'hurler avec les loups'. Il faut moderniser et mieux utiliser la police et la justice pour assurer la sécurité des Français dans le respect des libertés fondamentales. Les socialistes approuvent pleinement les mesures prises récemment par le gouvernement, mais nous savons aussi qu'il faut aller plus loin pour lutter contre les causes profondes de cette insécurité ressentie. C'est par le développement économique et social et par un ensemble de propositions fortes et cohérentes que le projet socialiste entend redonner confiance à la France.*

3.2 Donner un plus grand rôle au Plan

133. *Les difficultés de plus en plus grandes qui ont été recontrées au cours des dix dernières années dans les exercices de prévision à moyen terme sont venues conforter l'intérêt décroissant manifesté en France à propos de la planification. Or, loin de rendre le Plan inutile, l'instabilité de l'environnement international comme les ruptures liées à la mutation technologique rendent celui-ci encore plus nécessaire.*

134. *Le Plan doit être le lieu de confrontation des différentes visions d'avenir*

qu'ont les partenaires de la vie économique et sociale. La mutation technologique n'apparaît pas comme un fait isolé du reste de l'évolution de la société. Elle produit cette évolution et elle est produite par elle. C'est pourquoi il n'y a pas une modernisation de l'économie qui s'imposerait inéluctablement à toute politique mais au contraire il y a la politique socialiste que nous voulons voir traduite dans la modernisation. Cette traduction doit être débattue entre tous les acteurs sociaux, et le Plan constitue le lieu adéquat. Il est l'instrument de la démocratie économique et sociale.

135. *Mais il ne suffit pas de déterminer des objectifs. La nation doit aussi se doter des moyens. Si la modernisation ne peut être une fin en soi, elle n'est pas non plus véritablement un moyen. Le moyen d'agir est constitué par l'ensemble des politiques sectorielles que la nation entend voir conduire ainsi que par le cadre macroéconomique jugé compatible à tous moments avec l'état de la société française. S'il ne sert à rien de décréter un taux de croissance que l'on sait irréaliste, le Plan doit néanmoins se fonder sur la croissance économique la plus forte possible. En effet, l'histoire de notre pays montre combien les efforts de modernisation ont besoin d'un minimum de croissance pour entrer dans les faits. Dépassons le débat scolastique qui voudrait soit que seule la modernisation permette la croissance, soit que seule la croissance autorise la modernisation.*

136. *Le projet socialiste ne peut être mené à bien sans le Plan. Depuis 1981, celui-ci n'a pas reçu l'importance que les socialistes veulent lui donner. Le Plan doit exprimer la cohérence après avoir fait jaillir les préférences. Il doit avoir la possibilité d'imposer ses choix principaux. Il faut lui donner des moyens à la hauteur de l'enjeu.*

3.3 Favoriser la démocratie dans l'entreprise

137. *Si l'initiative du chef d'entreprise est primordiale, l'intervention des travailleurs représente une richesse, pas une contrainte. L'adaptation aux changements technologiques, l'efficience retrouvée, l'amélioration de la qualité, autant de domaines dans lesquels la capacité d'initiative de l'ensemble des travailleurs est essentielle.*

138. *Une vérité s'impose. Travailler sous la contrainte et par résignation, c'est diminuer les possibilités de chacun. Libérer les travailleurs pour les motiver, c'est changer le contenu du travail et modifier les rapports sociaux.*

139. *Les lois Auroux comme la loi de démocratisation du secteur public ont fourni un cadre juridique adéquat. Mais la modernisation de la société française ne peut s'opérer uniquement à l'aide d'un arsenal juridique, même si elle doit s'appuyer sur lui. C'est par la pratique de nouvelles*

relations sociales dans l'entreprise que la libération de cette dernière, que chacun prétend rechercher, pourra être obtenue.

140. *La négociation entre tous les partenaires doit porter sur un projet global de l'entreprise, sur sa stratégie, en fonction des choix effectués par le pays.*

141. *Concevoir l'entreprise comme une collectivité de travail, c'est notamment permettre aux travailleurs et aux organisations syndicales de donner leur avis sur la répartition des gains de productivité.*

142. *Quelle part réserver à l'investissement, à la recherche, à la formation, à la réorganisation et au réaménagement du travail, aux rémunérations? Voilà le changement à impulser qui assurerait aussi une croissance de la production et qui concrétiserait l'effort de modernisation. Il convient de favoriser le débat au plus près des réalités vécues, dans l'atelier, le bureau ou le service.*

3.4   Développer une dynamique locale

143. *Les espaces ouverts par les réformes de la décentralisation et de la planification doivent être utilisés. En dotant les collectivités locales des moyens de mener des politiques originales en matière d'emploi, non plus seulement 'défensives' mais aussi 'offensives', la planification régionale doit déboucher, par une association accrue de l'ensemble des partenaires au développement économique et social, sur une véritable dynamique de l'economie locale. Les associations et d'une façon plus générale l'ensemble de l'économie sociale peuvent y contribuer d'une façon décisive. Déjà en agriculture, les différentes formes d'association et d'entr'aide existantes permettent le maintien d'exploitations moyennes plus performantes. Ainsi, la logique économique n'est-elle plus seulement descendante, mais libère-t-elle les initiatives. L'Etat ne se décharge pas de ses responsabilités. Mais en rapprochant le niveau de la décision en matière économique, des besoins, en transférant des compétences aux collectivités territoriales – notamment en matière de formation professionnelle – il entend promouvoir un nouveau mode de développement local. Cette démarche est historique; elle doit être poursuivie, et les conséquences doivent en être tirées en termes de financement.*

3.5   Faciliter l'initiative culturelle

144. *Les dimensions économiques et sociales du changement ne sont pas les seules: l'initiative est aussi culturelle. La crise est aussi une profonde crise des valeurs et des modes de vie. Pour les socialistes, il n'y aura pas de transformation en profondeur si le domaine de la culture ne s'élargit pas et si la majorité des forces vives de la nation, en particulier le monde du travail, en demeure exclue.*

145. *C'est pourquoi la culture ne doit plus être considérée comme une activité marginale, passe-temps d'une élite favorisée par la fortune et l'éducation. Elle ne doit plus se limiter à une sphère étroite et consacrée: il faut reconnaître la pluralité des apports (cultures des régions, des groupes sociaux, des communautés et des ethnies) qui concourt à son enrichissement.*

146. *Pour les socialistes, la culture doit être présente dans toutes les institutions et sur tous les lieux: à l'école, dans l'entreprise, dans la vie quotidienne. Elle ne peut plus être isolée des autres activités humaines; comme la recherche scientifique, la création artistique et littéraire participe à l'avancée de notre société.*

147. *Elle ne peut non plus être séparée de l'économie: les industries de la culture et de la communication doivent être parmi les premières à contribuer à la création d'entreprises et d'emplois nouveaux.*

148. *La culture doit aussi être rendue à l'initiative des acteurs sociaux; la réussite de la décentralisation passe notamment par l'existence de multiples foyers de vie artistique et culturelle dans les régions; elle doit également favoriser toutes les formes de communication sociale qui peuvent être portées par les nouveaux médias.*

149. *C'est pourquoi, même en période de rigueur budgétaire, le maintien de l'effort culturel de l'Etat et des collectivités locales est un impératif pour les socialistes. Sans perspective culturelle, notre pays se préparerait un avenir où la technologie dominerait les individus sans leur donner les moyens et la chance de concevoir ensemble leur destin.*

3.6 Aller vers de nouvelles solidarités

150. *La modernisation de la France ne trouve son sens que dans une Europe plus unie, et dans un monde moins inégal.*

151. *L'Europe, et la France avec elle, est devant un choix:*

152.   *ou bien l'Europe se laissera imposer la nouvelle donne que les Etats-Unis veulent imposer: elle accepterait alors une vaste redistribution des cartes à l'échelle mondiale qui la rejetterait progressivement mais rapidement du centre vers la périphérie, au détriment du niveau de vie et de l'emploi de ses habitants, mais aussi au dépens de l'immense majorité des pays en voie de développement;*

153.   *ou bien elle maîtrisera les grandes mutations scientifiques et technologiques qui lui permettront de sauvegarder son indépendance et son rôle dans le monde.*

154. *Face à la polarisation croissante du monde autour des Etats-Unis,*

l'Europe se trouve confrontée à la maîtrise de son avenir. De sa réponse dépend le choix entre la poursuite de son développement autonome ou la chute lente vers la vassalisation.

155. *La coexistence de pays modernes au Nord et de situations de sous-développement, voire de famine, dans certains pays du Sud ne peut être tolérée et l'aide au Tiers-Monde doit être accrue.*

156. *Mais l'effort ne doit pas être purement quantitatif; il n'y aura pas de développement du Tiers-Monde sans prise en compte prioritaire de l'évolution des relations sociales à partir de la réalité des traditions et des cultures locales.*

157. *Dans le domaine des relations entre le Nord et le Sud, l'Europe peut et doit jouer un rôle autonome par rapport aux Etats-Unis comme elle l'a manifesté à l'occasion de la signature des accords de Lomé.*

CONCLUSION

158. *Les socialistes ont trouvé le 10 mai 1981 une société française en état de désordre. Certaines couches sociales étaient en désarroi; certaines idéologies égoïstes et chauvinistes commençaient à trouver des échos. La fin de la période giscardienne avait touché aux ressorts moraux mêmes du pays.*

159. *L'appareil de production était vétuste et inadapté, et les relations sociales connaissaient un grave retard. Il fallait donc assurer le fonctionnement d'une machine en mauvais état (en plus mauvais état sans doute que nous ne l'imaginions!), tout en préparant l'avenir.*

160. *Il fallait en effet faire face simultanément à deux tâches: ne pas sacrifier l'avenir au présent en refusant le déclin de la France, mais aussi ne pas différer l'amélioration des conditions de vie présentes des plus défavorisés. Les injustices n'étaient-elles pas criantes? Ne fallait-il pas, pour le Smic, le minimum vieillesse, l'aide aux handicapés, les allocations familiales, effectuer un effort de rattrapage?*

161. *En un mot, il a fallu tenir les deux bouts de la chaîne, faire face aux urgences du court terme et commencer aussi la construction de l'avenir. Et ceci dans une situation où ni les réformes de structures ni l'assainissement de notre économie ne pouvaient encore – mais aujourd'hui cela commence – nous donner des moyens nouveaux.*

162. *En effet, l'échec des politiques conservatrices menées avant mai 1981 avait singulièrement resserré nos marges de manoeuvre. Il faut en tenir compte lucidement.*

163. *Après la fin de la période gaullienne, la gestion de la droite a conduit continûment à l'affaiblissement de la France. Lorsqu'il y en a eu, les tentatives d'adaptation de notre économie ont le plus souvent sombré sous le poids des conservatismes qui avaient annexé le pouvoir politique ou ont échoué en raison de la prédominance de l'esprit de rente et de spéculation à court terme caractérisant habituellement le capitalisme français.*

164. *La droite a déclassé notre école, base pourtant de toute modernisation, laissé notre Université en déshérence, négligé notre recherche, qu'après le Front populaire De Gaulle avait fait renaître, accepté pour notre industrie un rôle de sous-traitant des groupes internationaux, regardé sans réagir le Tiers-Monde s'enfoncer dans la misère, laissé l'inflation imprégner nos structures. Elle s'est satisfaite d'un commerce extérieur structurellement déséquilibré et a laissé le chômage submerger notre société. Aggravation des inégalités, injustice fiscale, mais aussi appropriation de l'Etat par la technostructure, et soumission aux grands intérêts privés ont marqué cette période.*

165. *A tel point qu'aujourd'hui nul ne revendique plus la paternité de cette politique!*

166. *Aujourd'hui, malgré nombre d'insuffisances, dues notamment aux contraintes de la crise mondiale, il est certain que bien des avancées ont été faites – et de façon décisive – depuis mai 1981.*

167. *N'avons-nous pas réussi, tout de même, à améliorer significativement le sort des plus démunis, à redonner leur dignité et leurs droits aux travailleurs dans l'entreprise, à réaliser des réformes de structures dans notre industrie propres à assurer son avenir, à mettre en oeuvre la décentralisation si nécessaire et si attendue, à relancer la recherche scientifique, à ralentir l'inflation et la montée du chômage, à utilement contribuer à la construction européenne et à l'établissement d'un nouvel ordre économique mondial, à rétablir l'autorité de la France comme défenseur de la justice, de la liberté, des droits de l'homme et des droits des peuples?*

168. *Cela a été bien engagé mais il nous faut assurer solidement les bases de l'essor du pays en modernisant ses structures économiques comme son organisation sociale.*

169. *Pourtant, les indifférences, les réticences et les résistances que suscite notre politique doivent nous conduire à nous interroger. L'oeuvre à accomplir étant immense et urgente, avons-nous assez maîtrisé le rythme de nos réformes? Avons-nous bien hiérarchisé leurs priorités relatives? Avons-nous fait l'effort nécessaire pour moderniser notre administration et ses relations avec le citoyen, ses structures traditionnelles de pouvoir et l'image déformée de l'Etat qu'elle projette sur les citoyens? Avons-nous suffisamment été à l'écoute de certaines catégories sociales et notamment*

de la jeunesse? N'avons-nous pas trop cru qu'il suffisait de changer les lois pour changer le pays?

170. *Nous avons certainement sous-estimé l'état de notre appareil industriel, les difficultés de la politique sociale contractuelle et celles de la lutte pour l'emploi. Nous n'avons sans doute pas suffisamment utilisé les instruments que nous préconisions nous-mêmes et notamment la planification démocratique.*

171. *Tout ceci dans un contexte politique où les forces de droite attisent un climat difficile comme elles le font chaque fois que la gauche est au pouvoir. Tout ceci contre les forces de l'argent, du conservatisme, de l'archaïsme économique.*

172. *Légitimement fiers de l'oeuvre qui a été accomplie, nous sommes à la fois lucides devant nos insuffisances et décidés à continuer dans la voie de la modernisation et du progrès social. Obligés parfois de changer de rythme devant les difficultés du moment, nous n'avons pas pour autant abandonné nos valeurs ni notre idéal. Nous ne pouvons oublier que la situation de crise dans laquelle se trouve la planète doit être d'abord analysée comme un échec.*

173. **Echec à l'échelle de chaque pays industrialisé où l'exclusion des plus pauvres et des plus vulnérables est accentuée partout par les mutations technologiques.*

174. **Echec à l'échelle d'une planète où le Tiers-Monde fait de plus en plus les frais du développement des pays riches. L'échec cuisant du 'monologue Nord/Sud' se traduit par un accroissement des inégalités lourd de risques pour l'avenir.*

175. **Echec d'un système où les Etats-Unis ne parviennent pas à contrôler le réseau de pouvoir des sociétés multinationales.*

176. *Face au capitalisme, le socialisme reste pour nous le meilleur projet pour demain. Le monde communiste, replié sur lui-même, dominé par une hégémonie sans partage, maintient ses peuples hors de la liberté. Il a trahi ses idéaux. Il a fait preuve de sa triste inefficacité et de son caractère totalitaire.*

177. *Nous voulons maîtriser l'économique, non pour lui-même, mais pour en faire un instrument au service des hommes et des femmes de notre pays.*

178. *Réalistes et responsables, nous ne renions pas pour autant l'objectif d'une croissance durable pour bâtir une société plus juste.*

179. *Nous savons que le socialisme est né de la confluence de deux volontés. Celle d'oeuvrer pour que le progrès scientifique et technologique soit mis au service de l'homme, pour que les travailleurs soient les acteurs*

responsables et non pas les victimes et les dupes de l'essor économique.

180. *Nous sommes le parti des travailleurs, des créateurs, des hommes de progrès; nous oeuvrons pour la justice sociale. Le droit au travail reste pour nous un droit inaliénable et nous ne saurions nous résigner à la situation actuelle. Le Parti Socialiste estime que la lutte contre le chômage reste la priorité et c'est pour cela aussi que nous voulons la modernisation.*

181. *Pour nous, socialistes, la vie des sociétés humaines ne se conçoit pas comme une somme d'égos individuels livrés à l'affrontement incontrôlé. L'harmonie sociale ne se construira pas dans un laisser-faire qui n'est qu'un sauve-qui-peut.*

182. *En face de ce monde de plus en plus complexe, parfois trop technique, en mutation très rapide, le bien-être de l'individu reste notre but essentiel. L'épanouissement individuel indispensable et jamais négligé, le développement des talents multiples et divers, l'encouragement à l'initiative ne peuvent se faire qu'au milieu d'une société où l'individu joue pleinement son rôle collectif, où l'Etat est au service du citoyen, où il respecte l'individu tout en protégeant la collectivité, où il assure la loyauté du marché économique et la protection sociale de tous, une société de progrès, de justice, de fraternité, de liberté.*

Notes

1 Presidentialism and the Fifth Republic

1. I include in 'literature' not only academic writing but also political journalism, the writings and published speeches of politicians and activists, the publications of the political clubs, conferences and colloquia. The interrelation between these various forms in French political analysis and the high standard of much of the 'occasional' writings justify this inclusive definition. The 'themes' and 'approaches' – interpretative, chronologically descriptive, institutionally descriptive – will be conditioned in part by the traditional academic divisions such as constitutional law and executive-legislative relations and so on. As we shall see from this chapter, however, certain of the shifts in emphasis are the results of a deeper disquiet about the nature of the republic itself.

2. In this category we can include the hundreds of newspaper articles in the political columns in the 1958–62 period. For a typical example see M. Duverger on the institutional dangers of dyarchy (*Le Monde*, 12 and 13–14 May 1962). See also P. Mendès-France, *La république moderne* (Paris, 1962), R. Rémond, *La démocratie à refaire* (Paris, 1963) and the discussion of the republican tradition in D. Pickles, *The Fifth French Republic* (London, 1966, first published 1960) p. 8. For retrospective analyses of the same type, see G. Mollet, *Quinze ans après* (Paris, 1973) and F. Mitterrand, *Ma part de vérité* (Paris, 1969) p. 41.

3. See Mendès-France, *La république moderne*, pp. 15–16 and 22–23, F. L. Wilson, *The French Democratic Left* (Stanford, 1971) p. 67, and V. Wright, *The Government and Politics of France* (London, 1978) p. 151.

4. Republican support for de Gaulle was, of course, enacted as well as written. For supportive writing on the question of his republicanism see Sirius (H. Beuve–Méry), *Le Monde*, 8 January 1959, C. Mauriac, ibid., 2 May 1959, P–H. Simon, ibid., 14 May 1959, J. Fauvet, ibid., 13 May 1959. See also Duverger's assumption (ibid., 17–18 May 1959) that the 'république consulaire' would develop into a form akin to either Britain's parliamentary government or to those of the Third and Fourth Republics. See also L. Hamon, *De Gaulle dans la république* (Paris, 1958) pp. xvii and xxvii, R. Aron, *France: Steadfast and Changing* (Oxford, 1960) pp. 121 and 135–6, and P–H. Simon, *La France a la fièvre* (Paris, 1958) pp. 180–9. It was only later, after the Algerian crisis had been resolved, that the more problematic nature of regime development became a more pressing issue. (For representative examples of this change, see P. Viansson–Ponté, *Le Monde*, 8, 9, 10, 11 May 1962, M. Duverger, ibid., 12, 13–14 May 1962, P. Viannson–Ponté, ibid., 29, 30, 31 August 1962.)

5. The clearest example of this style is P. Viansson–Ponté, *Histoire de la république gaullienne*, 2 vols. (Paris, 1970–1). See also P. Williams and D. Goldey, *French Politicians and Elections* (Cambridge, 1970), J. Chapsal and A. Lancelot, *La vie politique en France depuis 1940* (Paris, 1975). This detailed chronological approach also informs more specific comment; see G. Suffert, *De Defferre à Mitterrand* (Paris, 1966) and the various analyses of elections and referendums of the *Cahiers de la fondation nationale des sciences politiques* (see bibliography). One of the major exceptions to this chronological rule is D. Pickles, *The Fifth French Republic* (London, 1966). Its institutional analyses make it a forerunner of the dominant style of 1970s literature. Its shifting emphases, however, support our argument, as does the striking admission in the preface to the 1966 edition: 'Once again, therefore, I can only express the hope that this edition will be up to date when it appears' (p. xi).

6. See, for example, the Club Jean Moulin, *Un parti pour la Gauche* (Paris, 1965), G. Defferre, *Un nouvel horizon* (Paris, 1965), A. Chandernagor, *Un parlement, pour quoi faire?* (Paris, 1967), C. Alphandery *et al.*, *Pour nationaliser l'Etat* (Paris, 1968).

7. See, for example, the collection of Mendès-France's speeches made around 1968, *Pour préparer l'avenir* (Paris, 1968).

8. P. Williams and M. Harrison, *Politics and Society in De Gaulle's Republic* (London, 1971).

9. The following is an indicative list of works, many of which contain a chronological element. What is significant, however, is that all of these works contain an overwhelming emphasis upon detailed 'synchronic' description: M. Anderson, *Government in France* (Oxford, 1970), P. Avril, *Politics in France* (Harmondsworth, 1969), R. Barillon *et al.*, *Dictionnaire de la constitution de la Ve République* (Paris, 1976), X. Beauchamps, *Un Etat dans l'Etat?* (Paris, 1976), P. Birnbaum, *Les sommets de l'Etat* (Paris, 1977), J. Blondel, *The Government of France* (London, 1974), F. Ridley and J. Blondel, *Public Administration in France* (London, 1969), M. Crozier, *La société bloquée* (Paris, 1970), C. Debbasch, *La France de Pompidou* (Paris, 1974), J. R. Frears, *France in the Giscard Presidency* (London, 1981), D. L. Hanley, A. P. Kerr and N. H. Waites, *Contemporary France: Politics and Society since 1945* (London, 1980), J. Hayward, *The One and Indivisible French Republic* (London, 1973, second edition, 1983), G. Lord, *The French Budgetary Process* (California, 1973), H. Machin, *The Prefect in French Public Administration* (London, 1977), J. Massot, *La présidence de la république en France* (Paris, 1977), *Le chef du gouvernement en France* (Paris, 1979), J. Rivoli, *Le budget de l'Etat* (Paris, 1978), E. Suleiman, *Politics, Power and Bureaucracy in France* (Princeton, 1974), V. Wright, *Conflict and Consensus in France* (London, 1979).

10. See in particular J–P. Jouary *et al.*, *Giscard et les idées: essai sur la guerre idéologique* (Paris, 1980), and N. Poulantzas, *Politique et classes sociales* (Paris, 1972).

11. Political memoirs have a long tradition in France. In the Fifth

Republic, these have often served the function of 'setting the record straight' or have been presented as personal manifestos of still-practising politicians. See, for example, J. Chaban-Delmas, *L'Ardeur* (Paris, 1975), and M. Jobert, *Mémoires d'avenir* (Paris, 1974). See also M. Cotta, *La VIᵉ république* (Paris, 1974), F. Giroud, *La comédie du pouvoir* (Paris, 1977), A. Salomon, *PS: la mise à nu* (Paris, 1980).

12. See, for example: Beauchamps, *Un Etat dans l'Etat?*, Birnbaum, *Les Sommets de l'Etat*, M. Charlot, *La persuasion politique* (Paris, 1970), Jouary *et al.*, *Giscard et les idées*, R–G. Schwartzenberg, *L'Etat spectacle* (Paris, 1977), Suleiman, *Politics, Power and Bureaucracy*.

13. P. Williams, *Crisis and Compromise* (London, 1972), D. Pickles, *France, the Fourth Republic* (London, 1958).

14. The tendency to call the Fifth Republic a republican monarchy or an elective monarchy only further begs the crucial questions.

15. R. Michels, *Political Parties* (New York, 1959) Part 6, M. Duverger, *Political Parties* (London, 1967) book 1, part 3, and G. Sartori, *Parties and Party Systems* (Cambridge, 1977) part 1, Chapter 4.

16. A. Krivine, *La farce électorale* (Paris, 1969), and Poulantzas, *Politique et classes sociales*.

17. The State/Republic opposition is sometimes presented as even more unstable in that it is argued that the statist tradition predates and dominates the republican tradition in French political life. See Anderson, *Government in France*, p. 1. On interpretations of the development – both linear and dialectical – of republicanism see B. D. Graham, 'Theories of the French Party System under the Third Republic', *Political Studies*, 12, 1 (February 1964) pp. 21–32.

18. Hostility to unrepresentative authoritarianism is largely derived from Montesquieu. (See *De l'esprit des lois*, Vol. 1 (Paris, 1973) pp. 11–23.) Even though the terms of reference have shifted to the Left (for Montesquieu, ideal representation was constitutional monarchy) the principle of opposition to despotism is the same.

19. It is significant in this context that throughout the first half of 1959, after the SFIO had moved into opposition to de Gaulle's government, all the major attacks in *Le Populaire* were against Debré (the Prime Minister) and not de Gaulle, and yet it was the latter who was defining the nature of the new republic.

20. It is the case that it was de Gaulle's *style* (of speech, gesture and disdain) which was one of the major factors in the Left's divided and shifting opposition to him from 1946 and again from 1958 onwards.

21. Acceptance of the presidency involves a wide range of degrees of acceptance. The only major figures who consistently disdained the presidency were Mendès-France and Mollet. Even these two, however, supported the claims of others to the office.

22. Wright, *The Government and Politics of France* (1978) pp. 124–50.

23. See J. Charlot, *The Gaullist Phenomenon* (London, 1971) pp. 63–4 and p. 83n. See also O. Kircheimer, 'The Transformation of West European Party Systems', in J. Lapalombara and M. Weiner (eds), *Political Parties and Political Development* (Princeton, 1966) pp. 177–200.

2 Political Leadership and Political Theory

1. In the French tradition this form of regime categorisation is derived
    from both Montesquieu and Rousseau, both of whom elaborated their
    political theories in the context of the refutation of another category
    (despotism).
2. Normative, even though mutable. A good example of this republican
    mutability is the addition of a socio-economic dimension to the
    Déclaration des droits de l'homme et du citoyen, incorporated into the
    1946 Constitution, and the stress upon economic planning within the
    framework of the Republic since the pre-war period. Republicanism
    has even incorporated into itself notions of elite competition,
    corporatism and the political reality of the media, but has never
    elaborated a convincing response to the enduring phenomenon of
    personal leadership.
3. For a typical example of this preoccupation with 'dyarchy', see M.
    Duverger in *Le Monde*, 14 May 1962.
4. See in particular de Gaulle's press conference of 31 January 1964 (*Le
    Monde*, 2–3 February 1964).
5. *The Eighteenth Brumaire* was first published in 1852. The references in
    this chapter are to the 1977 Moscow publishing house edition.
6. Ibid., p. 6.
7. Ibid., p. 13.
8. Ibid., p. 12.
9. Ibid., p. 17.
10. Ibid., p. 107.
11. L. Trotsky, *The Revolution Betrayed* (New York, 1972).
12. Ibid., p. 2.
13. Ibid., p. 277. See also p. 278 and p. 290.
14. Ibid., p. 93.
15. Ibid., p. 274.
16. See in particular ibid., p. 278.
17. Ibid., p. 278.
18. Marx, *The Eighteenth Brumaire*, pp. 10–11.
19. For a discussion of the ambiguity in the use of the term 'rational' in the
    social sciences see S. Lukes, *Essays in Social Theory* (London, 1978)
    chapter 6 and in particular p. 132 n. 58, and W. Runciman, 'The
    sociological explanation of "religious" beliefs', *Archives européennes
    de sociologie*, 10, 2 (1969) pp. 149–91.
20. M. Weber, *The Theory of Social and Economic Organization* (New
    York, 1964) p. 358. See also M. Weber, *Wirtschaft und Gesellschaft*,
    vol. 1. '"Charisma" soll eine als ausseralltäglich (urssprünglich,
    sowohl bei Propheten wie bei therapeutischen wie bei Rechts-Weisen
    wie bei Jagdfürern wie bei Kriegshelden: als magisch bedingt)
    geltende Qualität einer Persönlickkeit heissen, um derentwillen sie als
    mit übernatürlichen oder übermenschlichen oder mindestens spe-
    zifisch ausseralltäglichen, nicht jedem andern zugänglichen Kräften
    oder Eigenschaften begabt oder als gottgesandt oder als vorbildlich
    und deshalb als "Fürer" gewertet wird. Wie die betreffende Qualität

gewertet wird. Wie die betreffende Qualität von irgendeinem ethischen, ästhetischen oder sonstigen Standpunkt aus "objektiv" richtig zu bewerten sein *würde*, ist natürlich dabei begrifflich völlig gleichgültig: darauf allein, wie sie tatsächlich von den charismatisch Beherrschten, den "Anhängern", bewertet *wird*, kommt es an.' (M. Weber, *Wirtschaft und Gesellschaft*, vol. 1 (Köln: Kiepenheuer & Witsch, 1964) p. 179).

21. Weber, *Social and Economic Organization*, pp. 366 and 387.
22. For a representative example of a critical approach to the theoretical adequacy of the term see C. Ake, 'Charismatic Legitimation and Political Integration', *Comparative Studies in Society and History*, vol. 9 (1966) pp. 1–13.
23. For an opposite view see S. W. Eisenstadt, *Max Weber on Charisma and Institution Building* (Chicago, 1974) p. ix.
24. Weber, *Social and Economic Organization*.
25. Our notion of personalism therefore has little to do with Mounier's notion of personalist individualism. (See E. Mounier, *Communisme, anarchie et personnalisme* (Paris, 1966). In French political discourse personalism normally signifies Mounier's notion although reference to an idea akin to the sense we give to personalism can be found very occasionally. See for example L. Blum, *A l'échelle humaine* (Switzerland, n.d.) p. 72 and A. Siegfried, *Le Monde*, 12 November 1958.
26. I define a rally discursively, not organisationally. We are not, therefore, concerned with its actual or possible organisational form. In political discourse, a claim is made that a particular political organisation or group of people is collectively transcendental, or else potentially so, inasmuch as it can respond appropriately to a rally 'call' (*appel*).
27. By 'symbol', I mean more or less what Edelman calls a 'condensation symbol': something which becomes the focus of, and thereby attributes meaning to, a multiplicity of emotions (see M. Edelman, *The Symbolic Uses of Politics* (Urbana, 1964) p. 6. See also pp. 7 and 11). Edelman's definition, however, explains the symbol's function, but not its dynamism.

4 Discourse and Tradition: The Communists

1. There was also a *rapport* on *la moralité* given by Jean Kanapa, which balanced the liberal atmosphere of the congress to a certain extent. For a discussion of it see *Le Quotidien de Paris*, 4 February 1976.
2. For comments upon the origins of the abandonment of the term see E. Balibar, *et al.*, *Ouvrons la fenêtre, camarades!* (Paris, 1979) p. 45, A. Fontaine, *Le Monde*, 4 February 1976; J. Elleinstein, *Une certaine idée du communisme* (Paris, 1979), p. 63; P. Laurent, *Le PCF comme il est* (Paris, 1978) p. 37; P. Daix, *Le Quotidien de Paris*, 9 February 1976; A. Lecoeur, *Le PCF: continuité dans le changement* (Paris, 1977), pp. 109–30.
3. *Le Monde*, 9 January 1976.

4. At the 19th Congress in February 1970 the term '*je*' is virtually non-existent. At the 21st Congress '*je*' is used fewer than twenty times.
5. In this analytical section all the page references, given after quotations, refer to the pamphlet: *Pour une avancée démocratique: Rapport au XXIIIe Congrès du Parti communiste français* (Paris, 1979). Line references are not given, but almost all of the quotations follow chronologically.
6. There is also a suggestion here of the final struggle itself (c.f. '*sera le genre humain*' of *L'Internationale*).
7. The idea, when assessing the USSR, of the globally positive balance sheet had been in use in the party from late 1974 (see P. Robrieux, *Histoire intérieure du Parti Communiste*, vol. 3 (Paris, 1982) p. 219). The term was also used at the Vitry meeting with the intellectuals in December 1978.
8. It is worth noting, moreover, that Peugeot–Sochaux was one of the major sites of confrontation during the events of May and June 1968.
9. 'Right' and 'Left' are possibly inappropriate expressions to use to describe a democratic centralist party. One may say, however, that ideologically Eurocommunism corresponded to a 'Right' within the party, represented doctrinally by Elleinstein. A more strictly Leninist 'Left' was represented in the 1970s by the group that formed around Althusser.
10. *Le Monde*, 30 June 1972.
11. This recommendation is an indication of the thematic stress created by this mode of discourse. Note that Marchais inserts a statement about the importance of the CGT after his reference to the *cellules d'entreprises*, thus indicating an awareness of a logical problem in reconciling this formulation with the principle that the trade union is more important than the party at factory level.

5 Tradition and Innovation: The Communists

1. G. Marchais, *L'Espoir au présent* (Paris, 1980).

6 Discourse and Organisation: The Socialists

1. *Pour le socialisme: le livre des Assises du Socialisme* (Paris, 1974); Motion C, 'Redonner ses chances à la gauche', *Le Poing et la Rose*, no. 79 (February 1979), 'Motions nationales d'orientation'. All page and line references to the texts and speeches of the *Assises* will be bracketed after quotations. For example, (58/38) refers to page 58, line 38 of *Pour le socialisme*. In Motion C, all paragraphs have been numbered for convenient reference to Appendix 1. In this and the next chapter 'Socialist' refers specifically to the party, 'socialist' to the wider movement.
2. See *Pour le socialisme*, pp. 6–7.
3. Ibid., p. 7.
4. Ibid.
5. Ibid.

6. Ibid., pp. 6–7.
7. *Le Monde*, 18 June 1974.
8. *Le Quotidien de Paris*, 17 June 1974.
9. *Le Nouvel Observateur*, 16 September 1974.
10. *L'Express*, 7 October 1974.
11. *Le Quotidien de Paris*, 12 June 1974.
12. *Projet*, no. 88, September 1974.
13. Rocard's sense of urgency, however, had been directed, not at the PS, but at the PSU.
14. The first *composante* (PS) had 900 delegates, the second (PSU), 300, and the third (CFDT), 300. The organising committees were equally distributed.
15. See V. Propp, *Morphology of the Folktale* (Austin, 1968).
16. See Mitterrand's *appel* of May (*Pour le socialisme*, p. 7).
17. In the final vote at the Metz congress, the proportions of the votes attracted by the four motions in contention were:
    Motion A (Mitterrand), 46.99 per cent
    Motion B (Mauroy),   16.81 per cent
    Motion C (Rocard),   21.26 per cent
    Motion E (CERES),   14.94 per cent
18. *Le Poing et la Rose*, no. 79 (February 1979).
19. Motion E (CERES), for example, emphasises that only two '*lignes*' or strategies are possible: the Union of the Left or '*Une nouvelle troisième force*'. The implication is that the authors of Motion C (Rocardians) represent an opportunist social democracy. (*Le Poing et la Rose* no. 79 (February 1979) p. 25.)
20. I refer ambiguously to the authorship of Motion C. It was signed in the normal way by a selection of supporters from all federations, and therefore represented the Rocardian *courant* as a whole. The drawing up of the motion was a collective effort in which Michel Rocard, Patrick Viveret and Jean–François Merle played a considerable part. The implied personalism of the motion is unmistakable, however, (i) because it uses a style necessary to a personalist/socialist rally and (ii) because it does not question the presidential principles of the Republic. Symbolically, the motion is a call by Rocard and a claim to vision.
21. The *Projet Socialiste* is distinct from the *projet de société* of the 1974 *Assises*. Work upon it began after the legislative elections of 1978 as a collective undertaking in the party. After the Metz Congress, the elaboration of the text was taken over by J.–P. Chevènement. The final text was published as *Projet Socialiste: pour la France des années 80* (Paris, 1980). For an analysis of the text see A. Salomon, *P.S.: la mise à nu* (Paris, 1980) pp. 221–5.
22. This was one of the first and most widely used slogans of the party after 1971. It was also the title of a party publication which predated the Common Programme (*Changer la vie: programme de gouvernement du parti socialiste* (Paris, 1972)).
23. The phrase '*les faits sont têtus*' is a good illustration of the conflation of a social democratic style of realism and revolutionary intent. It could

well be imagined as the statement of a Centrist politician and is, in fact, generally accredited to Lenin.

24. This idea of logical consequence is reinforced generally in this part of the text by a series of other linking expressions: '*Dans le même esprit*' (143); '*C'est la conséquence des observations qui précèdent*' (153); '*Le même souci... doit nous conduire*' (157); '*Cela vaut aussi pour*' (161); '*cela suppose*' (167); '*Cela suppose aussi*' (168); '*C'est une des conditions nécessaires à la victoire de la gauche*' (169).

7 Organisation and 'Modernisation': The Socialists

1. The corpus includes:
   'Convention nationale: Modernisation et progrès social: textes prépar-atoires au débat', *Le Poing et la Rose*, no. 111, November 1984. (The references in the present chapter refer to the text of the convention resolution in this issue, which also contains a short preface by Jospin, 4 resolution amendments and a 'tribune libre');
   'Modernisation et progrès social. Convention nationale, Evry, 15 et 16 décembre 1984', *Le Poing et la Rose*, supplement to no. 228, January 1985. (This text includes extracts from the oral contributions, the text of the resolution, the results of the vote (text passed by 6793 to 86, 460 abstentions. All amendments rejected));
   copies of complete contributions to the debate of Laurent Fabius, Lionel Jospin (second intervention), and Michel Rocard. The paragraphs of the resolution have been numbered for convenient reference to Appendix 2.

Indicative Bibliography

Notes

1. Bibliographical sources are cited separately for each chapter (Chapters 4 and 5, 6 and 7 have been grouped together). These divisions affect two areas of reference: i) Sources which relate to more than one chapter but in differing degrees. These have been cited in the most relevant bibliography; ii) Sources which relate equally to more than one chapter. These have been given double entries.
2. Sources on the general historical background to the period have not been included in the bibliographies except where they have been cited in the text or in footnotes, or else are of special significance. Journal articles have also been omitted.

1 Historical Review

ALPHANDERY, C. *et al.*, *Pour nationaliser l'Etat* (Paris: Seuil, 1968).
ANDERSON, M., *Government in France* (Oxford: Pergamon, 1970).
ANGELI, C. *et al.*, *Les héritiers du Général* (Paris: Denoel, 1969).
APPARU, J.-P., *La droite d'aujourd'hui* (Paris: Albin Michel, 1979).
ARON, R., *France: Steadfast and Changing* (Oxford University Press, 1960).
AVRIL, P., *Politics in France* (Harmondsworth: Penguin, 1969).
BAECQUE, F. de, *L'Administration centrale de la France* (Paris: A. Colin, 1973).
BARILLON, R., *et al.*, *Dictionnaire de la constitution de la Ve République* (Paris: Cujas, 1976).
BARRÈS, P., *Charles de Gaulle* (Paris: Hachette, 1941).
BEAUCHAMPS, X., *Un Etat dans l'Etat?* (Paris: Bordas, 1976).
BIRNBAUM, P., *Les sommets de l'etat* (Paris, Seuil, 1977).
BLONDEL, J., *The Government of France* (London: Methuen, 1974).
Cahiers de la fondation nationale des sciences politiques: *Le référendum de septembre et les élections de novembre 1958* (Paris: Presses de la FNSP et A. Colin, 1960).
Cahiers de la fondation nationale des sciences politiques: *Le référendum d'octobre et les élections de novembre 1962* (Paris: Presse de la FNSP et A. Colin, 1965).
CAHM, E., *Péguy et le nationalisme français* (Paris: Librairie Minard, 1972).
CHAPSAL, J. and A. LANCELOT, *La vie politique en France depuis 1940* (Paris: PUF, 1975).
CHARLOT, J., *Le phénomène gaulliste* (Paris: Fayard, 1970).
Club Jean Moulin, *L'Etat et le citoyen* (Paris: Seuil, 1961).
Les constitutions de la France depuis 1789 (Paris: Garnier-Flammarion, 1970).
COTTA, M., *La VIe république* (Paris: Flammarion, 1974).

CROZIER, M., *La société bloquée* (Paris: Seuil, 1970).
DEBBASCH, C., *La France de Pompidou* (Paris: PUF, 1974).
DEBRÉ, J.-L., *Les idées constitutionnelles du général de Gaulle* (Paris: Pichon, 1974).
DEBRÉ, M., *Ces princes qui nous gouvernent...* (Paris: Plon, 1957).
DEBRÉ, M., *Une certaine idée de la France* (Paris: Fayard, 1972).
DEBU-BRIDEL, J., *De Gaulle contestataire* (Paris: Plon, 1970).
DREYFUS, F-G., *De Gaulle et le gaullisme* (Paris: PUF, 1982).
DROZDOWSKI, G., 'La critique des partis politiques par le général de Gaulle', D.E.S. dissertation, University of Paris II, 1973.
DUPUIS, G. *et al.*, *Le conseil constitutionnel* (Paris: A. Colin, 1970).
DUPUIS, G. *et al.*, *Organigrammes des institutions françaises* (Paris: A. Colin, 1971).
DUVERGER, M., *La VIᵉ République et le régime présidentiel* (Paris: Fayard, 1961).
EHRMANN, H., *Politics in France* (Boston: Little, Brown, 1971).
FREARS, J. R., *France in the Giscard Presidency* (London: George Allen & Unwin, 1981).
GAULLE, C. de, *Le fil de l'épée* (Paris: Berger–Levrault, 1944; Livre de poche, 1973).
GAULLE, C. de, *Mémoires de guerre: l'appel, 1940–1946* (Paris: Plon, 1954).
GAULLE, C. de, *Discours et messages: pendant la guerre, 1940–1946* (Paris: Plon, 1970).
GAULLE, C. de, *Discours et messages: dans l'attente, 1946–1958* (Paris: Plon, 1970).
GAULLE, C. de, *Discours et messages: avec le renouveau, 1958–1962* (Paris: Plon, 1970).
GIROUD, F., *La comédie du pouvoir* (Paris: Fayard, 1977).
GOGUEL, F. and A. GROSSER, *La politique en France* (Paris: A. Colin, 1981).
HAMON, L., *De Gaulle dans la république* (Paris: Plon, 1958).
HANLEY, D. L., A. P. KERR and N. M. WAITES, *Contemporary France: Politics and Society since 1945* (London: Routledge & Kegan Paul, 1980).
HAYWARD, J., *Private Interests and Public Policy* (London: Longman, 1966).
HAYWARD, J., *The One and Indivisible French Republic* (London: Weidenfeld & Nicolson, 1973, revised 2nd edn 1983).
Institut Charles de Gaulle, *Approches de la philosophie politique de général de Gaulle* (Paris: Editions Cujas, 1983).
JOUARY, J.-P., G. PÉLACHAUD and B. VASSEUR, *Giscard et les idées: essai sur la guerre idéologique* (Paris: Editions sociales, 1980).
JULLIARD, J., *La quatrième république* (Paris: Calmann–Lévy, 1968).
KESSLER, M.-C., *Le conseil d'Etat* (Paris: A. Colin, 1968).
LACOUTURE, J.,*De Gaulle* (Paris: Seuil, 1969).
LORD, G., *The French Budgetary Process* (Los Angeles: University of California Press, 1973).
MACHIN, H., *The Prefect in French Public Administration* (London: Croom Helm, 1977).

MAITROT, J.-C. and J.-D. SICAULT, *Les conférences de presse du général de Gaulle* (Paris: PUF, 1969).

MALRAUX, A., *Les chênes qu'on abat...* (Paris: Gallimard, 1971).

MASSOT, J., *La présidence de la république en France* (Paris: La documentation française, 1977).

MASSOT, J., *Le chef du gouvernement en France* (Paris: La documentation française, 1979).

MAURIAC, C., *The Other de Gaulle* (London: Angus & Robertson, 1973).

MENDÈS-FRANCE, P., *La république moderne* (Paris: Gallimard, 1962).

MENDÈS-FRANCE, P., *Pour préparer l'avenir* (Paris: Denoel, 1968).

NEGRIN, P., *Le conseil d'Etat et la vie publique en France depuis 1958* (Paris: PUF, 1968).

NICOLET, C., *L'Idée républicaine en France* (London: Gallimard, 1982).

NORA, P., *Les lieux de mémoire: la république* (Paris: Gallimard, 1985).

PICKLES, D., *France, the Fourth Republic* (London: Methuen, 1958).

PICKLES, D., *The Fifth French Republic* (London: Methuen, 1966).

POMPIDOU, G., *Le noeud gordien* (Paris: Plon, 1974).

QUATTROCCHI, A. and T. NAIRN, *The Beginning of the End: France, May 1968* (London: Panther, 1968).

RÉMOND, R., *La droite en France* (Paris: Aubier, 1963).

RÉMOND, R. et al., *La démocratie à refaire* (Paris: Editions ouvrières, 1963).

RIDLEY, F. and J. BLONDEL, *Public Administration in France* (London: Routledge & Kegan Paul, 1969).

RIVOLI, J., *Le budget de l'Etat* (Paris: Seuil, 1978).

SEALE, P. and S. McCONVILLE, *French Revolution 1968* (Harmondsworth: Penguin, 1968).

SIEGFRIED, A., *De la IVe à la Ve république* (Paris: Grasset, 1968).

SIMON, P.-H., *La France a la fièvre* (Paris: Seuil, 1958).

SOUSTELLE, J., *L'espérance trahie* (Paris: Editions de l'Alma, 1962).

SULEIMAN, E., *Politics, Power and Bureaucracy in France* (New Jersey: Princeton UP, 1974).

TOUCHARD, J., *Le Gaullisme* (Paris: Seuil, 1969).

VIANSSON-PONTÉ, P., *Histoire de la république gaullienne*, 2 vols (Paris: Fayard, 1970–1).

WILLIAMS, P., *Wars, Plots and Scandals in Post-War France* (Cambridge University Press, 1970).

WILLIAMS, P., *Crisis and Compromise* (London: Longman, 1972).

WILLIAMS, P. and D. GOLDEY, *French Politicians and Elections 1951–1969* (Cambridge University Press, 1970).

WILLIAMS, P. and M. HARRISON, *Politics and Society in De Gaulle's Republic* (London: Longman, 1971).

WRIGHT, G., *The Reshaping of French Democracy* (London: Methuen, 1950).

WRIGHT, V., *The Government and Politics of France* (London: Hutchinson, 1978).

WRIGHT, V. (ed.), *Conflict and Consensus in France* (London: Frank Cass, 1979).

2 Theory

ADORNO, T. *et al.*, *The Authoritarian Personality* (New York and London: Harper & Row, 1950).

AGULHON, M., *Marianne into Battle: Republican Imagery and Symbolism in France, 1789–1880* (Cambridge University Press, 1981).

ARON, R., *De la condition historique de la sociologie: leçon inaugurale au collège de France* (Paris: Gallimard, 1970).

ARON, R., *Main Currents in Sociological Thought*, 2 vols (London: Pelican, 1972).

AUSTIN, J. L., *How to do Things with Words* (Oxford: Clarendon Press, 1975).

BACHELARD, G., *The Poetics of Space* (Boston, Mass.: Orion Press, 1964).

BAILEY, F. G., *Stratagems and Spoils* (Oxford: Blackwell, 1969).

BELL, D. S., *Contemporary French Political Parties* (London: Croom Helm, 1982).

BENOIST, L., *Signes, symboles et mythes* (Paris: PUF, 1977).

BIRNBAUM, P., *Le pouvoir politique* (Paris: Dalloz, 1975).

BLOCH, M. (ed.), *Political Language and Oratory in Traditional Society* (London: Academic Press, 1975).

BORELLA, F., *Les partis politiques* (Paris: Seuil, 1974).

BRAUD, P., *Le comportement électoral en France* (Paris: PUF, 1973).

BURNS, J. M., *Leadership* (New York: Harper & Row, 1978).

BURTON, F. and P. CARLEN, *Official Discourse* (London: Routledge & Kegan Paul, 1979).

BYRNE, G. C. *et al.*, *Politics in Western European Democracies: Patterns & Problems* (New York: John Wiley, 1971).

CAHM, E., *Politics and Society in Contemporary France* (London: Harrap, 1972).

CASSIRER, E., *The Myth of the State* (New Haven, Conn.: Yale University Press, 1967).

CERNY, P., *The Politics of Grandeur* (Cambridge University Press, 1980).

CHARLESWORTH, J. C. (ed.), *Contemporary Political Analysis* (New York: Collier Macmillan, 1967).

CHARLOT, M., *La persuasion politique* (Paris: A. Colin, 1970).

COMTE, A., *A General View of Positivism* (New York: Speller & Sons, 1957).

CORBETT, P., *Ideologies* (London: Hutchinson, 1965).

COTTERET, J.-M., *Gouvernants et gouvernés* (Paris: PUF, 1973).

DEBRAY, R., *Le scribe: genèse du politique* (Paris: Grasset, 1980).

DOGAN, M. and R. ROSE (eds), *European Politics: A Reader* (London: Macmillan, 1971).

DONZELOT, J., *The Policing of Families* (London: Hutchinson, 1980).

DUNCAN, H. D., *Symbols in Society* (New York: Oxford University Press, 1968).

DURAND, G., *L'imagination symbolique* (Paris: PUF, 1964).

DURKHEIM, E., *The Elementary Forms of Religious Life* (London: George Allen & Unwin, 1976).

DUVERGER, M., *Political Parties* (London: Methuen, 1967).
EDELMAN, M., *The Symbolic Uses of Politics* (Urbana: University of Illinois Press, 1964).
EINAUDI, M. and F. GOGUEL, *Christian Democracy in France and Italy* (Indiana: University of Notre Dame Press, 1952).
EISENSTADT, S. W. (ed.), *Max Weber on Charisma and Institution Building* (University of Chicago Press, 1974).
ELLUL, J., *The New Demons* (London: Mowbrays, 1975).
FOUCAULT, M., *Les mots et les choses* (Paris: Gallimard, 1966).
FREARS, J. R., *Political Parties and Elections in the French Fifth Republic* (London: Hurst, 1977).
GEERTZ, C. *et al.*, *The Interpretation of Cultures* (New York: Basic Books Inc., 1973).
GELLNER, E., *Legitimation of Belief* (Cambridge University Press, 1974).
GENNEP, A. van, *The Rites of Passage* (London: Routledge & Kegan Paul, 1965).
GERTH, H. H. and C. W. MILLS, *From Max Weber* (London: Routledge & Kegan Paul, 1977).
GIDDENS, A., *Politics and Sociology in the Thought of Max Weber* (London: Macmillan, 1972).
GIDDENS, A., *Studies in Social and Political Theory* (London: Hutchinson & Co., 1977).
GIDDENS, A., *Central Problems in Social Theory* (London: Macmillan, 1979).
GINER, S., *Mass Society* (London: Martin Robertson, 1976).
GISCARD d'ESTAING, V., *Démocratie Française* (Paris: Fayard, 1976).
GRISONI, D. (ed.), *Politiques de la Philosophie* (Paris: Grasset, 1976).
GUILLAUME, M., *Le Capital et son double* (Paris: PUF, 1975).
GUILLEBARD, J.-C., *Les années orphelines 1968–1978* (Paris: Seuil, 1978).
HABERMAS, J., *Legitimation Crisis* (London: Heinemann, 1976).
HENIG, S. and J. PINDER (eds), *European Political Parties* (London: George Allen & Unwin, 1969).
HIRST, P., *On Law and Ideology* (London: Macmillan, 1979).
HOFFMAN, S., 'Heroic Leadership: the case of Modern France', in L. J. Edinger, *Political Leadership in Industrial Societies* (New York: John Wiley & Sons, 1967).
IRVING, R., *Christian Democracy in France* (London: George Allen & Unwin, 1973).
JUNG, C. G., *Modern Man in Search of a Soul* (London: Routledge & Kegan Paul, 1966).
KOHN, H., *The Idea of Nationalism* (New York: Macmillan, 1961).
KRIVINE, A., *La farce électorale* (Paris: Seuil, 1969).
KUHN, T. S., *The Structure of Scientific Revolutions* (University of Chicago Press, 1970).
LANCELOT, A., *La participation des Français à la politique* (Paris: PUF, 1971).
LAPALOMBARA, J. and M. WEINER (eds), *Political Parties and Political Development* (New Jersey: Princeton, 1966).

LARRAIN, J., *The Concept of Ideology* (London: Hutchinson, 1979).

LASSWELL, H. *et al.*, *Language of Politics* (Cambridge, Mass.: MIT Press, 1965).

LAWSON, K., *The Comparative Study of Political Parties* (New York: St Martins Press, 1976).

LÉVI–STRAUSS, C., *Structural Anthropology* (London: Allen Lane, The Penguin Press, 1968).

LIPSET, S. M., *Political Man* (London: Heinemann, 1976).

LOYE, D., *The Leadership Passion* (San Francisco: Jossey-Bass, 1977).

LUKES, S., *Essays in Social Theory* (London: Macmillan, 1978).

MACHIAVELLI, N., *The Prince* (London: J. M. Dent, 1960).

MACRAE, D., *Parliament, Parties and Society in France 1946–1958* (London: Macmillan, 1967).

MAN, H. de, *The Psychology of Socialism* (London: George Allen & Unwin, 1928).

MANNHEIM, K., *Ideology and Utopia* (London: Routledge & Kegan Paul, 1960).

MARCUSE, H., *Eros and Civilisation* (Boston: Beacon Press, 1974).

MARX, K., *The German Ideology* (London: Lawrence & Wishart, 1970).

MARX, K., *Preface and Introduction to a Contribution to the Critique of Political Economy* (Peking: Foreign Languages Press, 1976).

MARX, K., *Wages, Prices & Profit* (Moscow: Progress Publishers, 1976).

MARX, K., *The Civil War in France* (Peking: Foreign Languages Press, 1977).

MARX, K., *The Eighteenth Brumaire of Louis Bonaparte* (Moscow: Progress Publishers, 1977).

MARX, K., *Grundrisse* (Harmondsworth: Penguin, 1977).

MARX, K. and F. ENGELS, *The Communist Manifesto* (Harmondsworth: Penguin, 1967).

MAURRAS, C., *Enquête sur la monarchie* (Paris: Fayard, 1925(?), first published 1900).

MEHLMAN, J., *Revolution and Repetition: Marx/Hugo/Balzac* (Los Angeles: University of California Press, 1977).

MICHELAT, G. and M. SIMON, *Classe, religion et comportement politique* (Paris: Presse de la fondation nationale de sciences politiques, 1977).

MICHELS, R., *Political Parties* (New York: Dover, 1959).

MILIBAND, R., *The State in Capitalist Society* (London: Quartet, 1973).

MILL, J. S., *On Liberty* (London: Longman, Green, Longman, Roberts & Green, 1864).

MILL, J. S., *On Representative Government* (London: Longmans, Green & Co., 1865).

MILLS, C. W., *The Sociological Imagination* (New York: Oxford University Press, 1959).

MILLS, C. W., *The Power Elite* (New York: Oxford University Press, 1971).

MONTESQUIEU, C. de Secondat, Baron de, *De l'esprit des lois*, 2 vols (Paris: Garnier, 1973).

MURRAY, H. G., *Myth and Mythmaking* (New York: Braziller, 1960).

NEEDHAM, R., *Reconnaissances* (University of Toronto Press, 1980).

NETTLAU, M., *L'histoire de l'anarchie* (Paris(?): Editions du Cercle, 1971).

NIETZSCHE, F., *The Twilight of the Idols. The Antichrist* (Edinburgh: Foulis, 1911).

OUTHWAITE, W., *Verstehen: Understanding Social Life* (London: George Allen & Unwin, 1975).

PARSONS, T., *The Structure of Social Action*, 2 vols (New York: Free Press, 1968).

PENNIMAN, H. *et al.*, *France at the Polls, the Presidential Elections of 1974* (Institute for Public Polling Research, USA, 1975).

PLAMENATZ, J., *Ideology* (London: Macmillan, 1970).

POPPER, K., *The Poverty of Historicism* (London: Routledge & Kegan Paul, 1976).

POULANTZAS, N., *Politique et classes sociales*, 2 vols (Paris: Maspero, 1972).

POULANTZAS, N., *Les classes sociales dans le capitalisme aujourd'hui* (Paris: Seuil, 1974).

POULANTZAS, N., *L'Etat, le pouvoir, le socialisme* (Paris: PUF, 1978).

PROUDHON, P.–J., *Qu'est-ce que la propriété?* (Paris: Garnier–Flammarion, 1966).

REICH, W., *The Mass Psychology of Fascism* (Harmondsworth: Penguin, 1978).

RIESMAN, D., *The Lonely Crowd* (London: Yale University Press, 1978).

ROBERTSON, D., *A Theory of Party Competition* (London: John Wiley, 1976).

ROUSSEAU, J.–J., *Du contrat social* (Paris: Garnier–Flammarion, 1966).

ROUSSEAU, J.–J., *Discours sur les sciences et les arts. Discours sur l'origine et les fondements de l'inégalité parmi les hommes* (Paris: Garnier–Flammarion, 1971).

SAINT-JUST, L.–A., *Théorie politique* (Paris: Seuil, 1976).

SARTORI, G., *Parties and Party Systems* (Cambridge University Press, 1977).

SARTRE, J.–P., *Critique de la raison dialectique* (Paris: Gallimard, 1960).

SCHATTSNEIDER, E., *Party Government* (New York: Rinehart, 1942).

SCHUMPETER, J. A., *Capitalism, Socialism and Democracy* (London: George Allen & Unwin, 1979).

SERVAN-SCHREIBER, J.–J., *The American Challenge* (London: Pelican, 1969).

SIEGFRIED, A., *Tableau politique de la France de l'ouest sous la IIIe République* (Paris: A. Colin, 1964).

SMITH, G., *Politics in Western Europe* (London: Heinemann, 1972).

SPERBER, D., *Rethinking Symbolism* (Cambridge University Press, 1975).

STOETZL, J. and A. GIRARD, *Les sondages d'opinion publique* (Paris: PUF, 1973).

TAMBIAH, S. J., 'Form & Meaning of Magical Acts', in R. Horton, *et al.*, *Modes of Thought* (London: Faber & Faber, 1973).

TROTSKY, L., *The Revolution Betrayed* (New York: Pathfinder Press, 1972).

TUCKER, R. C., *Philosophy and Myth in Karl Marx* (Cambridge University Press, 1972).

TUDOR, H., *Political Myth* (London: Pall Mall, 1972).

TURNER, V. W., *The Ritual Process* (London: Routledge & Kegan Paul, 1969).

TYLER, S. (ed.), *Cognitive Anthropology* (New York: Holt, Rinehart & Winston Inc., 1969).

WEBER, M., *The Theory of Social and Economic Organization* (New York: Free Press, 1964).

WILLIAMS, R., *Marxism and Literature* (Oxford University Press, 1977).

3 Methodology

ABOU–WAFIA, S., 'Le message impressif à travers les discours de Valéry Giscard d'Estaing', DESS dissertation, University of Paris I, 1978.

BARDIN, L., *L'analyse de contenu* (Paris: PUF, 1977).

BARRY, B., *Political Argument* (London: Routledge & Kegan Paul, 1965).

BARTHES, R., *Mythologies* (St Albans: Paladin, 1976).

CARSWELL, E. (ed.), *The Social Context of Messages* (New York: Academic Press, 1971).

Centre universitaire de recherches administratives et politiques de Picardie, *Discours et idéologie* (Paris: PUF, 1980).

CHERRY, C., *On Human Communication* (Cambridge, Mass.: MIT Press, 1965).

CHOMSKY, N., *Aspects of a Theory of Syntax* (Cambridge, Mass.: MIT Press, 1965).

COTTERET, J.–M. and R. MOREAU, *Le vocabulaire du général de Gaulle* (Paris: A. Colin, 1969).

COWARD, R. and J. ELLIS, *Language and Materialism: Developments in Semiology and the Theory of the Subject* (London: Routledge & Kegan Paul, 1977).

CRETIN, M. and M. REINHARD, ' "Démocratie française": essai d'une nouvelle approche de l'analyse de contenu par l'étude des réseaux', DESS dissertation, University of Paris I, 1978.

DELAHAYE, Y., *L'Europe sous les mots* (Paris: Payot, 1979).

DUCROT, P., *Dire et ne pas dire: Principes de sémantique linguistique* (Paris: Hermann, 1972).

DURANDIN, G., *Les fondements du mensonge* (Paris: Flammarion, 1972).

FONTANIER, P., *Les figures du discours* (Paris: Flammarion, 1968).

FOUCAULT, M., *L'Ordre du discours* (Paris: Gallimard, 1971).

GALL, A.–E., 'Analyse du discours de la gauche non-communiste', DESS dissertation, University of Paris I, 1978.

GOLDMAN, L., *Pour une sociologie du roman* (Paris: Gallimard, 1973).

GRITTI, J., *Elle court, elle court, la rumeur* (Ottawa: Stanké, 1978).

GROUD, H., 'Le langage politique: l'exemple de l'élection présidentielle de 1974', DESS dissertation, University of Paris II, 1975.

HYMAN, S. E., *The Tangled Bank: Darwin, Marx, Frazer and Freud as Imaginative Writers* (New York: Grosset & Dunlap, 1966).

JAURÈS, A.–B., *La lutte contre l'inflation et le chômage sous la Ve République: d'après les commentaires de la presse française et des ministres V. Giscard d'Estaing et R. Barre* (Paris: Imprimerie Jouve, 1980).

LABBÉ, D., *Le discours communiste* (Paris: Presse de la Fondation nationale des sciences politiques, 1977).

MILLER, G., *Les pousse-au-jouir du Maréchal Pétain* (Paris: Seuil, 1975).

PROPP, V., *Morphology of the Folktale* (Austin: University of Texas Press, 1968).

REAGAN, C. E. (ed.), *Studies in the Philosophy of Paul Ricoeur* (Ohio University Press, 1979).

RICHARDS, I. A., *The Philosophy of Rhetoric* (Oxford University Press, 1976).

RICOEUR, P., *La métaphore vive* (Paris: Seuil, 1975).

ROCHE, J., *Le style des candidats à la présidence de la République, 1965, 1969* (Toulouse: Privat, 1971).

SMITH, A. G. *et al.*, *Communication and Culture* (New York: Holt, Rinehart & Winston, 1966).

4 & 5 Parti Communiste Français

Primary Sources
Newspapers and Periodicals

Cahiers du communisme, 1976, 1979 (Paris, monthly).
L'Humanité (Paris, daily).

Statutes, Congress Rapports and Resolutions
'Les statuts du parti communiste français', in *Cahiers du communisme* (June–July 1979) 405–21.
XIXᵉ Congrès: rapport du comité central (Paris, 1970).
XXIᵉ Congrès: rapport du comité central; résolution (Paris, 1974).
XXIIᵉ Congrès: rapport du comité central; résolution (Paris, 1976).
XXIIIᵉ Congrès: rapport du comité central (Paris, 1979).
XXIIIᵉ Congrès: résolution (Paris, 1979).

Other Publications of the Parti Communiste Français
'Femmes, pour changer votre vie'. Speech by Georges Marchais (Paris, 1977).
'L'Information de Georges Marchais aux intellectuels communistes réunis à Vitry les 9–10 décembre 1978' (Paris, 1979).
(See also 'Parti communiste français' in secondary sources.)

Secondary Sources
ADLER, A. *et al.*, *L'URSS et nous* (Paris: Editions sociales, 1978).

ALEXANDRE, P., *Le roman de la gauche* (Paris: Plon, 1977).

ALTHUSSER, L., *Ce qui ne peut plus durer dans le parti communiste* (Paris: Maspero, 1978).

BALIBAR, E., G. BOIS, G. LABICA and J.-P. LEFEBVRE, *Ouvrons la fenêtre, camarades!* (Paris: Maspero, 1979).

BENOIST, J.-M., *Chronique de décomposition du PCF* (Paris: Editions de la Table Ronde, 1979).

BERNSTEIN, E., *Evolutionary Socialism* (London: ILP, 1909).

BESANÇON, A., *The Intellectual Origins of Leninism* (Oxford: Blackwell, 1981).

BLUME, D. *et al.*, *Histoire du réformisme en France depuis 1920*, 2 vols (Paris: Editions sociales, 1976).

BOCCARA, P., *Etudes sur le capitalisme monopoliste d'Etat: sa crise et son issue* (Paris: Editions sociales, 1977).

BRINTON, M., *The Bolsheviks and Workers' Control* (London: Solidarity, 1970).

BRUNET, J.-P., *Histoire du PCF* (Paris: PUF, 1982).

BUFFIN, D. and D. GERBAUD, *Les Communistes* (Paris: Albin Michel, 1981).

BURLES, J., *Le Parti communiste dans la société française* (Paris: Editions sociales, 1979).

CARRILLO, S., *'Eurocommunism' and the State* (London: Lawrence & Wishart, 1977).

CAUTE, D., *The Left in Europe* (London: Weidenfeld & Nicholson, 1966).

CLAUDIN, F., *L'Eurocommunisme* (Paris: Maspero, 1977).

CLAVAUD, F. and G. MARCHAIS, *Les communistes et les paysans* (Paris: Editions sociales, 1972).

CLIFF, T., *Rosa Luxemburg* (London: Bookmarks Publishing Cooperative, 1980).

CUTLER, A. *et al.*, *Marx's Capital and Capitalism today*, 2 vols (London: Routledge & Kegan Paul, 1978).

DAIX, P., *La crise du PCF* (Paris: Seuil, 1978).

DREYFUS, G., *Histoire des gauches en France 1940–1975* (Paris: Grasset,1975).

DUHAMEL, O., *La gauche et la Vᵉ République* (Paris: PUF, 1980).

ELLEINSTEIN, J., *Le PC* (Paris: Grasset, 1976).

ELLEINSTEIN, J., *Une certaine idée du communisme* (Paris: Julliard, 1979).

FEJTÖ, F., *Dictionnaire des partis communistes et des mouvements révolutionnaires* (Tournai: Casterman, 1971).

FEMIA, J., *Gramsci's Political Thought: Hegemony, Consciousness, and the Revolutionary Process* (Oxford: Clarendon Press, 1981).

FIZBIN, H., *Les bouches s'ouvrent* (Paris: Grasset, 1980).

FRENKIEL, P., 'Le PCF et les sondages d'opinion 1964–1971', DESS dissertation, University of Paris I, 1972.

GAUCHER, R., *Histoire secrète du Parti communiste français 1920–1974* (Paris: Albin Michel, 1974).

GRAMSCI, A., *The Modern Prince and Other Writings* (New York: International Publishers, 1978).

GRAMSCI, A., *Selections from Political Writings 1921–1926* (London: Lawrence & Wishart, 1978).

GRAMSCI, A., *Selections from the Prison Notebooks* (London: Lawrence & Wishart, 1978).

GUÉRIN, D., *Rosa Luxemburg et la spontanéité révolutionnaire* (Paris: Flammarion, 1971).

JAY, M., *The Dialectical Imagination: The History of the Frankfurt School and the Institute of Social Research 1923–50* (London: Heinemann, 1976).

JOHNSON, R. W., *The Long March of the French Left* (London: Weidenfeld & Nicolson, 1981).

JOLL, J., *The Second International 1889–1914* (London: Weidenfeld & Nicolson, 1955).

KAUTSKY, K., *Social Democracy versus Communism* (New York: The Rand School Press, 1946).

KILMINSTER, R., *Praxis and Method: A Sociological Dialogue with Lukacs, Gramsci and the early Frankfurt School* (London: Routledge & Kegan Paul, 1979).

KRIEGEL, A., *Les communistes français* (Paris: Seuil, 1968).

KRIEGEL, A., *Un autre communisme?* (Paris: Hachette, 1977).

LAURENT, P., *Le PCF comme il est* (Paris: Editions sociales, 1978).

LECOEUR, A., *Le PCF: continuité dans le changement* (Paris: Laffont, 1977).

LEFORT, C., *Eléments d'une critique de la bureaucratie* (Paris: Gallimard, 1979).

LEFRANC, G., *Les gauches en France 1789–1972* (Paris: Payot, 1973).

LEFRANC, G., *Le syndicalisme en France* (Paris: PUF, 1975).

LENIN, V. I., *Essential Works of Lenin: What is to be done? Imperialism, the Highest Stage of Capitalism. The State and Revolution* (New York: Bantam, 1966).

LENIN, V. I., *'Left-Wing' Communism, an Infantile Disorder* (Moscow: Progress Publishers, 1975).

LENIN, V. I., *The State and Revolution* (Moscow: Progress Publishers, 1977).

LUXEMBURG, R., *Reform or Revolution* (New York: Pathfinder Press, 1973).

MANCEAUX, M. and J. DONZELOT, *Cours, camarade, le PCF est derrière toi* (Paris: Gallimard, 1974).

MANDEL, E., *From Stalinism to Eurocommunism* (London: New Left Books, 1978).

MAO TSE-TUNG, *Quotations from Chairman Mao Tse-Tung* (Peking: Foreign Languages Press, 1968).

MAO TSE-TUNG, *Why is it that Red Political Power can Exist in China?* (Peking: Foreign Languages Press, 1968).

MARCELLESI, J.-B., *Le Congrès de Tours* (Paris: Le Pavillon, 1971).

MARCHAIS, G., *Qu'est-ce que le parti communiste français?* (Paris: Editions sociales, 1974).

MARCHAIS, G., *Parlons franchement* (Paris: Grasset et Pasquelle, 1977).

MARCHAIS, G., *L'Espoir au présent* (Paris: Editions sociales, 1980).

MARX, K. and F. ENGELS, *Selected Works*, vol. 2 (Moscow: Foreign Languages Publishing House, 1958).

MORGAN, R. P., *The German Social Democrats and the First International, 1864–72* (Cambridge University Press, 1965).

MOUFFE, C. (ed.), *Gramsci and Marxist Theory* (London: Routledge & Kegan Paul, 1979).

NUGENT, N. and D. LOWE, *The Left in France* (London: Macmillan, 1982).

Parti Communiste Français, *Manifeste du Parti Communiste Français, pour une démocratie avancée, pour une France socialiste* (Paris: Editions sociales, 1969).

Parti Communiste Français, *Changer de Cap* (Paris: Editions sociales, 1971).

Parti Communiste Français, *Traité marxiste d'économie politique: Le capitalisme monopoliste d'Etat*, 2 vols (Paris: Editions sociales, 1976).

Parti Communiste Français, *Programme commun de gouvernement actualisé* (Paris: Editions sociales, 1978).

Parti Communiste Français and Parti Socialiste, *Programme commun de gouvernement* (Paris: Editions sociales, 1972).

PLAMENATZ, J., *German Marxism and Russian Communism* (London: Longmans, 1961).

PLEKHANOV, G., *Fundamental Problems of Marxism* (London: Lawrence & Wishart, 1969).

POPEREN, J., *L'Unité de la gauche 1965–1973* (Paris: Fayard, 1975).

POPPER, K. R., *The Open Society and its Enemies, Hegel & Marx*, vol. 2 (London: Routledge & Kegan Paul, 1962).

POSTER, M., *Sartre's Marxism* (London: Pluto Press, 1979).

ROBRIEUX, P., *Thorez: Vie secrète et vie publique* (Paris: Fayard, 1975).

ROBRIEUX, P., *Histoire intérieure du Parti Communiste, 1972–1982*, vol. 3 (Paris: Fayard, 1982).

RONY, J., *Trente ans de parti: Un communiste s'interroge* (Paris: Christian Bourgeois, 1978).

ROSENBERG, A., *The History of Bolshevism* (New York: Doubleday, 1967).

RUSSELL, B., *The Practice and Theory of Bolshevism* (London: George Allen and Unwin, 1962).

SOREL, G., *Réflexions sur la violence* (Paris: Editions Marcel Rivière, 1972).

STALIN, J., *Works*, vol. 6 (London: Lawrence & Wishart, 1953).

TANDLER, N., *L'Impossible biographie de Georges Marchais* (Paris: Editions Albatross, 1980).

TARTAKOWSKY, D., *Une histoire du PCF (Paris: PUF, 1982).*

TROTSKY, L., *Social Democracy and the Wars of Intervention in Russia 1918–21* (London: New Park Publishers, 1975).

WALTER, G., *Histoire du Parti communiste français* (Paris: Aimery Somogy, 1948).

WILLIAMS, S.(ed.), *Socialism in France* (London: Pinter, 1983).

6 & 7 Parti Socialiste

Primary Sources
Newspapers and Periodicals
Le Poing et la Rose (Paris, monthly).
Le Populaire de Paris 1959 (Paris, daily).
L'Unité (Paris, weekly).

Statutes, Rules, Rapports, Congress Motions
37ᵉ Congrès national: Projet de déclaration de principes et de statuts, includes 'Déclaration commune des organisations socialistes', 13 January 1905 (*Parti socialiste* (SFIO), Paris, 1945).
Règlement du parti, supplement to 'Bulletin intérieur', no. 68 (January 1954).
Parti socialiste: Déclaration de principes; statuts (Paris, 197–).
55ᵉ Congrès national: rapports (Parti socialiste (SFIO), Paris, 1965).
'Congrès national du Parti socialiste: Motions et contributions', *Le Poing et la Rose,* no. 37 (January 1975).
'Motion nationale d'orientation', *Le Poing et la Rose,* no. 38 (February 1975) pp. 3–6.
'Contribution des Fédérations au débat', *Le Poing et la Rose,* no. 60 (April 1977).
'Congrès du Parti socialiste: Motions nationales d'orientation', *Le Poing et la Rose,* no. 62 (June 1977).
'Motion finale de politique générale', *Le Poing et la Rose,* no. 63 (July 1977) pp. 12–23.
'Contributions au débat', *Le Poing et la Rose,* no. 78 (January 1979).
'Congrès du Parti socialiste: Motions nationales d'orientation', *Le Poing et la Rose,* no. 79 (February 1979).
'Textes de références du Parti socialiste', *Le Poing et la Rose,* no. 82 (June 1979).
' "Modernisation et progrès social". Convention nationale', *Le Poing et la Rose,* no. 111 (November 1984).
' "Modernisation et progrès social". Convention nationale', *Le Poing et la Rose,* supplement to no. 228 (January 1985).

Secondary Sources
ALEXANDRE, P., *Le roman de la gauche* (Paris: Plon, 1977).
Assises du socialisme, Pour le socialisme (Paris: Stock, 1974).
AUDRY, C., *Léon Blum ou la politique du juste* (Paris: Denoel, 1955).
BELL, D. S. and B. CRIDDLE, *The French Socialist Party. Resurgence and Victory* (Oxford University Press, 1984).
BIZOT, J.-F., *Au Parti des Socialistes* (Paris: Grasset, 1975).
BLUM, L., 'Le problème de la participation' in *L'Oeuvre, 1928–1934,* pp. 114–37 (Paris: Albin Michel, 1955–72).
BLUM, L., 'Notes sur la doctrine' and 'Discours au XXXVIIIᵉ congrès' in *L'Oeuvre, 1943–1947,* pp. 271–88 (Paris: Albin Michel, 1955–72).
BLUM, L., *A l'échelle humaine* (Mermod, Switzerland, n.d.).
CAUTE, D., *The Left in Europe* (London: Weidenfeld & Nicolson, 1966).
CHANDERNAGOR, A., *Un parlement, pour quoi faire?* (Paris: Gallimard, 1967).
CHEVÈNEMENT, J.-P. and D. MOTCHANE, *Clefs pour le Socialisme* (Paris: Seghers, 1973).
Club Jean Moulin, *Un parti pour la Gauche* (Paris: Seuil, 1965).
CODDING, G. A. and W. SAFRAN, *Ideology and Politics: The Socialist Party of France* (Boulder, Colorado: Westview Press, 1979).
COLTON, J., *Léon Blum. Humanist in Politics* (New York: Alfred A. Knopf, 1966).

DEFFERRE, G., *Un nouvel horizon* (Paris: Gallimard, 1965).

DEPREUX, E., *Servitude et grandeur du PSU* (Paris: Syros, 1974).

DESJARDINS, T., *François Mitterrand: un socialiste gaullien* (Paris: Hachette, 1978).

DREYFUS, F., *Histoire des gauches en France; 1940–1975* (Paris: Grasset, 1975).

DUHAMEL, A., *La république de Mitterrand* (Paris: Grasset, 1982).

DUHAMEL, O., *La gauche et la Ve République* (Paris: PUF, 1980).

EVIN, K., *Michel Rocard ou l'art du possible* (Paris: J.–C. Simeon, 1979).

Faire, *Qu'est-ce que la social-démocratie?* (Paris: Seuil, 1979).

FRANCE, S., 'Gaston Defferre's candidature for the Presidency of the French Republic, with special reference to his programme for the creation of the Fédération Démocrate Socialiste, May–June 1965', MA dissertation, University of Sussex, 1966.

GAY, P., *The Dilemma of Democratic Socialism* (New York: Columbia University Press, 1962).

GERSTLÉ, J., *Le langage des socialistes* (Paris: Stanké, 1979).

GRAHAM, B. D., *The French Socialists and Tripartisme, 1944–47* (Canberra: ANU, 1965).

GUIDONI, P., *Histoire du nouveau parti socialiste* (Paris: Tema, 1973).

HAMON, H. and P. ROTMAN, *L'effet Rocard* (Paris: Stock, 1980).

HAUSS, C., *The New Left in France: The Unified Socialist Party* (Westport, Connecticut: Greenwood Press, 1978).

HOWORTH, J., *Edouard Vaillant* (Paris: Syros, 1982).

HURTIG, C., *De la SFIO au nouveau parti socialiste* (Paris: A. Colin, 1970).

ILLICH, I., *Toward a History of Needs* (New York: Pantheon, 1978).

JAURÈS, J., *L'armée nouvelle* (Paris: L'Humanité, 1915).

JAURÈS, J. and J. GUESDE, *Les deux méthodes: conférence, Lille, 1900* (Paris: Les éditions de la liberté, 1945).

JOHNSON, R. W., *The Long March of the French Left* (London: Macmillan, 1981).

JOXE, P., *Le Parti Socialiste (changer la vie)* (Paris: Epi, 1973).

JUDT, T., *Socialism in Provence, 1871–1914* (Cambridge University Press, 1979).

LABBÉ, D., *François Mitterrand. Essai sur le discours* (Paris: La pensée sauvage, 1983).

LACOUTURE, J., *Léon Blum* (Paris: Seuil, 1977).

LEFRANC, G., *Le mouvement socialiste sous la 3e République, 1875–1940* (Paris: Payot, 1963).

LEFRANC, G., *Les gauches en France, 1789–1972* (Paris: Payot, 1973).

LIGOU, D., *Histoire du socialisme en France, 1871–1961* (Paris: PUF, 1962).

MACSHANE, D., *François Mitterrand. A Political Odyssey* (London: Quartet, 1982).

MAIRE, E., *Reconstruire l'espoir* (Paris: Seuil, 1980).

MAIRE, E. and J. JULLIARD, *La CFDT d'aujourd'hui* (Paris: Seuil, 1975).

MAUROY, P., *C'est ici le chemin* (Paris: Flammarion, 1982).

296   *Indicative Bibliography*

MAYER, D., *Pour une histoire de la gauche* (Paris: Plon, 1969).
MITTERRAND, F., *Ma part de vérité* (Paris: Fayard, 1969).
MITTERRAND, F., *Un socialisme du possible* (Paris: Seuil, 1970).
MITTERRAND, F., *La Rose au poing* (Paris: Flammarion, 1973).
MITTERRAND, F., *La Paille et le Grain* (Paris: Flammarion, 1975).
MITTERRAND, F., *Politique*, 2 vols (Paris: Fayard, 1977 and 1982).
MOLLET, G., *Quinze ans après: la constitution de 1958* (Paris: Albin Michel, 1973).
NOLAND, A., *The Founding of the French Socialist Party* (Harvard University Press, 1956).
NUGENT, N. and D. LOWE, *The Left in France* (London: Macmillan, 1982).
Parti communiste français and Parti socialiste, *Programme commun de gouvernement* (Paris: Editions sociales, 1972).
Parti Socialiste, *Projet socialiste* (Paris: Club Socialiste du Livre, 1980).
PEASE, M., *Jean Jaurès: Socialist and humanitarian* (London: Headley, 1916).
PFISTER, T., *Les Socialistes* (Paris: Albin Michel, 1977).
PHILIP, A., *Les Socialistes* (Paris: Seuil, 1967).
POPEREN, J., *L'unité de la gauche; 1965–1973* (Paris: Fayard, 1975).
PORTELLI, H., *Le socialisme français tel qu'il est* (Paris: PUF, 1980).
ROCARD, M., *Le PSU* (Paris: Seuil, 1969).
ROCARD, M., *Parler vrai* (Paris: Seuil, 1979).
SALOMON, A., *P.S.: La mise à nu* (Paris: Laffont, 1980).
SCHIFRES, M., *La CFDT des militants* (Paris: Stock, 1975).
SHIFRES, M. and M. SARAZIN, *L'Elysée de Mitterrand. Secrets de la maison du Prince* (Paris: Moreau, 1985).
SIMMONS, H., *French Socialists in Search of a Role, 1956–1967* (New York: Cornell University Press, 1970).
SUFFERT, G., *De Defferre à Mitterrand* (Paris: Seuil, 1966).
WEINSTEIN, H. R., *Jean Jaurès: A Study of Patriotism in the French Socialist Movement* (New York: Octagon, 1973).
WILLIAMS, S. (ed.), *Socialism in France* (London: F. Pinter, 1983).
WILSON, F. L., *The French Democratic Left, 1963–1969* (Stanford University Press, 1971).
YSMAL, C., *La carrière politique de Gaston Defferre* (Paris: Presse de la FNSP, 1965).
YSMAL, C., *Defferre Parle (18 décembre 1963–25 juin 1965)* (Paris: Presse de la FNSP, 1966).
ZEVAÈS, A., *Le Socialisme en France depuis 1871* (Paris: Fasquelle, 1908).
ZEVAÈS, A., *Les Guesdistes* (Paris: Marcel Rivière, 1911).

Index

QUEEN MARY
COLLEGE
LIBRARY

WITHDRAWN
FROM STOCK
QMUL LIBRARY

WITHDRAWN
FROM STOCK
QMUL LIBRARY